FOREWORD

This book is both the record of a friendship and the portrait of a man and his mind—the speculations and activities, the large theories, the small irritations, and, perhaps most surprising to many readers, the extraordinarily playful spirit of a great poet. It is also, although it was not intended to be, a gradually unfolding and unguarded autobiography.

The volume contains many poems which differ considerably from later published versions; furthermore, it includes poems and impromptu verses which do not appear in any of Robert Frost's collections. Some of the poems have become anthological favorites; others are highly personal, lightly jocular, and even broad burlesques; but all are the spontaneous and unique expressions of a personality unlike any other.

Although Frost never pretended to be a literary critic, many of his letters are illuminated with appraisals not to be found in books of criticism. The comments on his contemporaries are keen and sometimes cruel. On the other hand, he was always more than generous to my critical as well as my creative writings, and so appreciative of my early championship in his behalf that he overrated it.

As his letters grew more intimate they also grew freer in form and style. The spelling of the later correspondence is whimsical; the punctuation becomes more arbitrary; commas are treated cavalierly; abbreviation marks are generally ignored. In these printed pages spelling, punctuation—or lack of it—and purposeful distortions are preserved. Footnotes printed in text type are Frost's own annotations; those in brackets are mine.

—Louis Untermeyer

THE LETTERS OF ROBERT FROST TO LOUIS UNTERMEYER

THE LETTERS OF

Robert Frost

TO LOUIS UNTERMEYER

JONATHAN CAPE THIRTY BEDFORD SQUARE LONDON

FIRST PUBLISHED IN GREAT BRITAIN 1964
COPYRIGHT © 1963 BY LOUIS UNTERMEYER AND THE ESTATE OF ROBERT
FROST, ALFRED C. EDWARDS, EXECUTOR

Grateful acknowledgment is made to The Macmillan
Company, New York, for permission to quote from
Robert Frost's "Introduction" to *King Jasper* by
Edwin Arlington Robinson; and to the Louis
Untermeyer Collection in the Library of Congress
for copies of the letters and drawings

Design and typography by Ernst Reichl

PRINTED IN GREAT BRITAIN BY
LOWE & BRYDONE (PRINTERS) LTD, LONDON
ON PAPER MADE BY JOHN DICKINSON & CO.
BOUND BY A. W. BAIN & CO. LTD, LONDON

THE LETTERS

It is now fifty years since I first came across the name of Robert Frost. It was signed to two poems in the December, 1913, issue of a new quarterly, Poetry and Drama, edited by the poet Harold Monro and issued at his Poetry Bookshop in London. Since the magazine, for which I was a sporadic fieldworker, was exclusively British I assumed that the unknown Frost, appearing in the company of such well-known Georgians as Rupert Brooke, W. W. Gibson, and Lascelles Abercrombie, was a minor member of their group. But it was incredible that the two poems could have been written by a tyro; moreover, "The Fear" and "A Hundred Collars" were distinctly un-British. The ideas in both poems were universal enough. The dramatic situation in the former may have happened anywhere, and the place names in the latter may have been picked up by a visitor with a good ear for quaintness. Yet there was something more local than local color here, a native turn of thought and a matching colloquial idiom that was unmistakably that of New rather than Old England.

I expressed my puzzlement to Lascelles Abercrombie, with whom I had been corresponding about his somber Emblems of Love and Speculative Dialogues. From his characteristic address, The Gallows, Ryton, Dymock, Gloucester, Abercrombie informed me that Robert Frost was a forty-year-old American poet, domiciled in the neighborhood. Later I learned that Frost, who had made a bare living as a farmer and sometime teacher, and no possible living as a poet, had gone to England partly to try himself against another background and partly because his wife,

Elinor, said she wanted "to live under thatch." There were four children—a son Carol, and three daughters, Lesley, Irma, and Marjorie—and the Frosts, who had sailed from Boston in August, 1912, settled temporarily in Beaconsfield, a small town in rural Buckinghamshire. Except for an occasional trip to London, they went nowhere for a year; then, almost atavistically, they turned again to farming, this time at Little Iddens, Ledbury, Hereford-shire, a bit to the north of Abercrombie's Dymock. Besides Abercrombie, Robert made friends with W. W. Gibson and, especially, Edward Thomas, who was so inspired by Frost that he turned away from his travel books and other potboilers to write poetry—"Did anyone ever begin to be a poet at thirty-six in the shade?" he wrote to Eleanor Farjeon—it was Thomas who planned to follow Frost to America and would have done so had he not been killed on the battlefield of Arras.

Thirty years passed before I learned the extent of Robert's American heritage. A cousin, Joseph William Frost, who had left his Boston practice to become a flight surgeon, informed me that the original homestead of the Frosts in America is at Frost Garrison in Eliot, Maine; that the family settled there in 1660; that ten generations of the same name, including all Robert's ancestors, had lived there; and that the two garrisons used in the French and Indian Wars are "in as fine a state of preservation as Robert himself."

It would be gratifying for me to believe that I was the first to discover Robert Frost's peculiar differences as a poet. But I was, at best, only one of the first to recognize his unique touch and tone of voice. In 1913 A Boy's Will had been published in England and, though it did not make much of a stir, it was praised by several of the severer critics, including Ezra Pound, who reviewed the book, sent some of Robert's manuscripts to Harriet Monroe's Poetry magazine, and tried to get him to join Pound's own Imagist group. The following year, when North of Boston was published, the praise was not only more general but less reserved. Edward Thomas wrote in the Daily News:

> This is one of the most revolutionary books of modern times, but one of the quietest and least aggressive. It speaks, and it is poetry.... These poems are revolutionary because they lack the

exaggeration of rhetoric, and even at first sight appear to lack the poetic intensity of which rhetoric is an imitation. . . . They succeed in being plain though not mean, in reminding us of poetry without being falsely 'poetical' ... Within the space of a hundred lines or so of blank verse it would be hard to compress more rural character and relevant scenery; impossible, perhaps, to do so with less sense of compression and more lightness, unity, and breadth.

Alfred Harcourt, editorial manager of Henry Holt and Company, who became Frost's publisher, brought North of Boston over from England and, knowing of my interest in the work, gave me a copy. At that time I was superintending my family's jewelry manufacturing establishment in Newark, New Jersey; but, during the hours I stole from my partners, I was writing poetry with one hand and criticising it with the other for the Chicago Evening Post. My review of North of Boston, along with Amy Lowell's critique in the New Republic, greeted Robert Frost when the First World War brought him back to the United States on Washington's Birthday in 1915. I wrote to him a few days after his arrival and, about a fortnight later, received the first of his letters.

THE LETTERS OF ROBERT FROST TO LOUIS UNTERMEYER

Dear Mr. Untermeyer:

What must you think of a silence as long as this to a letter as
good as that? But let me tell you by way of what places the letter has
just reached me: the office of The New Republic; the office of Henry
Holt; South Fork, Penna; Wildwood N.J., and Philadelphia. Such
is the fact, though I can't prove it by the envelope which has been
travelling some of the time in other envelopes.

Your cordiality is especially warming. There's not a person in New
York I should have had more pleasure in meeting than Louis
Untermeyer. For I was already feeling a good deal acquainted with
you from having heard your name so often mentioned under a certain
thatch roof in Ryton Dymock Gloucestershire England.

You make me wonder if I hadn't better get back to New York in
a month or two. I can just see and hear myself having a good time
with you somewhere where there's not too much noise of the city. I
could tell you a lot about Abercrombie.

You are all too good about "North of Boston."

Sincerely yours,

Robert Frost

 ˙ You weren't thinking of coming to Boston in May, were you? I
believe I am expected there somewhere round the fifth.

R.F.

*[The first line of the following letter refers to an article I had written,
one of the first printed in the United States which assigned a definite place in American poetry to Robert Frost. It made the not too
startling point that there was no such thing as an unpoetic subject,
although there were plenty of unpoetic poets, and that there were
always ideas, moods, and situations waiting for poetry to express.
The article appeared in the book section of the Chicago Evening
Post; the literary editor at that time (whom Frost wanted to thank)
was Llewllyn Jones.*

*The reference to a book in the third paragraph is to my second
and youthfully hortatory volume of poems, Challenge, which had
been published a few months previously in my twenty-ninth year.]*

3

Littleton   N.H.
April 3,   1915

Dear Untermeyer:

There are a dozen things in your article that I should like to thank you for in detail, but I must stop for just one of them now. You make the point that there must be many poetical moods that haven't been reduced to poetry. Thanks most of all for seeing that, and saying it in a review of a book by me.

You see so well the necessity of our being generous to each other as fellow artists. I probably don't deserve all your praise, but you'll never be the poorer for having uttered it, and trust my enemies to discount it where it needs discounting.

I am in your book almost as I write and full of the large spirit of it. You are the same in your letters, in your reviewing, and in your poetry. Really I knew you in England. I admire and envy you for knowing what you want to urge in prose and verse. I shall love your book.

All this is in haste. My chief object in writing is to get you word in time that I am to be at Sylvester Baxter's, 42 Murray Hill Road Malden Mass on April 4. On April 5 I shall be at Tufts College. On April 6 and on for several days at Baxter's again. Will you look me up there?—or call me up? Baxter would be glad to have you come to see us both. I did think, though, that I should like it if we could steal away somewhere by ourselves.

Yours ever
Robert Frost

I must thank Jones.

[As the last paragraph of the preceding letter suggests, we met at Sylvester Baxter's in Malden, Massachusetts, and stole off for a long talk. It was some months before we became Louis and Robert to each other, but a rapport if not an intimacy had been established. I attended some of his first public appearances and suffered with him. He was painfully aware and somewhat frightened of audiences, a self-consciousness from which he rarely freed himself—he never would dine or even converse with his hosts before a lecture. Actually, he never lectured. He talked and, as he grew more at ease with people, talked in what seemed a haphazard assortment of comments that developed into a shrewd commentary on poetry as it related

to the state of the world. He never "recited" his poems; he "said" them—sometimes, especially if they were new or short, he "said" them twice. "Would you like to hear me say that one again?" he would inquire.

I wrote about some of his readings in Boston and elsewhere; in Brooklyn I introduced him to the audience at the Academy of Music. Shortly after, I received the following note with a copy of the English first edition of North of Boston.

Although Frost kept away from the literati, he liked to hear gossip of the literary circles in New York, and this I was glad to furnish. The reference to eating "at the same table with Ella and even to listen for a moment to what she thinks" was prompted by such an item of gossip. The occasion was a dinner of the Poetry Society of America, and Ella was Ella Wheeler Wilcox, the popular and much-syndicated author of Poems of Passion, Poems of Pleasure, Poems of Power, etc. I remember her as a heavy woman with badly bleached hair, a faded Golden Girl in a gold-embroidered dress copied, she told me, from "an authentic picture of the Greek Muse." She also told me that I was mistaken about the New Poets—"they can only experiment with words. The great thing in poetry is beyond them." The great thing, of course, was Passion—the capital was distinctly pronounced.]

[Some time in Spring, 1915]

Dear Untermeyer—

Have this from me with my love. Your faith has made it yours.

I suppose it is good for a poet to be required to eat at the same table with Ella and even to listen for a moment to what she thinks. It is the sort of experience that can only come to him while he is on earth.

Down with our enemies and down with the drinks (before Bryan shuts off the supply of the latter and packs us off to The Hague with the former.)

I'll write again soon.

Yours ever
Robert Frost

[At thirty I was a junior member of my father's and uncle's firm of jewelry manufacturers; but I was also a contributing editor of The

Masses, a magazine which declared it was directed against "rigidity and dogma wherever it is found, a magazine whose final policy is to do as it pleases and conciliate nobody—*not even its readers.*" It was a publication "with no respect for the respectable," and it was run by a group of bohemian Socialists who considered themselves revolutionaries but who were horrified by its successor, the uncompromisingly Communistic New Masses. The group of coöperating editors of the old Masses included such artists as John Sloan, Stuart Davis, and Art Young, and such writers as Max Eastman, Floyd Dell, and John Reed.

Our headquarters were in Greenwich Village—it would have been a cowardly concession to the bourgeoisie to have had them anywhere else—and it was there I took Frost (we had dispensed with "Mr.") to meet my associates. He liked them. He refused to think of them as revolutionists; he considered them romantic rather than radical. It was more or less the way he considered himself. Years later he wrote:

> I never dared be radical when young
> For fear it would make me conservative when old.

My emotional intransigence did not bother him. What bothered him at that time was that I was on the defensive about his poetry. There had been some niggling criticism about his "farm poems," a sneer at "The Tuft of Flowers" to the effect that a good mower does not mow weeds, and a gibe that Frost had left America, like other expatriates, to get a reputation abroad. As he wrote, he had given up hope of getting a reputation of any sort by the time he was thirty-seven.

"I've just got home out of that." "That" was a short lecture trip— or, to be more exact, a brief series of talks and readings which he gave with some pleasure but with much apprehension.]

Littleton   N.H.
May 16   1915

Dear Untermeyer

I've just got home out of that.

Blow in with any breezy news you will. You know I see nothing here.

You needn't be afraid of being too romantic for me—you or your friends. I liked you all as I found you sprinkled through the Masses. It's all sorts of a world.

6

Call your attention to the fact that the author of A Tuft of Flowers forestalled the cynic by having the mower mow the weeds which are worse forage than the butterfly weed: item that it is the country custom to mow everything—the weeds to keep them from seeding. The cynic attitude toward poetry is not as safe as it looks.

Call your attention to the fact that there are no signs that I coveted a British-made reputation. At thirty-seven I had pretty well despaired of a reputation of any make. I went to England to write and be poor without further scandal in the family.

Comfort me with apples.

You are a lot of fun as Owen Hatteras* and something of a terror. I'm glad you didn't bite me.

Contrary to what I thought was the understanding, Ellery Sedgwick is still hanging on to Birches.

You have seen me—well where you have seen me, and if you can still remain my friend, all I can say is that—well I remain yours

R. F.

P.S. I ought to say dammit that the farm I was to have had for a thousand dollars has gone up a hundred or two owing to the owner's having seen my picture in the paper. You can see how that might be.

[In common with most poets, Robert Frost was ambivalent about criticism. He wanted to ignore it, but he also wanted to know what was being said about his work. Until I discovered that a derogatory line spoiled all his pleasure in an otherwise laudatory review, I sent him newspaper clippings from time to time. He grew particularly annoyed at what he called "the game of categories" and the effort to pin him down as a traditional romanticist or a resentful realist.

Besides acting as a sporadic clipping service, I offered to market some of his new poems. This, however, was, if not presumptuous, unnecessary, for the unknown poet had returned to America to find himself well known to the publishers. He was "sponsored" by Ellery Sedgwick, editor of the Atlantic Monthly, and soon he was much sought after.

*[Owen Hatteras was a pseudonym under which H.L. Mencken, George Jean Nathan, and Willard Huntington Wright contributed "pertinent and impertinent" epigrams to The Smart Set. I occasionally sent in a squib or two which appeared under the fancy nom de plume.]

The "Robinson" referred to is Robert's fellow New Englander, the poet Edwin Arlington Robinson.

The Garnett mentioned in the same paragraph as Ellery was the critic and essayist Edward Garnett, son of Dr. Richard Garnett, who had been superintendent of the Reading Room in the British Museum, and father of the novelist, David Garnett.

The invitation contained in the last paragraph was happily accepted. It marked the first of many visits to mountain homes in New Hampshire and Vermont.]

Franconia   N.H.
June 8   1915

You Louis U!

I believe you like to see me suffer—I do it so nobly.

It reduces itself to this, that I am native, I set up to be a poet, and am generally set down for a realist. I'll tell you how you can tell whether I am the last or not: find out how I fell in love. The realist always falls in love with a girl he has grown up and gone to school with, the romanticist with a new girl from "off somewhere." That's not to say that they don't both fall in love with the respective girls for what they don't know about them. Mystery draws both on; only in the case of the romantic it is a more obvious mystery—a less mysterious mystery.

Pretty lively news about the festering free versers and the new magazine of poetry. It seems to me you could have used to advantage at the paragraph-ends some such refrain as "The Bowery, the Bowery! I'll never go there any more."

I see be the papers that you have been disporting yourself cognito at something springy and festive got up by the classes; so you needn't try to deny it. I see it stated, though, that you weren't allowed to read any of your poetry there. That was probably salutary.

A thousand copies is a lot of any book of poetry to sell. Five hundred is more of an edition than many a good man sells in England. Big reputations are made on smaller sales. I venture to say that Abercrombie has never sold over three hundred of anything, yet his name is a word of awe in high places over there. I wonder how well Robinson does with his books?

Do you know, I think that a book ought to sell. Nothing is quite honest that is not commercial. Mind you I don't put it that everything commercial is honest.

The beauty of your book is that the poems in it all get together and say something with one accord. It's a long way from you down to the ladies (they are mostly ladies in this country) who find difficulty in making the lines in one poem get together like that.

The three poems you have interested yourself in are with Ellery to stay. Ellery has said it: he is going to be good to me. He is even going to print the article by my new-found friend Garnett. He says it overpraises me, but never mind, it may not hurt me: he has never known a man's head turned when his hair was turned already.

But—if you would, try to sell something else, when I am sure I have something.

We are not fast in our place yet. But this is where we want to live and, unless something hangs us up, here we shall live, and here if you will stand a sort of camping out we want you to come and see us— you and your wife, on your way to or from Ogonquit—and this summer. Make it a week or so. I wonder if you care for the mountains. Lafe, the mountain (alt. 5000 f.), not the man, stands right in front of us. We are all pine on this farm. Apples are not a success where the winter temperature sometimes drops to 40 below.

Yours ever

R.F.

Tell me if you will come.

[As the last line of the following letter implies, Frost was overly conscious of "enemies." Most of these were fancied and his animad-versions were not to be taken too seriously. Any poet identified with "the new poetry" was a potential rival and, hence, an enemy. Edgar Lee Masters, author of the much-reviewed, sensational Spoon River Anthology, was one of these. A less formidable contender for public notice was James Oppenheim, whose Songs for the New Age had recently appeared.

The letter also reveals Frost's distrust of poetic diction and words which, decorative but inert, substituted for thought and action. Literature consisted, he maintained in a memorable passage, of "words that have become deeds."]

Franconia   N.H.

July 8   1915

Dear Untermeyer

I think Spoon River is perfectly all right for them as likes it: and that is saying a good deal for a book I am not supposed to have seen. Why have you never sent along the copy you promised? And there was a book of Oppenheim's I was to have had.

Forgive me my nonsense as I also forgive the nonsense of those who think they talk sense. All I insist on is that nothing is quite honest that is not commercial. You needn't take that as said in character. Of course I don't mean by that that it isn't true. Nothing is true except as a man or men adhere to it—to live for it, to spend themselves on it, to die for it. Not to argue for it! There's no greater mistake than to look on fighting as a form of argument. To <u>fight</u> is to leave words and act as if you believed—to <u>act</u> as if you believed. Sometimes I have my doubts of words altogether and I ask myself what is the place of them. They are worse than nothing unless they do something, unless they amount to deeds as in ultimatums and war crys. They must be flat and final like the showdown in poker from which there is no appeal. My definition of literature would be just this, words that have become deeds.

Remember all I say is said in character. I urge nothing.

It is as well that you shouldn't come here now. Because we are not really here ourselves yet. I am milking a cow or two and otherwise acting as if the farm were mine, but I haven't felt secure enough in it to have fetched my furniture or to have laid out any money on repairs. I have to wait on the decision of a guardian in these matters. The guardian holds a few hundred dollars in trust for me which, if he thinks best, he can lend me to buy the farm with. And if not, not. Don't tell my critics of this lest it should prejudice them against my unfortunate books.

You will be just beaching—quenching your "speed in the slushy sand"—your New York speed. Take it easy and don't upon any consideration look for copy—as dear old Wilfrid Gibson does wherever he goes. Once we were coming home from some country races, what they call point-to-point races, when he asked me uneasily "I didn't see a thing there I could use, did you?" He counted the day lost and only asked consolation in learning that I had lost it too.

Those troubles rather told on me in my last six months in England. Now I can forget them in a couple of cows that have to be anchored at both ends as a boat ought to be when you fish for perch and pout.

I'll bet there is nearly as much water here today as there is where you are. And we care personally. We have to care. We have a garden we don't want drowned. We easily fall into bitter apostrophe when the weather goes wrong—we don't stop to ask whom to. We talk on. I can't help thinking it is good for us after all those years detachment and disinterestedness.

Iron cross for you if you kill more than so many of my enemies at once.

Yours ever
Robert Frost

[I don't remember how (or why) I humored Frost about his supposedly "bad" letter, but I do remember Richard Burton. Said to have been a descendant of the famous English translator of The Arabian Nights, Burton was the author of a dozen books of undistinguished prose and almost as many volumes of amiable verse forgotten as soon as read. I recall one volume, however, because of an incredibly mawkish poem about Shakespeare running "Across the fields to Anne"—a line which served as the refrain for seven simpering stanzas beginning:

> *How often in the summer-tide,*
> *His graver business set aside,*
> *Has stripling Will, the thoughtful-eyed,*
> > *As to the pipe of Pan,*
> *Stepped blithesomely with lover's pride*
> *Across the fields to Anne.*

The volume which contained this gem was entitled Dumb in June, and when I suggested that Burton should have been, Frost commented, "He was."

"Willitscan" shows Robert's little-known but definite predilection for playing: "Will it scan?"]

Franconia   N.H.
July 20   1915

My dear Untermeyer:

You do just right to humor me when I am like that: one of my wife's relatives married into a family in which there was a taint of insanity.

That was a bad letter I wrote you the other day and what was worse I sent it. I don't remember what I said in it, but it was naught. Always give a fellow another chance when he behaves badly, and still another chance after that. Never draw a line beyond which you won't allow a friend or anyone else to go. It is the mark of a small mind to draw the line anywhere.

I wrote of everything, I believe, but what was really bothering me, which was no more important a person than Richard Burton— poor dear—author of the mortal line (I don't lie): The Sough of winds in Immemorial trees (caps not his), which brings together in some sort of relation the two worst poeticisms of our poetical bankruptcy. Why should I mind Richard, you say. I don't mind him today. But I did two or three days ago while his offense was still fresh on the floor. He had been writing to a common friend a pious wish that, for my own sake, I weren't quite so "daringly radical." It's the damned hypocrisy of his "daringly" that seems like the whole nation against me. You see the force of it and you smell the device. It makes him seem to speak as a well-wisher. Torment his picture.

I come to you with this sorrow because you are a young feller with enough oil in your feathers to shed it for me. My own feathers are drying up with age. (Figure not necessarily drawn from the barnyard.)

Remember this if you are still in the water: There is no help in a wave when you are coming back to shore tired out. It will be going your way. For a moment you will be lifted up with hope on the crest of it. But it carries nothing with it. It will go forward itself, but leave you to the mercy of any current. It is a hateful delusion when you are desperate for solid ground under your feet.

Poem—what? Willitscan?

You will be glad to hear that my cows and I have composed our differences and I now milk them anchored at one end only. They have accepted me as their milker in place of the calves. The trouble was that I wasn't enough like the calves, which are black and ring-streaked, to impersonate them. And I lacked some of the calves' little ways. I was easily known for a changeling.

Isn't it the usual thing to wind up a bucolic like this with an Ah here we touch the realities of life? Let's make a list of the realist things we know.

We have a maple tree we call the Torch on the farm. We'll be lighting it about the time you come.

Yorn

R.F.

[Six months passed before we called each other by our first names; after that there was no question about formalities. Our friendship grew not only firmer but gayer. Robert's way of putting it was both teasing and touching. "I shan't be at ease till we are on emotional terms where there is no more controversy neither is there any danger of crediting one or the other with more or less than we mean."

Apart from my admiration for Robert's poetry, which never failed to excite as much as move me, what endeared him to me was his irrepressible sense of play. It was a rich and surprising playfulness, unexpected and almost unknown to the readers of his monologues, a delight in fooling for its own sake, a drollery that ranged from literary badinage to absurdly bland double meanings and wildly nonsensical puns.

"W.S.B.'s anthology" was the 1915 number of William Stanley Braithwaite's Anthology of Magazine Verse. Braithwaite, an American Negro poet and critic, began his collections of magazine verse in 1913 and, after publishing seventeen volumes, discontinued the series in 1929. Robert had seen some of the parodies with which I had been afflicting my friends and fellow poets. Holt's published them a few months later under the title "—and Other Poets."]

Franconia   N.H.

Sept 9   1915

Dear Louis

Let me call you that in the hope of softening a little the light with which you burn too bright for these old eyes. You mustn't be so intellectual with me. I shan't be at ease till we are on emotional terms where there is no more controversy neither is there any danger of crediting one or the other with more or less than we mean. Then we shall know when we are fooling because we shall be always fooling like a pair gay with love. We shan't mean anything too profoundly much except perhaps that we are friends and that nothing else matters between friends. That is the only sincerity: all else is an approximation. It sounds like the loss of something, and it is—of competition, of the

1 3

sharpening of wits and of the criticisms that makes us look to ourselves. But friendship is like that: it may not be as strengthening as enmity, and then again it may. At any rate it is different. The beauty of enmity is in insecurity; the beauty of friendship is in security.

Even here I am only fooling my way along as I was in the poems in The Atlantic (particularly in The Road Not Taken) as I was in what I said about Spoon River. I trust my meaning is not too hidden in any of these places. I can't help my way of coming at things.

It grieved me a little that you shouldn't have felt that what I wanted to say about Masters but couldn't say because it would sound strange coming from me—couldn't say in so many words at least—was that he was too romantic for my taste, and by romantic I'm afraid I mean among other things false-realistic. Such are my limitations. But don't scold me. It is a small matter. It's but a qualification moreover of a real liking for the book. I like it better for what it is than for what a lot of people take it for.

But Lord why waste time in the realms of neither here nor there!

And you are naught with all that nonsense about being in W.S.B's anthology so that you can review it in The Post. Your fault is that you are too active-minded. You may be as nimble as you please when you move; but most of the time you must plan to lie still. Otherwise you will think of something that is nothing. Only those thoughts are worth anything that we have in despite of our indolence. You mustn't larrup your faculties under penalty of being unreal. You mustn't intend to have an idea strike you any more than to have an automobile. Then if the auto strikes you—

And as for your parodies—why, you are a child if you think I mind them. They are not my kind of fooling; but they are a constituted kind and of course much better than mine. The best of your parody of me was that it left me in no doubt as to where I was hit. I'll bet not half a dozen people can tell who was hit and where he was hit by my Road Not Taken.

What would you say if you were to see me for a moment in New York before we see you here? I may have to take a run in on business with the Holts on or about the twenty fifth. I should wish to avoid the many, but if it came right you might give me a glimpse of your Clement Wood and your James Oppenheim.

With the devout Tennysonian wish that that which I have written

here may He within Himself make pure (I refuse to look back at it)
I am, my dear Poet,

Sinceriously yours

Robert Frost

Franconia   N.H.
Sept 24   1915

Dear Louis:

This is to be a business trip and I shall be with Harcourt (of
Holts) most of the time. We are seeing what can be done to save me
from Madam Nutt.* I set up to be practical, but I have got my
business into the conventional entanglement of the conventionally
unpractical poet.

As I say, I shall be in Harcourts hands and at his home for a day
or two. Then I shall have a day with you—perhaps a night too if you
have the room vacant you spoke of. I must not be gone from my
cows very long.

It was Longfellow and not Whittier who wrote Felicia Hemans.

Yours ever

Robert Frost

Franconia   N.H.
Nov. 1   1915

Tell me, Louis,

While it is uppermost in my mind what, when you are doing the
high critical, do you mean by "overtones" in poetry.
Don't, whatever you do, force an explanation. If you don't mean
anything, frankly say so. On the other hand if you mean something,
don't for the sake of being clever or seeming to be modest, don't I beg
of you protest that you don't mean anything. It is the truth I am
after in this as in all things. A wet blanket, now, on your cleverness.
I must know certain things to a certainty before I go me into the

---

*[Madam Nutt took over the business of David Nutt, the English publisher under
whose imprint A Boy's Will and North of Boston had been issued. I gathered later
that she felt that it was enough to publish a little-known poet; to pay him seemed
superfluous.]

world next week to preach the gospel of sound, which is, as you remember, take care of the sound and the sense will take care of itself.

Or if you don't know what you mean yourself when you speak or anyone else speaks of overtones, what do you suppose Amy Lowell, for instance and to be specific but at the same time not too personal, may mean? The question comes very near the heart of life for me. Yet let me not scare you out of your casual ease by my impressiveness. The situation requires that you should speak from what comes first to your mind. Be your limpid self in speaking. (I spare you the peroration. You get my drift.)

Let's see was there anything else I felt as deeply about that wouldn't seem like anticlimax coming after. Oh, there was Ellery. I didn't find him anywhere in Boston as I came through, which served me right for not sending word ahead. I said nothing and went to bed in the north-bound sleeper for home. Ellery doesn't even know I was gunning for him.

Are you coming to Boston somewhere round the 27th to meet me and see The Am. Dram. Soc. (Ink.) put on The Death of the Hired and Home Burial? I may not be there and then again I may.

Tell your wife that some day I am going to write you a family letter beginning Mes enfants in which I will undertake to make it clear to you why an old man would so much rather see people cunning than clever.

Ollers urn

R.F.

But I seem to see little or nothing of that book with your Swimmers in it.

Franconia   N.H.
November 11   1915

Dear Louis

Its all right then: there's nothing in the term that will make any difference in what I am about to say. I only wanted to be sure before I went ahead. It's just one of those bad analogies that obliterates the distinction between poetry and music. I knew you were well informed (as well as clever) and would be able to tell me everything. I never meant to imply that I had caught you talking of

"overtones" (even in undertones)—never! I don't know what I may
have said. I may have said anything and meant nothing or the very
opposite—just as I may have said you were clever when you weren't
even educated. You and I are not clever, Louis: we are cunning, one
with the cunning of race the other with the cunning of insanity.
(All women are cunning with the cunning of sex.)

Anybody can tell you are cunning by the way you phrase
yourself on the subject of Braithwaite's five best poems. The
selection "staggers you." That is to say you don't say it is not good and
you won't say you don't know what good is. You seem to allow that
the poems have merit, though you don't see it. They have none.
Amy's is just nothing to the eye, ear, or peritoneum. How completely
outside of herself she gets and how completely outside of everybody
else she keeps. She executes a frightfulness. Somewhere else she brings
in the Peeping-Tom idea. The Adventurer is a Blissful Carman—a
voice from the nineties. Mosher would like it. But to be novel you
have to revive something older than the nineties. Susanner simply
bothers me. A priori I ought to like any latter-day poem that uses the
word "bawdy." I don't know why I don't like this one unless it is
because it purports to make me think. A bawdy poem should go as
easy as a song: "In Amsterdam there lived a maid," frinstance.

But why try to discriminate in this world? It ill becomes the author
of poems not to like the other fellows' poems, because the more he
doesn't like the other people's poems the more he seems to his
suspectors to like his own. Me for Hudson Bay!

And whatever we do, Louis, let us never take the Poet as a
subject, as if so in love with the idea of being a poet that we don't
realize that in Who's Who poets are rated lower than aldermen. A
man has a right to be a poet if he can climb into the Poetry Society,
but he needn't go calling himself sticky names like Gayheart in public.

I wish you wouldn't keep reminding me of the poetry societies I
belong to.

Can you drore pitchers? Let me do you one of our new home (not
yet finished or begun) on the Shores of Hudson Bay.

I profess myself an idealist in pictorial art. I have four children
who are enhanced as I take it by not being represented in the picture.
Art has ever been my lifelong solace when things have been going
wrong at the front. The object with the long matted hair is me
neglecting the fur business to go fishing on the immemorial sea

HUDSON'S
BAY

incarnadine—I might as well have said neglecting one thing to do another, as always. How it all comes back to me from the future. (It would come forward to me from the past, you!) The boat is named the New Moon to put it in the moon series with Henrick Hudson's Half Moon. The dog is behind the house barking at an Indian or something mysterious astir in the forest of Eld. My wife—I don't mean to desert my wife: she is there too—is cooking linseed doughnuts in bear grease. Nearest neighbors—not any. Nearest library—Carnegie at Newhernhut. You come too.

R. F.

As you say, few of these poets are much bothered by anything that is in them. I wish you would give them all Hell and relieve my feelings without involving me in the odium of seeming jealous of anybody. You have a scourging pen. Scourge away.

[Besides editing and publishing his annual Anthology of Magazine Verse, William Stanley Braithwaite reviewed poetry for the Boston Transcript and summed up what he considered the most notable achievements of each season. Robert was amused and a little irritated by Braithwaite's choices. He found Amy Lowell lacking in humor as well as the humanities, working herself into fits of spurious excitement, "motion as a substitute for emotion." Bliss Carman, co-author with Richard Hovey of Songs from Vagabondia, was a popular poet of the eighteen-nineties, and Thomas B. Mosher was an arty publisher of the same period. "Susanner" is the central figure of Wallace Stevens' "Peter Quince at the Clavier"—"Susanna's music touched the bawdy strings." "Gayheart: A Story of Defeat," written by Dana Burnet, was praised by Braithwaite as unquestionably one of the best poems of the year.]

Franconia   N.H.

Decem 3   [1915]

Dear Louis:

I think I told you what we were in for. But we are not in for it any longer. We have just passed through one of those family crises that leave nothing to show for themselves. We are lucky in all being still alive. I am nurse, cook, and chambermaid to the crowd, and that discouraged it would do my enemies (see roster of the Poetry Society of America) good to see me.

Sometime I will do as you tell me—write a little more poetry and a little prose too. Not now.

You needn't tell anyone I am so down or I shall have everybody on top of me. You know what a wolf-pack we are.

Goobye—goobye

R.F.

It's a joy to me that you have come in with us.* Let's start a great period in American letters. (Some people in Boston don't like my levity in such remarks as that.) Harcourt is the best ever.

Franconia   N.H.

December 22   1915

Dear Louis:

Sometime at a worse season I will tell you what I think of Braithwaite and having said so much to pollute this letter I will break off here and begin over on a fresh sheet which I will mail under a separate cover.

Nobody's but yours

R.

*["Us" was Henry Holt and Company, who, in 1919, under the aegis of Alfred Harcourt, became my publisher. Harcourt also became my friend, and I went with him when he founded his own firm.]

[Franconia   N.H.
December 24   1915]

(With a water-color drawing of pine trees by Lesley Frost)

CHRISTMAS TREES*

The city had withdrawn into itself
And left at last the country to the country;
When between whirls of snow not come to lie
And whirls of faded foliage not yet laid
There drove one day a stranger to my door
Who did in country fashion in that there
He sat and waited till he drew us out,
A-buttoning coats, to ask him who he was.
He proved to be the town come back to look
For something in the country he had left
And could not do without and keep his Christmas.
He asked if I would sell my Christmas trees;
My woods—the young fir balsams like a place
Where houses all are churches and have spires.
I doubt if I was tempted for a moment
To sell them off their feet to go in cars
And leave the slope behind the house all bare
Where the sun shines now no warmer than the moon.
I'd hate to have them know it if I was.
Yet who would have his trees but as the trees
Of others are and who refuse for them
Trial by market that all things must come to?
I dallied so much with the thought of selling.
Then whether from mistaken courtesy
And fear to seem too short of speech or whether
From hope of hearing good of what was mine
I said, "I wonder are there trees enough
To make it worth your while."
                                        He saw a chance.
"I could soon tell how many they ought to cut—
You let me look them over."
                                        "You could look.
But don't expect I'm going to let you have them."

Pasture they spring in, some in clumps too close
That lop each other and leave few branches green.

*[This differs in many details from the printed version.]

"No good to me," he said. But not a few
Stood solitary and had equal boughs
All round and round. He nodded Yes to those
Or paused to say beneath some lovelier one
With the buyer's moderation "That would do."
We climbed the pasture on the south, crossed over,
And came down on the north.

       He said "A thousand."
"A thousand Christmas trees!—at what apiece?"
"A thousand trees would come to thirty dollars."
Then I was certain I had never meant
To let him have them. Never show surprise!
But thirty dollars seemed so small beside
The extent of pasture I should strip, three cents—
For that was what it figured out a tree—
Three cents so small beside the dollar friends
I should be writing to within the hour
Would pay in cities for good trees like those,
Regular vestry-trees whole Sunday Schools
Could hang enough on to pick off enough.

A thousand Christmas trees I didn't know I had!
And looked at from the other fellows eyes
Worth three cents more to give away than sell
(A simple calculation will show that).
Too bad I cannot lay one in a letter.
I can't help wishing I could send you one
In wishing you herewith

      A <u>Merry</u> Christmas

For a few Untermeyers (three to be exact)
    from
  a many Frosts (six to be exact)

       [Franconia, N.H.
       January 1, 1916]

Dear Louis:
 Mind you I haven't read Fannie [Stearns Davis] and I haven't
read Braithwaite's g.d. book—I got one of the children to read it for
me and tell me about it. All that saved the fat obstacle from the

worst fate that overtakes paper was your name and mine on the flyleaf.

No, I didn't read the book. I'll tell you what I did do, though. I took the Midnight Horror out of Littleton not long ago, and on the train with me I had about as many good-looking boys and girls as there are great poets in the book. They were of the Lisbon High School which had just beaten at basket-ball for a second time the Littleton High School. And they were yelling glad. And this is what they kept saying all together and out loud: it came somewhere near expressing my feelings, though at the same time it shocked me: since as you know I am not a swearing man: I couldn't help liking the liberty taken in the rhyme: all the old rhyme pairs are so worn out that I'm ready to permit anything for the sake of a fresh combination: this was a new one to me—it may not be to you: well here goes: I mustn't put you off any longer: this is what the good looking children said:

> Lisbon once—Lisbon twice!
> Holy jumping Jesus Christ!

Maybe you don't like me to talk this way. I can see that I am going to make enemies if I keep on. Still that won't be anything new or strange. I had nothing but enemies three years ago this Christmas.

Why go into details? Granted that there are a few good poems in the book—I read yours and liked it because it says something, first felt and then unfolded in thought as the poem wrote itself. That's what makes a poem. A poem is never a put-up job so to speak. It begins as a lump in the throat, a sense of wrong, a homesickness, a lovesickness. It is never a thought to begin with. It is at its best when it is a tantalizing vagueness. It finds its thought and succeeds, or doesn't find it and comes to nothing. It finds its thought or makes its thought. I suppose it finds it lying around with others not so much to its purpose in a more or less full mind. That's why it oftener comes to nothing in youth before experience has filled the mind with thoughts. It may be a big big emotion then and yet finds nothing it can embody in. It finds the thought and the thought finds the words. Let's say again: A poem particularly must not begin with thought first.

Say! When I get started! What?

Thanks for your defense in The Call. You and I have got inside of each others breast works. I shall be glad when you can like anything I do. But don't feel obliged to like it (I know you won't—you are an honest man). I mean to hang on to you as a friend whatever you have to say of my poetry.

I shall come to see you if I stop more than three hours in New York. That dinner comes just wrong. I have engagements for a little money on the day before it and the day after—and, by rights, just on it.

I'm glad for your wife she has found a backer in Amy Lowell. I'm hoping to be more and more her backer when I see more of her work. There's an opening there she's making for herself—I don't mean with any person or persons—I mean in a realm.

You mustn't mind me. Some days you would think I knew it all, to see me on paper. In reality I am only a poor man on ration. Its a hard winter and I'm hard up and sometimes I harden my heart against nearly everything.

You came into our Christmas to make us a good deal happier. We're all your friends—friends of all of you.

If there were no God—but there is one, that's just the point— he's come back at the smell of blood on his altars—and he hasn't come back in pieces (two or more) like Biela's comet the last time it turned up—He is still One.

R. F.

Looking for the Yale Review and that puts me in mind of something else to thank you for, but not this time—later.

[Robert was unusually bitter about Braithwaite. But if the anthologist's bad taste put Robert in a bad temper, it also made him consider what makes a poem. A year or two later I excerpted the passage beginning "A poem is never a put-up job ... It begins as a lump in the throat, a sense of wrong, a homesickness, a lovesickness." It has since appeared in many textbooks as a poet's clue to the sources of poetry.]

[Franconia,   N.H.
January 7,   1916]

Dear Louis:

Will you tell me who Willa Sibert Cather is?* Is the name a man's? That's what I want particularly to know. Is he (or she) some poet I ought to have read?

R. F.

[The Poetry Society of America was a hodgepodge of well-meaning "melancholy trillers and thrillers" (Cummings' caustic phrase), middle-aged dilettanti who had had an occasional bit of verse published in some out-of-the-way magazine—Mencken called them "dessicated ladies of both sexes"—and a very few genuine poets. Many years later Robert was to become its Honorary President and was to be its honored guest at dinners given to celebrate another medal or award. But in 1916 the poet who discarded rhetoric and the grand opera manner in favor of a colloquial idiom was regarded with suspicion by the mediocrities who considered themselves arbiters of "the poetic tradition." I am afraid that I gave him a rather malicious report of one of their meetings during which his name was bandied about by those who constituted themselves the Old Guard. I also fear that I hoped to rouse if not to rile the best and most misfit poet in the stuffy Society.]

Franconia   N.H.
Feb 3,   1916.

Dear Louis:—

Just to protest that though in bed with the temperature of a setting hen I ain't a'goin' to die to please

> Ella Wheeler Wilcox
> Robert Underwood Johnson
> Richard Le Gallienne
> Abbie Farwell Browne
> Benjamin R. C. Low

*[The question of Willa Cather's identity was both ingenuous and genuine. Although her most famous novel, My Ántonia, had not yet appeared, three other volumes of prose had been published. But Robert had heard of her only as a poet, for it was with a book of poems, April Twilights, that she had made her debut.]

1916

    Brian Hooker
    Joyce Kilmer
    Cale Young Rice
    Florence Earle Coates
    Richard Burton
    Arthur Guiterman
    Olive Tilford Dargan
      or any other
    Old-believer,
    Whatsoever.

                            R.F.
                        (by Lesley)

*[The dedication to Robert, mentioned in the next letter, was in
These Times, a collection of poems published in 1917. Odell Shepard
and "a Stark Youth" (the novelist and drama critic, Stark Young)
were among those who made speeches at a Poetry Society meeting.
The family references are to my only brother, Martin, my first wife,
Jean Starr, and my son Richard. To prove I was a good jeweler, I
had sent Robert's wife, Elinor, a necklace I had designed, and, to
prove I was a poet, it had been accompanied by a sonnet.]*

                      Franconia   NH
                      February 28   1916

Friend of the Poor and Neglected:

Your dedication if I get it will make up to me for many things I
haven't had in life. You seem bent on being good to me whether I
deserve it or not—as I think I have said before. (Never mind, so long
as no one else has said it. But perhaps your wife has or some one of
your friends who is acquainted with the facts of the case, viz. my
unworthiness and your generosity.) I shall accept the poems and ask
no question. And all that are no worse than "Swimmers" I promise
to read and love for their own sake as well as yours. And the next
time we are in New York together won't we open a bottle of the
Illor Wellor Wheelcox brand of apricot cocktail on it!

I'm sorry for your brother. I hope he comes out right soon. Is it
the brother I met that night?—that night! If so and I may claim
acquaintance, remember me to him.

God deliver me even from having been where I would have had to
treat as my superior the likes of O. Shepard and a Stark Youth. I'm
glad Jean made hay. I should like to hear her read some time, but
where there were no particular drawbacks.

25

Looking over your letter again has just given me an idea for a suicide poem of my own in which a butcher by trade kills himself, cuts himself up, and distributes the pieces in corners and closets from garret to cellar. Very gruesome—also mysterious till you know the solution. Classification: historical pastoral.

Your guess would be that the order is wrong and he cut himself up and then killed himself. I have known of such a case. The victim— but I spare you the details. The motive was to cast suspicion on an enemy. The scene was a sawmill where there were things enough to cut with. I don't like this story. No chance for psychological gags. Some day I'll do you the other. And there's the tale of the dentist and the illegal operation. I forget what to call it. I guess I won't write it till I get a good name for it. A Dream of Julius Caesar. How would that be?

I was thinking I would let Benét have the poem you spoke of. It was among those I sent to Harcourt, was it? I must ask it back. Benét had an idea it would do for his chimerical scheme. You don't dislike it, then? I mean the poem—not the chimerical scheme. Any chimerical scheme is good per se.

You wait till I start roasting friends when I go on the road next fall with my stock lecture "New Sound in Poetry"! Of course something may interfere to prevent my going. Let's hope so.

We are all well of some things but we are sick of some others. Something that appeared in The Post a week or so ago nearly finished us. But the necklace came and it was all lovely. And thanks for the sonnet. Hit 'em again.

You tell Dick that I will talk moon to him next time if I have to talk in verse to do it.

Always yours
R.F.

A sonnet comes about as near being a cube to the eye—or at least a square as any poetic form we have. But you want me to believe it <u>isn't</u> cubism!

[Baxter's question (fifth paragraph of the next letter) concerned a remark I had been making in my lectures on "Modern American Poetry" about Robert Frost's being one of our three most important and most recognizably native poets. Later I named the other two: Walt Whitman and Emily Dickinson.

*The quotation about Heraclitus in the same paragraph is a take-off
on William Johnson Cory's paraphrase of Callimachus.]*

Franconia   N.H.

March 21   1916

Dear Louis:

I wish I could remember where-all I've been in the past week or
so and who-all I've baptized into my heresies. Here I am home again
in disgrace with those who see through me and ready with pen and
the same kind of note paper to resume inkling. You first!

I'm glad you found it in you to give Robinson his due because he
gave you yours, you devil, the night of the Poetry Meal. The way he
snickered over you was the next best thing to you there, confirming
me in what I had about made up my mind was the best quality in his
books. You are only more witty than he.

Sometimes I think you are a blinding flash—as in that preface to
"—and Other Poets." And don't think that because I don't think
you as successful with me as with Masefield, Yeats, Lindsay, Masters,
Pound, and some others I don't like the whole book as well as any
part of it. There ain't been no such book for brilliance.

I'm too faint with the pleasure you give me with your Review of
Reviews review to meet it with objection. I can't help suspecting you
know what you are talking about. You speak not without having had
time to think me over.

Baxter axt me the same question he asked you as to your three
and whether you meant them dead or alive. I shall tell him Riley,
Ella, and me, and all congenitally dead from the waist up. "They told
me, Heraclitus, they told me I was dead. They brought me bitter
tears to hear and bitter news to shed."

And Harold Goddard Rugg is a young librarian at Dartmouth
who, it's a safe guess, has been writing to you to ask you some such
question as Baxter's. I slept with him when I was at Hanover for my
lecture in the winter (as distinguished from the spring if it ever
comes); so naturally he has an interest in finding out what he was
entertaining unawares.

Very zeroic weather here yet.

Probability of our being in New York week after next.

All yours by this time

R.

[The next letter again discloses Robert's characteristic blend—perhaps alternation is the better word—of wildness and seriousness, of prankish nonsense and bitter sense. The talk about his future is as fantastic as the references to his past, as is the grim conclusion that "it's all over at thirty." Unlike Edgar Lee Masters, the fancied "hated rival" whose work after Spoon River Anthology marked an unsteady decline, Robert was just beginning—the lyrics in the forthcoming Mountain Interval were to surprise those who, having discovered North of Boston, thought of him only as a writer of blank-verse narratives.

The "sample" ("Old Age") from the "fourth book" is, of course, pure teasing. It has never appeared anywhere in print. Pitchblende might have been a provocative title, but Robert was only leg-pulling when he mentioned it; it was the pastoral rather than the mineral earthiness that was suggested by the title poem of his fourth volume, New Hampshire.

Toward the end of the third paragraph, Robert says that someone asks: "Have you done that Phi Beta Kappa poem yet?" This refers to "The Bonfire," his eclogue which he read in 1916 at Harvard.

"Toop"—Robert's brusquely punning footnote—is what he wryly considered himself worth: two-penny.]

[Franconia,   N.H.
May 4,   1916]

Dear Old Louis

When I have borne in memory what has tamed Great Poets, hey? Am I to be blamed etc? No you ain't. Or as Browning (masc.) has it:

> That was I that died last night
> When there shone no moon at all
> Nor to pierce the strained and tight
> Tent of heaven one planet small.
> Might was dead and so was Right.

Not to be any more obvious than I have to be to set at rest your brotherly fears for my future which I have no doubt you assume to be somehow or other wrapped up in me, I am going to tell you something I never but once let out of the bag before and that was just after I reached London and before I had begun to value myself for what I was worth.* It is a very damaging secret and you may not

*(Toop.)

28

thank me for taking you into it when I tell you that I have often wished I could be sure that the other sharer of it had perished in the war. It is this: The poet in me died nearly ten years ago. Fortunately he had run through several phases, four to be exact, all well-defined, before he went. The calf I was in the nineties I merely take to market. I am become my own salesman. Two of my phases you have been so—what shall I say—as to like. Take care that you don't get your mouth set to declare the other two (as I release them) a falling off of power, for that is what they can't be whatever else they may be, since they were almost inextricably mixed with the first two in the writing and only my sagacity has separated or sorted them in the afterthought for putting on the market. Did you ever hear of quite such a case of Scotch-Yankee calculation? You should have seen the look on the face of the Englishman I first confessed this to! I won't name him lest it should bring you two together. While he has never actually betrayed me, he has made himself an enemy of me and all my works. He regards me as a little heinous. As you look back don't you see how a lot of things I have said begin to take meaning from this? Well...

But anyway you are freed from anxiety about my running all to philosophy. It makes no difference what I run to now. I needn't be the least bit tender of myself. Of course I'm glad it's all up with Masters, my hated rival. He wasn't foresighted enough, I'll bet, to provide against the evil day that is come to him. He failed to take warning from the example of Shelley who philosophized and died young. But me, the day I did The Trial by Existence (Boy's Will) says I to myself, this is the way of all flesh. I was not much over twenty, but I was wise for my years. I knew then that it was a race between me the poet and that in me that would be flirting with the entelechies or the coming on of that in me. I must get as much done as possible before thirty. I tell you, Louis, it's all over at thirty. People expect us to keep right on and it is as well to have something to show for our time on earth. Anyway that was the way I thought I might feel. And I took measures accordingly. And now my time is my own. I have myself all in a strong box where I can unfold as a personality at discretion. Someone asks with a teasing eye, "Have you done that Phi Beta Kappa poem yet?" "No, I don't know that I have, as you may say." "You seem not to be particularly uneasy about it." "Oh,

that's because I know where it's coming from, don't you know."
Great effect of strength and mastery!

Now you know more about me than anyone else knows except that
Londoner we won't count because he may be dead of a lachrymous.

And don't think mention of the war is anything to go by. I could
give you proof that twenty years ago in a small book I did on Boeme
and the Technique of Sincerity I was saying "The heroic emotions,
like all the rest of the emotions, never know when they ought to be
felt after the first time. Either they will be felt too soon or too late
from fear of being felt too soon."

Ever thine

R.F.

I must give you a sample from the fourth book, "Pitchblende."
As a matter of fact and to be perfectly honest with you there is a
fifth unnamed as yet, the only one unnamed (the third has been long
known as "Mountain Interval") and I think the most surprising of
the lot (circa 1903). But none of that now.

OLD AGE

My old uncle is long and narrow.
And when he starts to rise
After his after-dinner nap
I think to myself
He may do it this once more
But this is the last time.
He lets one leg slip off the lounge
And fall to the floor.
But still he lies
And looks to God through the ceiling.
The next thing is to get to his outside elbow
And so to a sitting posture
And so to his feet.
I avert my eyes for him till he does it.
Once I said from the heart,
"What is it, Uncle?—
Pain or just weakness?
Can't we do anything for it?"
He said "It's Specific Gravity"
"Do you mean by that that it's grave?"
"No, not as bad as that yet, child,
But it's the Grave coming on."

Then I knew he didn't mean Seriousness
When he said Gravity.
Old age may not be kittenish
But it is not necessarily serious.

R. F.

Someone writes to tell me that the Poetry Society had one of my poems to abuse in manuscript the other night. Absolutely without my knowledge and consent. I don't mind their abuse, but I do mind their trying to make it look as if I was fool enough to come before them for judgment except with something I had cooked up for their limitations. Protest for me, will you? I wonder how in the world they got the manuscript.

[Robert always insisted on the difference between being a rebel and a radical. He argued that a radical was tied far more unquestionably to a program and a rigid set of principles than a reactionary, whereas a rebel was free—free to denounce any political party, propaganda, creed, or cant. As a rebel, he was willing to be the rejected and rejecting individual, isolated, speculating sorrowfully on man's eagerness to "belong," to trade individuality for group "togetherness" and mass conformity.

At this time his letters sounded many variations on the theme of foes and friends. I was, of course, touched by the evidences of a friendship which grew continually closer and warmer, and I was also amused by his mock fulminations against his enemies.

It was in the spirit of mockery—"I sort of fool along"—that he sent me a parody of a lecture prospectus. He had given several "talks" after his return to America—he was the most provocative and most penetrating of talkers—but, although for many years it was a way of supporting his farm and his family, lecturing was a kind of public torture. He could never get himself to prepare the customary "descriptive list" of subjects and even refused to confine himself to a set of titles. A self-adulating circular put out by the elderly poet Edwin Markham set him off—it "made me wonder if I hadn't a series of lectures in me that I could give."

Enclosed with the following letter was a broad burlesque of what lecture committees liked and what he could never get himself to do. The combination of plain fact and fancy fooling presents a practically unknown Frost. The reference to his "immersing" himself

in White Wyandottes conceals a more or less serious grief of un-
gratified chicken farming.]

Franconia   N.H.
May 24   1916

Dear Old Louis:

Seriously I am fooling. And so are you with your crocodile
you'llyou'llations. Come off. I thought you and we was going to be
rebels together. And being rebels doesn't mean being radical; it
means being reckless like Eva Tanguay.* It means busting something
just when everybody begins to think it so sacred it's safe. (See Rheims
Cathedral—next time you're in France.)

These folks that get on by logical steps like a fly that's climbed out
of the molasses a little way up the side of the cup—them I have no
use for. I'm all for abruption. There is no gift like that of suddenly
turning up somewhere else. I like a young fellow as says, "My
father's generation thought that, did they? Well that was the Hell of
a way to think, wasn't it? Let's think something else for a change." A
disconnective young fellow with a plenty of extrication in his make-up.
You bet your sweet life. What would the editors of the Masses say
to such onprincipled—what shall I call it?

The only sorrow is that I ain't as reckless as I used to be. That is
to say not in as many departments.

The sacred theory that you may not have theories is one I might
not hesitate to lay hands on. But dear me it will have to wait till I
have a day off. There's the planting to think of and the Phibetakappa
poem and I can't tell you what all.

Meanwhile and till I can go to join him here's a sigh and a tear
for poor old Masters. That stuff on the outside of Sandburg's book is
enough to prove my original suspicion, not that Masters is just dead
but that he was never very much alive. A fellow that's that way can't
ever have been any other way. But we won't labor that. We won't
labor or belabor anything and so we shall save ourselves from all
things dire. Nothing but what I am "forced to think", forced to feel,
forced to say, so help me, my contempt for everything and
everybody but a few real friends.

*[Eva Tanguay, a vaudeville performer who popularized a song of recklessness, "I
Don't Care."]

You are of the realest of these. Who else has struck for me so often in swift succession. I had seen what you wrote in Masses. The devil of it is I am getting so I rather expect it of you. Don't fail me!

Markham's circular made me wonder if I hadn't a series of lectures in me that I could give. So I blocked out a few. They are not much like what I have been giving for my salt. And yet perhaps they are or nearer it than the set talks I would give for instance in school. I sort of fool along.

And by the way I'm going to teach for a week or so at a summer school in July.

And by the way I'm going to do something in Philadelphia on June 1st—I can't tell what till I get there. I can't stop in New York because there is sickness and trouble here at home that I must hurry back to. You will come over to Boston when I go down for June 19th (I think it is). I take you at your word.

Don't mind me, but let me carry on for a rest. We haven't got to be a blasted thing, now, have we? Let's make it easy for each other.

Always yours

R.

I have liked James' book.* It has more things of heaven and earth in it than Sandburg's.

[Enclosure]

ANYBODY WANT TO HEAR R. FROST ON ANYTHING?
Partial List of Subjects in Stock:

BOOTY. Derivation of the word from beauty. Two words interchangeable in age of bride-snatching. Poetry, the bride of elemental nature. Richard Le Gallienne. Kale Young Rice. Edith Thomas. Etc.

THE UNATTAINABLE. How much ought a poet get for showing (Hamlet, Act III, Scene 2) in public? How much is fifty dollars? Are the English overpaid? Masefield. Yeats. Noyes. Base suggestion that poetry is as often gloating over what you have as hankering after what you haven't. Strabismus and Idealismus.

POETRY AND SCIENCE. Is the conflict irreconcilable? How long will

*[James Oppenheim's *Songs for the New Age*.]

the war last? Piece of Utrecht and other memorable pieces. Aphasia. Pompadour. Nell Gwyn. Resolved that evolution is like walking on a rolling barrel. The walker isn't so much interested in where the barrel is going as he is in keeping on top of it. The Labyrinthodont. The Sozodont. The Cotoledon. The Dodecahedron. The Plesiosaurus. The Thesaurus (and Rhyming Dictionary). The Megatheorem. The Pterodactyl. The Spondee. And the Concordance.

THE INEVITABLE: AND HOW TO POSTPONE OR AVOID IT. How to keep from attaining what you don't want. Query: If what Shelley meant by Prometheus wasn't the philosophizing poet, Shelley himself? The world's gain could he have stood fate off for one year. Two years. Five years. Ten years. Futility of speculation.

THE HARRISON LAW. Some dull opiate to the drains. Swinburne's famous adjuration to his sister: "Swallow, my sister; oh, sister, swallow!" Picture: We were the first that ever burst; or the danger of mixing drinks. Jamaica Ginger. A plain talk to druggists. Given in England under the title: A plain talk to chymists.

MOANISM AND SWOUNDING. On larruping an emotion. Men's tears tragic, women's a nuisance. Heightening. In this I make it clear—by repeated assertions—that I can use any adjective that anyone else can.

NEW HAMPSHIRE GOLD. Adventure with an examining doctor for an insurance company who, after looking me over and taking samples of me, decided I was just the romantic kind he could unload a small wild farm on because it was blessed with a gold mine that had been worked to the extent of producing three wedding and engagement rings. The moral being that I am not romantic.

TRUE STORY OF MY LIFE. Stealing pigs from the stockyards in San Francisco. Learned to whistle at five. At ten abandoned senatorial ambitions in order to come to New York, but settled in New Hampshire by mistake on account of the high rents in both places. Invention of cotton gin. Supersedes potato whisky. A bobbin boy in the mills of Lawrence. Nailing shanks. Rose Marie. La Gioconda. Astrolabe. Novum Organum. David Harum. Visit General Electric Company, Synecdoche, N.Y. Advance theory of matter (what's the matter?) that becomes an obsession. Try to stop thinking by immersing myself in White Wyandottes. "North of Boston." Address Poetry Society at Great Poetry Meal. Decline. Later works. Don't seem to die. Attempt to write "Crossing the Bar."

34

(International copyright.) Time: three hours. Very intimate and baffling.

(NOTE): Some of these lectures are more intelligible if taken in combination with all the rest together the same afternoon or evening.

Dollar a minute or sixty minutes for fifty dollars. I have to ask a little more where I introduce my adjectives immediately after, instead of before, my nouns—as in The House Disorderly.

Lists of nouns and adjectives I am accustomed to use furnished in advance to guard against surprise.

[During the spring of 1916 a group of young writers met frequently to discuss the launching of a new magazine which, unlike The Masses, would place emphasis on the cultural and national rather than on the socialistic and sociological point of view. We were fortunate in finding a (temporary) backer, and the first issue of The Seven Arts appeared in November. James Oppenheim was the editor, Waldo Frank the associate editor, and there was an Advisory Board of contributing editors which consisted of Van Wyck Brooks, Robert Edmond Jones, and a few others, including Robert (as indicated in his letter of June 6, 1916) and myself. We planned to set the Mississippi (or at least the Hudson) on fire, and we flourished our opening statement in the style of a manifesto: "It is our faith and the faith of many that we are living in the first days of a renascent period, a time which means for America the coming of that national consciousness which is the beginning of greatness."

In spite of our resolution to steer clear of politics we could not avoid the war. We offended the government (and, worse, our sponsor) by anti-war articles; we became a war casualty. The Seven Arts suspended publication at the end of our first year. Robert's "The Bonfire" (a poem which caused much comment because of a line, "War is for everyone, for children too.") appeared in the first number; his "A Way Out" (a tensely compacted one-act play) in the fourth.]

Franconia   N.H.
June 6   1916

Dear Louis:

Count me in of course. It sounds to me. What couldn't you hope to do to R. Burton, T. Garrison, and the like with an engine of that range? Death to the dead ones!

Never give up trying to make me "a prominent New Englander" till you make me one. Think of me as an Advisory Board! <u>Cave poetam</u>* when he gets a little power in his hands.

No, but seriousness aside, I should like nothing better than having some little part in your enterprise.

You don't mean that I should work—very hard, anyway, except hemming and hawing and rubbing up my spectacles in my best Supreme Court manner.

I seen your Post impression of me and have forgiven you, since you speak of it, your mixing me up with Masters. Next time you mention me in the Catalogue of the Ships put me in a different boat from the mighty Chicagoan. We are two separate aJackses.

This is more haste than is good for me at my age—but the habits of a lifetime, my child, the habits of a lifetime...

I'll tell you more when I know more myself.

Always yours

R.

[Undated]

Dear Louis:

What disheartened me about this Bonfire was that it made everybody think or so many think that it was saying something on one side or the other of a "question of the day." Dammit.

What should you say?

More anon. I'm just off to Plymouth for a week's work.

Love your country,

As allers

R.F.

[After graduating from Lawrence (Massachusetts) High School in his eighteenth year, Robert had passed half his entrance examinations for Harvard; but his grandmother disliked Harvard and he was sent to Dartmouth. He quit Dartmouth almost as soon as he entered it and stayed away from institutionalized education until he was nearly twenty-three. This time he went to Harvard and exposed himself to formal studies for about two years, but again neglected to graduate. He was forty-two when he received the first of his academic

---

*[Beware of the poet.]

honors, and was chosen to deliver the Phi Beta Kappa poem at
Harvard in 1916.

"Harriette" is Harriet Monroe, who had founded Poetry: A Mag-
azine of Verse and who was championing Vachel Lindsay's poetry,
a combination of religion and ragtime—someone said it was the
Gospel preached through a hot saxophone. "King Solomon" is
Lindsay's "King Solomon and the Queen of Sheba," the third
"chant" in what Lindsay called "The Booker Washington Trilogy."
The first two poems in the incongruous series are "Simon Legree: A
Negro Sermon" and "John Brown."

Carol was Robert's only living son.]

Franconia N.H.
June 15 1916

Dear Louis:

This is it.* I don't advise your coming over to hear me. There is an
orator you might care to hear, though I have made a point of not
learning who he is, in order to be beforehand with him in case he
should be up to ignoring poetry in the person of me. He is doubtless
a statesman—and I know these statesmen.

I've been keeping under cover a couple of things called An
Axe-helve and The Bonfire for this occasion. Neither of them except
by a stretch of the words can be called either timely or appropriate.
That much may be said in their favor. One is old old and the other is
new and so older than the first because it is written by an older man.

Thanks for a glimpse of Harriette in mid career. Of course I can
do nothing with King Solomon because it is not self-expressing.
Simon I agree will do for fun with the children, but you will admit
that it is a very cheap gallop of verses. The way John Brown gets
into the Negro folk-thought affects me. Vachel is at least more
interesting than a lot of us.

Of yours I like better the second, though you may not expect it
of me from what you know of my own work. I am emboldened by
that. It tells me why we are friends.

It was no very lyric time at Baxter's. I was there to see about
taking Carol to Mrs. Baxter's brother who is a specialist of the lungs.
They have been extraordinarily good about Carol. All distinctions
are off.

*[Ticket of admission, Phi Beta Kappa, Sanders Theatre, June 19, 1916.]

If you do come over—but I don't advise you to this time. I shan't be myself and I shall be pull-hauling in every direction. I can let you see the poems in MS one at a time and you can stand them that way.

Always yours

Robert F

James Oppenheim says he doesn't know what I am talking about in my letter to him, but he can get an explanation out of you. Don't you give it to him. I am trying to cultivate a little obscurity to save myself from the crowd.

Franconia   N.H.
July 17   1916

Dear Louis:

There are as many as four hypothetical questions I should like to put to you if I didn't have to do it in writing. One is as to inversions, whether they are all of one kind; another is as to a poem I have here in pickle which the same I hadn't any doubts of till I used it as a Phi Beta Kapper and almost scared myself out of conceit with it; another is as to a play I wrote once and might under certain circumstances and if I was sure you weren't overstocked with plays already, offer for an early number of The Seven Arts; and another still is as to the advisability of memorializing Harriet Monroe on the subject of the poem she seems to assume I entered in the late poetry Event of the Poetry Society. It dirks me to have anyone suspect me for a moment of having appealed to Wheeler* for judgment, and of course I should like nothing better than to have it generally known that I was the only living poet that Wheeler cared enough for to want to have him appear as if appealing to Wheeler for judgment.

Shall I begin or have I said enough? as Milton's Elder Brother hath it. Don't you think I'd better wait a day or two to see if I won't feel fluenter before attempting to formulate such important questions?

Harcourt has been and gone. He says I am out this fall with a book to be known as Mountain Interval.

Last year I advised you on waves. A word on sharks. I always find it efficacious in dealing with the Suns-of-Gons to keep the body

*[Wheeler was the old-guard president of the Poetry Society.]

exactly at right angles with the line of their smile. When they turn
on their side and smile perpendicularly in the act of biting, the body
must be thrown instantly to a horizontal position as in floating so that
they shall be warded off by bumping their own noses. There must be
no hesitation. And remember the body must never be presented
either end on. That is said to be fatal: as are also a few other things
I'm too plug inert to go into here, among them speculation, theory,
and all uncertainty.

Luck to "The Seven." Couldn't a poem be done on them to
demonstrate, as in Wordsworth, that they <u>are</u> Seven, though several
of them have gone to heaven. Anyway it could do no harm to use for
a legend on the title page: "Kind Master, we are Seven." Are they
seven honestly? I never counted them. Well there may be seven arts;
but there are only two voices.

> To voyses ah there, won is of the see,
> Won of the mountings, Louis, you and me.

Love to you all.

Never doubt me yours

R. F.

[Once established as "one of America's leading new poets," Robert
was showered not only with honors but also with manuscripts. It
seemed that every unrecognized (and sometimes well-known) poet
wanted his seal of approval. The poem referred to in the next letter
was a confused semi-autobiographical narrative by a professor whom
I had met on one of my lecture tours. I had incautiously referred to
my friendship with Robert, and the professor, who later turned on
both of us for failing to acclaim him, prevailed upon me to act as
intermediary for his work.]

Wonalancet N. H.

Aug 1 1916

Dear Louis:

That ere poem has been forwarded from Franconia to Plymouth
to here and I'm just confronted with it. Give me a moment longer.
I'm afraid the theme doesn't come clear enough to make me sure it
is anything. Tell me in two words what you think it says as a whole

and let me see if it agrees with what I think I get out of it. I have
my doubts.

In hot haste

R.F.

Franconia   N.H.

Aug 7   1916

Dear Louis:

Help me, will you? Harcourt sent me this to develop into
something about myself and I find that I can do nothing with it. It
ain't that I'm overnice. I simply don't seem to know how to
advertise my own work. It may be because I can't find anything
good enough to say. Man that is born of woman is apt to be as vain
as his mother. I turn to you. Just a few touches to this are wanted.
The sentences don't run clear enough. Some of the items of comment
are all right, but I'm not sure that the aspersion toward the end on
North of B. ought to stand as it is. "As hard and lovely (lonely?) as in
some of the poems in" it might better read. I have been counting
and I find that seven out of fifteen of the poems in N. of Boston are
almost humorous—four are almost jokes: The Mountain, A Hundred
Collars, The Code, The Generations of Men. It won't do to go
into all of that. But something saving could be said.

But I want to leave the whole thing to you. Won't you sketch it
freshly and then let me make the compromise with what A.H. has
done? Of course if you think this good enough, why we'll let it stand.

You had my letter as to Robinson's poem. I must confess the
thing bothers me. It seems to me to state nothing that I can state
after him in words of my own. There are good owlish things in it as
always with Robinson. But it's only a fairly good poem as a whole. I
shouldn't say <u>not</u> to publish it. You want to hold Robinson. He will
be giving you something better than this if you get him coming. And
I dare say its better than much you will have to accept. But
probably you ask no more of me than my opinion of the poem as a
poem. It's dubious.

I really think you may like my one-act play. It can wait till a little later. I'd like to have a poem in the first number of The Seven so that it would be out ahead of the book.

In hot haste but yours as ever

R. F.

[The "this" referred to in the opening sentences of the preceding letter was a circular that Alfred Harcourt had prepared in connection with Mountain Interval and which he wanted Robert to amplify or, at least, to approve. I was easily persuaded to do the enlarging.

After putting together the best of his new poems in The Man Against the Sky, Edwin Arlington Robinson had kept out a long soliloquy which he offered to The Seven Arts. It was a tired and tiring piece of work, but the editorial staff was hesitant about declining it. Robert's report prompted the negative decision. Instead of the Robinson poem, the February, 1917, issue of the magazine contained Frost's grim one-act play, A Way Out. The play not only recreated two antagonists—the rough snarl of The Stranger contrasted with old Asa Gorrill's piping drawl—but also projected a tragic absurdity taking place in a closed-in atmosphere of terror.]

Franconia   N. H.
Aug 8   1916

Dear Louis:

I had written you my last letter before either of your last two came.

Fifty is all right for The Bonfire. I'm glad you and James liked it.

As to Robinson's poem, it still seems to me splay or something. Regarded as an attack of early-marriage nerves, it seems even a little funny. But what I say stands: it's probably better than a good many poems you will have to print if you are going to print poetry at all. And I suppose you want to hang on to Robinson. Don't mind my not being enthusiastic over him in this particular poem. I'm willing to be counted with those on the fence.

The pennant for Boston in both leagues!

Love to yous

R. F.

Thanks for writing your address on your envelope. It's so long since I have seen it that I was needing confirmation of my recollection of it.

Franconia   N.H.
Sept 9   1916

Dear Louis:

Here a few bonafide addresses. There are more to follow.
Beautiful day or two.
Winter in the morning air though, and migratory impulses.

I promise you the play before long. You have no idea how I am kept from work by pleasant people. They don't seem to care a damn what they leave of me.

You and Jean are still without the youngster, I suppose, and will have to continue to be a while longer. Hard on you and on him. Bad time.

Bless you in haste.

R.

[Franconia,   N.H.
October 2,   1916]

Dear Louis

You couldn't come out here for that talk?

Your bluly

R.

Franconia   N.H.
October 13   1916

Dear Louis:

I can't make any of these seem very important. "Prelude" may be one or two things. I'm sure the rest are nothing distinct. The adjectives taken anywhere give the case away. It cost no effort of any kind to bring "vagrant" to "hair" nor "garish" to "day" nor "sultry" to "summer." They were all there already. Somebody fetched them sometime from a good way, no doubt, at considerable expense of spirit; but it wasn't Clement Wood. It's the same all the way through: Clement gets out of it too easily. He simply ought to be made to learn (without being told) that he must narrow down to what he actually catches himself at, to what he finds himself forced to think, feel, say, and do in mid-career. It will reduce his output for a while. It will make him feel pretty fragmentary—as if he hadn't enough to round out a whole of anything. Then let him be as fragmentary as he feels.

The last two lines of "Prelude" are bad. I should wish to get rid of "As I lie aching for the touch of you," as well.

Sorry to have to say it of Clement.

R. F.

[The "these" referred to in the preceding letter were several poems by Clement Wood which Robert read at my special request for possible publication in The Seven Arts.

Clement Wood, a renegade Southerner, had come to New York from Birmingham, Alabama, where, after succeeding Justice Hugo Black as presiding magistrate of the Central Recorder's Court, he had been removed "for lack of the judicial temperament." (He had made the political error of sending the state's Lieutenant Governor to jail for contempt of court.) He was twenty-six, three years younger than myself, when I met him in 1914, and we became close friends. I liked his unflagging buoyancy and admired his insurgent spirit. At that time he was earning his living by teaching, writing squibs, and waiting on restaurant tables—he declared that he liked to serve Negroes, for it freed him from the "taint of Alabama."

Later he became successful in a variety of fields. Composers favored his lively lyrics, especially "Shortnin' Bread" and "The Glory Road"; he won prizes for poems in the style of Vachel Lindsay; he edited a rhyming dictionary and a poet's handbook; he put together popularizations of psychology, about seventy volumes on science and literature for a five-cent Little Blue Book Series, turned out made-to-order biographies for wealthy nonentities, and bought an extensive place in the Helderbergs near Albany on the proceeds of indefatigable hack work. He died at sixty-two in 1950.]

[Undated
November, 1916]

Extracts from the diary of a backwoods poet kept at intervals during the period of The High Cost of Living. (Rotogravure.)

October 15

This day hunted bear without success.

October 16

(The handwriting of the next entry is shaky.)
This day hunted bear without success.

October 17

(The handwriting now becomes a scrawl.)
This day hunted bear without success.

October 27

(The handwriting is almost illegible by this time.)
This day hunted bear without success.

November 1

(The handwriting is an almost meaningless scribble.)
This day hunted bear without—

November 8

(In a jumble of wild and ecstatic capitals.)
HEWS ELECTED! SAVED ! ! ! ! ! !

In the entry of November 1 there is a pathetic reference
(almost illegible) to having spent the day in bed reading the
Sears Roebuck catalogue.

*[The preceding letter is undated, but the last "entry" in the "diary"
points to November, 1916, as the probable date. In 1912 Charles
Evans Hughes, lawyer and statesman, had refused to be a candidate
for the presidency, but in 1916 he resigned from the Supreme Court
to run as the Republican candidate against Woodrow Wilson.
Robert's bear-hunting backwoodsman was desperate and inaccurate;
in spite of the enthusiastic finale, Hughes was not elected.]*

[Franconia, N.H.
November 14, 1916]

Dear Louis

If I agree to look in on you for one day, the twenty-third or
twenty-fourth of the month, that is next week, will you promise not
to let a soul know of my being in town? I want to see you, but there
are a lot of people I like but don't want to see because I simply can't

44

afford the distraction in my now state of mind. What they don't hear of my being in town won't hurt their feelings.

I have been in no mood to meet De la Mare. He is one of the open questions with me like what to do with Mexico. He has only treated Edward Thomas, to whom he owes more than half, measurably well. Personally I am indifferent about him and have been these three years. Don't think I asked Harcourt to do The Listeners on De la Mare's account. The sum of it is that without much to go on I suspect that the man who rhymes with Delaware is a bit of a British snob and will bear fighting shy of. I shall <u>probably</u> have to invite him here, because my mother was so sure she had taught me manners and I shouldn't want her to be mistaken. But I'm almost sure he scorns America and has only come over for what he can get out of us and against us. And I have his poems to save. If he is half as bad as I am afraid he is, he might spoil the poems. You know how many poems you have lost by meeting the man who wrote them. My not meeting De la Mare in England was rather accidentally on purpose.

The magazine was right. I'll leave it to talk over with you. I'll just say now that your part in it was as brilliant as any. The preface to your Heine won't be the worst of it: you needn't prepare me for it with anything deprecatory.

I have been in the depths without a diving-suit. Surely you won't mind my taking a little common ordinary satisfaction in the election of Wilson. You don't think such things matter for yourself.

I am even helped by the way New Hampshire went. Make allowances for me. As a child I did what I could by marching and shouting and burning oil to throw the country to Cleveland in '84. And I lived to vote for Debs!

R.

[Robert had mixed feelings about the English. Many years later, in his eighties, he was to receive honorary degrees from Oxford and Cambridge, but in his forties he was convinced that the average Englishman considered an American something less than average. Even (or especially) the more-than-average Britisher frequently regarded his transatlantic cousin with the polite condescension of which James Russell Lowell had complained almost half a century before Robert. This explains his attitude to De la Mare, the least chauvinistic of authors, whose poetry Robert had brought to the attention of Alfred Harcourt and which Holt was to publish.

The English writer closest to Robert's heart and mind was Edward Thomas; but, in spite of Robert's opinion, Thomas' influence on De la Mare is questionable.]

[Franconia, N.H.
November 20, 1916]

Dear Louis

Unless something breaks it will be Friday night with you. Alfred wants you and me to ride with him Friday day. But probably he told you when you were in there coruscating.

And won't we give things a going over!

Play under one arm.

Yours stealthily

R

Franconia [N.H.]
Octodecem [1916]

Dear Louis

A breeze discovered my open book
And began to flutter the leaves to look
For a poem about the season, Spring.
I tried to tell her "There's no such thing."

For whom would a poem on Spring be by?
The breeze disdained to make reply.
And a cloud-shadow crossed her face
For fear I should make her pass the place.

P.S. I just thought you ought to know it whether it was so or not.

R.

Franconia N.H.
Dec 14 [1916]

Dear Louis:

Try you again. I undertake to be in New York not later than Wednesday next to stay till I see you for a talk. I have had a lot of

love letters in print from you but they are not the same thing as
seeing you. I go to work for a living in two or three weeks and then
goodbye to friends and poetry for awhile. I must tell you about it.
Damn writing.

Love me forever,

R.

[Franconia, N.H.
January 1, 1917]

Dear Louis:

You gave us a good part of our good Christmas. We are a
bejeweled family.

And speaking of families, how like the family affairs we flatter
ourselves we only find in country villages was that shop of yours I had
a glimpse of in the middle of the greatest city in the world where
everybody seemed to know everybody else if everybody wasn't quite
related to everybody else.* I should be jealous of you for having such
an institution in a modern city where it doesn't belong according to
all our theories, if I wasn't so fond of seeing our theories knocked
into cocked hats. What I like about Bergson and Fabre is that they
have bothered our evolutionism so much with the cases of instinct
they have brought up. You get more credit for thinking if you restate
formulae or cite cases that fall in easily under formulae, but all the
fun is outside saying things that suggest formulae that won't
formulate—that almost but don't quite formulate. I should like to be
so subtle at this game as to seem to the casual person altogether
obvious. The casual person would assume that I meant nothing or
else I came near enough meaning something he was familiar with to
mean it for all practical purposes. Well well well.

R.

I have never known you better than you are in A Side Street. It is
the solid stuff, especially from "I see them there" on to the end. You
are so clever you have to be careful about not cheating yourself about
your rhyme words. You can make yourself think they are not there
just for the rhyme when they really are. Lowell perishes of just that

*[The crowded offices of the family's jewelry factory.]

self-deception. Your rhymes justify this time very well. Excuse this troubling thought. A Side Street is a lovely thing.

Address me at Amherst next.

R.

[It was easy enough to give small presents of jewelry if you were a jeweler, especially if you were (as I was) managing a factory that produced medium-priced lockets, lavallières, linkbuttons, and brooches. The factory was in Newark, New Jersey, but our offices were in New York, and Robert relished the paradox of my trying to inject socialistic ideas in a business owned by small but stubborn industrialists. Besides my father, the family firm included two uncles and four cousins who regarded me with disapprobation if not active dislike, the more so since this poetry-struck junior partner was the only one who had been able to run the factory without an annual loss.

"A Side Street" is a poem which, unfortunately, scarcely deserves Robert's praise.]

Amherst   Mass
February 8   1917

Dear Louis:

The Girl with All Those Names* got hers—and poetic justice is done—the eternal verities are verified. Now she can kiss anything she pleases.

You don't tell me, though!—I won't believe she writes poetry about kissing dead Adonis anywhere. Anywhere in America!

<u>Me art hakes Anna numness panes me cents.</u>

Go in and kill them all off with my love.

The latest thing in the schools is to know that you have nothing to say in the days of thy youth, but that those days may well be put in learning how to say something 'gainst when the evil days draw near when thou shalt have something to say. Damn these separations of the form from the substance. I don't know how long I could stand them.

No Chicago this trip. The dates were too sprawling. At most three or four days were all I had a right to steal from the college.

*[Blanche Shoemaker Wagstaff.]

Thumbs down to Mr. Brown. I don't seem to know who he would be unless he is the fellow who tried to pull my leg once by mentioning you. His poetry may be good, but I don't like his business methods.

Roedker (spell him!) is another story. He was all round London knocking at preferment's door, but he kept within the decencies and I'm glad if you find one of his poems to like.

I'm going to have you out here before long to give us what for and see how we live.

I ain't so sanguine about the war as you are. I'm getting ready to use it to advertise my last book. Goodbye—R. F.

[At this time I had begun to think of putting together anthologies of modern American and British poetry. The accent was to be on the "new" poetry but was to stress substance rather than form. Robert liked the idea, although he was skeptical about some of the candidates considered for inclusion. The anthology—a miscellaneous mixture of a little good poetry and a great deal of mediocre verse, an olla putrida of which I was ashamed as soon as it was in print— appeared two years later.]

> Amherst Mass
> February 13 1917

Dear Louis:

Would you want to let me have one of the best of your good poems to see how much I could get you for it from some friends of mine who are publishing a magazine in Philadelphia. The magazine is mostly given up to themselves, all amateurs, but they think they want one poem a month by a professional poet, so to speak, to be to them for an example. The money they will give is not the whole point if it is any of it. They are good folks having a good time and I'm not sure that nothing will come of their venture. Masefield gave them their head poem for the first number. I gave them one for the second. Will you come in for my sake their sake your own sake or God's sake?

> Yours for business
>
> R.

Amherst   Mass
Feb 20   [1917]

Dear Louis:

Vision of you whirling me terribly by the ankle round and round
your head (never stopping to recover your derby which you have
knocked off) as you advance to the demolition of our masters.
Hit 'im with me! I suppose it mayn't do me as much good as it does
him harm; but it has to be.

I forgot you. There is you to consider too. Will it do you any
good? Or don't you care? I ought to be able to stand it if you can.

Clement Wood took an inclement little slap at me in a letter
yestre'en. Nothing serious, only just as much as to say (unasked) you
write poetry, Robbie Frost, and so do I, and just as you don't like all I
write, so I don't like all you write—me publisher is Gomme. He
wood, Would he, claim equality with me? More claimant than
Clement. What are you going to do with him when his book is sent
you for review? It is bound to be bad in any binding.

The magazine I begged a poem for is The Forge. Masefield set it
going. Otto Mallory, 1427 Spruce St, Philadelphia, edits it and I
think it asks nothing of poets in general: it aims at a good time for a
dozen or twenty people who intend to fill its pages themselves. They
are none of them writers by profession and I believe they are none of
them as yet jealous rivals of the likes of you and me. They are comfortable people to get along with. Where we come in is at my suggestion
with one poem a number for them to emulate. They had already had
a poem by Masefield and one by me when I made the suggestion.
They have paid me too well for mine. I can see something here that I
don't see in some other ventures.

As I said on the envelope of my last, When is your book?

Hoping to receive a copy I am,

I may say I Am.

I mean—well never mind what I mean. Only I don't mean any play
on the name of the Deity.

*[The phrase about "the demolition of our masters" in the first para-
graph of the preceding letter contains another of Robert's concealed
puns. I had written enthusiastically about Edgar Lee Masters' Spoon
River Anthology, but the success of that pessimistic yet penetrating*

work dulled the author to all criticism, especially self-criticism. Between 1916 and 1940 he published some thirty-six volumes of good, bad, and derivative prose and verse, considerably more than one book a year. Masters' Songs and Satires and The Great Valley, which followed immediately upon Spoon River Anthology, seemed a lamentable letdown, and my review of the books cited Robert as a contrasting example of the poet who refused to be rushed into print and run to the market place.]

[Amherst, Mass.
March 13, 1917]

Dear Louis:

Your Post review encourages me to think I ought to keep writing. You believe in me and I do too. I wonder if we are both wrong.

I may still go to Chicago. I am in fact promising to go this week— 14th and 15th. I last saw the city in 1885. Where were you in 1885?

I don't know what I think of teaching again after once having put all that behind me.

War will settle many things in many a man's private affairs. That much may be safely said of it.

Waiting for your book, I am,
Yours while I wait

Robert

Amherst   [Mass.]
March 28   [1917]

Dear Louis:

Everywhere I dip into the book,* pleasure—and no uncertain pleasure such as tortures me in the reading of most books lately. The book came on my birthday which was not observed as a holiday in this state: I had to work just as on any other day and so I have had no time for more than dipping. But I can see it's a full-flavored book as delightful as self-indulgence. It's still all before me. I have something special to live for for a week or two.

*[These Times, my third volume of poems, was dedicated to Robert.]

The preface* is another thing. That is brilliant. You ought not to do any more journalism and I only let you go on doing it because you represent the cause so well at the front: we need you to fight for us: I don't know what we should do if you dropped out of the fighting line. But you really ought to be let off for more important prose, not to mention your poetry at all.

I'm not very angry with you for what you did to Breathweight. Only I wonder if he's worth your pains. Perhaps he is. We are taught that we must try not to look down on anyone.

I'm going home for a few days to see how the house is coming on for next year. I'll take your book in my bag. The next one will be waiting for me here when I get back I suppose.

Both of them are going to have a go, I predict. You're going to stand out more and more. I see you loom!

But whether you loomed more or less, came or went, I believe I should continue

Yours always

Robert

I must see about those poems. They'll want one of them down there in Philadelphia. But there's some hitch about the magazine; The Forge it's called. I'll get after Mallory.

R.

[No address
April 1,   1917]

Dear Louis

I'm sick as hell of this Stark Young imbroglio and I'm thinking of going out and getting shot where it will do some good. Before I do anything so desperate, however, I'd like to take a run down to you for a little talk with you on what kind of a book it is you have been dedicating to me. It's all full of lovely things in a strong clear sound. Erskine was welcome to praise you with all the praises. But you know in your heart that I like you better than he does and with better understanding. Therefore you didn't let him get you away from me.

*[An article entitled "The New Spirit in American Poetry," which was to serve as the keynote to a comprehensive résumé published two years later.]

You dedicated your book to me instead of to him. And I take it that by dedicating it to me as a poet (who know another poet when I see one) and in addition to that as a person, you meant that long after I cease to be a poet you will be sticking to me as a person and a personal friend. This poetry ain't all there is between us, is it now? Because if it is I shall surely not be dissuaded from going out as aforesaid and getting shot where it will do some good.

I am going to take Elinor and get down to see you next week probably, but if not next week then the week after. Till then suffer with me in what I have got into. It is the incredibility of it!

But never mind me.

R.

[From 1917 to 1920 Robert was Professor of English Literature at Amherst College. He was not altogether happy there during this period. He dreaded campus politics but, much against his will, found himself involved. At that time there was some trouble about Stark Young, who was on the faculty before he gave up teaching to become a drama critic, essayist, and novelist. Another teacher, John Erskine was one of the most versatile men of the times. Besides being Columbia University's favorite professor, he was a concert pianist, a poet, a satirical novelist, a co-editor of the Cambridge History of American Literature, and a book reviewer who, much to my gratification, spoke highly of my poetry.]

Amerced   [Mass.]
4/22   17

Dear Louis:

This is the upshot of my little action between friends. I thought I was going to give you more money for your poems than most editors give and I thought I was going to give The Forge some real poetry. I guess I was intended by nature to mind my own business. Mallory's letter explains itself with the help of the one touch I've given it with the pen. Will you read it in my exhonoration and then return it so that I can send it to Amy.* I don't know when I have done as much

*[Amy Lowell, whom Robert had also persuaded to submit a poem to Mallory's magazine. The Forge suspended publication.]

mischief where my intentions were so good. You may forgive me,
but Amy never!

Why, I'm utterly glad of Erskine's admiration for your work and
I was only being jealous not of you but of him for what he said of you.
I was pretending to think that I was in danger of losing you because
somebody had got ahead of me in praising you. I was melancholy
when I wrote and disposed to play with sad things. I'm still melancholy.
He may be stark young but I'll say this if he was much stark younger
I should go stark crazy before I got back to my side hill. He has spoiled
everything here that the coming of the war hasn't spoiled. And he's
so foxy about it. He walks up close to me on the street and passes
candy from his pockets to mine like a collier passing coal to a warship
at sea. It makes everybody think that he must say with sorrow everything he says against me when he loves me so much in spite of all. But
it will make a melodrama.

When I have time I mean to make you my particular list of
your poems.

Don't mind your Clement Wood and I won't mind Stark Young.
You did him more than justice.

Never again will I write you so troublous a letter as this—not
though I live ten lives of mortal men.

Always yours

Robert Frost

Amherst   [Mass.]

May 7   [1917]

Dear Louis

Just two words to ask you if you can't stay a day or two with us.
Everything has gone to pieces with the coming of the war or I should
arrange about the lecture. The boys are pretty well gone glimmering
a gun.

Say you'll stay.

R.

Trust you don't see too much in Davies.* He's overrated.

*[W. H. Davies, the English lyric poet, whom I had characterized as a simplified
Blake composing a one-syllable Primer of Innocence.]

[The Masses, a magazine devoted to a liberal interpretation of arts and letters, a fusion (or confusion) of Socialism and Bohemianism, had faltered and fumbled along for about five years when suddenly the Post Office refused to allow it the use of the mails. The journal, of which I was a contributing editor, was openly pacifist and maintained that the war was a bad war and would be followed by a worse peace. The First World War hysteria was at its worst in America, where, unlike embroiled Europeans, Americans had little to fear and less to lose.

What at any other time might have been castigated as effrontery in 1917 was condemned as treachery. The staff of The Masses was indicted on two counts: (1) "conspiring to effect insubordination and/or mutiny in the armed and naval forces of the United States," and (2) "conspiring to obstruct enlistment and recruiting." The staff—Max Eastman, Floyd Dell, Art Young, and others, including myself—refused to take the charges seriously until we found ourselves in court. As the trial proceeded, it became evident to the most prejudiced juror that writers and artists as divided as we were could not possibly have been conspirators, and that what really was on trial was the issue of a free press. Since the prosecution was unable to prove any conspiratorial intent, the judge declared a mistrial. A second trial ended in a disagreement, and a reorganized Masses appeared as The Liberator.

Robert liked some of the individual members of The Masses, but he did not like the magazine; most of all he disliked my being a part of it. He was always against "movements," "causes," cliques, groups, social workers of any kind—he called them "gangs of do-gooders." Yet, as the next letter proves, although he was opposed to the "crowd" and felt I had no right to be a member of it, he would have gone into court to defend me even against myself. Fortunately, this was not necessary; but I regret that Robert's biographers were cheated of the chance to picture him forensically moving a stolid judge and jury to tears.]

Franconia   Once More
July 15   1917

Dear Louis

I do hope they will take a good look and see how practically out of that crowd you are before they decide to do anything harsh that will simply drop you back into it for good and all. This without prejudice to the crowd. But you know how it is when anything is climbing up a wall out of anywhere: the best thing to do is to let him alone: you touch him with a finger to help him or boost him and all he does is let go and flop back down into whatever it was he was climbing out of and drying off from to have it all to do over again if he doesn't land feet up and die of discouragement.

I feel that this is a critical moment with you. You need expert watching. If the Postmaster General jugs you and starts despitefully using you I am coming down to N.Y. as a sort of lay lawyer to defend you as Thoreau offered to defend John Brown. I can say things for you that you will be too cussèd to say for yourself. And they will be truer things than you would say yourself. That is the mischief. Say go ahead and let them lock you up. I'd like to see if I wouldn't be rather eloquent in such a situation. Your youth, your genius, your only child, your only wife, your sincerity that would rather be right and appear wrong than appear right and be wrong or even than appear right and be right, what you said you would do if Teddy went over with an army—why with such a chance I'll bet you another five cents I could wring tears from yourself to hear yourself described, make you fall forward in the prisoner's box and weep on the balustrade. (You see I am familiar with court proceedings, having recently sat with the judge of the Criminal Court of Pennsylvania at the trial of a—well, Braithwaite, if you will pardon the euphemism—for stealing twelve Dominicks.)

Not to make too light of what may be proving a serious matter, let me beg of you to be good at your age before the evil days draw nigh, and let who will be clever. You can discuss with the children the difference between formal liberty, which is a state structure like the Parthenon in all parts consistent with itself, and scott-free impulse which is nothing but what everything comes from and everything is built out of when it cools off a little and hardens enough for the builders to cut and handle it. Eloquent! My stars!

We'll do as Elinor says in her letter unless you insist on something else.

Always yours

R.F.

[*Shortly after the United States declared war on Germany, April 6, 1917, President Wilson sent Elihu Root to Russia. Root's mission* was to persuade the so-called revolutionary but actually moderate Kerenski government to wage war more vigorously than before. For a while it seemed that he had succeeded, but Root's efforts came to nothing when the Bolsheviks under Lenin took over the government by a coup d'état in November, 1917. Within a month the new regime offered the Germans an armistice, and by the end of the year withdrew from the war.

In August, before an armistice was contemplated, Root had reason to be hopeful if not sanguine of the outcome, and Robert shared his optimism about the survival of middle-class government in Russia. Robert was not given to prophecy; he preferred to be wrong by himself rather than be right with the shifting—he would have said "shifty"—mob. "Everybody is entitled to three guesses, and this is one of mine." He hated those too ready to conform and he despised compromisers. "What I love best in man is definiteness of position."

The Nevinson pictures referred to at the end of the letter are those by C. R. W. Nevinson, the British artist who painted a number of Futurist pictures shortly after 1912. "Max" is Max Eastman.]

Franconia   N.H.
August 18   1917

Dear Louis:

Let me not argue with you as to what Root saw in Russia to inspire confidence, but let me instead tell you what I think he thinks will happen in Russia and not only in Russia but in every other country in the world. I have very little in common with Root, but, though I come at things from almost an opposite direction from him, still my guess is his guess on this war. Middle class government, which is to say liberal democratic government, has won a seat in Russia and it is going to keep its seat for the duration of the war and share with us in the end in a solid out-and-out middle class triumph such as the Germans enjoyed when they marched into Paris. The lower class seeing nothing in all this for itself may do its worst to create diversions, but it will fail. This may be the last war between bounded nations in the old fashioned patriotism. The next war may be between class and class. But this one will be to the end what it was in the beginning, a struggle for commercial supremacy between nations. I will not guess further ahead than that. The lower class will kick a little on street corners and where it can find a chance in journalistic corners. But it will be suppressed—more and more brutally suppressed as the middle class gains in confidence and sees its title clearer. We are still surer of nationality than we are of anything else in the world—ninety nine million of us are in this country. I don't say this to discourage you— merely to define my position to myself. Live in hope or fear of your revolution. You will see no revolution this time even in Germany until Germany goes down with a perceptible crash, and I'm not so sure you'll see one there even then. Everybody is entitled to three guesses, and this is one of mine. You can have my other two to add to your own three. You'll need that many as you keep shifting your position to adjust yourself to events that will be going continually against you.

Sometime the world will try cutting the middle class out of our middle. But my mind misgives me that the experiment will fail just as the eighteenth century experiment of getting rid of the lowest class by cutting it out and dumping it on distant islands failed. You know how the lowest class renewed itself from somewhere as fast as it was cut out.

What I love best in man is definiteness of position. I don't care what the position is so long as it is definite enough. I mean I don't half care. Take a position and try it out no matter who sets up to call you an unhanged traitor. My God how I adore some people who stand right out in history with distinct meaning.

We wept for you a little (which is a lot for us) as you went out of sight down the road—we actually wept.

Yours for all the higher forms of excitement

Robert Frost

Those Nevinson pictures were beautiful in the way they found material for futurist treatment.

And much that Max says is true. But we are concerned, for the moment, with predicting what will come true.

Amherst   Mass
October 27   1917

Dear Louis:

Under separate cover I have told you why I ain't got no sympathy for your total loss of all the arts. You tried to have too many at the present price of certified milk. Why would you be a pig instead of something like a horse or a cow that only has one in a litter, albeit with six legs sometimes, for I have seen such in my old mad glad circus-going days. But that's all put behind me since I discovered that do or say my damndest I can't be other than orthodox in politics love and religion: I can't escape salvation: I can't burn if I was born into this world to shine without heat. And I try not to think of it as often as I can lest in the general deliquescence I should find myself a party to the literature of irresponsible, boy-again, freedom. No, I can promise you that whatever else I write or may have been writing for the last twenty-five years to disprove Amy's theory that I never got anything except out of the soil of New England, there's one thing I shan't write in the past, present, or future, and that is glad mad stuff or mad glad stuff. The conviction closes in on me that I was cast for gloom as the sparks fly upward, I was about to say: I am of deep shadow all compact like onion within onion and the savor of me is oil of tears. I have heard laughter by daylight when I thought it was my own because at that moment when it broke I had parted my lips to take food. Just so I have been afraid of myself and caught at my throat when I thought I was making some terrible din of a mill whistle that happened to come on the same instant with the opening of my mouth to yawn. But I have not laughed. No man can tell you the sound or the way of my laughter. I have neighed at night in the woods behind a house like vampires. But there are no vampires, there are no ghouls, there no demons, there is nothing but me. And I have all the dead New England things held back by one hand as by a dam in the long deep wooded valley of Whippoorwill, where, many as they are, though, they do not flow together by their own weight more than so many piled-up chairs—(and, by the way, your two chairs have come). I hold them easily—too easily for assurance that they will go with a rush when I let them go. I may have to extricate them one by one and throw them. If so I shall throw them with what imaginative excess I am capable of, already past the height of my powers (see Amy the next time you are in Boston).

I suppose it's a safe bet that the form your pacifism, your Protean pacifism, takes at this moment is "Down with Mitchel." Next it will be—you say! Do you see these transmogrifications more than one or two ahead? Aw say, be a nationalist. By the love you bear Teddy!

Yours while you're still bad enough to need me,

Robert Frost

[As related on an earlier page, The Seven Arts ceased to exist after its twelfth issue—which explains Robert's reference to my "total loss of all the arts." The event scarcely explains the mock-gloomy ruminations, but it gave him the opportunity to take one more slap at Amy Lowell and head into a grimly fantastic soliloquy.

The information "under separate cover" (a letter which followed within a week) turned out to be a limerick; I believe the only one which Robert ever wrote. The pun in the last line not only plays on the name of Randolph Bourne but implies what many people had suspected: that Bourne's brilliant, half-despairing, half-defiant articles in The Seven Arts ("The Collapse of American Strategy," "Twilight of Idols," "Below the Battle") had hastened the magazine's demise.]

[Amherst, Mass.
November 3, 1917]

Dear Louis:

This under separate cover, under cover of darkness in fact, not because I am ashamed of the sentiment, but because I haven't time in the press of reading Religio Medici to polish it off as I like to polish things off:

THE SEVEN ARTS

In the Dawn of Creation that morning
I remember I gave you fair warning
The Arts are but Six!
You add Politics
And the Seven will all die a-Bourneing.
R.F.

I am sitting in both the chairs at once and thinking of no one but Jean and you. And Dick! I'm thinking of Dick of course too. Tell Dick, Gee I wish I had some one to bet with on the election. Well, he and I can bet on it after it's over sometime when I'm down there.

R.F.

[The next letter is Robert's first attempt to get his biography straight. In Tendencies in Modern American Poetry, which had just appeared, Amy Lowell devoted the second chapter to Robert Frost—the first chapter was about E. A. Robinson. Robert never liked Amy Lowell's estimate. He shrugged at the comparison with Robinson

("Mr. Robinson is one of the most intellectual poets writing in America today; Mr. Frost is one of the most intuitive"); but, although he appreciated her praise, he resented the picture of himself as a disillusioned rustic who had portrayed an arid and decaying New England ("His people are leftovers of the old stock, morbid, pursued by phantoms, slowly sinking into insanity"), a country poet who turned monologues into melodramas—she misread the quiet anticlimax of "The Fear" and thought it ended in murder or madness—and who had no sense of humor. ("Mr. Frost is a kindly and genial poet, but he is never either whimsical or quaint. For this reason I find his people untrue to type in one important particular. In none of them do we find that pungency of thought or expression which is so ingrained in the New England temper.")]

Amherst   Mass

November 7   1917

Dear Louis:

Do you want to be the repository of one or two facts that Amy leaves out of account?

For twenty-five out of the first forty years of my life I lived in San Francisco, Lawrence, Mass., Boston, Cambridge, Mass., New York, and Beaconsfield, a suburb of London.

For seven I lived in the villages of Salem, Derry, and Plymouth, New Hampshire.

For eight I lived on a farm at Derry though part of that time I was teaching in the Academy there.

I began to read to myself at thirteen. Before that time I had been a poor scholar and had staid out of school all I could. At about that time I began to take first place in my classes.

I read my first poem at 15, wrote my first poem at 16, wrote My Butterfly at eighteen. That was my first poem published.

With Elinor I shared the valedictory honor when I graduated from the High School at Lawrence, Mass.

I was among the first men at Amy's brother's old college during my two years there, winning a considerable scholarship. In those days I used to suspect I was looked on as more or less of a grind—though as a matter of fact I was always rather athletic. I ran well. I played on town school ball teams and on the High School football team. I had my share of fights, the last a rather public one in Lawrence in 1896 that cost me the humiliation of going into court and a ten dollar fine.

It is not fair to farmers to make me out a very good or laborious farmer. I have known hard times, but no special shovel-slavery. I dreamed my way through all sorts of fortunes without any realizing sense of what I was enduring. You should have seen me, I wish I could have seen myself, when I was working in the Arlington Mills at Lawrence, working in the shoe shop in Salem N.H., tramping and beating my way on trains down South, reporting on a Lawrence paper, promoting for a Shakespearean reader (whom I abandoned because, after trying him on a distinguished audience I got him in Boston, I decided he wasn't truly great!) Nothing seemed to come within a row of apple trees of where I really lived. I was so far from being discouraged by my failure to get anywhere that I only dimly realized that anyone else was discouraged by it. This is where the countryman came in: I would work at almost anything rather well for a while, but every once in so often I had to run off for a walk in the woods or for a term's teaching in a lonely district school or a summer's work haying or picking fruit on a farm or cutting heels in a shed by the woods in Salem. Gee Whiz, I should say I was just the most everyday sort of person except for the way I didn't mind looking unambitious as much as you would mind, for example. Of course it's no credit to me. I knew what I was about well enough and was pretty sure where I would come out.

Amy is welcome to make me out anything she pleases. I have decided I like her and, since she likes me, anything she says will do so long as it is entertaining. She has been trying to lay at my door all the little slips she has made in the paper on me. She gets it all wrong about me and Gibson and Abercrombie for example. I knew neither of those fellows till North of Boston was all written. All I wrote in the neighborhood of those two was part of Mountain Interval. I doubt if she is right in making me so grim, not to say morbid. I may not be funny enough for Life or Punch, but I have sense of humor enough, I must believe, to laugh when the joke is on me as it is in some of this book of Amy's.

I really like least her mistake about Elinor. That's an unpardonable attempt to do her as the conventional helpmeet of genius. Elinor has never been of any earthly use to me. She hasn't cared whether I went to school or worked or earned anything. She has resisted every inch of the way my efforts to get money. She is not too sure that she cares about my reputation. She wouldn't lift a hand or have me lift a hand to increase my reputation or even save it. And this isn't all from devotion to my art at its highest. She seems to have the same weakness I have for a life that goes rather poetically; only I should say she is worse than I. It isn't what might be expected to come from such a life—poetry that she is after. And it isn't that she doesn't think I am a good poet either. She always knew I was a good poet, but that was between her and me, and there I think she would have liked it if it had remained at least until we were dead. I don't know that I can make you understand the kind of person. Catch her getting any satisfaction out of what her housekeeping may have done to feed a poet! Rats! She hates housekeeping. She has worked because the work has piled on top of her. But she hasn't pretended to like house-work even for my sake. If she has liked anything it has been what I may call living it on the high. She's especially wary of honors that derogate from the poetic life she fancies us living. What a cheap common unindividualized picture Amy makes of her. But, as I say, never mind. Amy means well and perhaps you will come to our rescue without coming in conflict with Amy or contradicting her to her face.

I wish for a joke I could do myself, shifting the trees entirely from the Yankee realist to the Scotch symbolist.

Burn this if you think you ought for my protection.

Always yours

R.

Department of English
Amherst College
Amherst, Massachusetts
December 1   1917

Dear Louis:

I seize this department stationery to give you a new sense of what a merely important person I am become in my decline from greatness. Will you please by return boastage make us knowing to any honors or emollients you have been unable to understand from under?

I notice that there are a number of poems by various people in the magazines for last month and this month—or rather I assume there are: I haven't looked to see.

Answers in full to all your recent questions by telegram are going forward to you by slow fright.

Always and forever yours

Robert

[December 24, 1917
Christmas Eve]

Ah, my dear Louis—

[Robert's only extended parody was "inspired" by Vachel Lindsay. Vachel was barnstorming across the country, exciting startled audiences with his rolling and robustious chants. "My new brand of poetry," he confided, "is pink lemonade and firecrackers at a County Fair: a loud noise and a bright sunset tint." He regarded these chants as an expression of the community; he pleaded for collaborators and liked nothing better than a session with his fellow poets when he could persuade them to improvise or build ballads by group accretion. On one occasion, when Sara Teasdale, Robert, and myself were present, he proposed that we should all write poems on one theme and have them published simultaneously in an issue of Poetry: A Magazine of Verse.

"Have you a specific subject in mind?" asked Robert.

"Yes," said Vachel promptly. "John L. Sullivan."

We laughed, but Vachel was serious. To him Sullivan was not merely a figure of strength but a symbol of burly Americanism, blood brother of Andrew Jackson, one of the native gods not yet enshrined. We wanted to humor Vachel; but Sara, who had been hailed as a laureate of love, felt that a lyrical apostrophe to the champion heavyweight was more than she could manage. I volunteered to write the first verse for her. It began:

> Corbett kissed me in his stride;
>   Kilrain in the hall;
> But John L. merely sighed and sighed,
>   And never kissed at all.

And that, we thought, was the end of it. I had forgotten all about the talk of a John L. Sullivan Anthology when, without warning or explanation, Robert enclosed his "contribution" in a letter dated February 18, 1918. His parody was both criticism and burlesque of Vachel's "General William Booth Enters Into Heaven"; he even had fun with Vachel's subtitle and stage direction: "To be sung to the tune of 'The Blood of the Lamb' with indicated instruments."

Vachel did not take our skits to heart—he certainly did not take them amiss—but he could not bear to give up the idea. His poem, "John L. Sullivan, The Strong Boy of Boston," another creation of what Vachel called "the Higher Vaudeville," is one of his most characteristic expressions. Instead of being bellicose, it is nostalgic, even tender, a period piece with a background of history and muffled histrionics. To show that he bore us no ill will for failing to join his pugilistic crusade, he dedicated the poem "To Louis Untermeyer and Robert Frost."]

Am. [Mass.]

Feb. 18 [1918]

Dear Louis:

Elinor is just a little afraid from my report of your paper on Thomas that you haven't said all you can in his praise. Like him all you can. It was little but condescension he got from that gang over there. Have your reservations in the first part, but if you could make the last part bulk a little larger by naming or even quoting a few more of the good things—

Always yours

R.F.

Enclosed see if you can find my poem for the Sullivan Garland.

[Enclosure]

JOHN L. SULLIVAN ENTERS HEAVEN

(To be sung to the tune of "Heaven Overarches You and Me")

Sullivan arrived at the very lowest Heaven
Which is sometimes mistaken for the very highest Hell,
Where barkeeps, pugilists, jockeys, and gamblers
And the women corresponding (if there are any) dwell.
　They done queer things, but they done 'em on the level,
　And thus they escape the jurisdiction of the Devil.

65

Sullivan felt, and he couldn't find his ticket.
He thought for a moment he would have to go to Hell.
But the gatekeeper told him, "You don't need a ticket:
Everybody knows you: Your name's John L.
    There's a lot of fighting characters been setting up waiting
    To see if you were up to your mundane rating."

Sullivan asked, "They've been setting up to see me?"
And the gatekeeper answered, "They have like Hell!
They've been setting up to try you, and see if they can lick you,
And settle who's who in the Fields of Asphodel.
    So you may as well be ready to take them all on—
    Hercules and Pollux and the whole doggone.

"Fraternity of sluggers, I mean the first-raters
(We send the second-raters to entertain Hell).
I seen Herc's hands all wound with lead and leather
Till they looked like the balls on a great dumb-bell.
    He's mad because the deeds you matched his with
    Were sound printed facts, while his were just myth."

Sullivan said "I guess I'm in for trouble."
He cracked the gate a little and then said "Hell!
I hope I ain't expected to take all them together.
If I take them in succession I'll be doing damn well.
    I wish I'd staid in Boston or Chelsea, and would of
    If I'd had the least encouragement to think I could of."

The gatekeeper said "You don't need to worry;
The way to do's to rush them and give them sudden Hell.
They've been so purged of earthliness they don't weigh nothing
While you weigh something, and will for a spell.
    They've nothing to sustain them but their jealousy of you,
    While you still feel the good of Boston beans, you do."

Sullivan burst into Heaven roaring.
The devils beyond the board fences of Hell
Put the whites of their eyes to crannies and knotholes
To see who was driving the angels pell-mell.
    They said 'twas the greatest punch of all times.
    Ring the bells of Heaven! Sound the gladsome chimes!

                                                    R.F.

This can only be read successfully by the author. You can read it
yourself from the book for the price of the book: one dollar. You can

66

hear the author read it for one hundred dollars. It is worth the difference.

[Robert's fondness for play assumed many forms, including private jokes and (as in the next letter) perverse parodies. The letter, ostensibly written by me to him, is a double lampoon: a mockery of my style, complete with an irrelevant pun, and a burlesque of Philip Dru, Administrator: A Story of Tomorrow.

Philip Dru, a cross between a novel and a political romance, was published anonymously in 1912. The author's secret was not well kept; the cognoscenti knew the book had been written by Colonel Edward M. House, statesman, diplomat, and specialist in foreign affairs. Although Woodrow Wilson had offered him a choice of cabinet positions, House refused any office; instead he became President Wilson's chief adviser—Wilson spoke of him as "my other independent self"—and the reforms adumbrated in Philip Dru deeply impressed the President. It is these proposed changes which Robert ridicules so intimately and so satirically in "my" letter.]

Date to suit
[Franconia,   N.H.
June 6,   1918]

Dear Robt

Sorry you found nothing in The Liberator you inordinately liked but my attack on Masters. I can see how you must like that for personal reasons; and as a matter of fact it was a pretty piece of writing, especially the first part of it, which I rather liked myself. But on the whole the merits of the magazine as an aphrodisiac were thrown away on you. To the pure all things are poor.

I can just know how the very naughty love story of Philip Dru will put you off the main interest of the book which is poetical and right in your line. Yes my dear Robt you were disposed from that early San Francisco training to a life of intrigue and machination. Love is a kickshaw and dalliance naught, but give you a field like poetry that calls to the pulling of wires and the manipulation of ropes, to the climbing of every black reviewer's back stairs for preferment, and you are there with a suit case in both hands "like an old stone savage armed." (I know you don't mind my quoting from your published works.) I wish I could say something to prepare you for what is before you in Philip Dru. There is no more to it than this: Philip meets Gloria (so named from the umbrella goods of commerce) quite properly through her brother, a classmate at West Point. Nothing to take exception to thus far. They walk out into a Mexican desert together. She faints from the heat. He has to carry her and in carrying her loses his sight from the alkali dust he kicks up as he stumbles along with his precious burden. Nothing is insinuated of his having overstepped the proprieties at this time. Neither has anything to reproach the other with. I can't believe that Col. House means Philip to have carried her other than as a perfect gentleman else how would she have consented to come to dinner with Philip (and Col. House too, for I make no doubt Col. House was at the dinner if anyone was) that memorable day after Philip's great victory over the armies of plutocracy? Unless he did nothing he ought not to do, how was Gloria left wondering all those years while he was busy reforming the U.S.A. and tout le monde and hadn't time to see much of her whether he loved her or not. You must remember that this isn't a novel by Hardy where every little accident has a significance in sex. In the end when he honorably can marry her, when all his obligations to the state are discharged, that is to say when he has a minute to spare, he looks around for Gloria and marries her. That's another thing that makes me almost sure that the desert episode was quite all right—at least that it is possible to put a good construction on it in the work of a man like Col. House: Philip's love sounds so like true love—the love that would not be so much loved it not honor more.

But whatever you make of Philip's relations with women (and I have pretty well covered them in the foregoing) for your own sake don't let them blind you to the beauty of such poetry as that of Col. House's chapter on reforming our burial practices. You can plainly hear the voice of Col. House saying to his good friend the President after the war is over and the captains and the kings are licked: And now, Woodrow, what do you say to our doing away with this awful habit of letting dead people down into a hole in the ground and throwing earth into their coffin lid when it would seem so much pleasanter to gather as friends and relatives and see them shoved into a fiery oven and cooked to ashes. Next after the social revolution (I am sorry it had to be so bloody—over a million killed wounded and missing—I can't help wondering where the missing went) next after the social revolution nothing is so dear to me as cremation. And I think chewing is a good thing too. Don't you think something could be done about that. Couldn't the noon hour of the laboring classes be lengthened say ten minutes with the express understanding that unless the actual time consumed in consumption—but I leave to you the formulation of the statute. I never thought when I was half the age I am now that I would ever have a chance to put a notion into practice just because I found I couldn't put it into words. And say, Woodrow, what's the matter with making a law that if anyone dreams a dream often enough to indicate that there's something he wants that he can't have and don't dare to ask for but if he submits his dream in writing to the department of Labor and Parturition and it be found that what he says is true and he really has the dream and often enough to be called habitual and nothing else will take the place of what is lacking in his life, such as more furniture or a different wife or a reputation as a novelist or a kind of food that will agree with him. Well then what do you say, Woodrow, if some other department that shall hereinafter be provided for and gotten up and authorized by Congress shall do everything in its power to make that man happy. Do you feel with me in these aspirations?"

Please legitimatize by signing on this line

[Robert believed so inexorably in the life of poetry that he did not want a poet to write anything but poetry. Although he was repeatedly asked to write critical articles, he steadfastly refused to write prose; he even rejected his publisher's request for a volume to contain his lectures. My alternation of creative writing with critical appraisals seemed to him not only a temporizing but a betrayal.]

Franconia   N.H.
June 27   1918

Dear Louis:

Why when you can write poetry like Jerusalem Delivered will you continue to mess with the Masses (or is it mass with the messes?) Is it because I <u>am</u> an aristocrat as someone in a review accused me of being that I so object to your social revolutionary antics? No it is

because I am as ambitious for you as a mother. Haven't I told you
once that your social revolution, yes and my world war, are nothing
but politics which is a game you and I know what we think of when
we see partisans of the old line at it. Politics is a joke because it is as
speculative as philosophy. I lump them together, politics and
philosophy, as things a young fellow might toy with in his salad days.
Once on a time I fooled with philosophy myself—wrote a little book
in fact (which may you never see) on Staving Off Results, the theme
being the result of staving off results. But, dear me, you, and
everybody, I thought you were putting away childish things. You are
President of a manufacturing concern now. What do you want to be—
President of the U.S.? That's where your political agitation will land
you if you don't watch out. And then what will Dick think of his
father? Will he think he's farther? I axe you. We all want you to be a
poet. Poetry is the only wildness excusable in a person who has
attained to your dignities, and that for the simple reason that it's the
only wildness that can be hoped to carry you beyond those dignities.
It may not carry you beyond them, but ah it may. (Privately I
think it has carried you already, but it's not to my purpose to say so
here.) We want you to immortalize. Don't for God's sake spoil
everything for us by turning out a Philip Dru. (By the way I didn't
tell you Huebsch* writes he suspects you of having written Philip.)
Be great.

　　To be frank I'm not much in favor of your going on with your
book of criticism just now when the whole world is doing books of
criticisms. That's another thing I oppose you in. You just deliberately
lose yourself in the ruck of Phelpses† and all. Of course you can do it
to tease me, making a virtue of humility all the way. But it's foolish
and it's dangerous. You should know better what you are after. For
my part I live in fear lest I shall get so I can't tell politics and
criticism from the warmth that called and clasped me to my kind. It
wouldn't hurt you to cultivate the same fear in yourself.

　　If you really value that letter of Vachel's you put yourself in my
power by letting me have it. You'll have to be mighty good to get it

---

*[B. W. Huebsch, the publisher who, later, became one of the board of The Viking
Press.]

†[William Lyon Phelps, Professor of English Literature at Yale, a volatile and indis-
criminate enthusiast, best known on the lecture platform as a popularizer of culture.]

back. Would you be willing to abandon politics to get it back? And criticism? I've about made up my mind you'll have to.

Now don't run tattling to Jean about my cruelty. She'll just take my side if you do. What does she want of anything but the poet in you?

Tell Dick hurrah for the Fourth. Tell him I'm what I call a Fourth-of-July American and what does he call himself?

Forever yours

Robt Frost

Robt—perfect passive participle, preferred by some to form ending in ed.

[Except for the last cryptic paragraph, which harks back to my writing reviews and criticism at a time when I should have been writing poems, the next letter is a frolic of wit and wildness. Robert's father had been a politician in San Francisco—William Prescott Frost was a States' Rights man and a campaigner for the Democrats; as a boy, Robert had seen enough of politics to be thoroughly disillusioned by its inanities as well as its chicaneries. Here, going off on a high-flying spree of nonsense, he reduces the political scene to a welter of absurdity, including implied puns on reformers, radicals, and radishes.]

Franconia N.H.

July 13 1918

Dear Louis:

You may say of me if you like that when Allen B. Thurman Samuel J. Tilden and David Bennett Hill had read to them what I proposed (in a prospective) to write about the campaign of '76, '80, and '84 disrespectively if they didn't come across, all three sat down with one bump on the same park bench and cried. But wait till I tell you what they cried. They cried: "Blackmail! We will have to come across, or I believe the little cuss will be as a good as his word. He has all the qualifications: he can write: he was born in time to speak from personal knowledge: he is unscrupulous in his origin: his grandfather was out in Shay's Rebellion: and his father was a delegate

to the convention at Cincinatti that nominated General Hancock
and a close friend of that Buckley the blind boss of San Francisco
who died a fugitive from justice in Hawaii before the Yankee
Imperialists stole the islands from Queen Liliahhowdoyouspellher.
This menacing boy was one of the plain people whom Garfield was
survived by in 1881 when he was shot by Gitteau where stands the
brass star in the floor of the R.R. station in Baltimore (which see),
whom McKinley was survived by when he was shot by Emma's
admirer, the youthful Czolgosz at the Pan American Exposition at
Bluffalo, got up to disarm the suspicion of the small American Reps.
that what we were after was them. We have of course to steer a
course about midway between treasonable and the libellous in these
days when all courts tend to degenerate into courts martial; but we say
it without fear of consequences, we had far rather pension this boy
here and now right out of the public pocket, than see him launched
with all his inside knowledge, his gift of frankness and his love of the
picturesque on an Epic of Politics that unless something intervened
to stop it might go on forever. Absolutely fatal as was the loss of the
electoral votes of Florida and Louisiana, there are worse things in
the world (and out of it too for the matter of that) than being
robbed by an umpire especially since in the election of 1876 we had
our own weakness chiefly to blame in not having made a more
thorough job of disfranchising the nigger. No this boy knows too
much. He has lived through more times already than the Wandering
Jew. Better infanticide than homocide: shall we kill him now? All
those in favor of this result make it none by the usual motion."

So they cried like push-cart pedlars in a side street. Then having
cried they wept. Like the true Democrats it is hoped to make the
world safe for, they managed this without handkerchiefs, dashing the
tears from their eyes and noses with the back of fists, all except
Allen Thurman who used his symbolic red bandanna, the democratic
theory of which in the campaign of 1892 was that one copy of it will
last a life time: it will take care of a nose running with grief or a cold,
a nose bleeding with love or a fight: a snap in the wind as it is pulled
endwise from the pocket and it is as presentable as if it had been to
the laundry: no one could tell whether the last thing had in it was a
cold or a nose bleed. We hardly made the most of Thurman's red
bandanna though reference to the public prints of that day will

convince you that we did not fail to correlate it with the way Thomas Jefferson rode to his inaugural alone and tied his horse to a post outside the White House with his own hand.

You are free to use any or all of the foregoing you can make head or tail of except what Thurman Tilden and Hill as with one voice cried, which I consider so tributary that I am reserving it to have it cut on my tombstone as a surprise to my enemies and critics, and I'd a little rather not have it released till then. A public character has got to keep something up his sleeve for when he is dead.

Anybody must be a baby not to see from my origin in such corruption that I am really strong meat for men, though I advertently admit that Masters may be a great man too. Moreover though I mewed my infancy among political bosses and in party bigotry, it must never fail to be mentioned once an hour or so while the world lasts that I have always liked reformers who went in for radishes. You knew I gave Henry George his start. I remember once, when I was a very small boy, going to his house in San Francisco and before dinner or supper going with him to a very sandy garden to get radishes. (I state but the truth).

That's the kind of a hairpin I am, if posterity asks you anything about me. I have been associated to my lasting good with all the reformers from him to you—all the reformers at any rate who go in for radishes. But all the time it has been my purpose to keep away from as many poets as I could and not hurt their feelings.

And by the way I should hardly want to prescribe for your radishes without seeing them. I have always found it dangerous and unsatisfactory to prescribe for or treat radishes in absentia. Only as an emergency measure, you might try thinning them to four feet apart in the row if your row is not less than four feet in length, and then consult Davies the tree specialist. They may be suffering from crevices (so called) in which case the crevices should be scraped out, treated with some reliable anti-sceptic and filled with cement. You must act at once, as the life of a radish is very short at best and they will have gone by or been eaten before you can make them comfortable. Whatever you do, don't be persuaded to spray them with Paris green too immediately before you eat them. Better salt than Paris green if you think you must eat them.

I concede that your criticism will differ from their's in <u>being</u> criticism, but how will people know this if you publish yours in the same year with theirs?

Robt Frost

Next letter will deal with the Maria Halpin scandal, campaign of '84.*

~~Amherst   Mass~~

Calcutta Bombay   Indiana

August 19—approximately [1918]

Dear Louis:

While I am I and you are you, you are never to doubt me; and I promise never to doubt you except as to your sanity. You are wise and clever and deep and wide and noble and impulsive (look at the way you made friends with the lower classes of Franconia in the person of Pearley last summer. He borrowed your "These Times" from me the minute your back was turned and has decided to keep it, he likes it so well with your inscription in it) and having conceded so much I should think I might have earned the right to go further in attribution and say that you are mad too—divinely mad in the common every day sense of the word, though if you were to ask me whom at, I should just have to create a diversion by asking in turn if the locution "whom at" doesn't fall on your ears a little—what shall I say? You're not mad at me and I'm not mad at you. We are agreed on too many things for that, especially in wanting all the freedom we can get before prohibition becomes national. I for my part still get all that's good for me though I have to confess by resort to constantly lower and more humiliating subterfuge. I haven't fallen so low as going to Poetical Dinners or Jay Writtenhome's† At House however and I don't think you have. At any rate I think I can stay away from them if it will help you to stay away and lead a cleaner life. Stick to your writing my child. You write so well. Etc. Etc.

---

*[Maria Halpin was said to be Grover Cleveland's "girl friend"; he was reputed to be the father of her illegitimate child. The presidential campaign of 1884 made much of the scandal.]

†[Jessie B. Rittenhouse, a minor poet, founder and secretary of the Poetry Society of America, and cultivator of a soi-disant salon.]

74

No, but seriousness aside, I shan't have time for anything in Poetry Carnival Week. I have you and Alfred to see and a lot of other hard work to cram into a few days. And it does seem to me you do the reviewing better and better. It has no business to be thrown off as mere reviewing. It is criticism and you know it and it ought to be done in a form that declares itself.

Believe me or not, I am
Rabindranath Tagore

P. S. I forgot to say damn your politics. Was there something else?

[Much of the next letter is a puzzle of paradoxes. It was rumored that Robert was seriously ill, that he had come out publicly against Spoon River Anthology, that several old subscribers for the Atlantic Monthly had objected to the way in which the magazine was favoring "the new poetry," particularly Frost's. His answer to my queries about these matters is a mixture of pseudo-formality and pseudo-philosophic banter. The matter of his illness is resumed in the letter of January 4, 1919.]

Franconia   N.H.
August Something   [1918]

Dear Untermeyer

Was it you were asking about my liver? Thanks but I ain't got no liver—and only one lung. There can't be anything the matter with what I ain't got. What ails me is what in high poetic parlance is known as an unposthume of the spirit; for which you will probably have to see Beaumont and Fletcher though you may find it in Stephen and Percy. The Poetic Drama! Oh my God!

That sounds like a person who knows what he doesn't like and I always hold that we get forward as much by hating as by loving—just as in swimming we advance as much by kicking with our feet as by reaching with our hands. But I can't say for certain that I don't like Spoon River. I believe I do like it in a way. I should be able to tell you better if you hadn't asked me. I could wish it weren't so nearly the ordinary thing in its attitude toward respectability. How shall we treat respectability? That is not for me to say: I am not treating it. All I know with any conviction is that an idea has to be a little new to be at all true and if you say a thing three times it ceases to be so. Mind you I am not finding fault—I never am—only—to be frank, the book chews tobacco I'm afraid. Perhaps that's <u>why</u> I like it.

So if you're looking for anything out of me on the subject that you can use against me, you will have to wait till next time. So much depends on the clothes a man has on when he speaks that I would rather, if you don't mind, defer handing down an opinion on my fellow in art till I have you here with me and can deliver myself by word of mouth.

You are coming before many months now. I hope the ground will be wet, so that we can have a bonfire of spruce boughs to talk around. This is a lovely region. It is away off.

If you knew the true inwardness of what The Atlantic has just been through for my sake! When everything else gives out there will still be the story of Me and The Atlantic to write a book on. One good thing: it will be well documented.

I am going to thank Wood for all that lively stuff the next thing I do.

Wishing you a merry Christmas I am,

"Not worth a breakfast in the cheapest country under the cope."

Robert Frost

Franc: [N.H.]
Sept. 16 '18

O Dear Louis

Comfort me with a Hartmann* picture, console me with anything you can say, for I am desolate and sick of the whole business. How shall I sing the John L. song that Vachel requires of me? Open thine eyes eterne and sphere them round and see if there is anything left to do thats worth a breakfast in the cheapest country under the cope. Till when I stand pat while this machine is to me.

Yourn
Robert Frost

[Illness seems to have been the topic of several of our letters at this time. In October, 1918, I was in bed for a while and wrote that it

---

*[C. Bertram Hartmann, friend and artist, one of whose water colors I had sent to decorate the living room in Franconia.]

was now my turn to be sick. I even set a date to my fanciful demise, and asked Robert to get to work on an obituary.]

[Amherst, Mass.
October 28, 1918]

Dear Louis

I have made a bad start in medias res on that obituary con amore, but before I can go any further I shall have to know at whose hands or of what you are concluding on Dec 17 if I remember rightly. I find it will make a difference in my wording which it is to be a case of, influenza, war, or the critics. It is just possible that you do not know yourself definitely, but then how can you be so definite about the date? Is there something here that I should be able to figure out for myself if I were as wise as a New Yorker and as harmless as I am? Ought I to be able to diagnose the disease, that is to say, from the length of its run from the beginning of the end to the end? Too long. for influenza it seems too short for most of the critics I have heard of or for due process of law. The government hasn't sent you as a gentle hint a snakeskin sausage with gunpowder stuffing and the motto "We leave it to you?" Such times we live in in the twilight of the subter-gods! Not that I want you on my account to feel that you must go ahead and die because you have sent out your announcements and invited people to the funeral. I hate to have my friends feel committed to anything. I should hate to have the Kaiser feel committed to this war. He must quit just the moment he has had enough and I shant think much or any the less of him (that would be impossible), though I must confess it is in his honor, you may tell my friend Dick if you see him, that we have gone into half-yellow. So please excuse this stationery.

Tubby serious. This is a war college and I am teaching war issues: so it's a lucky thing I have always taken a sensible view of the universe and everything in it. Otherwise I might have to knuckle to the war department were it ever so little or else go to jail like good old Gene Debs. I am out to see a world full of small-fry democracies even if we have to fill them two deep or even three deep in some places.

Lesley is worse than I am. She is manufacturing hydroplanes with the Curtiss company and I'm afraid if she wasn't so fond of seeing people licked, anybody licked, she might want to see the war go on forever. In other words she is one of the interests.

Too much war! I swear if there's another war on top of this one I shall refuse to know anything about it. I have ordered all my papers and magazines discontinued after July 4, 1919. No more politics for me in this world, once I am sure all throwns are throne down.

Commend me to everybody. What fun we'll have when we can get back to poetry, and the form of things is once more all or nearly all. Me heart celebrates. Let's go to Palestine for a visit at least. Shall we fix it up?

Blessed if we don't.
R.F.

Amherst   Mass
November 4   1918

Dear Louis:

More to us than many letters, however wild, will be the sight of you twain drawing rein, stalling your engine, breaking your car, or what you like to call it, before our door in Main St. Our number is 19 of that ilk: our telephone number 468 W; our names respectively as professor and author Robert Lee Frost and Robert Frost.

> "Come as the waves come when
> Navies are stranded!
> Come for the soul is free!"

It is just the same about you as it is about Peace; the minute we let ourselves think we can have it we cease to be able to wait for it: we give way to our longing entirely and are of no more use to anybody for anything.

For God's sake don't disappoint us. And please plan to stay more than a day or two. Please—if I say please won't you?

> There's twa fat hens upo' the coop
> Been fed this month or mair.

Well death to them, thraw their necks about, feed for the welcome guessed!

Waitfully watching
Robert Frost

Amerced   [Mass.]
[Jan. 4]   1919

Dear Louis:

Here it is as late as this (1919 A.D.), and I don't know whether or not I'm strong enough to write a letter yet. The only way I can tell that I haven't died and gone to heaven is by the fact that everything is just the same as it was on earth (all my family round me and all that) only worse, whereas, as I had been brought up in Swedenborgianism to believe, everything should be the same only better. Two possibilities remain: either I have died and gone to Hell or I haven't died. Therefore I haven't died. And that's the only reason I haven't. I was sick enough to die and no doubt I deserved to die. The only question in my mind is could the world have got along without me. I leave it to you to whom I think I may safely leave it.

We'll assume then in what follows that I am alive—however unlively it may sound. I can't tell whether it is my voice speaking or my bones creaking. What bones are they that rub together so unpleasantly in the middle of you in extreme emaciation? You ought to hear them in me when I make a sweeping gesture as in tennis or oratory or attempt to dance à la Russe some such classic as Integer Vitae. But why try to dance such a poem, you may say, till I feel more integral. Why not confine myself to the Rubáiyát? Why not simply confine myself?

Let's see what was I going to say.

Oh I guess first I shall have to ask you to call your red friends off von Moschzisker. I don't want his house in Philadelphia bombed again. Do you hear? Bomb somebody that's shown some want of sympathy with the down-most man as it used to be called. He's the most sensible decent sort—the Judge is. Isn't there some mistake don't you suppose?

Yes you can have the bad shoes parable. It's Ojibway I think—think.

I have read the way you say I would write Integer Vitae and I promise you I will do my best to write it that way when I write it so as not to make you a liar. Everybody says it's the living breathing image of my idiom. It ought not be hard to live up to. I will bear it in mind. Mine was good but probably not quite so good as Robinson's and Davies', n'est ce pas?

And by the way I saw a dazzler of yours quoted from Braithwaite's Anth in the Boston Herald.

George Whicher* liked Jean's book best of all he's seen lately. I'm to tell her personally how much I liked it when I get strong enough to lay it on with a baseball bat. I liked it all right.

Lola was so-so.† She tries a little harder than Emerson would have us try. Easy does it.

Pelle was good reading. But none of it was any news. Not a phrase but was old story. It was the insight that was remarkable and the nearness to the life. Form is with the rich, material with the poor, though to the poor it sometimes may seem that material is just what they lack to eat and cover their backs with. The rich are too vague from their remoteness from things ever to make realizing artists. Things belong to the poor by their having to come to grips with things daily. And that's a good one on the poor. They are the only realists. Things are theirs and no one's else, though of course it is forbidden the poor to eat or wear the things. Well there I go and I mustn't. Sometime I must copy you out a poem I did on Bolshevism in 1911 as I saw it spectral over Lawrence at the time of the strike. It will show you where I was.

What times they are. Jack Reed will tell you this month who licked the Germans but will he tell you next month who didn't lick Lloyd George in the English elections? If the poor promised themselves no more than vengeance in the oncoming revolution I'd be with them. It's all their nonsense about making a better or even a different world that I can't stand. The damned fools!—only less damned than the God damned fools over them who have made and made such a mess of industrialism. Requiescat! I started mildly enough: where have I got to!

> Let's resolve to be good anyway.
>> Your petitioner
>>> Rob't Frost

[Robert's illness, rumored to be tubercular, was diagnosed as influenza; he suffered from it during the last four months of 1918 and he was still ailing in January, 1919.

*[Professor of English at Amherst College.]
†[Lola Ridge, a poet who mingled sociology with metaphysics.]

Robert knew Von Moschzisker and he also knew that I knew nothing about the bombing of the Judge's house. The reference to my "red friends" was another teasing gibe about my association with such radicals as Max Eastman and Floyd Dell.

The "bad shoes parable" emanated from a talk that Robert gave on what might be considered "native" in poetry. Mary Austin, Natalie Curtis, and others were causing a stir with books purporting to prove that the basic American rhythm was that of the Indian and that our most indigenous poetry was in what they called the Amerindian song. Robert was one of those who maintained that, stirring as the Indian songs may be to the Indians, they were not, and could not be, part of our cultural heritage. He proved this by reading three different versions of one Indian chant which, according to the three translators, incorporated three differing symbols and meant three different things.

An occasional translator, I was also a part-time parodist. A volume entitled Including Horace began with a set of paraphrases of the Horatian "Integer Vitae" ode rendered in the manner of twenty-five poets, including Robert Herrick, Robert Browning, Robert Bridges, and Robert Frost. Robert liked the Robinson pastiche better than my transplanting of the Sabine woods to his own New Hampshire acres.

Pelle the Conqueror was a book I had sent Robert after one of our arguments about the labor movement. The Danish novelist, Martin Andersen Nexø, was frankly a propagandist, but his passionate convictions and his innate narrative power made Pelle a kind of social epic.]

[Amherst, Mass.
Feb. 17, 1919]

Dear Louis:

I'm sorry to have to put off New York again, but what's the use of saying so till I am prepared to "do different."

Part of the enclosed is intended for a little surprise. I ask you can any original first gift however unexpected give you half the pleasure that you must get from the return of anything as long given up for lost as Vachel's Edgar Lee Letter* (so called from henceforth).

I can't say that I am not satisfied with the Thomas article. In our

---

*[This refers to a long letter, dated May 13, 1918, which Vachel Lindsay had written me in praise of Edgar Lee Masters.]

hearts we both wanted you to write it as you saw it. I'm credibly told that there's something about me the British prefer not to have mentioned in connection with Thomas. If so you will have bothered them by what you have written. They seem to think it must diminish their poet to have him under obligations to an American. And yet he knew and freely and generously said that it was not only in verse-theory but in inspiration that he was my debtor. Of course it is all nothing. But no harm in bothering them in their conceit.

Lesley cites you and Jean for distinguished attentions. The family when next it convenes will doubtless make an appropriation—to buy you medals.

The family is terribly scattered for the moment. It gives me a foretaste of what it will be like when they are grown up and gone and I don't like it any better than I should. I suppose they will have to go their ways sometime. Well then I'm not going to stop them of course if it's fate. But I don't believe there's any law to keep me from turning from my own way to go after them along theirs. A father ought to have a right to follow, imitate and lose himself in the careers of his children. What would Bernard Shaw say?—I mean about the aged being dragged along by the young instead of the young being held back by the old?

I've got a word to you for one of these days, my friend, about these people who think you spend too much time thinking of me. You know you have exalted me. The question will soon be have you done it for nothing. Seeing you such a rich man they will suspect you have fattened your purse out of me. That will be the next thing. Let's destroy our check books so that they can't prove any money connection. I'd hate to have it go down to posterity that one poet had corrupted another with money. It would be unprecedented in the annals unless you count Amy's corruption of Braithwaite, and that's not a case of poet and poet so much as of poet and duodecaroon— something very special and never likely to happen again. I'll tell you something else we can do to throw the poetry society (lc) off the track. Let's meet and ignore each other in a public place on the very day Holt releases your book of criticism. Let's both act equally offended. Let's loudly refuse to be introduced to each other. Start cultivating the perpendicular wrinkles in front.

Meanwhile my love to you all from Dick up.

Robertus

*[I have been unable to find out whether Robert actually sent the
following wickedly ingenuous letter to the corresponding secretary
of the Poetry Society of America. I suspect that, in spite of his
assertion, the only copy of it is the one he sent to me.*

*George Sylvester Viereck, a latter-day Swinburnian, author of
Nineveh and Other Poems, My Flesh and Blood, The Nude in the
Mirror, etcetera, prided himself on being "the stormy petrel of
American literature." Accused of being a German agent during the
First World War, expelled from the Poetry Society and his name
dropped from Who's Who in America, he was a poet without a
license. The most devastating commentary on his much advertised
devilishness was written by John Reed to the tune of Gilbert and
Sullivan's "I Am the Monarch of the Sea":*

> O let us humbly bow the neck
> To George Sylvester Vi-er-eck,
> Who trolled us a merry little Continental stave
> Concerning the Belly and the Phallus and the Grave.]

Franconia   N.H.
April 3   1919

[Copy]

Dear Mrs. Perry
(Corresponding Sec.)
So I'm to be President of the Poetry Society because I wasn't at
your last meeting to say I wouldn't be President, just as I seem to be
expected at Wellesley on the eleventh for the simple reason that I
haven't said I wouldn't be there on the eleventh. Neither have I said
that I wouldn't be there on the twelfth or the thirteenth or the
fourteenth or any other day you have a mind to name. On the same
principle I suppose I am writing an epic because I haven't said I
wasn't and it has already made me a rich man because I haven't said it
hasn't and if I am a rich man I can go any distance in the train at
three cents a mile because I haven't said that as a sick man I'm not
able to. I must protest at this reverse way of being taken. Must I be
assumed guilty till I am proved innocent but more than that must I be
assumed guilty of every particular deed and thought that I haven't
specifically declared myself innocent of? (As for instance Maria
Halpin's baby.) *

*[See footnote on page 74.]

But seriously now do you think it was friendly of you all to make me an official when you must have seen how superstitious I am about holding office. I thought I saw a way out of it for us both in not accepting the Presidency you had imposed on me. I thought by silence I could sort of keep from myself what I was in for and in fact privately take the view that I was not a President while at the same time leaving you free to think that I <u>was</u> a President. Ingenious you see— and significant: it shows how anxious I am to please you as friends and fellow poets if not as member of any society. But it wouldn't do: you had to spoil it all and make the issue acute between us by proposing to lunch me formally on my job just as you would launch a ship. I may be nervous but I can't help seeing in it a conspiracy to shear me of any wild strength I may have left after two years of teaching in college. As Vachel would say "Let Samson be comin' into your mind."

With protestations of the warmest regard etc.

Robert Frost

Louis, I wanted you to have a picture of me struggling to climb out of what I have got into out onto the thin ice around me. The letter is a copy of one I am sending to Mrs. Perry on the occasion of her expecting me to lunch on the eleventh of the month because I haven't said I wouldn't come. Please put it up to posterity if I haven't done the best I could. Be my witness.

R.F.

Bids fair to rival the famous case of Vierick versus the Poetry Society of America, only mine illustrates the difficulty of staying out while his illustrates the difficulty of staying in.

R.F.

Franconia   N.H.
April 18   1919

Dear Louis

The point is that there isn't anybody in God's present world that's got such a mechanical mixture of poets real and unreal going round and round and over and over each other in his head and even shassaycrossways but always kept up off the bottom as the author of

The New Era in Poetry.* I was afraid that book would be too good
to be good for you. And it is. It is dangerous in two ways. It calls for
another book like it to pile on top of it about all the poets here and
in England taken together and it calls for it from you because you are
plainly the only one who knows enough to do it. And then on top of
that and before you are free to get back to writing your own poetry
again it calls for a third book, an anthology of this century that I wish
we could call The Laurels Wither on your Brow as a taunt to the
British. Of course we won't be indiscreet enough to name it that. Just
the same our purpose in it would be to show the British who's writing
the poetry now, i.e. "who's luny now." The preface will say that it takes
us over here to make a just anthology because, while the English like
doting islanders have been reading themselves and not us, we have
been reading both ourselves and them. We put you forward as
probably the only man of judgment in the arts who knows all the
poetry of all the poets there and here. Anybody can see you are that
and the fact imposes on you a duty you are not going to shirk. When
do we begin to round-up?

And the second danger of the book is that it will make you your
own worst rival.

All this apart from my personal satisfaction in the book, O thou
most generous one. You made the book and I may say that I also
made it if only in the sense in which I made the football team in school
and the last train at night. You achieved the book and I achieved
a place in it. It suffices for me. I wish you could say the book came out
in March. Otherwise March is a blank this year and my superstition
breaks down that I always get in some signal stroke of ambition in
March. Say it was in March and you make this March my best ever.

I follow you in nearly all your judgments and for so stupid a
person (without humor) in a surprisingly large number of your
brilliancies.

I have given you a name for your next book. My next is to be The
Bard Plymouth Rock by

The Plymouth Rock Barred

*[A preface to my The New Era in American Poetry, published in early 1919,
announced that the book was "an explanatory if not a conclusive summary of the
principal forces and figures of the period."]

Dear Louis:

I ask you to say the book came out in March, my birth month, and you confound me by making it on March 26 my exact birthday. You make me drunk with superstition. I am in love with chance and though as mischance it someday slay me yet will I and so forth.

You liked my Runaway. But we won't publish it yet a while. You can show it to anybody but editors. I should think Dick might like it. I suspect my kids really liked it, though Carol says it is not as good as my Well* (a copy of which I may decide to enclose for comparison since you have probably forgotten you once saw it on my porch in Franconia.)

Do you want to send George Whicher a copy of your book with your name written in it?

What's this madness of the mad Lesley over a college magazine? I hear the wild animal won a hoop race or a torch race or something round a flower pot.† The audience must have had time to get almost excited. So must the performers. Once all the way round a flower pot. I never was good at long distances myself.

Irma‡ rounded off her education nicely with her two weeks in New York.

You predict things for May. There is something uncertain about the word May per se. I don't care to predict for it. Still I doubt it will be marked by any particular occurrences anywhere of any particular nature. The time is not yet. I'm composing a poem with the refrain "Blow their bloody hats off." "Hats" you will observe. It is addressed to the wind not to the Bolshevike which are one and the same thing (nit). Pity me for not knowing what would set everything right. When I think of all the human pains that went to uplifting Pithecanthropus Erectus into the Piltdown man and the Piltdown man into the Neanderthal and the Neanderthal into the Heidelberg and him into the likes of me and Woodrow Wilson it makes me as

---

*[The poem was renamed "For Once, Then, Something."]

†[Lesley, Robert's eldest daughter, had won a prize as a chariot-racer in the Greek Games at Barnard College, which she was attending. I happened to be one of the judges.]

‡[Irma and Marjorie were Robert's other daughters.]

tired as sitting up all night on the job or doing it in my sleep. It seems looking backward as if it had been largely a matter of changing bones directly or indirectly. I'm afraid it was mostly indirectly. But why couldn't we try if it could be done this next time by attacking the bones directly after the Flathead Indians? Why by osteopathetic manipulation for example couldn't you for instance effect the next great change of me into Max Eastman or Jack Reed. (Let it be Max if I am going to be free to choose the particular freeman, free thinker, or free-for-all I have got to be.) Oh dear! I haven't got room to say what I wanted to about Prometheus and Polyphemus. But you can guess the rest from your knowledge.

R.F.

Franconia   [N.H.]
June 30   [1919]

Dear Looiss

Your Child's Garden of Erse hadn't escaped me. I've been having the Post regularly for some time so as to keep an eye on you in the Saturday number. I don't want to seem to avert my gaze from anything you do as if I were ashamed of you. Pun your damndest: I am not afraid of your compromising me. A mother can follow an erring son even to the gallows and beyond in tears to his grave in quick-lime without in anyway sharing in his guilt. So I should hope could a friend of my known devotion to you.

You are down there among the Daylight Savers letting off puns you don't intend and I am up here among the Anti Daylight Savers not writing the epics I do intend. It shows the difference between town and country.

One of the epics I intend is dental. I talked it up the other night to indicate what could be done that hadn't to my knowledge been done yet. If Amy has done it please apprize me and I won't go ahead with it, which will be easy enough as I wouldn't go ahead with it anyway. The Care of the Teeth is the name of the whole work and An Aseptic or Well-cleaned Cavity the name of the first chapter. I should want it to be expressive of the Major and Minor Satisfactions of a Dentist's Life. Shouldn't you? And I should want it to run serially in some good dentifrice's advertising. I feel that we are right at the turning point in these things: we are right at the shift of interest on the part both of the writer and reader from the literary section of the magazines to the advertising section. The serial epic of advertising will settle it in favor of the advertising section for good and all. I am ambitious to be the one to mark the final disappearance of the literary section: that is to say I could be ambitious to be that one if I had the least encouragement. Why don't you encourage me? Probably you want to know more about this epic of dentistry before you commit yourself to the project. Well it will be narrative of course as an epic should be. The plot is something I came across in the old days before success isolated me and cut me off from meeting ordinary people on equal terms. It is really no more than the life of a dentist I used to know who had gone out from a New England hill farm to learn dentistry and become dentist to a crowned head of South America, the Emperor Dom Pedro of Brazil. In the end he had retired to the New England hill farm with a pocket-full of Brazilian diamonds. Once Dom Pedro lent him to the king of Portugal for a while and he always averred that gold was so scarce in Portugal that he had to scrape a bit of it here and a bit there from out-of-the-way corners of the king's crown to fill the king's front teeth with: his back teeth he stopped up with Spanish cork. Consider the Americanniness of it all. American dentistry was our first and perhaps, till Mencken wrote The American Language, our only signal contribution to civilization. Our pride as a people rested on where our dentists had penetrated to.

Speaking of Mencken I can tell you what he would like to say if he had time to think it out. He would like to say that America isn't American enough for her authors to be very American yet. There may be a few fools trying to anticipate their future selves and write poetry as of 4000 A.D. so as to be more American than the facts warrant. But most of us are willing to take our lives as given us. About all we can do is write about things that have happened to us in America in the language we have grown up to in America. It's not so long ago that most of America except Jim Thorpe came from Europe—it was so short a time ago that it may be said to be coming yet. Look at me. Half of me has been here nine generations, the other half one generation: which makes me more representative I think than if I was altogether of old stock. I'm an ideal combination of been-here-since-the-beginning and just-come-over. My ideas may be such, most of them, as I could have got in Europe. They are over there as well as here. But what are the chances I didn't come by them honestly here where I lived totally immersed in them for thirty seven years before I saw Europe or much of anybody from Europe? If I got them in America I have faith that they are touched with Americanism. They may be European, but they have been here long enough to be tanned and freckled with the American sun.

Time we defined, I suppose, what it is to be American. Let's say it is never to have gone out of the country except to lick another country. That saves the soldiers, and when you come to consider it doesn't leave me out. No one except Mencken has ever accused me of having gone to England for anything but to get the better of the English.

And so I might go on writing nonsense indefinitely if I didn't see the end of this piece of paper just ahead.

Great scheme your textbook. It ought to have an unacademic chapter on versification. You are on the high school end. Lesley and I are writing—An Expressive First Reader for kids. Straight goods. Please include Death of Hired Man. Till further notice

Yours

R.F.

The Tuft of Flowers always seems to get people. Two other poems enclosed.

["A Child's Garden of Erse" is a caption I used for a review of a banal collection of Irish poetry—Robert's chiding me about my puns is the more amusing since it came from one who constantly delighted to play with the sound and sense of words. Even in his speculation on what is American, he could not resist the paronomastic appeal of "Americanniness."

"It's not so long ago that most of America except Jim Thorpe came from Europe"—Jim Thorpe, a football hero, was a full-blooded American Indian.]

Here are two new ones.

WRONG TO THE LIGHT*

Others taunt me with having knelt at well-curbs
Always wrong to the light, so never seeing
Deeper down in the well than where the water
Gives me back in a shining surface picture
Me myself in the summer heaven god-like
Looking out of a wreath of fern and cloud puffs.
Once when trying with chin against a well curb
I discerned, as I thought, beyond the picture,
Through the picture, a something white, uncertain,
Something more of the depths—and then I lost it:
Water came to rebuke the too clear water:
One drop fell from a fern, and lo, a ripple
Shook whatever it was lay there at bottom,
Blurred it, blotted it out. What was that whiteness?
Truth? A pebble of quartz? For once then something.

R.F.

FISH-LEAP FALL†

From further in the hills there came
A river to our kitchen door
To be the water of the house
And keep a snow-white kitchen floor.

The fall we made the river take
To catch the water in a dish
(It wasn't deep enough to dip)
Was good for us, but not for fish.

For when the trout came up in spring
And found a plunging wall to pass,
It meant, unless they met it right,
They glanced and landed in the grass.

*[This is what Robert originally called his "Well" poem. It appeared as "For Once, Then, Something" in New Hampshire.]
†[Robert toyed with the idea of putting this in a section entitled "Over Back" (a subtitle he subsequently used in A Witness Tree). It does not, however, appear in any of his volumes nor in his Complete Poems.]

I recollect one fingerling
That came ashore to dance it out;
And if he didn't like the death,
He'd better not have been a trout.

I found him faded in the heat.
But there was one I found in time
And put back in the water where
He wouldn't have the fall to climb.

R. F.

[Franconia, N.H.
August 4, 1919]

August!
How long
Gongula?*

[Franconia, N.H.
August 29, 1919]

Dear Louis

What we want to know before we go any further in any direction is are you home alive and getting well. Because if you're not what's the use of anything?

But if you are I may or I may not want to address myself in a few words to the subject of your two school books. Not that they need any ideas from me. That's my consolation: if I find I can't say anything to help you about them, they will probably be the better for it. As they stand I see their sufficient value. They easily beat what anyone else can do. Only I just don't want you to be too intemperate about the past. My efforts, should I rise and put forth any, would be toward begging you on bended knee to give the past half a show. (You'd think I was pleading for a lady <u>with</u> a past, but no, it is the past alone I am concerned for.)

Look what Amy's pig-eyed young bear-cat† done all over the Dial

---

*[This, a burlesque of Ezra Pound's early Imagist poem, "Papyrus," refers to a postponed visit which took place at the end of August.]
†[John Gould Fletcher, one of Amy Lowell's Imagist group. He was writing reviews as well as poetry and, at the time, was Amy Lowell's favorite protégé.]

for want of a little historical sense. Amy ought to be ashamed of him.
Right through his diapers! Let's withdraw from such society and go
into the maple sugar business. I swear!

Be good to Jean on our account.

More yours every time I see you

Robert Frost

*[One of the things in college courses which Robert fought hardest
was the effort to fit everything into conventional categories. He
particularly objected to those neat little cubbyholes: classical and
romantic, romantic and realistic. I happened to be present at a
round-table discussion with some of his students when he expatiated
on the theme of the next letter: "Every form of romance is but an
exhalation from some form of reality."]*

Amherst   Mass

October 15   1919

Dear Louis:

No need to tell you how sure I am that no one succeeds in any of
the arts without observing at least some one of the various realities.
That's the way he gets his originality whatever it comes to. He may
be as romantic as a girl of eighteen in subject matter and in vocabulary:
you'll find him trying to make it up to you in vocal reality or some
other reality. He must get back to the source of sanity and energy
somewhere. Every form of romance is but an exhalation from some
form of reality. The common speech is always giving off, you and I
know how, the special vocabulary of poetry. The same thing happens
with the tones of everyday talk. They have emanations of grandeur
and dignity and reverence and heroism and terror. No matter how
realistic we are we go up with these and float on them like charred
paper balancing on the updraft above a fire. That is to say the realist is
that much a romantic. The romanticist differs from the realist only in
being more romantic than he. He starts where the realist leaves off.
He refines on refinement and that's all he cares about refining on. He
still persists long after his refining touch becomes unperceptible.
Never mind if he is happy. Etc. etc. Here comes a boy I shall have to
go on with this to if I am to go on with it at all. Maybe it will prove to

be Everett Glass. Not for myself any more, do I think, but for boys we can only hope can make better use of it than I can. We are asked to believe that if I teach them enough they will go beyond me in accomplishment so that I can well afford to go no further myself.

Yours sadly

R.F.

Amassed Mass
Dec 8 1919

Dear Louis

That's a sturdy friend! I knew I could count on you not to doubt me even when appearances were most against me.

Brooks Moore* means nothing to me. Who is he? But Stork!†— both denotatively and connotatively! Not the father of twenty children, many of them twins, can show more perturbation than I at sound of that dread name. Stork! Almost more unwelcome to the married ear than cucoo even.

Had a good journey home with the illustrator of any books of mine hereafter to be illustrated.

Yours everly

Robertus

[During 1919 I had been gathering material for Modern British Poetry, a companion volume to Modern American Poetry. The collection was a tentative affair, a weak forerunner to the later and more voluminous editions. Unable to check certain little-known data, I turned to Robert to verify some of the chronology. Robert supplied the data with one exception and added a crude signature, a thumb print, and a "photograph"—the latter being a portrait of the grizzled veteran on the pfennig green stamp (1911 issue) of Bavaria. This made it "official."]

*[A misspelling of Brookes More, poet, brother of the American philosopher and essayist, Paul Elmer More.]
†[Charles Wharton Stork, critic, author, and sometimes poet. ·Editor of the Phila-delphia magazine Contemporary Verse (1917-1926).]

[Amherst,   Mass.
January 5,   1920]

Lascelles Abercrombie is approximately 38 years old
Wilfred W. Gibson*   ”   ”   42 ”   ”
D. H. Lawrence   ”   ”   ? ”   ”
F. S. Flint   ”   ”   32 ”   ”

* Isn't it Sturge Moore who says Wilfrid Gibson is older than most sheep, but not so old as the rose bush is; he is about as pretty as the former. Isn't it Tennyson who says D. H. Lawrence is old damsell, old and hard. Jean Ingelow says Lascelles Abercrombie is old, so old he can't write a letter. Flint, though young, is old enough to be the putative father of free verse in England.

Visaed for the State Dept.
(Signed in a badly shaken hand)
W. J. Bryan

[Amherst,   Mass.
Jan. 24,   1920]

Three more small ones.

THE LOCKLESS DOOR

It went many years,
But at last came a knock
And I thought of the door
With no lock to lock.

I blew out the light
I tiptoed the floor
And raised both hands
In prayer to the door.

But the knock came again.
My window was wide;
I climbed on the sill
And descended outside.

Back over the sill
I bade a "Come in"
To whoever the knock
At the door may have been.

So at a knock
I emptied my cage
To hide in the world
And alter my age.

R.F.

PLOWMEN

I hear men say to plow the snow.
They cannot mean to plant it though—
Unless in bitterness, to mock
At having cultivated rock.

R.

GOOD-BYE AND KEEP COLD*

This saying goodbye on the verge of the dark
And cold to an orchard so young in the bark
Reminds me of all that can happen to harm
An orchard away at the end of the farm
All winter cut off by a hill from the house.
I don't want it girdled by rabbit and mouse,
I don't want it dreamily nibbled for browse
By deer, and I don't want it budded by grouse.
(If certain it wouldn't be idle to call
I'd summon grouse rabbit and deer to the wall
And warn them away with a stick for a gun.)
I don't want it stirred by the heat of the sun.
(We made it secure against being I hope
By setting it out on a northerly slope.)
No orchard's the worse for the wintriest storm,
But one thing about it, it mustn't get warm.
"How often already you've had to be told
Keep cold, young orchard, Good-bye and keep cold.
Dread fifty above more than fifty below.
I have to be gone for a season or so
My business awhile is with different trees
Less carefully nurtured, less fruitful than these
And such as is done to their wood with an ax—
Maples and birches and tamaracks.

*[One of the poems which differ in a few details from the subsequent, printed version.]

95

I wish I could promise to lie in the night
And share in an orchard's arboreal plight
When slowly (and nobody comes with a light!)
Its heart sinks lower under the sod;
But something has to be left to God.

R. F.

Sow Shaftsbury Vete
February 8   [1920]

Dear Louis:

I crawled out (I was going to say out of going to The Cosmopolitan)*—I crawled out in the sun today and failing to cast any shadow, asked to be carried back to bed again. I guess it is the carving knife for mine: and I wouldn't care nearly so much if there was any advertisement in it. There is a Masters Mountain and right beside it a Frost Hollow hereabouts. What can be done to bring low the mountain and cast up the hollow? You say.

Yours
R.

Franconia   N.H.
March 12   [1920]

Dear Louis:

Honestly and truly this is what I dreamed last night. I'm not to blame for what I dream I hope.

I dreamed I had just been dining late at a conservative's who had made me a little uncomfortable by treating me as a radical—a little uncomfortable, not very. (You can't find anybody in these times who isn't more or less flattered by being regarded as a radical) I was standing on the street corner waiting for the last car when who should walk up to me out of the darkness to tell me the last car had gone more than an hour ago but you looking pretty well considering you looked for all the world in every detail like Martha Foote Crowe. The likeness was so exact that I don't know how I knew it was you except by the Current Opinion that you held devoutly to your breasts

*[The Cosmopolitan Club, at which Robert was scheduled to speak.]

like a prayer book. The next thing I remember we were away forward
in a debate in which I was trying hard to establish to the tune of

> "Watchman watchman don't take me
> Take that nigger behind the tree
> He stole gold and I stole brass"

that I was neither a radical nor a conservative. I had a strange inward
assurance that I was making my position perfectly clear because I
was speaking in a form of regular verse more or less acceptable to both
radicals and conservatives. I wish I could reproduce the verse here out
of the dream, but it seems to have got away from me. The important
thing is my argument. "Madman" I said, meaning of course Madam,
"I am willing that you should change everything in the world that
you want to change. You can hand me a list at any time and I will
cheerfully subscribe it. (English use of the verb acquired from
much reading of English authors.) But surely there are some things
you have neither strength nor inclination to change. Now all I ask is
the humble job of being allowed to hold on to the things you don't
want changed. There must be some?" I pressed you. "Aren't there?"

"I spuzso," you conceded reluctantly as if one didn't know what
they would be and wouldn't delay the action to find out then.

"In the general rush of change with almost everything going, I
should think there would be danger that some things would be carried
away that even the wildest revolutionary would be sorry to see
carried away. Well then that's where I come in. Delegate me to hold
on to those. 'Here hold these,' you could say. You would find me so
serviceable that never again would you hurt my feeling by calling me
a conservative. I should count my life not spent in vain if I were
permitted to sit and hold in my lap just one thing that conservatives
and radicals were alike agreed must be saved from being changed by
mistake in the general change of other things. I am interested in what
is to stay as it is; you are interested in what is not to stay as it is. We
can't split on that difference. We operate in mutually exclusive spheres
from which we can only bow across to each other in mutual appreciation. If I am a conservative it is the kind of conservative you want in
your pay to take care of what you don't want to take with you. And
just so if I am a radical it is the kind you can have no kick against
because I let you take with you all you care to load up with. The fact is
I am neither a conservative nor a radical and I refuse henceforth to be

called either. I am a strainer: I keep back the tea leaves and let the
tea flow through."

At this point you began to show signs of wanting to go back and
reconsider something you had been led by my eloquence in my own
desperate defence to pass over too easily.

"Let's see," says you, "what some of these things are you might
be trusted to hold while the rest of the world went forward."

"Or backward. Drive 'em in any direction you please. If the flame
has got to be bent, I don't care which way it bends. My interest is
to keep the candle from going over."

"You sound to me suspiciously open-minded. Don't care, do you,
whether we drive the world forward or backward. Think us capable
of driving it backward?"

"Don't get mad."

"It shows the prejudice I have suspected you of, against reform
and reformers."

"How so?" I asked to give you the trouble of putting an elusive
thought into words.

"But now I want the more to know what the things are you would
hold in your lap."

"You wouldn't mind my holding a lap-dog surely. You weren't
thinking of altering all the lap-dogs, I hope? Or I might hold a cat.
You weren't thinking of altering all the tomcats?"

I looked, and if you yourself weren't changing! A curtain
descended: there was a confused noise as of scenery being shifted;
the curtain rose, and you stood revealed in appearance intermediate
between Jessie Rittenhouse and Harriet Monroe.

"Anything personal intended by 'cats'?" you said.

And then a voice that was unmistakably Jean's said wearily "Louis,
Louis come to yourself."

"Coming", said a voice just as unmistakably yours, shrill but far
away as from the inmost inwards of yourself. Very ventriloquial.

The place seemed to be in Brookline.

It was unlabelled except for a street sign which read Heath Road.

I vow I have given it exactly as I dreamed it, especially the last
part of it where I wasn't laboring under the temptation of stretching
it to use up the note paper I happened to have in the house. You
ought to know how accurate it is. Where were you on the night of
March 11? Can you bring anyone to swear that you couldn't have been

on the streets with Martha Foote Crowe, Jessie Rittenhouse, and Harriet Monroe?

I stick to the position I dreamed I took. It looks to me fairly tenable. You want to blow the candle to see if it won't give more light. All right, let me hold the candle so you can give all your attention to blowing it carefully so as not to blow it out. And let me hold the matches too so that if you should blow it out we could form a society to relight it. (Just made it last the paper out.)

Everly yours

Robert Frost

Franconia   N.H.

March 21   1920

Dear Louis:

Is it nothing to you that no longer than ten years ago I was writing town poems like this:

THE PARLOR JOKE*

You won't hear unless I tell you
How the few to turn a penny
Built complete a modern city
Where there shouldn't have been any
And then conspired to fill it
With the miserable many.

They drew on Ellis Island.
They had but to raise a hand
To let the living deluge
On the basin of the land.
They did it just like nothing
In smiling self-command.

If you asked them their opinion
They declared the job as good
As when to fill the sluices
They turned the river flood;
Only then they dealt with water
And now with human blood.

*[This is not to be found in the *Complete Poems*. It appears only in A *Miscellany of American Poetry*, which I began editing in 1920.]

Then the few withdrew in order
To their villas on the hill
Where they watched from easy couches
The uneasy city fill.
"If it isn't good," they ventured,
"At least it isn't ill."

But with child and wife to think of
They weren't taking any chance.
So they fortified their windows
With a screen of potted plants,
And armed themselves from somewhere
With a manner and a glance.

You know how a bog of sphagnum
Beginning with a scum
Will climb the side of a mountain;
So the poor began to come
Climbing the hillside suburb
From the alley and the slum.

As the tenements crept nearer,
It pleased the rich to assume,
In humorous self-pity,
The mockery of gloom
Because the poor insisted
On wanting all the room.

And there it might have ended
In a feeble parlor joke,
Where a gentle retribution
Overtook the gentlefolk;
But that some beheld a vision:
Out of stench and steam and smoke,

Out of vapor of sweat and breathing
They saw materialize
Above the darkened city
Where the murmur never dies
A shape that had to cower
Not to knock against the skies.

They could see it through a curtain,
They could see it through a wall,
A lambent swaying presence

In wind and rain and all,
With its arms abroad in heaven
Like a scarecrow in a shawl.

There were some who thought they heard it
When it seemed to try to talk
But missed articulation
With a little hollow squawk
Up indistinct in the zenith
Like the note of the evening hawk.

Of things about the future
Its hollow chest was full;
Something about rebellion
And blood a dye for wool
And how you may pull the world down
If you know the prop to pull.

What to say to the wisdom
That could tempt a nation's fate
By invoking such a spirit
To reduce the labor rate!
Some people don't mind trouble
If it's trouble up-to-date.

Patented 1910 by R. (L.) Frost

Elinor has just come out flat-footed against God conceived either
as the fourth person seen with Shadrack, Meshack, and Tobedwego
in the fiery furnace or without help by the Virgin Mary. How about
as a Shelleyan principal or spirit coeternal with the rock part of
creation, I ask. Nonsense and you know it's nonsense, Rob Frost,
only you're afraid you'll have bad luck or lose your standing in the
community if you speak your mind. Spring, I say, returneth and the
maple sap is heard dripping in the buckets—(allow me to sell you a
couple. We can quote you the best white first-run sugar at a dollar
a pound unsight and unseen—futures.) Like a woman she says Pshaw.
You know how a woman says Pshaw—you with your uncanny
knowledge of your own wife. I took out an accident policy limited to
death by boiling in a sap pan, swore off on baths, and took up my
new life as a farmer today by absentmindedly boring a hole clear
through a two foot maple tree and out onto the other side. "Amatoor!"

all the leaves began to murmur. "Book-farmer!" Leaves is of course an anachronism—that well known figure of speech. There weren't any leaves as yet.

Think it over and do as the last line of Drummond's famous poem, "You won't..."*

R.F.

[Long before the following letter was written, Robert was greatly perturbed by hysterical outbursts on the part of his sister, Jeanie. His letters to the lawyer who settled his grandfather's estate and who was empowered to dole out the money, would, if ever published, throw further light on the difficulties.]

Franconia   N.H.
April 12   1920

Dear Louis:

I must have told you I have a sister Jeanie two or three years younger than myself. This is about her. It is not a story to tell everybody; but I want you to hear it if only so that you will understand why I am not as gay as I have been in my recent letters.

The police picked her up in Portland Maine the other day insane as nearly as we can make out on the subject of the war. She took the police for German officers carrying her off for immoral use. She took me for someone else when she saw me. She shouted to me by name to save her from whoever she thought I was in person.

I was prepared for this by what I saw of her a year ago (a year and a half ago) when she came to us at Amherst, a fugitive from a mob in a small town fifty miles away who were going to throw her into a mill pond for refusing to kiss the flag. She got Hell out of the war. She turned everything she could think of to express her abhorrence of it: pro-German, pacifist, internationalist, draft-obstructor, and seditionist.

She has always been antiphysical and a sensibilitist. I must say she was pretty well broken by the coarseness and brutality of the world

*[The rest of the admonition is an undecipherable scrawl. However, the poem to which Robert refers is William Henry Drummond's piece of humorous dialect verse, "The Wreck of the 'Julie Plante'" with its last line or, rather, its last two lines:

You can't get drown on Lac St. Pierre
So long you stay on shore.]

before the war was thought of. This was partly because she thought
she ought to be on principle. She has had very little use for me. I am
coarse for having had children and coarse for having wanted to
succeed a little. She made a birth in the family the occasion for writing
us once of the indelicacy of having children. Indelicacy was the word.
Long ago I disqualified myself for helping her through a rough world
by my obvious liking for the world's roughness.

But it took the war to put her beside herself, poor girl. Before that
came to show her what coarseness and brutality really were, she had
been satisfied to take it out in hysterics, though hysterics as time
went on of a more and more violent kind. I really think she thought
in her heart that nothing would do justice to the war but going insane
over it. She was willing to go almost too far to show her feeling about
it, the more so that she couldn't find anyone who would go far
enough. One half the world seemed unendurably bad and the other
half unendurably indifferent. She included me in the unendurably
indifferent. A mistake. I belong to the unendurably bad.

And I suppose I am a brute in that my nature refuses to carry
sympathy to the point of going crazy just because someone else goes
crazy, or of dying just because someone else dies. As I get older I find
it easier to lie awake nights over other people's troubles. But that's
as far as I go to date. In good time I will join them in death to show
our common humanity.

Always yours

Robert Frost

[In 1920 I began putting together a series of biennial collections
entitled A Miscellany of American Poetry. None of the inclusions
had previously appeared in book form. I was, however, less the
editor than the collector and compiler, for the foreword specifically
stated that each contributor to the volume was his own editor; "as
such, he has selected and arranged his own contributions." The
series ran to four volumes and it was abandoned only because the
correspondence entailed in obtaining the manuscripts and the time
consumed in putting the book together proved more than I could
manage. (I was still commuting from New York to Newark, where
I was in charge of the firm's jewelry factory.) The first number consisted of the most recent work of eleven poets. Robert finally decided on "Plowmen," "Good-bye and Keep Cold," "The Runaway,"

"The Parlor Joke," "Fragmentary Blue," and "The Lockless Door." Conrad Aiken (whose melancholy musings made Robert speak of "Comrad Aching") submitted the First Movement from "The Pilgrimage of Festus"; Sara Teasdale, recently married, sent a dozen heart-full if not heartbreaking lyrics; and Carl Sandburg appeared with twenty characteristically tough, tender, and cryptic compressions.

Lincoln MacVeagh, to whom Robert refers in the second paragraph of the next letter, had become managing editor at Holt's after Harcourt left to found his own firm. As indicated, Robert's trouble with English publishers lasted for years.

George F. Whicher, who taught at Amherst, was not only a highly esteemed teacher but a skilled translator, especially of Horace and the Goliard Poets. He became a close friend of Robert's as well as his colleague, and the two of them enjoyed the meeting with the English poet, Siegfried Sassoon, which I had arranged.

The "pome" mentioned in the concluding paragraph was finally called "The Need of Being Versed in Country Things," and was changed so that it ended:

One had to be versed in country things
Not to believe the phoebes wept.]

[Franconia,   N.H.
April 28,   1920]

Dear Louis:

The way it stands now I am in four deep with Harpers and I'm not sure that isn't four deeper than I wish I were in. The four are Fragmentary Blue, Place for a Third (namely Eliza), Goodbye and Keep Cold, and For Once Then Something (formerly Wrong to the Light). What do you want of me for the Misc? To tell you the truth I am feeling recessive for me and don't seem to know how I come to be publishing anything anyway. First you propose having I forget what and then A Parlor Joke and then A Star in a Stone Boat and then The Runaway: meaning that as a friend you are going to be delighted with anything I give you no matter how damaging it may prove to me as an author and to you as an editor. You know, you old skeezicks, you never managed to dislike heartily any poem I ever wrote except the one to E.T. and that is complicated with the war in such a way that you are afraid it may be a tract in favor of heroism. (But it isn't.) I hear you were down on the Cape seeing Comrad

Aching and I almost hope you found there what will make it easy to go without anything from me. Sarah you say is hastening East with a trunk full of Lyrics to My Husband In Different Places, Buenos Aires, Rosario Punta Arenas, etc. Carl has brought forth a mountain.

I'll tell you what puts me off the game a whole lot. It's the state of my affairs with publishers. MacVeagh spoiled all with Heinemann by making overtures to Mrs. Nutt without consulting him. Heinemann is put out and I am disappointed. My troubles over there aren't ended and my troubles here are pretty well begun. What's the use of writing stuff that I don't know who is to own in England or America. I am going to write drama after this and let poetry go to hell. But I don't say I will stay out of your Misc if I am committed. One poem more or less in print can't make much difference either way.

May see you in N.Y. before long or on neutral ground between there and here.

Whicher was wholly enthusiastic about Sassoon. You never saw my pome on The Importance of Being Versed in New England Ways. It ends:

> But one had to be versed in New England Ways
> Not to believe the Phoebes wept.

To our better acquaintance!

Robertus

Franc Again
May 14   1920

Dear Louis:

You know you can have anything you want of mine. The Harpers group will be out in July. What do you say to waiting for the two, in that you seem to like Goodbye and Keep Cold and Fragmentary Blue? A good story has attached to the Goodbye one. A friend of mine, an unsophisticated farmer and real estate agent at Amherst, handed a copy of it to the pomologists of the Agricultural College of Massachusetts to pass judgment on its pomological content. Their report was that pomologically it was all right, but poetically not: they would re-write it and make a better poem of it. Thus I get it on all sides now-a-days! How would it be to hold the Misc till we get the

agriculturalist's version to go with mine? At least it would be one more
poem to help fill my allotted space.

You did well not to send the thankless Bodenheim* to Europe.
You have enough uses for your money taking mortgages on my next
farm without patronizing poetry as she is written out of focus by the
villain of the Village. Have no compunction.

I am just back from as far south as New Milford where I had a
good talk with Lesley and had half a mind to summon you as per
your promise of a recent letter. If I am that far down again next week
land-looking as before would it be too much to call you to look at
the property I am thinking of buying? Anyway hold yourself ready to
be talked to on the telephone. Take a lozenge to clear your throat.

I have three or four houses on the possible list—one at Monson
Mass, one at West Springfield Mass, one at Winsted Conn, and one
at New Milford. The call of three is pretty much.

I got horribly kicked round for me as I rode. The agents, taking
me for I don't know what, descended on me with loud lies to pick my
bones. Little they suspected that it was the other way about and I
was gluttonously picking theirs for literary purposes. I have an old
poem on a real estate agent that only wants a little more material to
finish it and make it marketable. I'm not sure that they haven't
supplied it.

Tell Jean safety first: always ascribe any offensive I seem to say to
the Frostian humor: I am always joking. I don't believe I can have
told her not to write to Elinor, but if I did say not to of course I
must have been having my little joke however private. We folks are
not going to go back on you folks intentionally. It rests with you not
to let us do it unintentionally.

But I'll whisper you something that by and by I mean to say
above a whisper: I have about decided to throw off the light mask I
wear in public when Amy is the theme of conversation. I don't
believe she is anything but a fake, and I refuse longer to let her
wealth, social position, and the influence she has been able to
purchase and cozen, keep me from honestly bawling her out—that is,
when I am called on to speak! I shan't go out of my way to deal with
her yet awhile, though before all is done I shouldn't wonder if I tried

*[Maxwell Bodenheim, who characterized himself as a Greenwich Village Villon.
During his last years, he was a beggar and a vagabond, sleeping in the subways, charged
with vagrancy. He was murdered in a dingy rooming house in the Bowery.]

my hand at exposing her for a fool as well as fraud. Think of saying that as the French have based their free verse on Alexandrines so she has based her polyphonic prose on the rhythms of the periodic sentence of oratory. She couldn't get away with that if she hadn't us all corralled by her wealth and social position. What could "periodic" have to do with it. Periodic sentences have no particular rhythm. Periodic sentences are sentences in which the interest is suspended as in a plot story. Nonsense and charlatanry—that's all that kind of talk amounts to. I'm sure she guessed without looking it up that there must be something recurrent like beat or pulse implied in periodic. She knew ladies were periodic because they recurred monthly. She's loony—and so periodic by the moon herself. Feeling as I do you don't think it would be honester for me to refuse to be bound between the covers of the same book with her, do you?

I wish you could see the mts. now. Every one wears one great white mountain birch laid out giantesque in the ravine system on its side like a badge of the north country. I don't know that that is any inducement to you to come up.

Ever yours
Robert Fross

Please let me know to oncet if nearly all this meets with your approval.

Franconia, Last Moments
[June 3] 1920

Dear Louis:

All right then if you have a thousand dollars you can lend me please send it with your blessing to my brand new address Monson (Monson) Mass. some day this week.* I may have to ask you for some more in a month or so. The thousand will fix me up for the present. Gee I'm blue over this move to new scenes and neighbors. Encourage me in it as you always have in all things.

*[Robert loved Franconia not only because it was a haven during hay-fever time but also because it was the place where the family had been most at home. Nevertheless, he felt it was being infested with too many summer visitors, "condescending society folk," and he began looking for a new locale. A farm in Monson, Massachusetts, was one of the places he considered buying before he found the stone house he wanted in South Shaftsbury, Vermont.]

You'd think you might let me see some of the poems the rest of you are filling the Misc with. Are any of them half bad?

I am afraid I am trying to write too many plays at once for the good of the novel I am also writing. Never mind. It gives me a feeling of business if not of art. I wish I could throw style over: I seem slowed up by it. I don't know how it is with you.

Be as good as it is in your nature to be.

Yours ever
Robert Frost

Franconia   [N.H.]
June 19-20   1920

Dear Louis:

You remember the thousand dollars you lent me week before last. Well I always meant to repay you in full, but as day after day dragged by and my position seemed no stronger financially, I began to despair of ever being able to repay you even in part. I did my best to believe that as it is more blessed to give than to receive, so, obviously, it must be more blessed to receive than to give back. In vain. Nothing would comfort me. My New England upbringing had put me beyond help of such sophistries. Life was becoming serious, not to say a burden under the weight of owing you so much, when suddenly I had a saving thought, which was to apply the thousand dollars you had lent me in paying it back. Luckily I had the thousand intact. Isn't it funny? We have had one of the great affairs of the purse that will go jingling down through Am Lit—and all in the space of ten days elapsed time and neither of us one cent the worse off for the experience. In the supreme hour of trial you proved generous—you gave me all you had offered—and I proved grateful and honorable—I paid you back with thanks. We are out of the woods where we can crow. When we ask ourselves, as we must in our position, what boshterity will say of us in this transaction, we know beforehand what it will say. It will say that we were both perfect. Even our wives will say no less I think. Hurrah for our wives!

Suppose in my agony of debt I had sought forgetfulness like a drunkard by plunging deeper into debt and tried to borrow, say, of Harcourt Brace and Howe, of Henry Holt and Company, or both together, how would I have stood with boshterity? That's what you have to think of.

> O Thyme whose vurdicks mock our own
> The only righteous judge art thou.

I have decided several things that I will tell you about later. One of them is that I will probably go further off for my farm and fare cheaper. This came to me a trifle suddenly the day I got to Monson. The object in life is hard to keep in mind. I let it slip sometimes, but never for long—never for good and all anyway. In this instance it is apples bees fishing poetry high school and nine or ten rooms. Nothing else matters. Nearness to no particular city matters. Farming in style doesn't matter. Open fireplaces don't matter. Neither does my next book (as book). It would be interesting to make a list of all the things that don't matter and that I mean to consider less and less. We could have a bonfire and a ceremonial burning of them all some night when you come to see us in the Aroostook. The United States wouldn't be on the list. Wouldn't be, I say. I can promise to stay on this side of the Canadian line. I think too I can promise to keep out of teaching for a while, though I have had several invitations to come back to it since I pulled out of Amherst.

Fishing bees poetry apples nine rooms and a high school! All of which we now think are within our unaided means. So I am enclosing your thousand dollars, old friend, with a thousand thanks for the support it gave me when I was ambitious for a business farm at a business distance from big cities. Saved in time!

Ever thine
Robbered Frossed

Franconia   [N.H.]
[June 25,   1920]

Dear Louis:

You got the check yesterday I trust and here's the proof today.*
You must forgive the delay with both: I had been scattering myself all over the Six States—literally: I pared my fingernails in Winsted Conn, had my hair cut in Portland Maine, and a tooth out in Brattleboro Vt.

---

*[The proof pages of the first A *Miscellany of American Poetry*.]

Nothing but the last Resurrection will ever reassemble the disjected members. In the disintegration of body and soul you cannot blame me if I neglected my friends.

The proof only just came forward from Monson and I hasten to give it a dab and return it to you. No time to read anybody's but my own. Your Tadpole got me by the tail and twisted it. There seem to be eleven poets where there were ten. Is Fletcher the new one? Glad he's in. Couldn't you let Kreymborg* make the twelfth? Then we would all be poets in a friendly dozenship and could sign ourselves.

Yours dozenly

R.F.

Franconia N.H.

July 12 1920

Dear Louis:

Has Merrill Root been so foolish as to mention my name or the name of Amherst to make way for his poetry anywhere? You have something more than any resemblance you see in his poetry to connect him with me. The last I saw of his poetry it was pretty much his own and what wasn't his own wasn't mine I'm sure. I won't believe he has been coming under my influence after having got out from under my shadow. He never was a member of my class of geniuses anyway. I had him in an enormous crowd I read Gammer Gurton's Needle with and he has perhaps called at the house half a dozen times. I count him a friend, and just for that reason I have left him to break in among you poets without my doubtful help. Now that two or three of you have noticed him of your own motion I should think I could speak without prejudice to his chances. He's not in the same classification with Raymond Holden† whom I throw out the window onto your spear-points. I'm pretty sure he's a poet. It would please me a lot if you should see it as I see it. Max Eastman's good opinion ought to weigh with you if Harriet Monroe's doesn't. I say no more. But I think you ought to make your half-inclination whole and go in for Root, or rooting for Root, a little. He's some sort of a homely

---

*[Alfred Kreymborg, a poet-playwright, identified with the avant-garde movement.]
†[Raymond Holden was one of the most gifted of Robert's "boys." His first book, *Granite and Alabaster*, shows Robert's influence, but his subsequent poems and novels evince color and character of their own.]

devil of perversity that should commend itself more to you than to me. His father is a poor preacher and Merrill is himself a Quaker preaching, though not ordained, in orthodox pulpits. I don't know how he gets by in any pulpit with the radical stuff that froths out of him. He had his troubles as a conscientious objector before the fact, if you are not too tired of the breed.

But Raymond Holden. They say we poor expect the rich to consider the poor but when we are asked to consider the rich, we start talking a priori. One of the books I am writing at this moment is to be called On Looking into the Rich. Won't I consider them, though! I count myself peculiarly qualified for looking into them by my freedom from prejudice against them. Neither they nor their trappings make me the least bit embarrassed self-conscious or unhappy with the bitches and sons of bitches. I have come right up to them and looked in without fear and without even dislike. I believe I honestly liked them not only for themselves but for their money before I looked into them. I was just the one for doing them justice, I should say. But what have I seen in them? Well, the book tells that. Buy the book.

Yours everly
Robert Frost

You are the first person I have mentioned Merrill Root to in any terms.

[Although he had reservations about some of the poets, Robert was pleased with most of the first Miscellany of American Poetry. The references in the next letter need only a modicum of explanation. "The New Adam," "A Marriage," and "Intercession" were later incorporated in my The New Adam; the poem which Robert calls the "Pollywog" was an overwritten and overrhymed piece of whimsicality entitled "Boy and Tadpoles." "The Long Hill" and "Water Lilies" were two of Sara Teasdale's lyrical contributions. Vachel (Lindsay) had withdrawn two of his reverberating "chants"—he said he was tired of the sound of them—in favor of less characteristic and far less interesting incidental verses. Amy Lowell was represented by a mixed group in free verse; Robert particularly disliked her nine-page "Funeral Song for the Indian Chief Blackbird." James (Oppenheim) troubled him because of his psychoanalytical portrait-parable of Woodrow Wilson, "The Man Who Would Be God." *Edwin Arlington Robinson's* contribution was an eight-line poem, "The Dark Hills," which became famous. *Conrad Aiken's* "First Movement from 'The Pilgrimage of Festus'" ran to sixteen meditative pages; in the third and fourth sections, Festus, "planting beans in the early morning," has a long vision. "Shinleaf" was a poem I had dedicated to Robert.]

Franconia   N.H.
July 17   1920

Dear Louis:

If you have enough poems like The New Adam and A Marriage to make up a volume without the help of anything else of any other kind, you can set yourself so far apart from anyone else that you won't even need boundary lines let alone stone walls to mark you off. I don't know where else to look for that full-savoring sensuousness of thirty years that ploughs where twenty used to tickle. It would be one thing to do and of course you would do it well. Why plan to have a little of everything (as I'll bet you do) in your next book. Why not hew to the idea of your title, however small a book it leaves you for a dollar and a half? Don't have The Pollywog in it for instance. Save the Pollywog to go with The Frog when you shall write it.

Intercession is the lovely one of the lot. But I don't know that you want to be encouraged to be lovely in that sense. Being lovely might interfere with being energetic, which is what you always give the effect of being at your best even in such a thing as the Pollywog. And no matter whom you translate he comes through you energized and more energetic than he went in. It would be foolish not to reckon with that and not make yourself out of what you are.

While I am about it I may as well have my shot at the other contributors to your Misc. When shall I listen to anything I like better than The Long Hill and the Water Lilies. The perfect accent. And neither of them the least bit wrested to bring in Sappho or the bursting heart. You must forgive me for liking these two poems about as well as anything you have in the book.

Vachel I don't have to deal with because these poems have been withdrawn. I tried to read his Golden Whales aloud in company last night. It failed to get me by the hyperbolics.

All I want to say about Amy is she had better enquire of the Smithsonian Institute if the Indian or any other American but H.D. (and she's an expatriate) wails in the two separate vowels "a" and "i" after the Greeks. Her poem on the resolute young men you can't have too much of in this world reminds me of one on A Pair of Pants a lady of Europe wrote before the war made atrocities popular. She was said to dance it out as Duncan was then dancing verse. It went:

> We women are restricted to a glance
> At where the virile member bags the pants.

I only remember the authoress wasn't Felicia Hemans. Anyway Amy is more exciting when she calls for young men not incapable than when she takes five hundred thin lines to bury an Indian Chief on horseback. No to her. The Chief is buried all right.

Carl's idiom and lingo would be enough if there was nothing else in the book. He's a box of pen points. Gimme Aprons of Silence; Crapshooters; Man, the Man Hunter; Blue Island Intersection; and Pencils.

Robinson the cunning devil isn't forgetting his effects when he pretends to have only the one small poem to be lost among our many. I'd like to punish him for his selfish calculation if I could see where to strike. But I don't unless it is his calling the sunset a sound for the rhyme.

Fletcher is a whole lot better than I expected him to be. I have mixed him up too much with Amy to be fair to him.

There's a lot of good in Aiken. Maybe it's all good (though never the thriller that the Morning Song of Senlin is); but it is too formidable, especially for leading off with. Our misfortune more than his that his name begins with an A. You couldn't get him further into the book by arranging us in some other order on some other principle? Beans is a good Boston subject, and the beans are the best part of the poem. Wouldn't I be likely to say so?

James should have read again what Korah said to Moses and then written his denunciation of Woodrow. "You take too much upon you seeing all the congregation (namely the Senate) are holy everyone of them and the Lord is among them: wherefore then lift you up yourself above the congregation of the Lord?" "Is it a small thing that thou hast brought us up out of a land that floweth with milk and honey to kill us in the wilderness except thou make thyself altogether a prince over us?" You remember what happened to Korah and his friends and his wives and his sons and his little children. I was brought up on that.

There remains only Jean to speak of. Why will she let the spirit be dragged down sick by the sick body? If the spirit were sick in its own right I shouldn't be preaching this sermon. But it is the body uttering its sickness through the spirit—I can tell by the sound. I suppose I should distrust any sickness of the spirit as from the body unless I knew for certain that the body had a clean bill of health from the medical dept. A sick spirit in a sound body for me. It's a personal preference I am expressing. No doubt a sick spirit in a sick body has its honor and its reward. So much for the subject matter apart from the poeticality of the poetry. Of course I know the poems are truthful close and workmanlike.

If it were My Misc I'm pretty sure I would jumble the poetry in it. I'd begin with a real lady, say Jean or Sara; go over us once in one order and then in another. It would look less like the Georgian and it would get rid of Aiken's solid thing lying across the threshold.

Thanks from the heart for "Shinleaf." Some day when you have given me up as cold and ungrateful I shall requite it.

Ever yours
Robert Frost

Have you had a "bid" to a South Sea Island party to include Clarence Darrow, Frank Harris, Somebody Russell, Mary Pickford, Me and Edith Thomas? It is to raise vanilla and forget civilization at least till after election.

R.

[During the summer of 1920, several writers received letters from a Mr. H.G. Rhinehart of Los Angeles. The letters were differently worded but the import was the same. Mr. Rhinehart was sick of Western civilization and proposed to found a colony of kindred souls in one of the South Sea Islands. His group was to include, among others, the Socialist Charles Edward Russell, the lawyer Clarence Darrow, the teacher-anarchist Bayard Boyesen, and the novelist Frank Harris. Mr. Rhinehart informed us that he was a relative of a fullblooded native family on the island of Tahaa, that he had formally been made a member one New Year's Day at a family feast almost four thousand miles southwest of San Francisco, and, though he was writing from the Californian coast, his true home was in the Tahitian group, of which Papeete was the port of call. In the letter received by Robert, Mr. Rhinehart said that he had divorced himself from the white race in 1912 and had lived with the primitives ever since. ("O God, the years wasted living in Whiteland!") Appealing to the poet, Mr. Rhinehart continued:

> The pressure against your spirit must be very real. I suppose that you know that we, the U.S.A., have already taken Mexico. I have some evidence and the main reasons. How very wonderful— all in this Christian land. I want to grow flowers—the essence of the elements—with their eyes and spirit they make for me kindness and smiles and a God.

The opening paragraph of the letter drew a picture which only Gauguin could have attempted:

> Great artists never mixed such pots of paint as the sun and sea. They in mid-sea tropics have daily a new pot, a fresh hue. These are live things too virile for brush and canvas. By the lagoon a group of naturals, rich in joy and strength, sit about their night in a cocoanut-leaf song-house and breathe out pure notes 5,000 years old. There one feels the history of the human race. If one cares, one can verandah-sit with a faint smile—listen to the fronds of the nut-trees—let the trade winds fan and forget the hour, the day— forget all save a sooth-spirit. So sweet, so perfect to be far from the whiteman's fangs.

Mr. Rhinehart tempted us with "a primless park plantation" and with garlands of "roses dangling through space." Each of us were to have a hut to himself, a hut made of pleated bamboo with a roof of woven pandanus leaves ("waterproof for ten years"), a board floor, and a verandah. We were to feast upon tropical fruit and think of work only forty days in each year. There was to be no physical labor except that of "inoculating by hand" vanilla flowers, "tinted petals of white beauty, the world's one perfection." Mr. Rhinehart concluded, "If you cannot go, you might pass these papers to some quality friend who would be interested."

Diagonally over the margins of the letter Robert wrote a burlesque reply ("to be read with a foot-rule") and sent it to me.]

Franconia, N.H.
July 23, 1920

Dear Louis, My Quality Friend:

I have had to decline this invitation on the ground that I want to stay in the world a while longer to see what is going to happen. Hadn't seen any finality in the war; must hang around till I see some in politics. Also on the ground that I prefer to contract my skin diseases from white people as being more likely to be white diseases. My latest information from the South Seas is that this man's island is to be open island for pearls next year; in which case it will be full of divers and entertainment dives such as movies, con games, and shoot-the-chutes. It would be literary (almost) to run away from such things here only to run into them there ... I told him you would probably go, as you were retiring from the jewelry business, and if he couldn't get you he could try Edith Thomas, who seems about to retire from poetry and even life itself from sheer satisfaction with the good work she has been doing the last ten years. If you accept and go, make it a condition that President Wheeler (of the Poetry Society) shan't go and spill the vanilla beans.

Gee, I wish I were done with life so I could go where I please. But if I could go I shouldn't light out for anybody's cast-off islands in the Pacific. Rockwell Kent knew a trick worth two of that for press stuff. I should bar Charles Edward Russell if it were my funeral. And who is this Luke North that, so untrue to his name, Looked South? ... Neither do I understand how the intellectual keeps going unless it is by panning intellectuality like The Liberator. Catch on to the New Radicalism and vote for Harding. Anyway, welcome to the Beach.

Sinceriously
Robbered Frossed

Franconia   N.H.
September 18   1920

Dear Louis:

Still here more than anywhere else, though I now practically own a farm (all but paying for it) in South Shaftsbury Vermont and only one half of my family remains with me, one third of it being at Arlington Vermont in the manse and one sixth in New York campaigning, not for Cox, not for Harding (whom I should like to see elected if only I was surer he was anti-international), but for Melcher of the National Association of Book Publishers.

As for you, you are campaigning as always for the honest word in poetry. Poor old Clinton Scollard and Louis Ledoux when you take your knife in hand to make excision! It is hard for me not to go over to the criminal's side in the day of retribution. I can run with the hounds till the hare is overtaken, but I die with the hare when he dies. But never mind me. Have at the buggers. Pond* is in the bankruptcy courts and what bade fair to become the Disgustan Age of American Poetry from the influx of British Verse may yet turn out the Augustan.

Look at your Misc. Isn't she a beauty for cover and topography.† You needn't tell me you hadn't a hand in her make-up. From Harcourt Brace unhelped nothing like that ever. And I think five or six of your poets do themselves justice in it—five if you omit me. Harcourt is right in being proud of it. But make him send me two or three more copies of it. He only sent me two and I've had those taken away from me by force before I had time to inscribe them. What we want is sales but not to poor devils like me. I say sell to the rich till they are as poor as we are. That's the kind of a Socialist me and I trust The New Republic are at this writing. I deny that there is anything Bolshevist in my position. Let the New Republic clear its own skirts.

I set Merrill Root on you. Now see what <u>you</u> can do with him.

*[James B. Pond, head of a lecture bureau which specialized in bringing English lecturers to America.]

†[I don't know whether this is a mistake in spelling or (as I suspect) a purposeful confusion of geography and typography.]

See that he has a copy of Prof. Grenville's Manufacture of Verse* to begin with.

How about a movement to steer all the free versifiers to a country as free in name as Liberia?

I have various poems coming in different places, one of them a lyric written twenty years ago. I wonder if you can spot the old lyric. The editor of The—didn't. I'd bother you to read some stuff in MS, but I don't want to ravish you of your vacation freshness so soon.

Did you happen to notice the Songo River when you were sailing on it—how it ought to lend itself to song and poetry? Longfellow. took a stab at it before fountain pens were invented. Isn't it about due for a stab from someone else in the light of what we now know about everything?

Sinceriously

Robertus

"The Brick House"

Arlington,   Vermont

October 11   1920

Dear Louis:

I've been sick, joking aside. The trouble seems to be that I wasn't taken up carefully enough in Franconia nor replanted soon enough in South Shaftsbury. It has been a bad job of transplanting. I lost a lot of roots (the tap root entirely) and the roots I have left are pretty well impaired by too long exposure to the air out of the ground. You're a poet yourself and finely constituted; so you don't have to be told how it is with poets. The time of year too has been against me, let them say what they will in rural journalism. Even in the case of evergrins I find that the fall is <u>not</u> a favorable time for transplanting. And I'm not an evergrin. It has gone hard with me. You must excuse me if I don't find strength to fill pages with my admiration for your New Adam. I was curiously prescient about him, wasn't I? No "moth's kiss first" about him, is there? He ploughs and that's why he reads straight through as a book like a novel. The book

*[A fictitious book which I had outlined in a prospectus, and then reviewed. It made straight-faced fun of the Lush and Rhetorical Sonnet, the Mouth-filling and Mystical Ode, the Purple Patchwork Lyric, and the Crocus-crowded Georgian Pastoral.]

has one name and one nature. The effect of it all's so vivid that it makes me want to ask personal questions; but I don't ask them, mind you. Sometime I <u>will</u> tell you the three worst poems in the book when I have had more time to look for them. Someone else who admired the book as much as I, said the only fault he had to find with it was too much "breasts"—not too many, but too much. However I wouldn't pick out any one poem marred by the breast motive. It is one of our books of poetry.

I really don't know what's the matter with me unless it's what I say. I can lift anything anyone else can lift. I was wishing only last night Levinski would leave Carpentier* to me, and yet I seem barely able to be around.

Still I'm yours consciously

Robert Frost

[South Shaftsbury, Vt.
November 10, 1920]

Dear Louis:

I guess you'd better send any letters for me to Bennington, Vermont, R.F.D. No. 1, and leave the rest to the good God we talked all round the other night without liking to name him—such is our modesty in the spirit as compared with our immodesty in the flesh.

And oh but I was sorry we couldn't go with you to Mecca (since we are on the subject of religion and the flesh).† You might have spoken sooner I should think. As it was we didn't see how we could give up the idea of going to see the strike of the chorus and leading lady and the riot of the audience at the Lexington which we had bought tickets for. It was a beauty. We sat a restive hour after starting time and at nine o'clock a solitary man in citizen's clothes came before the curtain to ask us to bear with him five minutes longer: the trunk had been lost but was now found that contained what some lady was going to wear if she wore anything. At ten o'clock the same solitary figure a good deal aged with care reappeared in answer to a fierce and vindictive curtain call to say that it was all off: he had squared the chorus who had started the trouble only to end up

---

*[Popular pugilists of the day.]
†[A ceremony at the Mecca Temple in New York.]

in a run-in with the leading lady. He didn't know her name, but we could look it up on the program and remember her in our prayers as responsible for our misspent evening. When he denied his own leading lady in such words, someone behind or in the curtain gave an impetuous treble shriek of "Oh!—you beast!" and the curtain was agitated and a great wave ran its length. He had the infuriated audience all on its feet in front of him asking for its money back. He told them not tonight. He couldn't give them their money back because there was none in the box office, but if they would come to Allen and Fabian's the next day something would be done for them. Irma went to recover our eight dollars but all she saw was a fight between two women; she saw the color of no money. He only said what he said to save his life by getting us to go home. He had no money anywhere, poor man. Which just shows you you don't know enough to appreciate how well off you are yourself.

I doubt if we missed much by not hearing anybody sing, though judging from the way she shrieked the leading lady was a soprano— I won't say a good one because I don't know enough to know. We liked the riot and the place full of police. All that was wanting to round off my time in New York was a few bullets flying somewhere. I have to remember we saw a woman stoned in Van Dam St. three nights after election—not because she was a Magdalen but because she was a Democrat. All the little Italians were after her for Fiume and D'annunzio. She fought with them and stood them off facing the stones. She was middle aged. New York, New York!

I'm enclosing a poem or two for old times sake.

Yours

R.F.

THE ONSET

Always the same when on a fated night
At last the gathered snow lets down as white
As may be in dark woods and with a song
It shall not make again all winter long—
Of hissing on the yet uncovered ground.
I almost stumble looking up and round,
As one who overtaken by the end
Gives up his errand and lets death descend
Upon him where he is, with nothing done

To evil, no important triumph won
More than if life had never been begun.

Yet all the precedent is on my side:
I know that winter death has never tried
The earth but it has failed; the snow may heap
In long storms an undrifted four feet deep
As measured against maple, birch, and oak:
It cannot check the Peeper's silver croak;
And I shall see the snow all go down hill
In water of a slender April rill
That flashes tail through last year's withered brake
And dead weeds like a disappearing snake.
Nothing will be left white but here a birch
And there a clump of houses with a church.

Robert Frost

MISGIVING

All crying "We will go with you, O Wind,"
The foliage follow him leaf and stem.
But a sleep oppresses them as they go,
And they end by bidding him stay with them.

Since ever they flung abroad in spring
The leaves had promised themselves this flight,
Who now would fain seek sheltering wall
Or thicket or hollow place for the night.

And now they answer the summoning blast
With an ever vaguer and vaguer stir,
Or at utmost a little reluctant whirl
That leaves them no further than where they were.

I only hope that when I am free,
As they are free, to go in quest
Of the knowledge beyond the bounds of life
It may not seem better to me to rest.

R.F.

DUST OF SNOW

The way a crow
Shook down on me
The dust of snow
From a hemlock tree

Has given my heart
A change of mood
And saved some part
Of a day I had rued.

R.F.

*[The "one or two corrections in your Robert Frost" (third para-
graph of the next letter) are the emendations which Robert made in
a typescript I had sent him. It was an estimate, half chronology,
half critique, which I was about to publish. The poems to which
he refers in the second paragraph are those added to the amplified
(1921) edition of Modern American Poetry. The three new poems
included in his letter of November 12, 1920 ("The Onset," "Misgiving" and "Dust of Snow"), differ in a few minor details, chiefly
punctuation, from the printed versions.]*

South Shaftsbury   Vermont
November 12   1920

Dear Louis

I somewhat autocratically bade you address me when next you
wrote at Bennington this state. You will do well not to do as you were
told. Address me where you know I am viz at South Shaftsbury and
I will explain later.

I am not going to let the fact that my typewriter was left behind
me prevent my sending you a poem or three as per my promise given
in the draughty subway high above the roar of passing cars. Only
one is a candied date for place in your improved Anthropology of
Latter-day Poetry for Male and Female Colleges:—The Onset; and I
don't overurge that. It's a mistake to be too sure of the final rating of
your latest written and your latest out. I really can't seem to
entertain much doubt of A Tuft of Flowers, The Death of the Hired
Man, Mending Wall, Birches, Goodbye and Keep Cold, The
Runaway, and Fragmentary Blue. I'd like to think The Onset belongs
in that select company. But then so would I like to think everything
I ever wrote belonged. I'm a frail mortal.

One or two corrections in your Robert Frost. You say you want
the dates right. Let's be truthful about the farming: it didn't earn me
a living. Make it "a few years teaching at Derry and Plymouth, New
Hampshire," and "place" not "farm" in Gloucestershire. You are

welcome to any old golden opinions of me you like so long as you are particular about my facts.

Don't mind the one offending word in "Misgiving." It is a good poem I wrote years and years and years ago and am now just publishing in The Yale Review. Dust of Snow has no traps for unwary chronologists. It is simply a little poem done rather recently by me about as I am.

This is the last about myself for a long time let's hope. So try to reorganize.

Farewell

R. F.

So. Shaftsbury Vermont
December 5 1920

Dear Louis:

This is nothing except to apprize you that small watch of Switzerland (Tavannes) is running along very lovable and current on schedule time with new spring main introduced—if anything is to be said rather beforehand than retarde. So that it not failing I shall ought to catch train for New York by the forelock on Friday and Saturday and may easily see you a few momentoes. I hope for you.

Sincere wishes

Robert Frost

No sign up for Mr. D'Hell's novel work. Where is it you suppose?

[One of the advantages of being a manufacturing jeweler was that I could give small gifts, such as a Swiss watch, with a minimum of effort and expense. The Tavannes timekeeper came accompanied by a polyglot advertisement—which prompted Robert's broken-English reply to my inquiry as to its performance. "Mr. D'Hell's novel work" was Floyd Dell's semi-autobiographical Moon-Calf.]

South Shaftsbury Vermont
December 28 1920

Dear Louis:

Seriously now I am sick with disgust. My "shrill New England whang"! Am I shrill in speech thought or style? Does shrill or twang

(twang is probably meant) describe me or anything I have done? I can't help suffering from such words. But is it for me to defend myself from them? I had about forgotten the existence of the poetry society of america when you had another friend come in on me with the news that I had been elected a something in it. Of course it was without my knowledge and consent. You won't believe this. But Elinor will tell you I seldom get the society's printed letters and absolutely never open what I get. That is what I call exemplary. I am willing to speak defensively to you—but to not many others in this world. I'm capable of some humility with a friend. But ordinarily I'm a sufferingly proud devil. Maybe you'll tell me how I'll best score in the long run on the poetry society, by never mentioning it even to itself from this day forth or by noticing it so far as to ask it to resign me from the high office it has honored me with. And speaking of their honoring me with anything, that flock of pro-English sparrows, shall I honor them with a row?

But, oh, dear me there's better things to think of than our troubles. Our shrillness and our water pipes that ain't in all vanish in the thought of the picture you two sent us. We never had this sort of thing to make a house with before till Chapin* gave us the portrait of Elinor. The faint landscape is lovely.

The rug Elinor sent Jean has a story you mustn't attempt to imagine and do in verse yourself because I shall do it for you someday and call it Under Foot. The truth is more tragic than anything you can imagine. But I don't want to frighten you so you won't like to have it round.

I'll see that you have photographs of the bust, front and left cheek.

The only other news besides what you tell me (and by the way was Melvin right in ascribing the offensive words shrill and whang to Theodore Maynard?) † is the news that I have just had a cat named after me in Washington D.C. in the household of a friend of the outgoing administration (so I can't see how it can lead to political preferment.) I shall have to go ahead with my original plan to set my cap for Harding to alienate him from Edgar

*[James Chapin, the artist, and a good friend of the Frosts.]
†[Anglo-American poet and critic, author of some thirty books and vice-president of the Catholic Society of America.]

Saltus.* You stick to what you stick to in spite of what it is, and I stick to what I stick to because of what it is. I am the more flattering. Yours because of everything

Robert Frost

South Shaftsbury   Vt.
January 19   1921

Dear Louis:

Will you lend me exactly $150 for approximately three months? I believe you will, you generous soul; so I would be safe in thanking you in advance, if I were never going to write you another letter. But I am going to write you at least one more letter to enclose you a still better poem than I ever wrote before (naturally since I only wrote it last night, and our friend Wilbur Cross† says I improve with every stroke, that is, I grow surer without growing duller—see my recent poem Misgiving written fifteen years ago and now accepted by an editor for the first time) and I will keep the profuseness of my thanks till then (not fifteen years ago or the first time: you'll have to figure this out as best you can. I'm wanted on the telephone.)

Yours more than ever
Robert Frost

Notice the access of friendship

South Shaftsbury   Vermont
Jan 27   1921

Dear Louis—

Robert Frost is coming he says, with the accent on the says: but he says it by telegram which isn't very binding, especially on a sick person, if he should manage to be sick. He has started to be sick now.

*[Author of sensational novels in which, said Oscar Wilde, "passion struggles with grammar on every page." He was a favorite of President Harding and, according to Twentieth Century Authors, "seems to have had some effect on the literary style of his [President Harding's] state papers."]
†[Wilbur L. Cross, Professor at Yale, who established and edited the Yale Review, and later served four terms as Governor of Connecticut.]

The only question is, shall he continue to be sick till Feb. 23rd, or shall he get well, enjoy a period of good health, then get sick again in time to make his excuses. Let us pray for light on this subject. I write this by the hand of another, or rather I dictate it from a bed of pain.*

There is something I particularly want to ask you. What are the first names of Smith, the editor of "The Century," and Mitchell, the editor of "The Dial", respectively? I've got some excuses I want to make to them, too.

You can't honestly say that the Transcript-Braithwaite treated you any worse than the Post-Canby treated me and some other Americans in an article called "Ham and Eggs" Saturday. What are we going to do about such things?

More when I'm better.

Yours,
Robbed Frossed

South Shafts   Vt.
February 14   1921

Dear Louis:

I have since decided I meant the knife of the critics. Enclosed please look till you find one Valentine.†

R.F.

I gave out in the middle of cutting it out for you. Have Dick finish it.

South Shaftsbury   Vt
April 15   1921

My dear Louis:

My list to date has been The Brimming Cup, Miss Lulu Bett, Moon-Calf, Poor White, The Dark Mother, Main Street, and for

---

*[It was dictated to his daughter, Lesley, and signed, in a purposely shaky hand, by him.]
†[The "Valentine" turned out to be the corner of a high-school composition book. Robert had cut the design so that what was left of it was a lamp, a scroll, a wreath of laurel, a capitalized heading, HIGH COMPOSITION, and the legend, *Literature is an Avenue to Glory.*]

comparison The American (Henry James) and The Rise of Silas
Lapham. That's more novels for me in six months than I had read
before in six years. I guess you and Dorothy Fisher must have set me
to looking for something. Have I found it? The first half of Moon-Calf
is half a great book. The last half, the sinful half, didn't go down and
it was a surprise that it didn't. I should have expected Floyd to be
as convincing in his sins as in anything. I think he must have erred in
relying too implicitly for his effect on a bare statement of what he
had done. He wouldn't have thought anything good was good enough
to deliver so unvarnished. He was caught thinking that anything bad
was bad enough as it was in nature. He miscalculates our shockability.
He doesn't even seem plausible. He sounds hypothetical.

I don't think you did Sherwood Anderson's girl justice in an
otherwise first rate review of a first rate book. She wasn't
experimenting, poor thing. She was randoming, as Alisande hath it.
If she had been experimenting she would have had the courage to go
on as of right and wouldn't have let her father drive her into
marriage. The whole book's all right. You're not looking for a
wrapper slogan to put on it; so I can say boldly to you it is the
greatest novel since The Scarlet Letter, Little Women, and Ivanhoe.

Honestly now I'll bet you have kidded yourself into thinking the
Foreword to Main St. an ironic delicacy. Out here in the country
we think the illusion to Cannibal invading Carthage to enthrown the
Corner Grocer on the Sugar Barrel is the Sage Cheese. For Gods sake
don't <u>you</u> set up next as an authority on what ought to be done to
protect small towns from the ravages of sympathetic measles. Sink
Lewis told an interviewer I know that America would be all right in
twenty thousand years. But there won't be any America in twenty
thousand years. The most fervid patriots are satisfied to sing it: they
only expect the flags to "wave a thousand years." Small towns do buy
books: so what in Hell are the writers kicking about? Count me as in
favor of reforming a whole lot of things downward. I keep hearing of
Lewis wanting to better small town people. I'm for bettering or
battering them back where they belong. Too many of them get to
college.

Did I tell you what scared me out of Monson the evening I
arrived there to take possession of the farm by the Quarry? It was a
bevy of twenty college boys skylarking and swatting each other over
the heads with copies of The New Republic in front of the village

drug store. It was too early for them to be summer colonists and I
had it in the deed of the farm that there were to be no summer
colonists in Monson anyway. Says I to myself, says I, and lights out
for Boxford Mass, Rochester N.H., Brunswick, Waterford, Norway,
Harrison, and Skowhegan Maine. The only hotel in Monson has
bedroom doors that though they may be locked can be seen over and
under and I should say crawled over and under from the halls. Those
were engaging, so I engaged one door with room, looked at myself
credulously in the mirror, and then went out on the street to look for
excitement till my family should arrive on the load of furniture that
was coming to me. 'Twas graduation at the Academy; everyone was
shuffling reverently in white and black to some exercise that I as
an outsider couldn't be expected to know the importance of. I didn't
want to be an outsider. I was just on the point of mounting the
Soldiers Monument and applying in a loud voice to the community
at large to be taken in as soon as possible and treated as an insider
when I ran bang into my bevy of twenty college boys all obviously
out of tune with the village and not the least in the mood of its
pitiful little function. They probably thought they were laughing at
each other but what they were really laughing at was the notion of
their ever having taken the Academy Graduation as an end and aim.
At their colleges they had commencements, and there were even
things beyond commencements: Rhodes Scholarships if you won
them might take you to Oxford where you might hope to acquire a
contempt beyond any contempt for small things you could show
now. They knew now that there was nothing here that they would
not some day be able to scorn. I fled them as I had fled their like
thirty years before at Dartmouth. I never could bear the sunsuvbijches
belief that they were getting anywhere when they were getting
toward their degrees or had got anywhere when they had got them.
That's not it exactly; it was more their belief that they were leaving
anybody behind who was not getting toward their degrees. I
preferred to drop out of their company and be looked on as left
behind. Of course all I had to do not to be left behind was to have
one solitary idea that I could call my own in four years. That would be
one more than they would have.

To Hell with these memories! I went free from the Little
Collegers like Sinclair Lewis ages ago.

But the best writing of all is Coming Aphrodite. Now I'm envious.

We have had no such short story. You must agree with me. Every
stroke of it to the very last. I wept for the sheer perfection—and I'm
the fellow who won't allow artists to take artists for their subject.

Conrad Aiken's Punch didn't get down to anything or rise to
anything. I read it and that's saying a good deal for me. But it put it to
you too much à la Browning. The old inflection went against me.
I'll tell you a funny thing. I had a leap of the mind (such as they
call a hunch I suppose) just as I started to read that the two
unaccountable loves for such a monstrosity were going to prove
extreme refinements of lust, perversions of sophistication. That
proved nothing special. The real Immortal Liar was Munchausen. I
only remember him away from women. Had he exaggerated amours?
He should have a few.

You've been to Chicago while I've been to Canada. I read 'em
most of your School Anthology up there. It seemed to do them good.
The people liked the poems and I liked the people. Carl had been
before me and made the way easy with his slow smile and big banjo
on his knee. Let's try to get Lee Keedick to put us on his circuit in a
dual turn I have yet to think up—give me a minute to think, as
Charlotte said. The only thing you play on is words and the piano. I
excel on the penny whistle. Nothing to any of that. I have it! You
know we talked of a Collusive Stunt after Brooklyn.* What do you
say to working it up?—for next season—my nest is feathered for this.
Which puts me in mind I must send you a check when I know you're
home again. Be patient with Dick and Jean.

Sufficiently for one letter
Robert Frost

*You from the platform I from the audience at one stand, vice versa
at the next.

[Because Robert refused publishers' requests for commendations of
their books it was assumed he never read current novels. But, as
the foregoing letter shows, he was not only aware of such contemporary novelists as (in the order indicated by the titles of their books)
Dorothy Canfield Fisher, Zona Gale, Floyd Dell, Sherwood Anderson, Waldo Frank, and Sinclair Lewis, but he was also an appreci-
ator of their realistic fictions. Abjuring public criticism, he could

be coaxed into appraisals that were as surprising as they were private. "But the best writing of all is Coming Aphrodite. Now I'm envious." The envy was only feigned. Robert had become a whole-hearted admirer of Willa Cather, and her "Coming, Aphrodite!", the most memorable short story in Youth and the Bright Medusa, had roused him to a pitch of unreserved enthusiasm. "I wept for the sheer perfection."

"You know we talked of a Collusive Stunt after Brooklyn." A reading by Robert at the Brooklyn Academy of Music had been followed by a discussion which I had led. Afterward we joked about "teaming up" for a series of collaborations on and off the platform.]

South Shaftsbury   Vt
July 7   1921

Dear Louis:

No one put it into my head: I thought of it myself: there's that much good in me still, thought that's all there is. I mean there's that much thought for other people. The rest of me is swallowed up in thoughts of myself. All the time you were here I read and read to you from my own works. You were partly to blame. You let me, to try me to see how far I would go in my self-assertion. You were stringing me, so to speak. You gave me all the line you had on the reel. And I took it. But there's this redeeming consideration. It did occur to me of my own motion though not until too late that you also may have had works to read from and were only diffidently waiting to be asked like the decent person you are. I'll be damned. It shows how far we can get along in our egotism without noticing it. I'm a goner—or almost a goner. The terrible example of others I could name I haven't profited by any more than I have by the terrible example of people I have seen die.

> To prayer, to prayer I go—I think I go—
> I go to prayer
> Along a solemn corridor of woe
> And down a stair
> In every step of which I am abased;
> A cowl I wear,
> I wear a halter-rope about the waist,

I bear a candle-end put out with haste.
I go to prayer.*

I shouldn't wonder if my last end would be religious; I weary so of cutting back the asparagus bed of my faults. I wonder what it is about prayer. I have half a mind to try it. I'm going to try to be good, if it isn't too late. Let the columnists mock as they will.

Yours

RF

South Shaftsbury   Vt.

July 23   1921

Dear Louis:

It will be a hard book to displace from the schools.† It's a good one, and I say it who am as particular about the books I am praised in as I am about those I am condemned in. There's an income in that there book or I'm much mistaken. I don't want to get your hopes up too much, but I can't help telling you that a man named Fry has made more than a million dollars out of Fry's Geographies. If you do make a fortune, I speak now for a percentage. The percentage of benzoate of soda in jam would be all I should ask. All right, it's an agreement. If anyone else asks you for a share in the profits you tell them they had theirs in flattery—let them read the book—especially Edgar Lee M.

By the way I see that Mugsy McGraw‡ has taken on to his pitching staff a product of my special course in writing at Amherst. His name is Zink and he will tell you that it was I and no one else who taught him style and control. He owes me everything but his degree. And then people will question if anything comes of teaching English!

You were right about learning.

Fait'fully

Robert Frost

*[Not in the Complete Poems.]
†[The second edition of Modern American Poetry.]
‡[John J. McGraw, battling manager of the New York Giants baseball team.]

South Shaftsbury   Vt.
August 8   1921

Dear Louis:

It can hardly be denied that I am going in October to Ann Arbor
to become an idle-fellow of the University of Michigan for one year.
If you know of any evidence to the contrary for Heaven's sake turn
it in before it is too late. It looks as if I had been bought and paid
for by an ex-governor of the state of Michigan named Osborn. Tell
me it isn't true.

That small poem of Jean's in the Virginian hay-stack! I can't
lose it. Forty like it and time be damned. Nay twenty. Nay ten.
Excuse my neighing.

There's an important story about art, the refrain of which is
Has the cow calved yet. I wish you would look it up in Grimm or
Andersen. Let me know when you have found it and I will interpret
it to you. I am reminded of it by the fact that here I have been
waiting since July 28th and our cow hasn't calved yet so far as we can
determine by a microscopic examination of her pasture.

I have recently seen reason to believe that as a nation we are
being kept out of our greatness in literature by what I may call the
columnar attitude of mind, whether we write columns or only read
them. Our habit is to be smart and guarded. I am sailing on or about
July 1st 1922. What is there to hold me here?

I don't know what your Dick has done this summer, but our
Carol has found us a diamond (though but tourmaline) or so he
reports from up along. Sometime we'll make a party and christen it.
You be thinking of a good name.

Last night I read the Gospel according to John and I confess I
don't know what to think. Whicher has a theory that going to college
is the modern equivalent of retiring into the desert. Something
suggestive I like in the word desert. You remember that beautiful
line of Wilkie Collins in The Woman in White:

"Her son was drowned at Oxford at the age of eighteen."

Eighteen is just about the age at which most of them get
drowned at Harvard and Yale.

Carol wires that he camped out near a Latvian over against
Grafton Sunday. I wonder if this is a Latvian that Lenin would be
looking for. I understand Lenin expects to find himself long enough

armed presently to reach out and punish his enemies everywhere in all countries. I could easily scare myself thinking so sinisterly.

Tell this to our edgarly masters. The Baptist minister and his wife have one hoighty-toighty daughter and none other child and she is freshest of all flesh on earth and in her their one deloight (apologie to Yea Robinson). She's been fooling around with various and sundry, particularly with one Ross who is nineteen to her seventeen and, to have it over with, the minister caught Ross, dragged him before his wife, and made him marry his daughter. Now what as a sophisticated New Yorker and friend of Broun, Hackett, and Mencken would you suppose the town would make for a story out of a situation like this? Small towns ain't so very original in your scheme that they are likely to think more than one thing of marriages enforced. The small town this time decided that it must be the mother being sick was afraid she might die, and before she went wanted to see her daughter in off the range. And so it seems to have turned out—a maternal folly, nothing worse to the foulest imagination. No eight seven six or five months baby need be looked for. The next thing the mother did after safely placing her daughter was to exact an almost public promise from the minister that he would never marry again and then, instead of turning her face to the wall to die, started to get well with the doctor's permission (since her case was hopeless anyway) on Kickapoo Swamp Root Bitters. What I write to commend is the freedom of the village mind that could see all this as it was unhindered by age-long preconceptions.

Monroe says the buckwheat has been behaving very badly with the bees. It will be sweet for a few hours in the morning and then for the rest of the day unyielding. It has put the hives all out of temper. Ordinarily Monroe does what he likes with the bees, shakes them off the combs, sweeps them into heaps, and carries them in his bare hand without being stung. They stung him twenty five times when he walked between the hives where he had a perfect right to be. They came looking for him away on the porch of his house to sting him right before me. The buckwheat had just the same effect on them that that kind of woman has on a man. And that's no tale from Maeterlinck.

I was so careless as to say to Whicher that Yeats was one of the few poets we could read right through entire. It's not true. We can't afford to grant him more than his due. He's disposed to crowd the rest of us as it is. I looked to see. Even where all is contrived to look so choice and so chosen there are whole pages that are nothing. We're all human. There's not enough of any of us to make a whole good book.

I have planted or have caused to be planted a Boh tree in India to sit out the rest of the dance under when I shall have done with vanities: and this without knowing what a Boh tree is. It may shed rain, but will it shed lightning? Do I want it to? I go, incredible as it may seem to you. But before I go I want to see you to ask you several things. You have a wisdom that is of another race that I would fain draw on. Not now. Sometime. When I shall be moved to speak of it again. It is of the kind of tears I have wept lately. I have never heard of them. Let's throw away just about nine-tenths of what we have been and all that's columnar.

> Ever yours
> Robert Frost

[Robert had met and liked Franklin P. Adams who, as F.P.A., conducted a newspaper column of casual prose and verse called "Always in Good Humor" and, subsequently, "The Coming Tower," but he did not like "the columnar attitude of mind." He resented the quick disposals, the sophisticated town gossip, the smart clubbiness as much as he disliked conversing

> with a New York alec
> About the new school of the pseudo-phallic.

He was, however, not as disturbed as he implied. His threat to leave the country and sit beneath a Boh tree in India was, of course, a fantasy, an impromptu piece of fooling. The reference to Maeterlinck was prompted by the Belgian poet and dramatist's The Life of the Bee.*]*

> Franconia   N.H. (till
> September 15th only)
> August 20   1921

Dear Louis:

There was nothing the least invidious in my omission to mention your poem when I was mentioning Jean's. I didn't see that you had a poem in all that. Why didn't you tell me on the fly leaf? Now that I know you had one, I shall have to look it up when I get back to the book.

You understand that we are only going to Michigan and only for eight months. You're not losing us even for a while. You can come out there if you will condescend and we can come back here. Let us not consider ourselves separated. I may get neighborly with Henry Ford and get a chance to bring a new car for sale over the road from Detroit to New York now and then. It would save him freight and me passenger rates.

But I mustn't be columnar about it. How damaged we are by our newspapers.

I don't see how I am to get to New York and you and Aley and the ladies of the Cosmopolitan Club before I go. I was smothered with hay fever this year. I shall have to linger in Franconia till the last moment. Listen: it wouldn't be an awful sacrifice for a good healthy person like you to run up to see me here. Fine night trains at this time of year both ways. Aw say, do it. I'd like to look at these mts. once more through your eyes before I leave them more or less forever. Honestly! You want to look out or I may feel hurt.

Ever yours

Robert Frost

Franconia N.H.

September 5 1921

Dear Louis:

You've got my hopes up and you've got to come or I shall be disappointed forever. On the Friday night train. I must have another good talk with you before I go west in the military sense of the words. What am I doing this for? It's got all round that I am giving up New England and you.

Well I haven't.

R.

South Shaftsbury   Vt
September 26   1921

Dear Louis:

Re the poem of yours in the Virginian Free-for-All brought up to us on appeal we wish to say it is a good thing. Decision of the lower court (viz E.A. Robinson) sustained.

Do a whole lot of poems like that far from the question of love and labor. Leave the evils that can be remedied or even palliated. You are of age now to face essential Hell. Cease from the optimism as much that makes good as that sees good. Come with me into the place of tombs and outer darkness. When I say three begin gnashing your teeth.

I'm in earnest. Just as the only great art is inesthetic so the only morality is completely ascetic. I have been bad and a bad artist. I will retire soon to the place you wot of. Not now but soon. That is my last, my ultimate vileness, that I cannot make up my mind to go now where I must go sooner or later. I am frail.

> To prayer, to prayer I go
> (I think I go) I go to prayer—
> Along a granite corridor of woe
> And down a stair
> In every step of which I am abased.
> A rope I wear.
> I wear a halter rope about the waist.
> I bear a candle end put out with haste.
> I go to prayer*

Well this was waiting for me to get on at this corner. Today was on the calendars a thousand million years before they were printed. I seem to smile.

Yours yet awhile

R.F.

I hoped you might like James Chapin's defeated-looking microcephalus giant at the bottom of the picture.† This you understand is not particularly Paul but man with all the strength he needs and more strength than he has brains to know how to use. I

---

*[A slightly different version of the poem is in the letter of July 7, 1921.]
†[An illustration, more or less symbolic, for "Paul's Wife."]

have figured that out of my symbolics. But who said anything about an ogre or superman slumping heart-broken or overcome with raw food in front of his cave in the Arthur Davies' landscape. The writer proposes and the illustrator disposes. The picture strikes me as arty. I congratulate you on your taste.

> 1523 Washtenaw Ave
> Ann Arbor   Mich.
> [October 12,   1921]

Dear Louis:

Notice the address—in the middle of the second thousand. I may not write it on every letter any more than you do yours. Try not to lose me.

I agree with Mencken in much that he says of you. How true it is that friendship has made you blind to all fault in me and Carl Sandburg. You must learn to see us as we are. No you mustn't either. Isn't Mencken the ablest rotter we have almost? He makes me think of nothing but flight.

Not that I'm so very much good myself. But that's just it. I don't want to feel obliged to remember my sins everyday in fairness to such non-fur-bearing skunks as Mencken and a few others I could name. Oh I know they are intelligent and all that. That is to say they have heard of Freud. You don't need to tell me.

As for this place where I am, it is all right, but it lacks finality, as the Wandering Jew said. I have several other places yet to visit before I find rest. That it is a place on the map and not a state of the mind I shall someday come to for relief, I am persuaded from the number of times I have come Balboa-like on the truth and not been helped. Today, for example, I made the discovery for myself that it was a mistake to ask to be directed on the way by anyone I overtook or was overtaken by. If I didn't want to be embarrassed by his offering to go with me and see me on my way, the best person to ask was someone I met. It is a great truth and I had happened upon it. For a moment it eased my malady. But it wasn't enough to last beyond my determining why it was true. The old grief is back. "I'm bound away."

You escape H.D.* in prose. I see it as you see it more or less and more clearly with your confirmation. I'm glad I had you see the manuscript. I'm anxious to do such a person no injustice I don't have to from our common heritage of strife. Will you send the manuscript to

Marianne Moore
14 St. Lukes Place
New York City

and remember me to Jean and the children.

Always yours
Robert Frost

1523 Washtenaw Ave
Ann Arbor   Mich
[about October 15,   1921]

Dear Sir:

Please find enclosed one sent which you know what you can do with. And see here, as sure as you dun us again, you will lose our business.†

Believe me, viz
Robert Frost

1523 Washtenaw Ave
Ann Arbor   Michigan
November 23   1921

Dear Louis:

I'm so near dead of I don't know what all here that it wouldn't pay me to write much to you unless I was pretty sure you weren't dead there. So this'll be just a line or two to find out. It would be descent of you to acknowledge the resent scent I cent you. For God's

---

*[Hilda Doolittle, one of the original Imagist poets, who used only her initials as a signature.]

†[I had sent Robert a gold-handle knife which I had manufactured, and, since the superstition had it that a knife cuts friendship unless a copper coin is given in exchange, I demanded the penny.]

sake give some sign of animation besides the poems by Léonie
Adams you keep printing in the New Republic.*

To some I am known as the Guessed of this University because I
came as a riddle and was so soon solved. The fact that I was so soon
found out is uppermost in some minds. In other minds what I was
found out to be is uppermost, namely a radiator of the poetic spirit.
To them I am known as the Radiator. I differ from other radiators
not only in what I have to radiate but also in where I have to work.
Other radiators have to heat a room. I am expected to do something
else to all out of doors. I only tell you to clarify my own mind. If it
has come to this here let us face it. If I could will my job to you as
Roosevelt willed Taft the Presidency I sure would. I find I do my
best work on a diet of soft coal or carbide and water. My state
ranges through anabolical, katabolical, and diabolical. Temperature,
subnormal; which for a radiator is serious. Amy would tell you I was
never serious before.

Keep remembering me to Jean and Dick. They at least will
understand.

Radiantly

Robert Frost

Edgar Guessed of Detroit and I the Guessed of the University
were brought together in public on the field of the cloth of gold
yesterday and I wish you could have seen how happy it made the
onlookers and the committee of burghers, who had arranged for our
meeting. Eddie said significantly he knew Sylvester Baxter. I didn't
know what to answer, so I didn't take my thumb out of my mouth.
Eddie asked me to call Bill Benét off him. I sullenly refused to
interfere. I confess I didn't make a very good appearance. I looked
jealous to the representatives of the press. Oh and another thing, one
of your Liberator poets attacked me personally in the lobby of the
Statler Hotel because I had flopped by coming to live on Washtenaw
Avenue. He denounced me to a lot of people who afterward looked
me up in Who's Who to find out why I was worth denouncing. Gee,

*[I had "discovered" Léonie Adams while she was still an undergraduate member of
the class of 1922 at Barnard College and I was able to get her unprinted poems
published in the New Republic.]

some of your Liberator people must want to live on a grand street
pretty badly to take my living on one so bitterly.

*[Robert's official title during his stay at the University of Michigan
was Fellow in the Creative Arts, but he was familiarly known as
"Poet in Residence." He liked to play with the notion that as
guest at Ann Arbor he was supposed to be a counterpart if not a
colleague of Edgar A. ("Eddie") Guest, "America's Daily Laureate,"
the much-syndicated bard of "Home and the Kiddies," who lived
in nearby Detroit. "If I could will my job to you as Roosevelt willed
Taft the Presidency I sure would" turned out to be an accomplished
fact. Some years later I succeeded Robert as "radiator of the poetic
spirit" for two visits of a month each at the University of Michigan.]*

[Ann Arbor, Mich.
January 23, 1922]

Dear Louis:
I think, by gracious, I've lit upon something in free verse. But it's
so much better than anything I have seen in manuscript that I can
hardly believe my senses. I wish you'd look at it and tell me if I'm
not right. It's a story to read straight on. And it's no application of
any philosophy of the moment. It's a scot free delineation almost
from the word Go almost to the tape. I'm lost in wonder at the way
it keeps the ground and never soars. The ending regarded as a good
one couldn't be worse, regarded as a bad one couldn't be better. It
enters my armor where I didn't suspect there was a hole. It's a real
novel.

There are bad spots in it to get rid of. It would stand some cutting.
The four lyrics would have to come out. But that would be all right;
the author gives us leave to make alterations.

I'm going to send it to you by express. Get it back to me as
suddenly as possible. If it is missed too long, I don't know what they'll
think I'm up to. I've let it lie around unread too long as it is from
scepticism about new poetry in general.

Mind you I'm talking about a novel.

Ever yours
Robert Frost

[I wish I could remember what manuscript Robert is talking about in the previous letter; it is obviously a narrative in free verse which jolted him considerably, the more so since he always said he considered the writing of free verse equivalent to playing tennis with the net down. But memory refuses to react; there is not the faintest tintinnabulation of the smallest bell in the back of my mind. Somehow, perhaps because I retain no impression of it, I suspect the vers-libre novel was never published.]

Ann Arbor   Mich
January 30   1922

Dear Louis:

Hoping the enclosed specimen may find a place in your museum of malformations not too far from that far call you had to the South Seas I am

Yours truly
Robert Frost;

but if for any reason that is impossible (you may not have valued the call enough to preserve it in alcuhaul—you may even have closed out your museum to retire into Westchester County) hoping on the other hand that you will return the specimen to me intact I am for the second time in one letter

Yours truly
Robert Frost

P.S. If them young people* can't pull off anything, I'm going to see what I can do. I most dambly want to see you out here. I have a new plan for defeating the divine purpose that I want to unfold to you before I lose interest in it.

Hurry that manuscript back to me. I feel like a man speculating with money he holds in trust.

R. F.

Remember me to your wife and children. I saw your wife in The Bookman the other day. I thought she was looking very unusual. You must take good care of her. She acts to me like a person who was

*[The student organization in charge of bringing "outside" lecturers to the campus.]

just about to sing some more. I must say she sang a bookful last time.* Take care of her and she will take care of you. Believe me she has your best interests at heart. I'm sure of it. There, there. I didn't mean to strike the domestic note. You're not to cry. How emotional a poet it is at all! We all know you are happily married. There's no call for a demonstration. It's not yourself as a husband but the institution of marriage you are anxious to make out a case for? I can well believe it, knowing you as I do know you and what you have come through and up out of. But never you worry about the institution of marriage or any other institution for that matter. I'll take care of what institutions there are. And that just uses up my paper.

> Dept. of Minstrelsy   Official
> University of Michigan
> Ann Arbor
> [February 1,   1922]

Dear Louis:

Tell me about the book for this year.† You know I wanted you to let Gamaliel Bradford in with a poem or two even though you may not like him too much. How about Elinor Wylie? She's an entity all right. I hope she wasn't at the movies on Sunday night when the roof fell in. Sunday night at the movies was bad enough; and I hear she has been defying Jove's lightning in other ways. Is there any truth to the rumor? Or is she simply a highschoolma'am down among the senators and representatives?

What do you say if we start me off with Fire and Ice?—you seem to like that so well. After that I don't know what to say. You haven't seen The Gold Hesperidee and The Grindstone. I wish I could leave it to you to choose between them. But I don't know what has become of The Grindstone. The last I saw of it was in Farm and Fireside last year. I'm not sure you wouldn't like it better than The Gold Hesperidee. George Martin might be able to help you find it if you

---

*[Jean was studying voice in hopes of having a concert career.]
†[The second volume of the biennial A Miscellany of American Poetry. Three new poets were added to the original eleven: "H. D.," Alfred Kreymborg, and Edna St. Vincent Millay. Robert was represented by "Fire and Ice," "The Grindstone," "The Witch of Coös," "A Brook in the City," and "Design."]

thought it worth while. Martin is the editor of F. and F.

Let's see—what else is there? There's Paul's Wife and A Witch of Cöos to take one of. Did you see the Witch as remedied up at the last end in Harriet Monroe's Mag?

I'll send The Gold Hesperidee along for consideration. You'll want Design. The Nose Ring is for you, not particularly for anyone else. You won't want it in the book. Keep it till next year till I have a set like it.

Ever yours

R. F.

[Enclosure]

THE NOSE-RING

Honor's a ring in the nose that people give,
But it makes my sensitive nose more sensitive.
It makes me wince when I use my nose for a plow;
Where once I thought all thorns were on branch and bough,
Every root in the ground is thorny now.
Henceforth it seems I am not to get my girth
By going below the surface of the earth.
But let me get down again to the roots of things
And I will dispense with my honor in rings.

R. F.

[Besides "The Nose-Ring," not to be found among his published poems, Robert enclosed a reprint of a "poem" by one C.R.D.S. Oakford entitled "The Indices of Thought" and credited as follows: "From the novel, Society the Real Criminal."]

The thoughts of woman and of man,
Are always traced upon the hand:
Upon the face and in the eyes,
And o'er the feet and legs and thighs,
A million virile thoughts imbed
Within the hairs on a woman's head.
The babe imbibes a mother's thought,
When from her breast she takes a draught.
Thoughts planted in the brain's deep wells
Conceived in embryonic cells,
Develop into minds sublime,
That fill the corridors of time.

I had been talking more-or-less seriously about making a collection to be called The World's Worst Poetry. It was to contain some of the howling absurdities of Julia A. Moore, "The Sweet Singer of Michigan"; James B. Elmore, "The Bard of the Alamo" (Alamo, Indiana); J. Gordon Coogler, "The Laureate of Long Island"; Norris C. Spriggs, author of "Sprigs of Poetry"; James McIntyre "The Cheese Poet"; Carl Claudius' "Vicissitudes of an Esculent," a four-thousand-line rhymed epic in praise of the potato; a selection from the eight volumes of the "Poetical Works" by Mary Ann O'Byrne of Watervliet, New York; William McGonagall, who billed himself as "Poet and Tragedian"; along with some of the pretty puerilities of Wordsworth, Tennyson, and Tennyson's successor to the laureateship, Alfred Austin.

Robert submitted the couplets above for possible inclusion. He also inserted three letters in Mr. Oakford's title, so that "The Indices of Thought" became "The Indicences of Thought."]

[Ann Arbor,   Mich.
February 23,   1922]

Dear Louis:

You will come for what these children can offer you I hope. They should be encouraged and so should I.* I've got up this carnival for you, Carl, Amy, Vachel, and Bynner without anybody's knowing I was behind it. I had to be very indirect. I've said nothing to you about it because I wasn't sure it would be a go. Come and bring Jean and we'll have our semi-annual powwow in spite of fate and distance.

Always thine

R.F.

[Ann Arbor,   Mich.
March 12,   1922]

Dear Louis:

I think I should be for the Heine poem if I had to choose.† It cuts deeper with me just as A Deserter of the Desert cuts deeper than The

---

*[With Robert's guidance the student organization at the University of Michigan arranged a lecture series which included Carl Sandburg, Amy Lowell, Vachel Lindsay, Witter Bynner, and myself.]

†[A translation I had thought of printing in the Miscellany.]

Gold Hesperidee with you. I can see why, but life is too short and crowded to go into reasons in art.

Uki Osawa, Stella Brunt, et al.* must have assigned you a date by this time. They tell me they have done the best they can for you.

Let's see—was there anything else? If not, let's say so and quit for the moment.

Ever yours
Robert Frost

Thanks for what you said about Down the River.

[Ann Arbor,   Mich.
March 20,   1922]

Dear Louis

Will you send me with such haste as you are capable of, you slow old thing, one copy of your latest Modern American Poetry inscribed For Lois E. Whitcomb from Louis Untermeyer (if that is the way you still spell your name)?—also a couple of copies uninscribed? You can get them cheaper than I can if I don't get them from you for nothing. Put them down or charge them up to publicity. Anything you can do to praise Miss Whitcomb will please G.D. Eaton (concerning whom consult The Smart Set for March) and anything that pleases Eaton will give you standing with what Farrar says is the best college newspaper literary supplement in the United States—namely that of The Michigan Daily. A lot has to be done here for all of us to offset such a book as a man named Rankin (concerning whom consult The Smart Set for some other month) wrote about Dargan, Marks, Rice,† and the like to the almost total exclusion of you, me, and the like. The children (bless their bobbed heads) are on our side and only need a little encouragement in the way of a book inscribed with your name (which after all is nothing) to give us the victory. We'll

---

*[The student committee in charge of the arrangements of the University of Michigan's lecture program.]

†[A reviewer named Rankin (first name forgotten) published a brochure in praise of the accomplishments of Olive Tilford Dargan, Josephine Preston Peabody Marks, Cale Young Rice, and other forgotten sentimental poets.]

fix Rankin—or rather you will—or I will if you'll supply the books.
Let's see what else was there I had on my mind—
                                        In a hurry
                                                R.F.

                                        [Ann Arbor, Mich.
                                        April 4, 1922]
Dear Louis:
    You will just naturally spoil everything if you let those Detroit
Library people take you away from us. You were to have been the
piece of resistance, coming right in the middle of everybody, and we
wanted you for three nights running. A number of groups want to
entertain you (or vice versa).* Sandburg has done for himself by
arranging to get out of town to go to Detroit about three hours afte:
he gets here. The Detroit Librarians have butted in on purpose.
Detroit doesn't matter. I want you to do something to solidify poetry
here, so that in a year or two after they have flirted with a musician
and a sculptor, they will be sorry they didn't stick to poets and poetry.
Our art can do more to entertain them than any other art but foot-ball.
So let's entertain them unforgettably. Help me. It's not for myself
I'm thinking, for I am done with vanities, but of you or some other
poor devil when in rotation they get round to poetry again and are
looking for a poet to keep. You know the plan. I assume you do.
They are going right through the arts and then through them again
till someone or something cries out in pain or gives way.
    Stand by me. It is a biological necessity.
                                        Steadily yours
                                                Robertus

                                        [Ann Arbor, Mich.
                                        April 13, 1922]
Dear Louis:
    All right if that's the case. I haven't pretended to run this business.
Only I had heard complaints from everybody of how Carl Sandburg

*[Another group connected with the University had promised the Detroit librarians
that I would come over one of the evenings while I was in nearby Ann Arbor.]

had broken his promise to star for an evening with the Whimsies* and run away to the Detroit Librarians. I didn't know the Whimsies had themselves to blame. It is no great matter. You go to Detroit then only for Friday night.

Will you stay for a dinner at Dean Bursley's Sunday night then? Will you wire if you can?

People look forward to hearing you.

Hastily

R.

[Ann Arbor, Mich.

May 2, 1922]

Dear Louis:

People are still calling pitifully for you on the telephone and at the front door, and will not be consoled when I tell them you have gone to 310 West 100 St. New York City. They long to speak to you nose to nose and not through a medium such as the postal service. And can you blame them? You were their man and you done them brown.

And now dear Louis I want to ax you something privileged behind closed doors. Please don't give me that picture by Leon Makielski as being too expensive a gift, Elinor thinks, for your means when you are leaving business. I am buying The Red Tree for one hundred dollars and Elinor says that is a whole lot for the impulses of two men combined to have come to. Stet.

And, say, I find I have lost Conrad Aiken's address. Have you it. I'm in mortal worry lest he should go ahead with me in his anthology on the assumption that silence gives consent. Help me. Elinor will let you in this case, because it will cost you no more than a postage stamp which she says I needn't enclose. Ain't I bitter?

You heard about the auditorium at Mankato that caught fire of itself when I was on my way to set it on fire with my eloquence. Well, the seeds of fire you scattered around here slept till you had been gone a week and then broke out in several places at once, notably on the roof of the ell of this D'Ooge† house we live in. Nothing but the prompt

---

*[A student organization at the University of Michigan.]
†[Robert had rented a house from a Mrs. D'Ooge, sometimes known as the Doggie House. Robert disliked the place, the name, and the owner.]

action of Elinor in calling me, me in calling central, central in calling the firemen, and the firemen in coming saved the D'Ooge antiques and art photography. The inside of the ell roof was the most beautiful smooth sheet of pure yellow flame when I looked out to see if Elinor was telling the truth. So you see what poetry kindled.

Another good story and absolutely true: A drug store advertised on a window the confection of ice cream encased in chocolate known as Frost-bite. The book-store next door not to be out done advertised my books as Frost-Bark—Very Little Worse than His Bite.

Don't fail to send Conrad Aiken's address.

Keep me in right with Dick—at least till I can reassure him of my comparative interest in him next July.

Ever yours

Robertus

[Ann Arbor, Mich.

May 19, 1922]

Dear Louis:

No, Amy didn't displace you in our affections. You still hold the top of both batting and fielding lists. Amy upset a lamp and a water pitcher and was in turn herself upset when I told her what you said about the lumber-yard on her shoulder.* She called the janitor fool and damn fool to his face —this was out back before she went on—and she called Conrad (of the Whimsies) "boy" in the sense of slave. She and I were ten minutes before the whole audience, disentangling the lengthener wire on her lamp. As a show she was more or less successful. After it was all over she described Straus to some ladies, among them Mrs. Straus, as the fussy old professor who stood around and didn't help. Straus says she must have meant me. She laid about her. And in that respect she disappointed nobody. She only failed to live up to the specifications when she stole away from a house full of guests and came to my house to smoke her cigar in private. Her speaking and reading went well considering the uproarious start she made with the lamp and water. I never heard such spontaneous shouts

*[During a question-and-answer period, I had remarked that the controversial Amy Lowell carried not only a chip on her shoulder but an entire lumberyard.]

of laughter. Out in front she took it all well with plenty of talk
offhand and so passed for a first class sport.

I tell you all this to give you an idea of what you were better than.
You have survived the eliminations and must prepare to measure
strength with Vachel in the final.

Here are the proofs—and by the way I happened to notice when
I was reading from your Modern Am Poetry that you had left a line
out of Mending Wall: "There where it is we do not need the wall."
It just barely hurts the sense.

Perhaps you had better send the picture to South Shaftsbury,
though I confess I am almost too impatient to see it.

> Ever yours
>
> Robert Frost

> [South Shaftsbury, Vt.
>
> July 8,   1922]

Dear Louis

I wrote you a letter a week ago which you paid no attention to
because I never sent it. It was all about the way the distinguished
Greek and Latin Professor's Widow (pronounced Dogie as in The
Chisholm Trail) accused me out of a clear sky of having stolen or
otherwise nefariously made away with one of the five iron pisspots she
would swear she had distributed to the five bedrooms of the house she
rented to us in Ann Arbor. She wouldn't claim it was an Etruscan
vase. Neither was it Mycenaean or Knossian ware. Nevertheless it
represented a loss of fifty cents and she proposed to make a stink
about it if not in it. I haven't admitted that I could have stolen a thing
I no longer have any use for since I stopped drinking. If I did
anything with it, I probably took it out into society to make conversation and lost it. I remember trying hard to break it over Carl
Sandburg's head for his new mysticism and madness prepense—but
in vain. I may have dented it ten cents worth. I have asked her to let
the ton of coal we left her in the cellar go toward that.

I got too bitterly funny about the episode in my other letter.
I decided that I didn't mind the bitch as much as I made myself
appear. I'm served exactly right for having spent so much of my life

tolerating the lower and middle classes. I've been punished often enough in the past for pretending not to see what was wrong with the poor. This is the worst I ever got it for affecting to stand in with the comfortably off. Mencken wins. My democracy has been 99 per cent unrealization. I left the world when I was young for reasons I gradually came to forget. I returned to the world at thirty three (sharp) to see if I couldn't recover my reasons. I have recovered them all right, "and I am ready to depart" again. I believe I will take example of Uriel and withdraw into a cloud—of whiskers. You may find me pretty brushy when you come by later in the week. It will be for a sign.

I'll save my adventure with Hughes the Secretary of State to tell you on your visit.

Here's looking for you and Jean. Stay as long as the law allows when you come.

Pretty much as ever

R.F.

Fail to say much about this in reply. Everybody reads your brilliant letters here; and the girls haven't been let into my shame as yet. Wouldn't it jar you? This is what my year among the teachers comes to. It reads like a fable to express my prejudice against education.

Wolcott   Vermont nr Canada

January 1   [1922]*

Dear Louis

I walked as per prophesy till I had no feet left to write regular verse with (hence this free verse) and that proved to be just one hundred and twenty five miles largely on the trail. Here I am stranded without Elinor's permission to go on or come home. I slept out on the ground alone last night and the night before and soaked both

*[Dated January 1st, either by error or whimsicality; the letter was sent on September 1st. Robert and the children had gone on a Long Trail hike in August and September —January in Vermont is scarcely a hiking month and certainly no time to soak both feet in a running brook—and the context makes it obvious that this letter was written the day before the next letter from St. Johnsbury on September 2nd.]

my feet in a running brook all day. That was my final mistake. My
feet melted and disappeared down stream. Good bye

Graditudinously yours

R. F.

I should admit that the kids all did two hundred and twenty miles.
I let them leave me behind for a poor old father who could once
out-walk out-run and out-talk them but can now no more.

Saint Johnsbury   Vermont
nr. New Hampshire
[September 2,   1922]

Dear Louis:

Here I am out at St. Johnsbury that famous town (named) for
St Johnswort, having for my part achieved peace without victory. The
children made a record for the two hundred and twenty miles of
Vermont from Mass. to Canada. I am content that it is all in the
family though as for me personally the laurels wither on my brow as
of course they were bound to sooner or later. I am beginning to slip:
I may as well admit it gracefully and accept my dismissal to the minor
and bush leagues where no doubt I have several years of useful service
still before me as pinch hitter and slow coach.

While I have walked in pain, you have been dancing. Such is life.
I shouldn't want you to miss any pleasure or improvement on my
account. I trust you go back to the city with your mind made up, and
I wish you always peace with or without victory, as you like it, but at
all events peace. (You needn't think this is my wish for everyone
indiscriminately. I have many variations of the expression for various
cases. The Irish, for example I always wish victory without peace.)

Yours wilsonianually

R. F.

I have just learned of the death of Lord Northcliffe in my absence
in the woods—when my back was turned. I am naturally deeply
moved. When the cats away the mice will play.

Also hooray for Tilden!*

*[William Tilden was the American tennis champion. Tennis was a game of which
Robert was inordinately fond, not only as a spectator but as a very active participant.
He insisted on playing with me when he was in his seventies and, though I was twelve
years his junior, he usually won.]

[South Shaftsbury, Vt.
November 5, 1922]

Dear Louis:

If you really want to find out who wrote A Critical Fable* just
follow my advice and proceed as follows with Miss Amy Lowell. Tell
her you had it quite independently of me from a man named Ira Sibil
that it was Nathan Haskell Dole the well-known-in-Boston punster.
Say I seem to have heard the same thing from George Herbert Palmer
the well-known-in-Boston widower of Alice Freeman Palmer. Be
perfectly open and above-board if you want to get an appreciable rise
out of her. Don't be funny. Station someone with a red flag two or
three hundred yards on each side up and down the road to warn off the
traffic before you touch this off.

Gee some Boston this time. And now a long jump from where
John Stark licked the British in 1777 to where Andrew Jackson licked
them in 1814. After that Ann Arbor.

The Round Up† was all right if it went all right. John Farrar
told me people in stripping circles had liked pretty much everything
in it but James Oppenheim's contribution and mine—and mine was
all right as a short story. Another time I think I shall stay out. People
have a right not to like me exactly as I don't like Carl very well for the
moment. Your Roast is good. Now go ahead and cook in some form
or other everything in the Bible. You be serious for a while and I'll be
your parodist. Ghost Toasties or Manna Rechauffé; Fermented
Scapegoat's Milk. Bless you in all you undertake and forgive us our
irreverence toward you as we also forgive your irreverence toward us.
The only difference is that ours is less witty than yours and so
harder to forgive.

I am at present hard at work translating one language into another.

I wish I could see you on my way through New York for as I
have often told you I had rather see you once than write to you an
hundred thousand times—Biblical an. You see how thinking of the
Bible can corrupt the style.

*["A Critical Fable was published anonymously, and Miss Lowell played out a long
comedy of pretending that it had been written by someone else—first by Louis
Untermeyer, then by Leonard Bacon, then by an imaginary poet whom she had
invented for the occasion." From The Shock of Recognition by Edmund Wilson.]
†[The second issue of A Miscellany of American Poetry, which contained (see later
in the paragraph) my long pseudo-Oriental tapestry of a poem, "Roast Leviathan."]

Pathé News that ends this vaudeville show: In Detroit I was bidden to a feast with Eddy Guest; even so in Vermont I am bidden to a feast with Daniel Cady. Haply you never heard of Daniel Cady. Stop your ears with wax or you will hear. Today I was away on the mountain building a habitation enforced or reinforced against the hunting season. I heard in Rutland Vt. that the wife of the President of The Rutland Railroad regarded Dorothy Canfield as local talent and as such refused to be interested in her. "Why she hasn't a reputable publisher, has she?" was her question. Tell Harcourt that. The years we waste!

Believe me

Robert Frost

Complain your damndest that I don't write often; the fact remains that yours is the only address in the world that I can write right off without looking it up.

[South Shaftsbury, Vt.
November 8, 1922]

Dear Louis

I think in the book I am sending you Raymond Holden goes further than any of my boys to date; otherwise I wouldn't be sending it. You know how suspicious I am of these boys.

Ever yours

R.F.

South Shaftsbury, Vt.
[December 23] 1922

Dear Louis:

Don't go to Europe till I tell you something.* It's about poetry. It should always be Beautiful and Dimmed. I should advise you to attempt nothing further under the old rules. Let this be the last thing we take up when we meet, which should be next week.

*[I was arranging to stay a year or more in Europe. Jean was to make her concert debut in Vienna while I was to do research in German literature.]

Meanwhile a Merry Christmas to you and Jean Starr Untermeyer the poet and vocalist.

I am as adamant—I have decided to occupy the Ruhral Districts for an indefinite period.

Yours for Christmas

R.F.

[South Shaftsbury, Vt.
January 20, 1923]

Dear Louis:

Elinor thinks perhaps I ought not to send a letter like this. You judge for us. If you don't think I'll live to be sorry just put it into another envelope and send it along to Burton.*

I came home with grippe. Everybody has had it in the house and Irma has had pneumonia—yes. But it's all right now.

I ought to let one at Burton. If you'd like the fun of seeing me punch him I'll come down and punch.

Ever thine

R.

[Enclosure]

You little Rascol:

Save yourself trouble by presenting my side of the argument for me, would you? (My attention has just been called to what you have been doing in the Tribune.) Interview me without letting me know I was being interviewed, would you?

I saw you resented not having anything to say for yourself the other day, but it never entered my head that you would run right off and take it out on me in print.

I don't believe you did the right thing in using my merest casual talk to make an article of. I shall have to institute inquiries among my newspaper friends to find out. If you did the right thing, well and good; I shall have no more to say. But if you didn't, I shall have a lot to say.

I'm sure you made a platitudinous mess of my talk—and not just

*[Burton Rascoe, journalist and critic, who had written a caustic review of Robert's poetry and, worse, had misquoted him.]

154

wilfully to be smart. I saw the blood was ringing in your ears and you weren't likely to hear me straight if you heard me at all. I don't blame you for that. You were excited at meeting me for the first time.

You seem to think I talked about obscurity, when, to be exact, I didn't once use the word. I never use it. My mistake with the likes of you was not using it to exclude it. It always helps a schoolboy, I find from old experience, if, in telling him what it is I want him to apprehend, I tell him also what it isn't.

The thing I wanted you to apprehend was obscuration as Sir Thomas Browne hath it. Let me try again with you, proceeding this time by example, as is probably safest.

Suppose I say: Of all the newspaper men I ever met, you most nearly resemble a reporter I once talked with casually on the street just after I had paid ten dollars in court for having punched a mutual friend. I talked to him exactly as I talked to you, without the least suspicion that I was being interviewed. He must have taken sides with the mutual friend, for he ran right off to his office and published everything I had said as nearly as he chose to reproduce it.

There you have what I call obscuration. "I say no harm and I mean no harm," as the poet hath it; but the stupider you are the more meaning you will see where none is intended. The really intelligent will refuse to listen to such old-wives' indirection.

Or again, suppose I say: Just because you have won to a position where you can get even with people is no reason why you shouldn't perform face forward like a skunk, now is it? I only ask for information.

Or to "lay off" you personally for the moment, suppose I say: I learn that someone is bringing out an Anthology of the Best Lines of Modern Poetry. He proposes to run the lines more or less loosely together in a narrative and make them so much his own that anyone using them again will have to enclose them in double quotes, thus:

"'What sayest thou, old barrelful of lies?'"

" 'Not worth a breakfast in the cheapest country under the cope' "

"'Shall I go on, or have I said enough?'"

These three lines are from Chaucer, Shakespeare, and Milton respectively. Please verify.

Or suppose I say: Good sense is plebeian, but scarcely more plebeian than any sense at all. Both will be spurned in aristocratic circles this summer.

I thought you made very poor play with what I said about the obvious. The greatly obvious is that which I see the minute it is pointed out and only wonder I didn't see before it was pointed out. But there is a minor kind of obviousness I find very engaging. You illustrate it, when, after what passed between us, you hasten to say you like me but don't like my books. You will illustrate it again if, after reading this, you come out and say you like neither me nor my books, or you like my books but not me. Disregard that last: I mustn't be too subtle for you. But aren't you a trifle too obvious here for your own purpose? I am told on every hand that you want to be clever. Obviousness of this kind is almost the antithesis of cleverness. You should have defended your hero's work on one Sunday, and saved your attack on mine for another. You take all the sting out of your criticism by being so obvious in the sense of easy to see through. It won't do me the good you sincerely hoped it would.

You are probably right in thinking that much literature has been written to make fun of the reader. This my letter may have been. Do you remember what Webster said or implied about the farmer who hanged himself in a year of plenty because he was denied transportation for his grain?—or what Nemphrekepta said to Anubis?

When my reports are in on your conduct, I may be down to see you again.

I shall be tempted to print this letter some time, I am afraid. I hate to waste it on one reader. Should you decide to print it take no liberties with it. Be sure you print it whole.

Ever yours,
Robert Frost

[South Shaftsbury, Vt.
January 23, 1923]

Dear Louis:

You and Jean think such wrath ill becomes me. I'm over it now anyway. We won't send the letter to Burton the rat. My grounds for wanting to let him have both fists in succession in the middle of the face are chiefly that he stated me so much worse than I know how to state myself. That is the greatest outrage of small town or big town— misquotation. It flourishes worst, it seems, among these smart cosmopolites. But never mind.

We did have fun with Under the Tree.* Lesley had seen and liked it in MS in Chicago at Mrs. Moody's. Highly poetical and entrancingly gauche.

I'm glad you could say for the ambitious Raymond† what you did.

Ever yours

R.

Back to Ann.

[Ann Arbor, Mich.

February 5, 1923]

Dear Louis

It might be a good idea to call the explanatory poems Notes. I'm pretty sure to call the book New Hampshire. The Notes will be The Witch of Coos, The Census-taker, Paul's Wife, Wild Grapes, The Grindstone, The Ax-helve, The Star-splitter, Maple, The Witch of Grafton (praps), The Gold Hesperidee (praps), and anything else I can think of or may write before summer.

I'll go further and say that I may even bring out a volume of lyrics at the same time and refer to it in New Hampshire as The Star in the Stone-boat. I'm in a larking mood. I'll do almost anything for the sake of contraption.

I'm fearfully glad you've come to an understanding with MacVeagh. I think you two could learn to like each other in a way.

If it isn't too much like fishing, please tell fools like Maynard in your essay on me in what sense of the word many of my poems are praise. He says I never praise anything. Don't seem to contradict him or anyone else, but just point out how my undersaying and litotes is just as high praise in effect as someone's else oversaying hyperbole and superlative. Gee I hate to be so misunderstood.

I'm back out here as you may judge from the fact that last night I entertained a couple of young non-smokers till ten, went out calling till after midnight, and read through a novel in MS by Lawrence Conrad between then and six this morning. That takes rank with my

---

*[Under the Tree was Elizabeth Madox Roberts' first book, an amplification of a group of poems written when she was an undergraduate at the University of Chicago. Because of its artful artlessness it was highly praised.]

†[Raymond Holden.]

fourteen lectures in fourteen days and three hundred lines of blank verse between ten at night and noon the next day. I'm on a tear. Let who will be clever.

Let's see when was your date to come again? I'm wanting to see you. People all speak friendly of you and Jean.

I want to send you a copy of The Star-splitter. You don't care for The Gold Hesperidee. There's something the matter with the last of it. And you think it doesn't cut very deep.

I wonder how the Raymond Holden book is coming on.

Do you notice how little light Boston throws on the sky at night. She hasn't had a heavy weight champion since John L. Sullivan. Let's think of all we can say against her on Vachel's account.

Ever yours
Robert

[In the letter of February 5th Robert enclosed a Monthly Bulletin of the Michigan Authors Association. The bulletin was written in a "folksy" style and began:

GRACIOUS SAKES ALIVE! DID YOU MISS IT?

If you did you missed a wonderful talk by Professor Wenley. It was deep enough to intrigue the deepest thinkers ... DON'T MISS THE NEXT MEETING. "Day by day in every way our meetings are getting better and better."

There was much more in this vein, some of which Robert underlined. For example:

*James Oliver Curwood has completed his new novel, "The Alaskan." It is considered his best work and he has received the highest price ever paid to an American novelist for a novel of the same length ... Myrtella Southerland is completing a series of new poems for the newspaper syndicate ... Frederick Zeigen has left for Miami, Fla., with his family for the balance of the winter, where he will complete his new novel, "The Bishop Story." Mr. Zeigen has a winter home on the water front in Miami, where he does most of his writing. His last book of poems, "Stardust and Dandelions," was completed there last winter ... Edgar A. Guest's new book of poems, "All That Matters," has had an unexpectedly large sale. Eddie is improving every day ... *Robert Frost of Ann Arbor won the annual Poetry Magazine Prize for best work published in that magazine. Let us get better acquainted with you, Robert ... Every member of this Authors Association should spend at least five hours a day in creative* literary work. Are you doing this? ... *Send in your membership application today. Do not wait. Only the weakling hesitates!*

After the line about E.A. Guest's daily improvement Robert added a large exclamation mark. In front of the item about himself he inserted an asterisk and appended the following:

Became a member by default; i.e. because he didn't appear in time and refuse to become a member. He says no notice was formally served on him of the danger impending.]

[Ann Arbor, Mich.
February 12, 1923]

THE STAR-SPLITTER†

"You know Orion always comes up sideways.
Throwing a leg up over our fence of mountains,
And, rising on his hands, he looks in on me
Busy out doors by lantern light with something
I should have done by daylight and in fact
After the ground has frozen I should have done
Before it froze, and a wind throws a handful
Of waste leaves at my smoky lantern chimney
To make fun of my way of doing things,
Or else fun of Orion's having caught me.
Has a man, I should like to ask, no rights
These forces are obliged to pay respect to?"
So Bradford Kimball mingled reckless talk
Of heavenly stars and huggermugger farming
Till having failed at huggermugger farming,
He burned his house down for the fire-insurance
And spent the proceeds on a telescope
To satisfy a lifelong curiosity
About our place among the infinities.

"What do you want with one of those blamed things,"
I asked him well beforehand. "Don't you get one!"

"Don't call it blamed: there isn't anything
More blameless in the sense of being less
A weapon in our human fight," he said
"I'll have one if I sell my farm to buy it."

†[This first draft differs in several particulars from the printed version.]

There where he moved the rocks to plow the ground
And plowed between the rocks he couldn't move,
Few farms changed hands. So rather than spend years
Trying to sell his farm and then perhaps not selling,
He burned the house down for the fire-insurance
And bought a telescope with what it came to.

He had been heard to say a number of times,
"The best thing that we're put here for's to see.
The strongest thing that's given us to see with's
A telescope. Someone in every town
Seems to me owes it to the town to keep one.
In Littleton it may as well be me."
After such loose talk it was no surprise
When he came stumbling in the frozen ruts
One night and shouting "Help my home's on fire!"
Some threw their windows up, and one at one said
"Let them that set the fire put out the fire."
One at another, "Them or else their sons
Or sons' sons to the seventh generation."
Mean laughter was exchanged between the windows
To let him know we weren't the least imposed on
And he could wait: we'd see to him to-morrow.

But the first thing next morning we reflected
If one by one we counted people out
For the least sin, it wouldn't take us long
To get so we had no one left to live with.
For to be social is to be forgiving.
Our thief, the one who does our stealing from us
We don't cut off from coming to church suppers
But what we miss we go to him and ask for.
He always gives it back that is if still
Uneaten unused up or undisposed of.

It wouldn't do to be too hard on Brad
About his telescope. Beyond the age
Of being given one's gift for Christmas
He had to take the best way he knew how
To find himself in one. Well, all we said was,
He took a strange thing to be roguish over.

Some sympathy was wasted on the house
A good old-timer dating back along.
But a house isn't sentiment. The house

Didn't feel anything. And if it did
Why not regard it as a sacrifice
And an old-fashioned sacrifice by fire,
Instead of a new fashioned one at auction.

One may be a good man though a bad farmer.
Out of a house and so out of a farm
At one stroke (of a match) Brad joined the railroad
As under-ticket-agent for a living
Where his job when he wasn't selling tickets
Was setting out up track and down, not plants
As on a farm, but planets, evening stars
That varied in their hue from red to green
According to the safety or unsafety.

He got a good glass for six hundred dollars.
His new job gave him leisure for star-gazing.
Often he bid me come and have a look
Up the brass barrel, velvet black inside,
At a star quaking in the other end.
I recollect a night of broken clouds
And underfoot snow melted down to ice
And melting further in the wind to mud.
We spread our two legs as we spread its three,
Pointed our thoughts the way we pointed it
And standing at our leisure till the day broke
Said some of the best things we ever said.
That telescope was christened the Star-splitter
Because it didn't do a thing but split
A star in two or three the way you split
A globule of quicksilver in your hand
With one stroke of the finger.
It's a star-splitter if there ever was one
And ought to do some good if splitting stars
'S a thing to be compared with splitting wood.

But after all, as Brad himself would say,
Do we know any better where we are
And how it stands between the night tonight
And a man with a smoky lantern chimney,
How different from the way it ever stood?
I mean do we know for all our looking?

Robert Frost

WESTERN UNION
TELEGRAM

1923   MAR 15

DEB 114 11 1 EXTRA RUSH
  ANNARBOR MICH. 15 955A
LOUIS UNTERMEYER
  HOTEL PFISTER MILWAUKEE WIS
COME ON DON'T STAND TALKING ABOUT IT FRIDAY NINE THIRTY
  ROBERT FROST

[South Shaftsbury,   Vt.
May 2,   1923]

Dear Louis

Stop brittling if you don't want to be called brittleminded.*

And gee didn't it make me feel lonesome when my friends were counted by Farrar and found to come to just two, you and Gibson. Figures can't lie; but sleeping lions can if you let them: and I wish Farrar had let them. As long as I went unrealizing I was happy. But I suppose the day of reckoning had to come; and it was all day with me though I don't believe it can have taken Farrar all day just to count two unless it was a door-to-door canvas he made and it was a long way between the two doors. I cried myself to sleep that night. Just two friends, one of those about to leave me to go to England and the other in England already.

But candidly I am going to feel rather unsupported with you out of the country. There's something to what Johnny says. He has spoken a half truth. He is mistaken about Gibson. But he is right about you. Subtract you and what have I left? The worst of it is I have no faith in its being a merely temporary subtraction. It will be just like you to get drowned both going and coming. It's the good swimmers that always get drowned at sea, they say, whether because they are apt to be careless about falling overboard or because when the ship goes down they feel some delicacy about piling into the life boats. There seems to be something in swimming as in tennis that is

*[In an article on Robert, John Farrar had referred to me as one of his "brittle-minded" friends. H. G. Wells's *Mr. Britling Sees It Through* had been published a few years prior to the piece.]

162

incompatible with bad manners. Your wife won't thank me for this my raven's croakery on the eve of your putting out to sea—moaning of the far as Tennyson would call it. But if it is hard for her, think how hard it must be for me. I refuse to spare myself. Why should I spare her? We want the truth—the truth about friendship no less than about marriage.

When are you going?

That's good of Jean to stand by my little poem before all the world. Stopping by Woods on a Snowy Etc. is my best bid for remembrance. Jean's another friend; Farrar never thought of her.

Surely I'll have time to write you again. I must write you a nice letter for Abercrombie.*

Ever yours
Robert Frost

[South Shaftsbury, Vt.
June 9, 1923]

Dear Louis

Now look unless you tell me where you are over there I shall be driven to trying to reach you through the diplomatic service.

I'm home from Michigan but I haven't parted with the book to MacVeagh yet. Something's come over me.

Don't present the letter to Abercrombie unless you absolutely like it.

File your itinerary.

R.

[June 9, 1923]

Dear Lascelles†

The first I ever heard of Louis Untermeyer was from you; the first thing I ever read of his was in your shadowy library at The Gallows, Ryton (of terribly mixed memory); you introduced him to

---

*[Lascelles Abercrombie, the English poet and dramatist, one of the most eloquent and most underrated of the so-called Georgian group.]
†[In an envelope marked: For Lascelles Abercrombie England Introducing Louis Untermeyer.]

me when you knew more about him than I; I introduce him back to
you now that I know more about him than you know.

He is one of our best poets, especially in his first book Challenge
and in his latest Roast Leviathan, which you would be sure to like.
He is our best critic and so naturally a great admirer of your work.
It was only the other day that he brought me your Ham and Eggs. He
is my great friend and so not unnaturally a great admirer of my
work. In politics he is still somewhat the reckless idealist in spite of
all time and his wife, who is a sound thinker as well as a most
charming lady, have been able to do to make him see reason. He
puns, often successfully.

Most of this I tell you so that you will be good to him for his own
sake (and his wife's). I can hardly ask you to be good to him for my
sake without risk of presuming too much on how you may be
supposed to feel toward me after all these years of neither seeing each
other nor writing to each other. I trust you are still a little my friend
as I am

Much yours

Robert Frost

South Shaftsbury Vermont   U.S.A.

June 9   1923

*[The next letter is headed "Boston," but the reference to the woods
"(away down north of Bridgton)" and the wild ducks "quacking
foreninst me in the rapids of the river" make it apparent that, though
the letter was mailed from Boston, it was written in Maine during
one of Robert's visits to his sister Jeanie at the institution to which
she had been committed.]*

[Boston   Mass.

September 13,   1923]

Dear Louis

This is to prepare you on the only paper available in the Maine
woods (away down north of Bridgton) for a letter I contemplate
writing you. I don't want to come on you all at once after so long a
silence with the accumulations of that silence.

I'm going to give the first course I ever gave in philosophy next
year on judgments (or less technically Verdicts) in History,
Literature, and Religion—how they are made and how they stand.

As you see I am on my way into the church. What did I tole you, Doctor, if you went away and left me with nothing to lean on but God? It is too late to do anything about it now (at any rate by mail). You may as well accept it. But I do wish you could come home and mitigate a little the complications that are sure to ensue. That will be the burden of my letter when I write it. I shall go on to wish you were where I could invite you in on this job at least once in the year. You could be of great assistance in a course run as this will be by the case method or, as I like to put it, the illustration-first method.

And I'll tell you all about my next book in the letter when I write it. Already some of my staider friends have stuck at the levity of the title and of the forced use of notes. They say it doesn't seem like me but (with a sigh) after all they had felt that I was changing. O gee.

And I'll mention Europe in my letter too. Sure I will! I'll congratulate you on having found it wanting. I'll just lay in and do this matter of your not deserting us justice.

I'll write the letter next week. Meanwhile my love to you all.

Ever yours
Robert Frost

There's a wild duck quacking foreninst me in rapids of the river—six wild ducks! Lots of wild life here and some tame.

Amherst, Mass.   U.S.A.
November   1923

For Louis Untermeyer—this figment of his creative criticism.* He thought it into existence by publishing a review of it before it was written.

Robert Frost

[Amherst,   Mass.
March 10,   1924]

Dear Old Louis:

Since last I saw you I have come to the conclusion that style in prose or verse is that which indicates how the writer takes himself and

*[One of the first copies of New Hampshire that came off the press.]

what he is saying.* Let the sound of Stevenson go through your mind empty and you will realize that he never took himself other than as an amusement. Do the same with Swinburne and you will see that he took himself as a wonder. Many sensitive natures have plainly shown by their style that they took themselves lightly in self-defense. They are the ironists. Some fair to good writers have no style and so leave us ignorant of how they take themselves. But that is the one important thing to know: because on it depends our likes and dislikes. A novelist seems to be the only kind of writer who can make a name without a style: which is only one more reason for not bothering with the novel. I am not satisfied to let it go with the aphorism that the style is the man. The man's ideas would be some element then of his style. So would his deeds. But I would narrow the definition. His deeds are his deeds; his ideas are his ideas. His style is the way he carries himself toward his ideas and deeds. Mind you if he is down-spirited it will be all he can do to have the ideas without the carriage. The style is out of his superfluity. It is the mind skating circles round itself as it moves forward. Emerson had one of the noblest least egotistical of styles. By comparison with it Thoreau's was conceited, Whitman's bumptious. Carlyle's way of taking himself simply infuriates me. Longfellow took himself with the gentlest twinkle. I don't suppose you know his miracle play in The Golden Legend, or Birds of Killingworth, Simon Danz, or Othere.

I own any form of humor shows fear and inferiority. Irony is simply a kind of guardedness. So is a twinkle. It keeps the reader from criticism. Whittier, when he shows any style at all, is probably a greater person than Longfellow as he is lifted priestlike above consideration of the scornful. Belief is better than anything else, and it is best when rapt, above paying its respects to anybody's doubt whatsoever. At bottom the world isn't a joke. We only joke about it to avoid an issue with someone to let someone know that we know he's there with his questions: to disarm him by seeming to have heard and done justice to his side of the standing argument. Humor is the most engaging cowardice. With it myself I have been able to hold some of my enemy in play far out of gunshot.

There are people like John Gould Fletcher I would fain not have let in on myself; if I could have held them off all my life with smiles

*[Robert enlarged on this theme in his "Introduction" to E.A. Robinson's posthumous *King Jasper.*]

they could take as they pleased. But John G. pushed through my defenses. Let me tell you what happened. It was amusing. You might like to pass it along to Huebsch: you know him so well. You could quote this part of my letter word for word. Three months ago John Gould Fletcher wrote me saying "I learn you have a book out. I wish you would use your influence with Henry Holt & Co. to help me get a book out. I am sending them a manuscript." I spoke to Lincoln MacVeagh in the matter. He said he wouldn't publish John Gould Fletcher's book for two simple reasons: first because it wouldn't sell and second because he hated the kind of thing Fletcher wrote. I said I wouldn't ask him to publish it to get me a good review or save me from a bad one. Obviously he might have published Fletcher's book and charged it up to advertising mine. Maurice Firuski* knew about this and made haste to tell me the minute it was out that I had got the bad review in The Freeman. No doubt I deserved it on two counts that we needn't go into. But I can't excuse Fletcher his bad taste—worthy of Washington politics or New York business. Have I not written in New Hampshire that it's no wonder poets some times have to seem so much more businesslike than businessmen? It is because they are so much less sensitive from having overused their sensibilities. Men who have to feel for a living would unavoidably become altogether unfeeling except professionally. And The Freeman's part in it interests me. It just shows how hard it is for an American publication, however lofty its pretensions, to keep from lending itself to blackmail and corruption. Probably The Freeman is having the most superior editorials on the state of affairs in Washington. There endeth all that might concern the editors and publisher of The Freeman.

We haven't given up the idea of getting to France and England this summer. Amherst goes sadly, I'm afraid I have to admit. I'd like to look at it receding from the deck of an outward bound ship. The trouble seems to be the usual one in this world, to stop being crazy without falling stupid. But you know me, Al. I'm always on the point of jumping overboard because the ship is unseaworthy. Take my advice and never jump unless the ship is actually sinking or on fire. All ships are relatively unseaworthy.

*[A bookseller in Boston.]

G

You did not err. The story in <u>The Bookman</u> was Lesley's. But be more truthful than common. You never recognized it from any family resemblance. You had many clues to help you. The knowledge that Lesley was writing under an assumed name, the personal note on her devotion to stone-breaking in Vermont, and the name Leslie. You mustn't tell her any more that she repeats her father. The charge is dangerous to her further development. She has been held back long enough by our discretion and her own. It's time she let out in prose and verse. The bookstore she has contemplated is going to be a mistake if she is driven to it by our coolness to her in her art. I haven't wanted to do anything to excite her to creation. Anyone of mine who writes prose or verse shall be a self-starter. But neither do I want to hold her from it too much or too long. I know you'll sympathise with me in this as much as in anything I have at heart. I thought her story all poetry. I hadn't seen it before it was in print.

I wish I could see you and hear all about what you are getting done. And I hope Jean likes her voice better and better. One reason for our wanting to get over is to see you both off your native heath. It would be fun meeting there where we never met before, maybe a foretaste of our meeting in heaven by accident at a soirée of Mrs. God's. Mrs. Olds, the new President's wife, gives lots of soirées and dinners—if that's all that's needed.

Affectionately

Robert

[Amherst, Mass.
March 12, 1924]

Dear Louis

I sent you a long enough letter without this yesterday. Amusing to see Robinson squirm just like any ordinary person in a tight place trying to keep in with his neighbors. It goes down with Laura E. Richards. Funny motions life makes. We must try to be comparatively honest.

R. F.

[The letter of March 12, 1924, contained two clippings. Both were from a newspaper in Gardiner, Maine. The first, dated January 25, 1924, was headed: NEW ENGLAND'S INDIGNATION

AROUSED—EDWIN ARLINGTON ROBINSON'S POEM CONDEMNED—DAVID DARLING LOYAL CRITIC. It consisted of a letter from D. H. Darling to John W. Berry, Editor of the Gardiner Journal, complaining that Robinson's sonnet entitled "New England" had appeared in the London Outlook and Darling resented what he thought was a slur. "The British find rocks to heave at us without our help, and are 'on the target' often enough without our giving them the range." Contrary to Mr. Darling's assumption, Robinson had never submitted the poem to a London publisher; it had been reprinted from the December 1, 1923, issue of The Literary Digest.

The other clipping made this plain. It was explained in a letter from Laura E. Richards, author of many books for children, that Mr. Darling had misapprehended the intention of the sonnet. In reply to a query, Robinson himself wrote: "As for the sonnet on New England, your letter makes me wonder if you didn't read it the wrong way. It was supposed to be aimed at those who patronize New England."

In any case, it is obvious that Robert did not like the way the Northeast Corner was characterized by his fellow New Englander.]

South Shaftsbury   Vermont U.S.A.

August 12   1924

Dear Louis:

I haven't reported on Amherst yet. I found that the college does belong as charged to Mr. Dwight Morrow of J. P. Morgan & Co.—your bankers in Paris. But so does Smith College belong to Mrs. Dwight Morrow. They might belong to worse. The Morrows are the kind of rich who take good care of their playthings. Morrow is certainly intelligent and so liberal, he tells me, as to have sat in until very recently anyway at the councils of The New Republic. Mrs. Morrow is a member of the Poetry Society of America. Between them they have just put David Morton on the Amherst faculty, I am told over the telephone. The question of David Morton was worrying President Olds when I came away. He could have wished him a poet he knew more about. I couldn't help him much because I didn't know much myself. The Morrows pressed for Morton as the winner of some sort of Poetry Society prize. President Olds is not young. I have seen him worn out with running to New York all year for instructions and permissions.

The boys had been made uncommonly interesting to themselves by Meiklejohn.* They fancied themselves as thinkers. At Amherst you thought, while at other colleges you merely learned. (Wherefore if you love him, send your only son and child to Amherst.) I found that by thinking they meant stocking up with radical ideas, by learning they meant stocking up with conservative ideas—a harmless distinction, bless their simple hearts. I really liked them. It got so I called them the young intelligences—without offense. We got on like a set of cogwheels in a clock. They had picked up the idea somewhere that the time was past for the teacher to teach the pupil. From now on it was the thing for the pupil to teach himself using, as he saw fit, the teacher as an instrument. The understanding was that my leg was always on the table for anyone to seize me by that thought he could swing me as an instrument to teach himself with. So we had an amusing year. I should have had my picture taken just as I sat there patiently waiting, waiting for the youth to take education into their own hands and start the new world. Sometimes I laughed and sometimes I cried a little internally. I gave one course in reading and one course in philosophy, but they both came to the same thing. I was determined to have it out with my youngers and betters as to what thinking really was. We reached an agreement that most of what they had regarded as thinking, their own and other peoples, was nothing but voting—taking sides on an issue they had nothing to do with laying down. But not on that account did we despair. We went bravely to work to discover, not only if we couldn't have ideas, but if we hadn't had them, a few of them, at least, without knowing it. Many were ready to give up beaten and own themselves no thinkers in my sense of the word. They never set up to be original. They never pretended to put this and that together for themselves, never had a metaphor, never made an analogy. But they had, I knew. So I put them on the operating table and proceeded to take ideas they didn't know they had out of them as a prestidigitator takes rabbits and pigeons you have declared yourself innocent of out of your pockets trouserslegs and even mouth. Only a few resented being thus shown up and caught with the goods on them.

I went to Middlebury and put the finishing touch on myself and

*[Alexander Meiklejohn, a believer in "progressive education," had been President of Amherst before being dismissed for his liberal policies. Robert said that the college suffered from a case of Meiklejaundice.]

my teaching for the year. I speak literally. I am sick to death almost
with having gnothied* so many people. It seems to have come hardest
on my liver or kidneys this time: whereas in the old days the straight
teaching I did, wholly unpsychoanalytic, only ruined my first and
second stomachs, particularly the first, the one that I ruminated with.
I wasn't happy at Middlebury, the scene of my rather funny failure
last year with New Hampshire (the poem, not the book). The
Whichers were there, the old man Poetry Societist, George, and the
wives, and I was aware that for some reason they were not helping me
much. George is his father's son. He catches the germs of the people
he's with. I left him a protective wash against Meiklejaundice when
I came away. But he got the bug though in attenuated form, as is
like him.

Let's talk about something healthier. The farm goes rip-roaring
as no farm ever went with me. Carol has hired almost nothing done
this year. He has ploughed and done all the haying himself. Fun to
look on at—I always so dreamed of being a real farmer: and seeing
him one is almost the same as being one myself. My heart's in it with
him. I have to strive not to put my mind in and interfere with
advice. Let him go it. We've given him the farm outright, as I may
have told you. Lillian† is an unspoiled little girl easy to interest in
everything in the world. She's hard at it preserving a jar of something
for everyone of the 365 days in the year.

Lesley's store is well started. She ought to have some of your books
autographed. She'll have to wait for them, I suppose, till you get
home. I believe she is at the Williamstown Political Institute today
with her truck (called the Knapsack) full of appropriate books to
sell. She's almost too enterprising for her health. If you see anything
over there such as the little hand-carved figures in wood that might
add a touch to the shop, do buy it at my expense. She must have
atmosphere. You and Jean will like the place when you see it. The
address is The Open Book, 124 South St., Pittsfield, Mass.

Don't expect me in the Misc. this year if you don't want to make
me nervous. I'm jaded with the pulls on me that I can't answer to.
I've made up my mind that with a few people to abet me I won't do
one single thing in verse or out of it or with it till I God damn please
for the rest of my natural life. The same for prose. I'm not going to

*["gnothied": a punning play on the phrase "Know thyself."]
†[Carol's wife.]

write any more letters of obligation. I'm going to wait till I want to say a particular thing in a particular letter to a particular person if I wait till the Second Coming. What did I get into writing for if it wasn't for fun? This is my first letter under the new ruling. You may be sure it is no letter of obligation!

Ever yours
Robert Frost

[Amherst,   Mass.
April 10,   1925]

Dear Louis

Wouldn't it jar you to have this* brought up against you by a whole chorus of former classmates thirty three and a third years or one third of a century after the fact? I went to Lawrence prepared at worst to have some of my old unpaid debts thrown in my face. Here you have one of the first half dozen poems I ever wrote to a finish. I have got to confess to someone. It gives me strange powers of speech.

Still yours

R.

Miss Elsie Sergeant† wants to ask you about my weaknesses for a New Rep article. I showed her this myself.

CLASS HYMN—1892
LAWRENCE HIGH SCHOOL

Words by Robert L. Frost
Music by Beethoven

There is a nook among the alders
Still sleeping to the cat-bird's "Hush";
Below, a long stone-bridge is bending
Above a runnel's silent rush.

*["This" was a Class Hymn written in 1892 when Robert was not quite eighteen and at Lawrence High School. An interesting bit of juvenilia, it is reprinted after the letter.]

†[Elizabeth Shepley Sergeant was preparing a "profile" of Robert for *The New Republic*: "Robert Frost: A Good Greek out of New England." Thirty-five years later she published a full-length biographical study: *Robert Frost: The Trial by Existence*.]

A dreamer hither often wanders
And gathers many a snow-white stone;
   He weighs them, poised upon his fingers,
Divining each one's silvery tone.

He drops them! when the stream makes music,
Fair visions with its vault-voice swell;
   And so, for us, the future rises,
As thought-stones stir our heart's "Farewell!"

[*The second paragraph of the next letter concerns an imbroglio of birthday celebrations. Robert believed that he was born in 1875, and it was not until he was in his late sixties that he learned he had made himself younger by a year and that the registration of his birth showed that he was born in 1874. On March 26, 1925, his friends arranged a dinner at the Hotel Brevoort in New York to celebrate what they believed to be his fiftieth birthday; Willa Cather, Dorothy Canfield Fisher, and the Van Dorens were there, as well as all the available contributors to the biennial Miscellany. The only conspicuous absentee was Amy Lowell, who, unhappy about the way in which the English reviewers had dismissed the two-volume biography of Keats which had cost her so much energy, was "indisposed." In less than a fortnight, however, she was well enough to be the star performer at a sumptuous party which she gave at the Hotel Somerset in Boston to offset the criticisms and honor (somewhat belatedly) her own fiftieth birthday. Robert and I were literally summoned to appear; there were to be toasts and speeches, and we were to come to her manorial home in Brookline before the dinner so that Amy could tell us what to say. Our excuses were thin, but both of us declined to attend. A month later she suffered a stroke and died.*

The dream reference to my advising Robert to "Will your frosty mantle to Wilbert Snow" is another of Robert's word plays. It is also a reminder that I had included two of Snow's poems in one of my anthologies with the comment that his work was "obviously though perhaps unconsciously indebted to Robert Frost."]

So. Shaft. [Vt.]
[June 20, 1925]

Dear Louis

   It seems to me that's a very mature sentiment for an American of any age, that about your having gone back on everything but the

173

world. It can never be said again that living in Europe a year and five-twelfths with the Second Coming of Casanova did nothing for you. There are very few things so small that the least of us can't profit by them.

I suspect that what lies at the bottom of your Schmerz is your own dereliction in not having gone to her Keats Eats just before Amy died. She got it on us rather by dying just at a moment when we could be made to feel that we had perhaps judged her too hardly. Ever since childhood I have wanted my death to come in as effectively and affectingly. It helps always anyway it comes in a career of art. Whatever bolt you have shot you have still, as long as you are alive, that one in reserve. But, of course, it always does the most good on a world that has been treating you too unkindly.

I didn't rise to verse, but I did write a little compunctious prose to her ashes. And I did go before the assembled college to say in effect that really no one minded her outrageousness because it never thrust home: in life she didn't know where the feelings were to hurt them, any more than in poetry she knew where they were to touch them. I refused to weaken abjectly.

I dreamed that as I wandered by the way I was assured by you that I needn't worry any more to run hither and thither carrying favor with lectures and recitations: my mark was made as much as it was ever going to be made. I could go back like Cincinnatus to my plough. And you don't know what a relief it was. I wept with gratitude toward you. You mean to say, I cried, I am free to putter my days out without even writing any more if I don't want to write? What's the use of trying to beat Two Look at Two, you answered. Will your frosty mantle to Wilbert Snow. And with that you swung your 1917-model Something Apperson car into the Bennington-Brattleboro-Keene road for the Poetry Society at Peterboro. The souvenir pennons and bannerets all over your car were flapping Robinson, Aline Kilmer, Abbie Brown, etc. and you had on one of these new fashioned tail lights that kept winking Stop Stop Stop.

This dream could have been worked out more carefully to make it mean more if I had turned it over in my mind longer before I wrote it out. It will do well enough as it is for a Freudian diagnosis. It combines a good deal.

The first cousin of Waldo Frank and the third or fourth of Loeb the Darrow ward or charge came to me the other day with a tale of

just having broken away from his psychoanalyst after a scene in which he had handed the psychoanalyst a letter and made him read it while he waited. He said it was a very bitter letter full of technical terms. I asked him what had the psychoanalyst done, psychoanalyzed him? It seems he had done worse; he had introspectrosized him. At least, I said, he had supplied you with the language to deal with him in. He had and I made him eat it. Have you been—ah—sick, I suggested. My mother is a subnormal society has-been and last month my brother committed suicide. Why did your brother commit that? Because he was tired of the varnish business that belongs to the family and was engaged to be married to an already married woman. Strange that that hadn't occurred to me. The boy is a perfectly unobjectionable last year's graduate except for a poem as I remember it about Gods face being painted on the sunset sky. God's face painted! This must be some of this God-the-Mother cult. Unless he meant the Virgin Mary.

Captain Mattison, our postmaster, and a man who has been to France wanted to know of me what they had gone into court out in Tennessee for, to settle it once and for all who we were descended from, monkeys or the Virgin Mary? Speaking of the Virgin Mary.

And so I might sustain the theme indefinitely that you nor I nor nobody knows as much as he doesn't know. And that isn't all: there is nothing anybody knows, however absolutely, that isn't more or less vitiated as a fact by what he doesn't know. But of this more in my next book which I can't make up my mind about, whether to throw it to Holt, Harcourt, MacVeagh, or Knopf.

I recently ran across a biological fact that interested me, as facts go. It establishes exclusiveness much lower down in the scale than you would expect to find it. Exclusiveness in love. Way way down.

Exclusively yours

Robert Frost

Sugar Hill   N.H.
Aug. 31   1925

Dear Louis:

The best Aiken poem is probably Arachne, the best Benét the Wily Fawn (not the linsey Jesse), the best H D the Recording Angel and Richard Aldington, the best Eliot I or II or possibly III, the

best Fletcher To Hell with Whores (line 21), the best Kreymborg
Neighbors, the best Vachel Buffaloes, the best Amy her Communication to you or me (and by the way I hear there is a
British-started story going round that I shortened her life by not
liking her Keats. I think someone must have got me mixed up with
you), the best Edna Saint I (the rest are pretty bad except for line 8
in V and stanza 2 in VII), the best Ransome (as far as I've got)
Thinking Drinking, the best Robinson Gardiner Maine, the best
Sandburg Star Monkey (because when we stopped some one in a car
to ask him what he meant by crowding us into the ditch he promptly
answered "Oh ho yah hi yi yippy lulu the meaning was five six seven
five six seven"—just like that), the best Sara Teasdale On the South
Downs and There Will Be Stars, the best Jean (and I trust you are
being good to her) Bitter Bread and Midnight, the best you
Disenchantment and the Poetry Contest in Kansas, the best me The
Minor Bird and The Night Light. All of which is to prove to you
that though a poet I do read other people's poetry only I don't do it
as poet but as teacher of literature in Amherst, Michigan, and such
like places.

Honestly I hope you folks aren't going to pull anything
boneheaded. It will be a poor advertisement of my philosophy if it
won't keep my most intimate friends from getting unmarried. Think
how any foolishness on your part is going to involve me and cut out
the cheap talk. That is what I say unto you both.

We are enjoying a descent of bears upon this region. If we
survive it there should be much to tell. They are as thick as
caterpillars in a pest year. If you never hear from me again you will
know that I have probably been killed by a bear hunter for the
bounty on bears which is large enough to be worth taking any risk
for. $5. A baby bear was knocked on the head in our Tamarack. Six
of the Fobes sheep have been eaten. A mother and two cubs went up
the road by our house the other evening tearing down the small
cherry trees along the wall. You could see where one of the cubs had
wiped his bottom on a large stone and left traces of a diet of choke
cherries and blueberries. I almost got one cornered in our pasture last
night, but he lifted the wire and went under the fence. It is terrible.

Ever yours

Robert Frost

1926

[The 1925 Miscellany of American Poetry contained new poems by
the loosely affiliated group which had now grown to seventeen.
Robert's comments need a little amplification. What he called Conrad Aiken's "Arachne" was a grimly symbolic poem entitled "The
Wedding." William Rose Benét's "Wily Fawn" was "The Fawn
in the Snow"—Benét had recently married Elinor Wylie, who was
also represented in the collection. "Not the linsey Jesse" is a double
pun: "linsey" because, like linsey-woolsey, "Jesse James" was a
ballad made of common or coarse cloth; and also because its bois-
terous tone was like Vachel Lindsay's. "Let Zeus Record" by H.D.
(Hilda Doolittle) gave Robert the opportunity to speak lightly of
the Recording Angel and Richard Aldington, from whom she had
been divorced. One of T.S. Eliot's "Three Dream Songs" became
an integral part of "The Hollow Men." John Gould Fletcher's
major contribution was a turgid narrative, "Lazarus," but the poem
to which Robert refers was "Painted Women." Alfred Kreymborg's
"Neighbors" was one of "Seven Movements" devoted to birds.
"The best" Vachel Lindsay was his unusually short "The Flower-
Fed Buffaloes." "A Communication" by Amy Lowell was an ironic
gesture which, in spite of Robert's sly dig, was not addressed to
either him or me. Edna St. Vincent Millay, who had contributed to
the preceding volume eight of her finest sonnets, including the now
famous "What's this of death, from you who never will die?" "What
lips my lips have kissed, and where, and why," and "Euclid alone has
looked on Beauty bare," chose to be represented by a set of six childish but not really childlike verses, "From a Very Little Sphinx." John
Crowe Ransom had a generous representation: twenty poems which,
two years later, were the basis of his book Two Gentlemen in Bonds.
The poem of E.A. Robinson which struck Robert hardest and which
he characterized as Gardiner, Maine (where Robinson lived as a
child), was the controversial sonnet "New England." "Monkey of
Stars" was one of Carl Sandburg's wild mixtures of casual mysticism and quirky nonsense. The other references are self-explana-
tory.]

Ann Arbor   Mich.
February 11   1926

Dear Louis

We have been East two whole months with a sick Marjorie and
are now divided over her, Elinor having stayed on to take care of her

and I having come to Ann Arbor to make some show of teaching a little for my year's pay. I'm sad enough about Marj, but I am more busted up than sad. All this sickness and scatteration of the family is our fault and not our misfortune or I wouldn't admit it. It's a result and a judgement on us. We ought to have gone back farming years ago or we ought to have stayed farming when we knew we were well off.

I put my own discombobulation first to lead up unnoticably to yours. I've heard things about you that sound like suffering. And I must see you. I'm no authority on trouble for all the success you ascribe to me in settling Joseph Warren Beach's troubles in the day of them. I'm just your plain friend in favor of the unmelodramatic status quo. Not for me to argue anything where I don't know. I just want to hear you talk.

But I don't want my seeing you here or hereafter to have to depend on any arrangements I can make with an agent. Please no agents between us. You assign a day or two to visiting me on your way back and fix it up now with your agent yourself. Tell him you want such and such a date left blank in honor of me. It will make him respect me and wonder who I am that can be taken time out for so regardless of expense. I will do my best to have got you a lecture here and you can pass him his rake-off. But I don't want to bind myself to anything as I stand with the community at this moment from having rather pleasantly over-stayed my leave (as tacitly understood.) And I don't want to lose you in the machinery of your profession. Rather I would you had remained a jeweller to the poor than that you should get so platform proud as to be undealable with except through the heartlessness of agency.

I ain't foolin. The letters and forms of agents go entirely against my school of poetry. In many a college and town I have been told in so many words of the wonderful form that has to be filled out before you can meet the author of the latest life of Lincoln. It flatters me to have a few great men entirely offhand with me. I like to think I have got where they are.

J.W. really seems to have been serious in that marriage. I made up my mind he should be as serious as lay in me to make him! He rather played it on me the day he used me for a chaperone to sit in his Ford car for respectability while he stole off in whatever takes the place of alders in Minnesota. I could see he thought it was funny to

be so romantic at my expense. So to be equally funny and romantic at
his I went straight on from that moment, and inside of two days had
him sewed up in marriage for the rest of his life. I bought 'em
the only champaign I ever blew anyone to either epi or prothalamial.
I wanted to know who the laugh was on last. Really I'm glad now
if it was on no one. But you mustn't play lascivious tricks on me for a
literary man. I help hasten the consequences. One practical joke
deserves another. Of course mine was the more serious of the two. I
can be rather unthinking. One of my faults is a love of the excitement
of putting a thing through—or a person.

Propose me now some dates—please.

Ever yours
Robert Frost

*[Although there were no favorites among the Frost children,
Marjorie, the youngest and frailest, touched her parents most. Two
of the six children had died in infancy—there was a tubercular
strain in the family—and Marjorie was their greatest worry.*

*It was unfortunate that at this time I added my marital troubles to
Robert's cares. As Robert indicates in the preceding letter, he was
helpful in the romantic affairs of a well-known teacher at the University of Minnesota. I turned to Robert more for understanding
than for help. A protracted lecture trip in the midwest served as an
excuse to get away for a while; acceding to Robert's request, my
agent did not interpose when I went to Ann Arbor for a public
appearance as well as for the much-needed private talks.]*

[March 14, 1926]

A Drury for your Morton. And mind you I never even heard of
him before. I can't make out his name. Probably head-master of the
young aristocrats up there. I told him it was all very rush-me-off-my-
feet and friendly but it arose from a misunderstanding. It was very
likely my Phi Beta Kappa poem of 1916 come home to roost. But
that wasn't really a lapse into laureatism. It was no poem written for
the occasion. I'm a good fellow and all that, but I can't be seduced
by any such limited flattery as this. Thicker says I. Thicker. I'd
like to see my virtue really tried for once.

Louis, Louis. Don't talk to me about forgiveness. I'm not Peter
Rhadamanthus. I've simply felt my natural sorrow that two such

good friends of mine as you and Jean should be winding up your affairs. As I said before, I wish I could see you for a day. It couldn't do you any harm. I wouldn't even try to ground you in my philosophy and religion. I'm long since past my confidence in meddling. All my meddling but once has been more or less in the comic spirit anyway.

Say something expansive to all the Coxes for me. Tell Sidney to teach 'em up.

Be good according to your lights. (A man is as good as his lights I heard a butcher say).

Ever yours
R. F.

["A Drury for your Morton." Robert is pitting the headmaster of St. Paul's in Concord, New Hampshire, against the poet-pedagogue David Morton. Drury was distinguished as an essayist and greatly admired by those who came in contact with him.

The mention of the Coxes is another matter. Sidney Cox had been a good friend to Robert for years. They had met when Cox was in his early twenties, and Robert, in his late thirties, was teaching in Plymouth, New Hampshire. Their friendship grew when Cox became Professor of English at Dartmouth, and the ties were cemented when, in 1929, Cox printed his appreciation, Robert Frost: Original "Ordinary Man." A more psychological study of the poet, A Swinger of Birches, was published posthumously in 1957, eight years after Cox's death.]

[Ann Arbor, Mich.
May 3, 1926]

Dear Louis

Progressive in love, politics and religion, reactionary in education. You had to be reactionary in something to be human. I have given some minutes of my life to helping get the textbook where it couldn't be told from a book for a gentleman's library. I've lived to see some pretty good specimens of the advanced textbook, stripped to the bare text, freed entirely of "busy work" improvement-play and teachers' machinery. I accept school just as I accept the sonnet form or any other social convention: only it seems to be in me to want to make the school as un-schoollike as possible. I should like the books carried away from it not to have any dreary ma'amish connotations that would destine them to the attic or the second hand dealer's dump. But let not God consider me. I know damn well the subtle ways he turns and passes and turns again. All that can be said when my best friend and one of the best minds minding starts on the back track is that the laugh is at my expense. Teaching will be teaching after I have done my prettiest to translate it to an Elysian Academe. I don't pretend not to be a fool. Teaching is not really where I live anyway, come to think of it. So no wonder I am amused by the contretemps of your arriving at textbooks just when I was leaving them. I conclude that things like that don't matter between us—nor does anything else in a friendship dating back to Baxters high perched house in Malden and the Blaney dinner party on Beacon Hill in May 1915. Beseech you no trepidation before me. Go somewhere else to tremble if tremble you must about anything on earth. For all I know textbooks illustrated or unillustrated may be one of the best illustrations of my favorite truths that we keep coming back and back to. I've written about 'em.

It's a brilliant book, as I may say who have read everything in it but the list of teachers on your side. I don't know that I would have the least reservation about it if it could be contemptuously sold to teachers as an example of what everyone of them ought to be expected to do for himself but can't do, the poor fish.

Something in the first number of the unreactionary Masses made me notice your omission of Carmelite Jeffers. What is it about this bird? I keep hearing that the mightiest (Robinson and the Van Dorens) have fallen for him.

It is fine to be in a position to help the young comers like Laing and Schacht.

The Discoverer is one of the best poems you ever discovered.

You remember what I thought of Humbert Wolfe.

No Eliot, Gibson, Moody, Abercrombie. Oh well.

But I wish you might have kept Ridgely in.

You're not coming to lecture was a great blow to me. I counted on you to make it up to them for all I haven't done this year. It has been awful. And next year I expect to be anywhere. (In brackets confidentally I have my portfolio packed light to light out. I said I was going farming, and I'll be as good as my word. Meet me by moonlight five weeks from tonight in Vermont. I have a rendezvous with life.) To a mob of Whimsies who clamored about our house I explained that if lecturing had been all, but it was the combination of lecturing and being lectured that had kept you away. They mustn't blame you or me too much either. But, seriously, I needed you.

Other ratiocinations orally when we encounter. Gee I have just had an invoice of wisdom I'll bet you would give anything to get the benefit of before I have lost confidence in it by trying it on anybody else. I took it on a bad debt that has been owing me ever since I was in the hen and pullet business in Derry.

Tadpoles is always a good poem. And so is The One-hoss Shay. There's a laster and another laster. Happened to notice them.

I came within an ace of going to near Philadelphia to live last month. What?

There was a talk on philosophy that haired me up considerably here lately.

Carol is planting cultivated blueberries. Marj is very slow about getting up. Elinor takes her very much to heart.

Affectionately

R.

Did Cox tell you the state-wide trouble he was in? I hope he gets to Dartmouth.

[*Robert's twitting me about making a textbook (in the foregoing letter) was justified. Although Modern American Poetry and Modern British Poetry were used in the classroom, they were designed for pleasurable reading rather than for dubious teaching. I had never deliberately gone about the business of preparing a textbook until, prodded by my publisher and aided by various teachers, I published Yesterday and Today in 1926. Subtitled "A Comparative Anthology," it was divided into two parts, the nineteenth and the twentieth centuries, to emphasize contrasts as well as similarities in form, subject matter, style, and spirit. I agreed with Robert that poetry could not be taught but only "caught"; yet I convinced myself that a textbook which did not look like a textbook might persuade young people that poetry was made more for enjoyment than for study, and that they might want to keep it for their own when they were finished with high school.*

In spite of Robert's praise, the book turned out to be a compromise between the fresh and the overfamiliar, between the experimental and the little known. I had, for example, included Eliot,

Jeffers, and Abercrombie in the first draft, but I weakly yielded to the teachers' insistence that (in 1926) these poets presented too many hazards to the high-school sophomores who found even the most traditional poetry difficult.

As to the other particulars in Robert's letter: Alexander Laing and Marshall Schacht had just graduated from college and had been featured in Dartmouth Verse. "The Discoverer" was written by Nathalia Crane when she was twelve years old. Humbert Wolfe, the English poet who died in 1940, was a Deputy Secretary of the Ministry of Labor—he called himself "a most uncivil Civil servant" —a puckish essayist who was also a pungent lyricist. Besides being a poet and playwright of distinction, Ridgely Torrence was the poetry editor of the New Republic. "Tadpoles" was my overlong fantasy "Boy and Tadpoles."]

[Ann Arbor, Mich.
May 17, 1926]

Dear Louis:

Some of what you must have taken for ironies were the flattest simplicities. I really insist on nothing in education. My own preference any day would be a book like your Singing World for a textbook. (It happened to be lying where Marjorie had left it on the sofa when I sat down to read your letter.) The beautiful bare text for me. Teachers who don't know what to do with it, let them perish and lose their jobs. I don't allow for the existence of teachers who depend on "teachers' helps." But I dunnow! There are more people on earth than are provided for in my philosophy—latitudinarian though I try to be. I am willing to let you judge for me. So I said and I meant it. If there are teachers in quantity who need your help you must help them. Only do it as little as you can and withdrawingly so as to throw them finally on their own resources like the Philippine Islands when they shall be fit for independence (you know our national promise.)

I'll tell you what you could do to please me the next time. Where notes and suggestions for study (teachers' helps) seem inevitable you could offer them by word of preface as the merest samples of what the teachers are expected to get up for themselves. Of course there is matter for remark in poems. Nobody denies that. But it must be solemnly laid on everybody in this world to make his own observations and remarks. That's what we mean by thinking, and that's about all we mean. A teacher says to a pupil "Watch me notice a few things in the next few months: let's see you notice a few things too." But the teacher's observation must be genuinely his own. A little, if it is his own, will induce more mental action in his pupils than a great deal supplied him by you—you old wholesaler.

By the way "banter" struck me as one of the best words ever used to explain me.

We'll meet then soon.

It's shaping up apparently for me to earn my living by a couple of weeks at each of two or three colleges next year and be left free to settle down on the farm I was threatening to buy the last time I saw you in Pittsfield. Oh, you don't know how I'm spoiling for a place to do anything I like to the trees on. I haven't put the least bit of interest into my duties here. I've practically done nothing for anyone and I feel like an ingrate.

Ever yours

R.F.

[South Shaftsbury, Vt.
November 25, 1926]

Dear Louis:

This will be my eighth attempt on you since last we met: from which you may judge how hard you have made it for us, my old. The thing of it was to so word myself that by no shade of meaning I could be suspected of wanting to influence your decision.* Whatever you did at a time like this, it mustn't be the least bit for me. Of course this is only somewhat and not altogether like changing mounts at the halfway house. It is not the same matter of indifference to your friends and I won't say it is. Ladies aren't horses any more than cabbages are watches. You yourself didn't make the change without a pang of regret for the girl left behind. It's no fun being cast off. You saw that. In fact you showed a capacity all through for sustained suffering worthy of a Russian novelist. Let's chalk it up to

*[The decision concerned my separation and divorce from Jean and my marriage to Virginia Moore.]

184

your credit—to the credit of the whole human race—that you
didn't find you could do this invidious thing to Jean without turning
a hair. Nor will you blame us if we couldn't watch you do it without
turning a hair. Our pang of regret was of course less than yours,
but so also were our consolations and compensations infinitely less.
We hadn't the physical incentives [to] go ahead at all costs. We
weren't in the illusion of the flesh. It was an awkward moment and
we had to be careful not to speak discordantly. I can say all this now
when it is safely too late to do either good or harm. You see I keep off
the merits of the case entirely. Come right down to it, my theme is
nothing more nor less than my own selfish embarrassment in the
affair. But if you and Jean don't care enough to be dissociated in Art
and the Miscellany, I don't see why I should care.

I have been getting down on life lately for one reason or another.
The bread I cast upon the waters seems all coming home to roost at
once. My philosophy staggers in the breach. But what though my
button does lack a shirt—never you mind, roll on!*

About my part in Art and the Miscellany:† I'm in the middle of
sprinkling a bare handful right now over the magazines to pay for
Irma's marriage into the deserts of Kansas. There's one that has in
it a farmer saying

> "A sigh for every so many breath
> And for every so many sigh a death.
> That's what I always tell my wife
> Is the multiplication table of life."

I wish you could have that. But you can't—it's sold.

I'm in favor of The Flower Boat, too. I wish we could get the
original version from The Youth's Companion. My memory of the
last stanza is a little shaky. My list would be Lodged, The Flower
Boat and The Birthplace. Maybe I can spare the one act play in one
New England dialect. I mean The Cow's in the Corn. But let me

---

*[A burlesque of W. S. Gilbert's "To the Terrestrial Globe" ("Roll on, thou ball,
roll on"), which was a burlesque of Byron's "Roll on, thou deep and dark blue ocean,
roll!"]
†[The fourth volume of A Miscellany of American Poetry (1927), which, alpha-
betically arranged, began with Léonie Adams and ended with Elinor Wylie, contained Robert's "Sand Dunes," "The Flower-Boat," rescued from his youth, "The
Passing Glimpse," "Lodged," and "The Birthplace," which differs slightly from the
version sent with this letter.]

sell it if I can. I am short and discouraged. I must write you out
Lodged and The Birthplace. I enclose 'em.

Yours ever

Robert

South Shaftsbury Vermont
November 25   1926

LODGED

The rain to the wind said:
"You push and I'll pelt!"
They so smote the garden bed
That the flowers actually knelt,
And lay lodged—though not dead.
I know how the flowers felt.

R. F.

THE BIRTHPLACE

Here further up the mountain slope
Than there was ever any hope,
My father built beside a spring,
Strung chains of rock round everything,
Subdued the growth of earth to grass,
And brought our various lives to pass.
A dozen girls and boys we were.
The mountain seemed to like the stir,
And made of us a little while—
With always something in her smile.
Today she wouldn't know our name.
(No girl's of course has stayed the same.)
The mountain pushed us off her knees;
And now her lap is full of trees.

R. F.

[South Shaftsbury,   Vt.
May 3,   1927]

Dear Louis
    Jean assumes to ask for you both* if we have thrown you over.
Hell no. I was afraid my silence would begin to be misunderstood. If

*Seems funny for Jean to be asking for you. How much married to
you does she think she is? Women are too much for me.

1927

I was more silent with the pen than usual it was because I could think
of nothing adequate to say: I was willing to leave consolation and
advice to the author of the author of Elmer Gantry, I mean Alfred the
Sloganist.* You would have only to call on him to comfort you with
slogans and he would touch your various stops as skillfully as if you
were the public and he were just what he is. Can't I just hear him
inspiring what I see by the papers you have been free to say on the
subject of faith in life. Honestly it sounds like office talk. Om Mani
Padmi Hum. Which is to say the lotus flower has a center that means
something. So has Eugene O'Neill's Great God Brown to anybody
who prides himself on living in New York. Come to me if you want to
hear some small part of the truth. You are not bad except in the sense
that I am bad and a lot of others are bad. Don't mistake me as implying
there is no such thing as goodness anymore. You will hear it claimed
that esthetics is all there is of ethics. Nothing could be worse thinking,
as I could explain to you in full if I had time. There is such a thing as
badness. But as I say you are not bad. You are only in Dutch. You
haven't been prospered. I'm sorry for that, and you hold my sympathy
just so long as you keep from delivering in obiter dicta to the news-
mongers. Don't don't say things like that about faith in life where I can
come across them because they simply bust me all up in the seat of
philosophy. You are not responsible I know in the circumstances and
I wouldn't want you to be responsible. I should think less of you
if you were responsible. Only if you love me for Christ's sake
find some more poetic way of going irresponsible than in dub
sophistries. I'm hard on you—too hard. But you've got to stand this
and more from me. I wish we could meet somewhere by ourselves
for a twenty-four hour talk. It would have to be outside of New York.
How about Albany? I may not know much about God and man, but
by the hocus pocus I begin to think I know more about you than you
do yourself. You're the only person I ever said as much to. On
general principles I refuse to set up as an authority on other people.
I am no missionary. You may have noticed I gave you no advice when
you were in Ann Arbor. Perhaps I should have given you advice.
There's where I may have failed you. I've boasted lately in my teaching
relation with boys that I played neither the psychoanalyst nor the
confessor. I've kept at the level of polite conversation. But I don't
know, about my motives. How do I know that I haven't kept from

*[Alfred Harcourt.]

187

meddling for the real pleasure I take in seeing humanity go blameless to Hell.

Oh G! thinking of it all in these ways brings the woe all back in waves over me.

Still I'm yours

R.

I'd have you here if it weren't for Marj. And after all I'd like to be alone with you for a day.

[South Shaftsbury, Vt.
June 22, 1928]

Dear Louis:

I've read the book* more than I've read most books even by you. It's a good book, at its best in such things as Variations on a Childs Game and Jewish Lullaby, and in such other things as Disenchantment, Positano, and Critique of Pure Rhyme. How the accents bring you back. If hearing were all, the book would be enough. But it seems as if I must see you somewhere soon again either in Europe or America. Are you coming home right away or are you going to wait in Europe till I can look you up there when we get over in August (as we should if our purpose holds.)

If I haven't written in a long time, I suppose it is because I haven't found anything very easy to say. My spirit barely moves in letter writing anyway under its burden of laziness and disinclination. The least addition of sorrow or confusion to my load and I stop altogether. That's an amusing one you call Words Words Words. For a cent I would subscribe to the sentiment. The logic of everything lands you outside of it: the logic of poetry outside of poetry (I needn't tell you how); the logic of religion by nice gradations outside of Catholicism in Protestantism, outside of Protestantism in agnosticism, and finally outside of agnosticism in Watsonian behaviorism: the logic of love, outside of love (if it were only by physical exhaustion); the logic of strife, in China. But what leaves the heart in the mystery

*[*Burning Bush*, which was published when I was living in Europe.]

and the sting in death is the fact that when you have eliminated yourself by logic as clear out as Eenie meenie minne moe, then you are as good as in again. Which is one of several things that has led great men to suspect time and space and motion (however directed) and thought, of being vicious circles—vicious. We are what we are by elimination and by deflection from the straight line. Life is a fight we say and deify the prizefighter. We could go further and say life is a night-club and its presiding deity a <u>retired</u> prizefighter or Bouncer, bouncing us forever out.

I was arrested at your Koheleth. You and I think we know each other pretty well. But I wonder if you ever realize (I never did before) that a good way to distinguish between our natures would be in the way you have and I haven't searched in books and out of books for rooted convictions. The only time I ever wish I had convictions is when I am asked for the loan of them. I'm afraid all I see in books and going round is ideas to emulate—to try if I can't have the like of. The only thing that can disappoint me in the head is my own failure to learn to make metaphor. My ambition has been to have it said of me: He made a few connections. Sounds fearfully humble—the aspiration of mere craftsmanship. Never mind. It's fun to give the show away. My head may be second-rate. But I wasn't bidden to have a heart in vain. If my mind isn't bent on convictions, my heart seems set on a few human beings. Not many, but that makes my position all the more perilous. Friends and convictions—what's the difference? One ought to go in for neither or both.

It does me good to be where I can talk nonsense to you again. Some film has gone off my mind.

Always yours

R.

South Shaftsbury Vermont U S A
June 21   1928

SPEAKING OF METAPHOR

In going from room to room in the dark,
I reached out blindly to save my fall,
But neglected to close my arms in an arc.
The old door got inside my guard

And hit me a blow in the head so hard
I got my basic metaphor jarred.
All things still pair in metaphor
But not with the mates they had before.
I hardly know the world any more.

R.

[After a two-year struggle with love and conscience I was divorced from Virginia and remarried Jean. Trying to readjust myself to the old life in a new environment, I adopted two children, moved away from New York City, and bought a one-hundred-and-sixty-acre farm in the Adirondack mountains, not far from Robert's place in Vermont across Lake Champlain. The nearness was to be invaluable later on; but during the first summer, when I needed him badly, he, his wife, Elinor, and his daughter Marjorie were abroad. It gave me a mean satisfaction to learn that he did not enjoy his nostalgic sojourn in England—the man who had been his best friend over there, Edward Thomas, had died in battle; his other associates were scattered— and he definitely disliked Paris. Before the end of the year the Frosts were back in South Shaftsbury.]

Georgian House
Bury St.
London S.W.1*
October 11   1928

Dear Louis

Irma mentions your just having looked in on Carol at South Shaftsbury Vermont on your way to a farm of your own in the Adirondacs. And I was thinking of you and Jean as buried deep in the Black Forest of Germany. In fact I had written you a letter there that probably came too late, but even so may reach you by forwarding to America sooner than this. It was one of my sad mocking letters (with a picture of me by Watteau in it) and won't do you any good if you read it more than once. So disregard it and listen to me now saying seriously:

How much better if you had been a staid orthodox Jew and never

*We are going back to Paris for the first week of November. Address American Express 11 Rue Scribe Paris.

had run wild after a super-wisdom that doesn't exist. You are back
now where you started from and not one bit improved in mind or
spirit. The whole experiment has been a waste of time and energy.
You haven't found out anything that you didn't know before, that
we didn't all know before: and I won't listen to you if you say you
have. That's the one thing I can't stand from a person in your
predicament. For my sake, if you still care for me, don't talk about
having been chastened or having profited in any way. You've lost—
time, if nothing else. I've lost. We've all lost. Having admitted that,
let's say no more on the subject. I'd impose it as a penalty on you that
you shouldn't wax literary on what you have been through—turn it
to account in any way. I won't if you won't. It must be kept away
down under the surface where the great griefs belong. I don't mean
you must stop writing, but you must confine yourself to everything
else in the world but your own personal experience. I beg of you.
Honestly. The thought would be too much for me of all three of you
putting up a holler in verse about it all. The decencies forbid you
should score off it. Write a court drama of the IVth Dynasty. I
should think this was the point where you have almost got to leave off
being a subjective poet. That is if you care of me.

I'm coming back in a few weeks now and the first thing I'll do will
be to look you up for a good talk—not about the past but about the
future. Gee, it has been hideous—like going round and round you
with a gun trying to shoot an animal at your throat on top of you,
but not daring to put a shot in for fear of killing you. You had people
like Alfred who knew what to say to you. I didn't know what to say
then and I hardly do now. I think you and Jean on a farm most of the
time would be a good idea. But you ought to work hard outdoors and
in to keep from talking. I wish I knew a subject to assign you for a
book, and one for Jean too—a real labor like a Benét-Robinson-
Henderson epic—but it needn't be as heavy as that—though heavy.

I'd have struck off to see you in the Black Forest—only only only.
There was Marj, none too well. I couldn't have her too much
disturbed in the mind. I was in no position to act. Things are looking
up for us a little now. Marj seems not unhappy with the Fischbachers
at Sevres. And Elinor gains a little as she cheers up. Both she and
Marj have been in a serious condition.

I impose penalties. I'd almost like to prescribe a remedy. Thought
on in these bookish ways our lives go everywhichway. Don't look into

books to see yourself reflected. Avoid the mirror of books. Be as ordinary as you can till I can get there. This is first aid in the emergency. But you don't know what I'm talking about. I'll tell you when I come.

Ever yours

Robert

Midhurst
Hucclecote
Gloucester, England
[October 24, 1928]

Dear Louis:

I've been thinking my fastest about you lately with some renewal of hope to overtake your affairs as they begin to slow down. I almost feel at this moment as if I were abreast of you. Probably I'm not, but let me state you as I seem to have you now. By the time you get this letter very likely you'll have scooted like a rocket and left me as far behind as the eighteenth century. Experience ought to have taught me to be careful what I say about your women from a distance that gives too much time for things to happen before my letter reaches you. It takes courage to talk about relationships that are changing as fast as yours.

My judgment on you is that you have wronged yourself in all this business of alternating between two wives. You have been acting against your nature under pressure of the bad smart talk you have listened to and learned to share in in the society you have cultivated in your own New York salons (so to call them.) I've heard the mocking when I have been there and heard you lend yourself to it till I was ready to bet what would happen. None of it was right or wise or real. What I dread most now is that you will go on the assumption that, though it was folly and landed you in tragedy, it was on the way somewhere and somehow prepared you for greater and fuller life. Shut up. To hell with such comforts. It was all time and energy lost, as I have said before.

You have merely talked yourself out of your senses. I refuse to admit you were ravished out of your senses. You talked yourself out of them in your own parlor. For I heard you. Now you are yourself again by sheer weight of the honesty in your bones. Talk no more—unless you can talk unclever, unsophisticated, simple goodness. You tempt me to soak you in milk to renew your innocence. The funny positions people can talk themselves into in a lifetime of try-it-on talk.

Someone you know said to me in drink the other day:

Dyou blieve im marriage? Afer miwife died I got mix tup with a woman wanted me tmarry her. Ver attractive woman y understan. Had a child by her. Wouldn't marry her. Didn't want to. Think I ought to marry her?

Does she still want you to?

Shdoes—innaway. D you think ought to have married her before?

Has it caused her much pain—your not marrying her?

Sidible.

Well we have to consider whether decent marriage isn't a provision of the ages for causing the least possible pain between the sexes. The least possible is all I say.

Shwants to marry someone elsenow.

I thought you said she wanted to marry you.

Shwants to marry me first. Then get divorce n marry nother man.

I don't understand yet.

Marry me make tall reglar. Xplain it to him sos she won't have tell him. Thinks he'll like it better.

Wants you to marry her for his sake.

S bout it.

Louis Louis very few people that leave the good old folkways can keep from getting all mixed up in the mind. We can make raids and excursions into the wild, but it has to be from well kept strongholds. I think you think so now. Let's drop the whole subject.

Always yours

Robertus

South Shaftsbury   Vt.

January 6   1929

Dear Louis:

I didn't half see you in New York. I'm still sad and unsatisfied about you. I stick to it that talk does no good. It isn't talking with you I feel the need of but just being round with you till the present obliterates the past. Nothing I said down there had finality.

Nothing was a solution for you. You had no idea I thought it was.
It's lucky you haven't been seeing me or hearing from me the last
two years or you would have had as many false solutions as I have had
phases. I can't help seeking a solution for anybody in your
predicament. But it's just as well I shouldn't be where I could propose
every solution I think of. I mean I shouldn't be encouraged or allowed
to propose everyone. I don't believe in myself as a problem-solver.
Honestly. Though I can't help thinking at this moment that if Jean
only had the self-respect to act out in good faith her independence
of you you might, left to your own freedom of movement, find that
she was the only girl you wanted to live with. She drains you insensible
with her desperate demands on you. I told her that. I ought not to
be telling it to you: it might make the remedy less effective for you
to know about it. But never mind: nothing I say matters in a situation
that I thought in the first place was none of my business and have
now pretty well proved to have been none of my business. I'd just like
to see you adopting four children to run your Adirondack farm with.
But you wouldn't gratify me that much. You'd be afraid you were
amusing me.

Well, to hell with nearly everything—with everything but poetry,
politics, and true religion—and a few friends and relatives—a very few.
And I forgot farming. I bought a farm for myself for Christmas. One
hundred and fifty three acres in all, fifty in woods. The house a
poor little cottage of five rooms, two ordinary fireplaces, and one large
kitchen fireplace all in one central chimney as it was in the beginning.
The central chimney is the best part of it—that and the woods. You
mustn't be jealous, though jealousy is a passion I approve of and
attribute to angels. May I be guarded and watched over always by the
jealousy of a strong nature. It is better than arms around the body.
Jealousy alone gives me the sense of being held. My farm probably
doesn't compare with yours for view. But it looks away to the
north so that you would know you were in the mountains. We have
no trout brook, but there is a live spring that I am told should be made
into a trout pond. There is a small grove of white paper birches
doubling daylight. The woods are a little too far from the house. I
must bring them nearer by the power of music like Amphion or
Orpheus. It is an old occupation with me. The trees have learned that
they have to come where I play them to. I enjoy the power I find I

have over them. You must see us together, the trees dancing obedience to the poet (so called). You'll exclaim.

I ain't going to mention books this time.

Ever yours

Robert Frost

[South Shaftsbury, Vt.

August 12, 1929]

Dear Louis:

My farm is fast going back to wilderness—as fast as can be expected, the doctor and nurse would say. How is your farm? I ask out of politeness more than any real interest. My farm has got a considerable start of the cows in its pasture trees. Give it a year or two more unpastured and I doubt if it will ever be overtaken. Seventy-five years from now it will show a sugar bush to match yours. You wait! You are younger than I am, so I leave it to you to do the waiting. Meanwhile you ought to have to see all the H—L hinges there are in our farm house. In those we XL. In those we superiorate. Our barns are coming down little by little, a board at a time as the mood comes over Wade our poet in labour—at, I mean. And as the barns come down the view comes out. Our trickle (as compared with your torrent) has held its own through the drought with pristine vitality. Some are in favor of calling the farm The Trickle. Marjorie wants it called Nine Barns in memory of the barns it once had. But Prescott* has become accustomed to The Gully, and one hates to undeceive a child.

We're to meet then on and around the 27th. I had difficulty in fixing on a date because I hate to face eventualities at this time of year.

I'll have to write you out a copy of The Egg and the Machine: I have no one to type for me.

Lankes† is over at the Gully camping out. But I am afraid we are not giving him just the company he wants in Wade Van Dore.‡

---

*[Prescott, christened William Prescott after his grandfather and great-grandfather, was the son of Carol and Lillian La Batt Frost.]
†[J. J. Lankes, engraver, made many woodcuts for Robert's poems, including those in the limited edition of New Hampshire.]
‡[Wade Van Dore, one of Robert's "boys," was a sort of disciple who, at that time, earned his keep as Robert's part-time hired man.]

Wade has a good deal of the Wobbly* in him. He is burly, but he has a principled objection to work and the courage and ingenuity to dodge it. Lankes has a family of four to work for and Wade's emancipation rouses his wrath and jealousy. Also I'm afraid my moderate interest in Wade rouses his jealousy. It ought not to. My interest in Lankes is such a very different thing. Lankes is a wood-cutter and no mistake. Poor Wade has his place all to make. He is a strange boy. His mother tells us that his obediently doing what he is asked to do throws him into long cataleptic sleeps afterward. I gather that his verse comes out of some such sleeps. He says nothing about such things. I gather from watching him. He will go back to Kashabowie, his settlement north of Superior, in the fall and I shall have less to worry about.

Ever yours
Robert Frost

THE EGG AND THE MACHINE

He gave the solid rail a hateful kick.
From far away there came an answering tick;
And then another tick. He knew the code:
His hate had roused an engine up the road.
He wished when he had had the track alone
He had attacked it with a club or stone
And bent some rail wide open like a switch
So as to wreck the engine in the ditch.
Too late, though, now to throw it down the bank.
Its click was rising to a nearer clank.
Here it came breasting like a horse in skirts!
(He stood well back for fear of scalding squirts.)
Then for a moment there was only size,
Confusion, and a roar that drowned the cries
He raised against the gods in the machine.
Then once again the sand-bank lay serene.
The traveler's eye picked up a turtle trail,
Between the dotted feet a streak of tail,
And followed to where he made out vague,

*[Wobbly: a member of the Industrial Workers of the World (I.W.W.), sometimes used as a term of derision, as of a tramp.]

But certain signs of buried turtle egg;
And probing with one finger not too rough,
He found suspicious sand, and sure enough
The pocket of a little turtle mine.
If there was one egg in it, there were nine,
Torpedo-like, with shell of gritty leather
All packed in sand to wait the trump together.
"You'd better not disturb me any more,"
He told the distance. "I am armed for war.
The next machine that has the power to pass
Will get this plasm in its goggle glass."

Robert Lee Frost

[One of Robert's friends, James Wells, had as his hobby The Slide Mountain Press. In 1929, for its second publication, Robert let Wells print ninety-one copies of a comic poem which does not appear in any of the Frost volumes. He gave it a nursery-rhyme title, The Cow's in the Corn, and Wells entered into the joking spirit of the thing by presenting it in an elaborate format; the few short lines were spread over sixteen deckle-edged pages. An entire page was devoted to "characters in the play": Mrs. O'Toole and Mr. O'Toole. This note is Robert's title-page dedication, and the "play," including rhymed stage directions and introduction, follows.]

To Louis Untermeyer who can be safely trusted to discover for himself everything of beauty in this book except the fact that the paper used for it was made in Spain in the year 1720

This, my sole contribution to the Celtic Drama (no one so unromantic as not to have made at least one) illustrates the latter day tendency of all drama to become smaller and smaller and to be acted in smaller and smaller theatres to smaller and smaller audiences.

R.F.

A kitchen. Afternoon. Through all O'Toole
Behind an open paper reads Home Rule.
His wife irons clothes. She bears the family load.
A shout is heard from someone on the road.

Mrs. O'Toole.
Johnny, hear that? The cow is in the corn!

                    Mr. O'Toole.
I hear you say it.

                    Mrs. O'Toole.
Well then if you do
Why don't you go and drive her in the barn?

                    Mr. O'Toole.
I'm waiting; give me time.

                    Mrs. O'Toole.
Waiting, says you!
Waiting for what, God keep you always poor!
The cow is in the corn, I say again.

                    Mr. O'Toole.
Whose corn's she in?

                    Mrs. O'Toole.
Our own, you may be sure.

                    Mr. O'Toole.
Go drive her into someone else's then!

She lifts her flat iron at him. To escape her
He slightly elevates the open paper.
The cow's heard mooing through the window (right).
For curtain let the scene stay on till night.

                                    [South Shaftsbury,   Vt.
                                     June 5,   1930]

Dear Louis:
    I'd just like to know the man that wrote some of the pages in King
Mob. I wonder if I do. Come ahead and tell me.* He certainly
swings his metaphysics like not many we have, as where he says, all
so easy-like, the only mental thing in the whole universe that isn't an
analogy is a formula. It doesn't matter that he doesn't come out
anywhere. That would be to take sides for or against rain. We must

*[King Mob bore the name of Frank K. Notch, an obvious pseudonym which
amused Robert, whose home in New Hampshire had faced the Franconia Notch.
The author was Maurice Samuel, the brilliant journalist and novelist, born in
Rumania, whose adult life was divided between the United States and Israel.]

go into these questions when we meet this summer—don't count on it to be at Breadloaf.

Spank Joseph† one for me and don't run the risk of erring on the wrong side.

Ever yours
Robert Frost

Glengulch* South Shaftsbury Vermont
Elinor says say exactly when you three and the nurse are coming to visit us after June 25. This is serious or getting to be.

*Glen is Scotch, gulch is Californian.

[*Now that we were living near each other visits grew more frequent and, in consequence, letters were exchanged less regularly. Nevertheless, there was always something to be settled that had not been said. As the next letter indicates, Robert regarded Edwin Arlington Robinson with admiration tempered by many reservations. His introduction to Robinson's posthumous King Jasper is an almost perfect example of appreciation and critical balance. Although he and I differed sharply about the portrait of Shakespeare in "Ben Jonson Entertains a Man from Stratford," we agreed that Robinson's Arthurian cycle, and particularly his Tristram, which had been widely circulated by one of the leading book clubs, was a tortured analytical rewriting of Tennyson's limp Idylls of the King.*

(George) Roy Elliott, mentioned toward the end of the letter, George F. Whicher, and Otto Manthey-Zorn were Robert's closest friends on the Amherst faculty.]

[South Shaftsbury, Vt.
June 6, 1930]

Dear Louis

I am just starting to write letters again, letters or anything else, after a long sickness of public life; and my first halting letter shall be to you. I hardly know my own handwriting. I hardly know myself seated at a desk. Where have I been the last six months in abeyance? But where was I the eighteen years just preceding—the years I mean from

†[One of my adopted sons.]

H

1912 to 1930? In no very real dream. The book of all I ever wrote, when it comes out this fall, ought to do something toward accounting to me for those false years. But I have seen it in proof and it looked like no child of mine. I stared at it unloving. And I wonder what next. I don't want to raise sheep; I don't want to keep cows; I don't want to be called a farmer. Robinson spoiled farming for me when by doubting my farm he implied a greater claim on my part to being a farmer than I had ever made. The whole damn thing became disgusting in his romantic mouth. How utterly romantic the ener- vated old soak is. The way he thinks of poets in the Browningese of "Ben Jonson"! the way he thinks of cucolding lovers and cucold husbands in "Tristram"! Literary conventions! I feel as if I had been somewhere on hot air like a fire-balloon. Not with him altogether. I haven't more than half read him since "The Town Down the River." I simply couldn't lend a whole ear to all that Arthurian twaddle twiddled over after the Victorians. A poet is a person who thinks there is something special about a poet and about his loving one unattain- able woman. You'll usually find he takes the physical out on whores. I am defining a romantic poet—and there is no other kind. An unromantic poet is a self-contradiction like the democratic aristocrat that reads the Atlantic Monthly. Ink, mink, pepper, stink, I, am, out! I am not a poet. What am I then? Not a farmer—never was—never said I was. I've stayed your friend through several vicissitudes. A friend is something to be. Roy Elliot, the Humanist professional, asked me if I had written anything since I came home in April. Me! Write anything in two months! It used to take me ten years to write anything. And now that I have found myself out for an unromantic and so have no incentive, it should take me not less than twice as long.

Ever yours
Robert Frost

[In 1921, with Professor Wilfred Davison of Middlebury College as Dean and supported by the President-elect of Middlebury, Dr. Paul D. Moody, Robert became an active participant in the Bread Loaf School of English, located twelve miles up the mountain from the town of Middlebury on the College's mountain campus. In 1926, the Bread Loaf Writers' Conference was initiated by the publisher,

John Farrar, at Robert's suggestion. I came over from Elizabethtown in the Adirondack Mountains to join Robert, and, for many summers, was one of the "faculty" at Bread Loaf, Vermont.

Because of a real or fancied slight to Lesley, Robert had quarreled with Farrar. He referred to the Conference, to which inexperienced or frustrated writers came hoping to find a publisher, as the "Two Weeks Manuscript Sales Fair," and said that as a forum it was more like pig farming: a "Farrow session." Later Robert joined in the supplementary activities and became the tutelary god of Bread Loaf; but, at the time, he was scornful about "putting new limbs on crippled manuscripts so they could walk straight into the editorial rooms of The Atlantic Monthly."]

[South Shaftsbury, Vt.
July 14, 1930]

Dear Louis:

I am left out of the Two Weeks Manuscript Sales Fair as I had reason to suppose I would be. I thought perhaps it would be less embarrassing all round if I simply forgot to go to the earlier educational session at Bread Loaf. But I have been come after by Pres. Moody and flatteringly written after by our friend Gay to be present and help them dedicate the Memorial Library to Wilfred Davison on Monday July 21st. Pres. Moody said frankly that he saw no way but for the second session to go on commercial as it had begun. I judge he thought the two sessions could be kept like the right and left hand each from knowing what the other was doing. He asked me to think of the two as separate. They can't be separate, of course, and in the end belonging to one will mean belonging to both. But I don't care if it does in the end. This year can make no difference in principle, and I hate to put on airs that will hurt either Moody's feelings or Gay's. I agreed to go on the understanding that they would give you your choice of sessions. I knew you said you came a good deal to be there when I was. But of course we are going to see each other here right off anyway, and maybe it would be too ostentatious for you to desert the Farrow session because I was left out of it. You may be sure I don't mind your being with that gang for a visit if only as a spy and agent provocateur. You can't imagine how cleanly I have forgiven the Johnnie. The explanation is that I am at heart secretly tickled if I offended him unintentionally. I suppose it to have been unintentionally, because to this hour I don't know what my offense was. I am too cowardly to offend anybody intentionally and usually too skillfull to do it unintentionally. So I am stuck. I can't hurt anybody no matter how much he deserves it. When I do it is a triumph of the divinity that shapes our ends. It gives me a funny feeling I must say I like. I suppose it's a manly feeling, but I'm such a stranger to it I hardly know. Yes I came off so well with the Johnnie that I shan't care if you do treat him as if nothing had ever happened. I even evened the score between him and Lesley.

Another barn got out of the way last week. We'll be almost ready for you when you get here on the 26th. Remember comparisons are odious as between farms. King's X.

You are so afraid to cut wood at home I shall have to give you a chance to cut some here. I'll try you on the other end of the cross-cut saw with me. And may the best man faint from sheer sympathy with the live wood.

I heard from Raymond Holden for the first time in five years. And in the same mail I had a letter of another of our youngsters, Joseph Anthony, commending to my mercy (pronounced Marcy in the Adirondacks) a rhymed book of his called Casanova Jones. Have you seen it? What are you going to say to such indifferent nonsense from a boy you like? Accuse it of hypercleverness? But would that be honest?

Raymond wants to know if I have changed. Yes, I tell him as it happens within the month, into a conscientious answerer of every letter I get.

To show you how high life goes at our post office. At one time we had two countesses getting male there. One of them was Millicent Rogers, but she was only a countess by marriage and she undid herself by marrying an Argentinian and going to South America. The other one was seen loading a couple of boxes of loud-peeping day-old chickens into the back of her car the other day. That explained her. Plainly that's where she got her title, counting chickens before and after they were hatched.

Ever yours
Robert Frost

I haven't seen a newspaper since I started writing letters. I haven't heard a bit of news. I have recovered my pristine innocence in no time.

[North Bennington, Vt.
July 20, 1930]

Dear Louis

Here's this book back at once so it shan't get lost. And my! what a piece of ready writing. Elinor and I both read it with admiration for the way you hold a new book off at its distance for judgement. Genevieve Taggard did awfully well, all things considered, but it is exactly as you say about her. She doesn't make a case out for her man, and she would have had more fun in making it out that there was no man at all. In my biography I have it that Madam Martha was Emily's neither legitimate nor illegitimate child, parthenogenetic by the composite imago of all the men it might have been. Enough of this pretty soon.

I have read a good deal of your higher guide book and enjoyed reading it without the help of having been to the Black Forest. It may prove the last straw and break me of my habit of not going to Germany. I mean this. You make it all sound like just what I need in my present state of mind. I'd like to go and write a book in one of the corners you tell of. And I may yet.

If I don't see you at Middlebury no matter: you'll be here right away where we'll have each other's undivided attention. We'll talk Longfellow and Emerson. Longfellow was a true poet for anyone with the ears to judge poetry by ear. His size—well I haven't bothered to size him up yet any more than I have a lot of lyric people. Just go and listen to that passage about the Jew in the Prelude to one of the books. Emerson was great. Great great great. I wonder what kind of a book Michaud has written about him.

Till I hear you go into second coming up our hill.

Robert

South Shaftsbury   Vt

July 20   1930

["This book," which, in the previous letter, Robert damned with a faint stigma as "a piece of ready writing," was Genevieve Taggard's The Life and Mind of Emily Dickinson. *With a great deal of poetry and little plausibility, the author set out to prove that two men had been involved "in some very vital way with Emily's existence": Leonard Humphrey, her "beloved teacher," who died when she was twenty; and George Gould, frowned upon by her father who forbade*

meetings with her suitor, for whom she presumably renounced love and became a recluse. *Eight years later, in* This Was a Poet, *George F. Whicher, Robert's friend and Amherst colleague, was the first to cut through the obfuscations of the Emily Dickinson "mystery."*

"Madam Martha," one of Emily Dickinson's later editors, who regarded the poet as her exclusive property, was her niece, Martha Dickinson Bianchi.

The "higher guide book" mentioned in the second paragraph was my Blue Rhine=Black Forest, *a rambling account of a walking trip in Germany.*

Robert never wavered in his devotion to Longfellow, particularly as a story-telling lyricist, and to Emerson, not only for what he said but, even more, for the way he said it. Régis Michaud's book was Emerson: The Enraptured Yankee. *Like Carlyle, Michaud maintained that " 'The Conduct of Life' was Emerson's most important work," distilling the Emersonian essence of "life, transition, expansion, the spirit in full energy."]*

Franconia   N.H.
Sept. 6   1930

Dear Louis

I found your letter waiting for me when we got here tuckered at the end of the month. This is the latest we ever fled the plague since we began to be flees, in 1906 to be historic. One sickness and another in the family kept us till I could have cried out with the romantics that no artist should have a family. I could have, if the idea hadn't been so stale and unoriginal. I have been thinking about art lately (not with a capital A but with a capital F) and the conclusion I have reached is that it is the bodiless child of a perversion not necessarily but preferably major, such as embracery or godamee, but at least not getting married or not having children if married. Art is nothing but to get ashore out of the stream of animal perpetuations. It is systematically to get some fun out of sex without having to work for it. Hell, yes that must be so, so many fools seem to think so. If there's an idea that lends itself to facile spieling in our day equally well with that of evolution it is that of detachment (sic—R!)

About the preface to your book of earlier Ams. I very much want to read it. But I may as well wait till our visit which we want to make

you in a week or two—on the 18th to be exact. Elinor is inclined to think Jean is right about your property in the book. I should only be invading you if I came in. We see rosily, they really. That is why woman in our hours of need (uncertain coy and hard to please) should, even more than the dog or horse, be looked on as the Friend of Man. I'm serious about the book's being yours. You can consult with me and when I don't advise you wrong I'll advise you right about Poe Longfellow Bryant and Emerson, those four and no more. You'll have to go it alone on Lowell Whittier Drake Dana Freneau Wigglesworth Barlow Pierrepont and the rest. A lot of them were ladies then as a lot are now. I wonder if it wouldn't be found at any given time that most of the contemporary fit to go into an anthology was feminine. The girls keep it up and every now and then a boy whoops it up. Who wrote:

> I am a pebble and yield to none
> Were the vaunting words of a tiny stone.

<u>Ans</u>: Ought I to know? Wouldn't it, I mean, damage me more with the examiner to know than not to know. <u>Rerejoinder</u>: It certainly would with Thomas Edison.

I ought to say I should like to help with the selections from my big four. I should make no bones of cutting poems down to my taste. I just came on another poem Palgrave carved out of a longer one. It was one of Patmore's, "The sheep bell tolleth curfew time." Harriet Monroe rewrites living poets. Why shouldn't we dead poets?

Ever yours
Robert Frost

[The second paragraph of the preceding letter refers to a collection published in 1931, American Poetry from the Beginning to Whitman. Since Robert had instigated the idea more than a decade earlier, I had hoped to have him as a collaborator; we had made a tentative table of contents together. But, as indicated, he felt that his role should be limited to acting merely as consultant. As an adviser he was invaluable; he rediscovered forgotten poems and pointed out new values in his favorites. When the book appeared, it carried a dedication: "For Robert Frost, who prompted it on a mountain-farm in New Hampshire and who furnished the final cues on an Adirondack hillside twelve years later."]

[*In the 1920's I had become acquainted with Burges Johnson. A teacher at Vassar, Union, and other Eastern colleges, he was also a writer of light verse who, in 1931, compiled a New Rhyming Dictionary and Poets' Handbook. Johnson was particularly fond of parody, bouts-rimés, and other rhyming games. From time to time he planned "projects" to show what a series of arbitrarily rhymed words might suggest to different poets. In 1930 he asked me to make a sonnet preserving the order of the following words: "whole," "sweet," "greet," "goal," "roll," "feet," "neat," "soul," "sleep," "pass," "know," "deep," "alas," "go." Johnson also hoped that Robert would contribute to his "laboratory experiment."*

I don't know what happened to my example of word-juggling; I think I took it at least half seriously. But although Robert willingly complied, he burlesqued the whole idea. In his most puckish vein, he composed a piece of sober-sounding nonsense, twisting the words into double meanings and punning them into absurdity. The lines, with their comic transpositions, came in the letter of October 1, 1930.]

TROUBLE RHYMING

It sort of put my spirits in the	whole
When my Scotch friend from the adjoining	sweet
Came bursting in on us with "Greet, oh	greet!
Someone's been locked in a Chicago	goal (tr?)
Not just for robbing Croesus of his	roll,
But for inditing verse in rhymes and	feet.
No wonder Truslow Adams says we're	neat;
But if we're cattle we are not the	soul—
There's others capable of such a	sleep,
As the French say in English, or fox	pass,
As we might say in French, but ah, it's	know
Excuse for us that others sin as	deep.
A man, and not a pusil, not	alas,
I take my share of shame for Chica	go.

R.F.

[South Shaftsbury, Vt.
October 1, 1930]

Dear Mr. Untermeyer:

You wouldn't remember, but I met you shaking hands once in the West. Something shaky in your manner emboldens me to submit to your judgment my first sonnet for ages. May I leave it to you to say on this showing whether you think I ought to write any more for a while? I want you to take the entire responsibility for my future. I'll do as much for you sometime. I may say the sonnet is original except for the rhymes which were supplied in the set all set up by an agency in York State.

Sincerely yours
Robert Frost

Ps. I was formerly poet Laureate of Vermont, but they chucked me for cause.

R.F.

[During the early summer of 1931, I asked Robert to help me decide which of his poems should represent him in The Book of Living Verse: English and American Poetry from the Thirteenth Century to the Present Day and should also be added to a revised and amplified edition of Modern American Poetry. The request came at a bad time. The family was separated, attacked by serious illnesses, and riddled with worries. Lesley was hospitalized on Long Island. Marjorie, the youngest, had been forced to go to Colorado when tuberculosis, as had been feared, put a stop to her nursing studies at the Johns Hopkins Hospital. Lillian, Carol's wife, had also contracted tuberculosis; and Irma, whose young husband was away studying architecture, was suffering from spells of extreme nervousness. Nevertheless, Robert, aided by his wife, Elinor, found time to put down two lists of poems, the lyrics, and the monologues before he left for the West.]

Montauk Long Island
June 12   1931

Dear Louis

This is getting momentous. What we decide to put in here will go down to time. We don't want to make any more mistakes in selecting than we have to. Even I know that not all my poems are equally good. Neither are they all equally bad. Some like The Housekeeper are very much worse than others. Don't ask me to go into the terrible details. There are moments when I am overwhelmed under them as if my nature underneath a heap of jarring atoms lay. Jarring atoms is what they disintegrate into. But I mustn't give way

to such talk. It would be bad advertising with anybody but you. And today particularly I am in no mood to estimate myself or anything I ever did. Lesley is at the hospital in Southampton (L.I.) in ineffectual pain and has been for three days now. We don't understand what's the matter. The doctors say nothing's the matter. We'll be convinced of that after everything comes out all right. All our children are an anxiety at once it happens. Marj gains very slowly. Carol's wife (I haven't told you have I?) will have to be taken West for her lungs. Carol must sell his farm just when it is coming into productiveness. The orchards began blooming this year. Irma is on the strain of having a husband at college (John's one of these smart boys that shines in college: so that will probably come out all right). And here is Lesley in trouble too. Elinor just interrupted me to say on the telephone that it is bad but the worst of it is it doesn't get worse.

I hope you three are flourishing. In a day or two I'll write again about the poems. But first tell me a little more about it. How big is it going to be? Is it going to extend considerably beyond the lyrical? I judge so by your proposing some of my blank verse. But instance please.

Ever yours
Robert

[North Bennington, Vt.
July 9, 1931]

Dear Louis

Now for it or, as the lady said when required to swear in court. You ought not to make me, but if I must I must; so here goes Hellity damn! Elinor and I have cooked up a list anyone of which we will take sides with against you if you leave it out. This is the first time I ever helped anthologise myself. Next you'll have me helping you write my reviews. Besides the general list of all the poems we hate and can't bear to see you omit we have made out two trial sets for you to cock your eye at. They are offered as basises for discussion. Leave us talk things over. What do you say to deleting the second stanza of Tree at My Window for the sake of perfection? Does that keep the "head" in the last stanza from ringing as it should? I've always been a shade unsure about what the second stanza did to the poetic logic which is the thing I set above all things in poetry. The two changes in

An Old Man's Winter Night are obvious gains. I don't know where
"fill" crept in. It was originally "keep." "Fill" is a joke with the "heavy
breathing." Elinor and I both think the two best written of the long
ones are The Mountain and The Fear, the four richest in the human
are Snow, The Death of the Hired Man, Home Burial and The Black
Cottage. Respond.

I go to Bread Loaf for my one night tomorrow (Thursday), visit
Lillian at her sanitorium on Friday, and start with Elinor for Marjorie's on Tuesday. We are in many many troubles for the moment, so
many that grief loses its dignity and bursts out laughing. I toughen,
it seems to me. Of course I may be prejudiced in my own favor, but
if I keep on I think I can't be refused a chance for the heavyweight
crown. I have doubled up my fists at several lately that manifestly
didn't want any part of me. The secret of success in these encounters
is not to care for your eyes nose teeth or chin. I've found that out
late in life but not too late. I used to say yes I'm ready to fight, but
I don't want my teeth broken. Well, I was wrong. What reason had
I for not having my teeth broken? There was no reason. We were
brought up on principles of saving everything, ourselves included. The
war taught us a new gospel. My next book is to be called The Right
to Waste. The Right? The duty, the obligation, to waste everything,
time, material, and the man. I've a good mind to tell them so at Bread
Loaf while I am heated on the subject. But would it take root in such
ground and do either good or harm?

Perhaps you had better send your next letter to me in care of
Marjorie Frost, Mesa Vista, Boulder, Colorado.

Steadfastly yours
Robert Frost

Elinor's Choice of Shorter Ones

My November Guest
Storm Fear
Reluctance
Mowing
An Old Man's Winter Night
Birches
Putting in the Seed
Stopping by Woods
To Earthward

Two Look at Two
The Need of Being Versed in Country Things
Spring Pools
Tree at My Window
A Soldier
On Looking up by Chance at the Constellations

Mine Supplementary to Hers

The Tuft of Flowers
The Pasture
Hyla Brook
The Oven Bird
The Star in a Stone-boat
The Onset
Dust of Snow
Nothing Gold Can Stay
The Aim Was Song
The Runaway
Acquainted with the Night
Out Out

Elinor and I agree that the chief long ones are The Mountain, The Death of the Hired Man, The Fear, Home Burial, and Snow.

Suggested Set No. 1

My November Guest
Stopping by Woods on a Snowy Evening
Tree at My Window (1st, 3rd, & 4th stanzas) ("For" for "And.")
An Old Man's Winter Night ("need" for "what it was") ("keep" for "fill")
To Earthward, Star in a Stone-boat, or Two Look at Two
Snow, Home Burial, The Fear, The Mountain, or The Death of the Hired Man.

Suggested Set No. 2

Mowing
Stopping by Woods on a Snowy Evening
The Pasture
Tree at My Window (1st, 3rd, & 4th.)
Birches, The Star in a Stone-boat, or Two Look at Two
The Mountain, or Snow

[In July Robert and Elinor were in Boulder, Colorado, where Marjorie was being treated. They took her on a botanizing and picnicking trip to Evergreen, and, during his stay in the West, Robert defrayed some of the expenses by accepting lecture engagements through an agent he both disliked and distrusted. Meanwhile, Marjorie, who was writing poetry of delicate distinction, was helping Robert make the final choice of his poems to be added to those already appearing in the anthology The Book of Living Verse.

The "Ferris" about whom he inquired was Thomas Hornsby Ferril, a Denver journalist, editor, and poet, whose first book, High Passage, was published in 1926. Robert came to admire Ferril's combination of sharp regionalism and broad Americanism. A firm friendship, unbroken by distance, ensued; Ferril was one of the few recipients of a rhymed tribute from Robert:

> A man is as tall as his height
> Plus the height of his home town.
> I know a Denverite
> Who, measured from sea to crown,
> Is one mile five-foot-ten,
> And he swings a commensurate pen.

Robert's resentment of being managed ("I suppose lecturing for any agent is roughing it.") led him to abandon lecture bureaus of any kind, but it did not inhibit his pleasure in lecturing. He had overcome the nervousness preliminary to mounting the platform. Feeling his way through a talk until it assumed the shape of an essay, he could not help enjoying the rapprochement and the response with which audiences enjoyed him. His remarks between the reading of his poems were peppered with epigrams. Some of them found their way into poems; some of them came from fragments of midnight conversations—he was at his voluble best after 11:00 P.M. Others were suggested by letters he had been writing. Here are a few:

I am not an escapist; on the contrary, I am a pursuitist. I would rather cast an idea by implication than cast a ballot.

I am also a separatist. You can't mix things properly until you have separated them, unscrambled them from their original chaotic mixture and held them separate long enough to test their qualities and values.

Sometimes it strikes me that the writers of free verse got their idea from incorrect proof pages.

*I am against all the isms as being merely ideas in and out of favor.
The latest ideologies are formidable equations that resolve themselves into nothing more startling than that nothing equals nothing.*

*Louis Untermeyer could be run down by an automobile and then
write a poem as the ambulance bore him off. He writes with his
coat-tails flying.*

*There are three ages of man: first, when he learns to let go with his
hands; second, when he learns to let go with his heart; third, when
he learns to let go with his head. (This, rephrased in poetry, was the
climactic thought in "Wild Grapes.")]*

[Evergreen, Col.
August 1, 1931]

Dear Louis:

I am up here 8000 feet high, gasping for oxygen, my walk slow
and vague as in a world of unreality. Anything I say feels as if someone
else said it. I'm told it's not my heart but the size of my lungs that's
to blame. I always was a short distance runner even in my best days.
I did one hundred yards in eleven seconds, but hare and hounds was
an agony.

We came here to give Marj a vacation from the sanitorium. We're
having a fine time all to ourselves in spite of the uneases of altitude.
(Marj and I are the sufferers as it turns out, though Elinor was the
only one we feared for beforehand.) I clumb some of the nearer dirt
hills for the activity I need, leaving the rocky peaks and cliffs till I
renew my youth. I'm botanizing all over in an almost entirely
different flora. Up one ravine today there were masses of larkspur and
monkshood. It's a very flowery country. I'm a little too late for much
of it. I've just missed the yellow lady's slipper that seems as common
here as the pink slipper at home. Isn't it strange for me to be living
away off like this. Three weeks ago I was settled for a month but as
if forever in the sand-dunes of extreme Montauk. Such lengths our
children drag us to. I'm glad none of the family are foreign mission-
aries or we should be snatched back and forward very likely from
continent to continent instead of as now from state to state. I don't
care if God doesn't care.

Who is this Ferris poet in Denver? Is he one of your prospects?
He seems a pleasant boy. But I don't like Fisher the entrepreneur.

If I have to make a really western tour, someone will have to recommend a better agent than that man. I suppose lecturing for any agent is roughing it. I had a real run in with Fisher. I let him have me interviewed for his publicity twice on arrival, once in the station and once in a newspaper office, a place where in all my years of reading to people I have never gone for anything. On top of that I had to stand a lot of loud anxiety from him about his getting a big enough audience. Damn him. I was against his trying for one in the summer anyway. To hell with him for a bad sport. I can't think he lost much by the size of the crowd I saw in front of me. But I could wish he had. There was nothing handsome about his style. I shouldn't have got into this. I took the Colorado University thing weakly to pay our fare and then one thing led to another. Fisher has been soliciting me for a year or two. I was inclined to let him manage me for a California swing-round. He did himself out of a cool thousand by his inconsiderateness of my age and dignity.

I, we all, go back to Boulder next Wednesday for my talks to the summer school. I may live to be sorry I got into those. Sometimes I do well and then again I get too tired from the strain leading up to a performance. I mustn't complain of how Fisher manages me: I don't manage myself very well. I don't care if God doesn't care.

Elinor and Marj take your side about the second stanza in Tree at My Window. They say I can't leave it out. All I say is never show any version of a poem to your friends and relatives unless you are absolutely sure it is final.

All right then the list is

1. An Old Man's Winter Night
2. My November Guest (complete)
3. Stopping by Woods
4. Tree at My Window
6. Home Burial

And if you possibly can make (I hate to have it left out)

5. To Earthward.

I've numbered them in the order that would please me most. It is your selection with Elinor, Marj, and Me concurring. I'm willing

to stand or fall by it. Sometimes I almost cry I am afraid I am such a
bad poet. But tonight I don't care if God doesn't care.

Our best to you all three.

Ever yours
Robert Lee

Address ℅ Marjorie Frost
Mesa Vista
Boulder Colorado
July 28 1931

*[In the matter of "children and children's children" (first paragraph
of the next letter), Robert had become a grandfather when a boy was
born to Carol and Lillian.*

*As for the telescope, Robert had always had, so to speak, an eye
for one; in "The Star-splitter" he wrote affectionately about a man
who*

> *... burned his house down for the fire insurance*
> *And spent the proceeds on a telescope*
> *To satisfy a life-long curiosity*
> *About our place among the infinities.*

It made me happy to satisfy Robert's own curiosity.]

[South Shaftsbury, Vt.
September 23, 1931]

Dear Louis:

I'm back from settling the Rockies and Sierras with my children
and children's children or rather child. So as for that telescope, let'er
come. She will fill a life-long want, as you have reason to know from
having gone shopping with me for one once and witnessed my
heartbreak when we failed to find what you thought I could afford.
You more than anything else kept me from one then, whether from
too much sympathy with my family or too little sympathy with
me (at least on my scientific side). It is only poetic justice that you
should stand me one now so late in life. I will have it right here in
South Shaftsbury please. And let the most modest stars be prepared to
be looked right at. Frankly I had been getting near-sighted of late,
especially when it came to the N.Y. Telephone Directory, and I had

been thinking of going to the expense of a pair of pinch-noses, but how much better a monocle such as this you have thought up for me. With it I should be able to see you as a farmer. I mean I should be able farming in the Green Mts to see you farming in the Adirondacks. As a farmer I should be able to see you as a farmer. With a child on each knee ventriloquizing out of alternate corners of your mouth for both of them. My love to them, the poor little dears. I don't know what possessed me to take them in vain thus in our elderly affairs.

Before I forget it, I hope you won't leave Smart's Song of David wholly out of your book, nor Curran's "If sadly thinking with spirits sinking would more than drinking my cares compose—." Smart's is the only splendid poem in a century of wit. Curran is the fine old pre-Sin Fein Irish style that few will listen to now. I saw a poem by an American girl (Davies I believe her name was) that seemed to me one of those rarities that you get now and then from a nobody in particular, just as you did in the anonymous ballad days. It began "I sing of sorrow, I sing of weeping. I have no sorrow."* I wish you could have a look at it.

Ever yours
R.F.

Say isn't the Gerard Hopkins figment a caution to us who would be original. That book with all its notes is a mental exercise.

[South Shaftsbury, Vt.
October 26, 1931]

Dear Louis:
> The telescope has come and I am charmed.
> I don't see how on earth I ever farmed
> A day without a tool so all important.

---

*[The poem, written about 1917 by Mary Carolyn Davies, was one of a small set of lyrics entitled *A Girl's Songs*. The lines that Robert liked were called "Borrower" and ran:

I sing of sorrow,	From some .tomorrow
I sing of weeping.	Where it lies sleeping,
I have no sorrow.	Enough of sorrow
I only borrow	To sing of weeping.]

I have to tell you though (perhaps I oughtn't)
That come to get the barrel up and pointed
I can't see Hoover as the Lord's annointed;
I can't see E.A. Robinson's last book—
As yet—I'll have to have another look.
At first I couldn't even see the moon.
And that now just because there wasn't one;
There was, according to the almanac.
One whole night I was pretty well set back.
Perhaps the object glass demanded dusting
Or the small lenses needed readjusting;
Perhaps as in the picture I'm inclosing*
Some question of the day was interposing
Between me sinful and my hope of heaven.
But never mind, I didn't blaspheme even.
I had one of the two things Shakespeare wanted most.
Write on my tombstone for post-mortem boast:
I had—I had the other fellow's scope.
I need nobody else's art, I hope.†

P.S.   It will take another and entirely separate letter to tell you
how much more to me than much scope was the dedication of your
able book. I'm particularly proud of your handling of Longfellow
and Emerson, not mine a bit—all yours. Sometime I want to see you
do a small book (say four or five lectures long) on Our Predecessors
Now, or Our Past in our Present. And I liked the Yale Review poem
best of any lately. So did Cross; he told me when I saw him last week.

                                                                R.F.

*[The innermost part of the next letter—and a hard core it is—takes
off from James Truslow Adams' historical view of rebellion and the
frontier spirit and develops into Robert's speculations on the reasons*

*[The "picture" was a cartoon clipped from a newspaper. It showed a badly frightened
World staring through a telescope. The telescope was labeled "The Future" and the
object at the other end was marked "Soviet Russia." The cartoon was captioned
"Obscuring the View."]
†[Robert's telescopic pun derives from a line in Shakespeare's sonnet beginning,
"When in disgrace with fortune and men's eyes." The line is:

            Desiring this man's art, and that man's scope, ...

The playful couplets have never been printed.]

for America's lawlessness. Before this, however, Robert reinforces my decision to reject a poem by one of Percy Mackaye's daughters. Mackaye, poet and playwright, had sent it by way of Sara Teasdale, with a suggestion that Robert might also approve of it; moreover he implied that, since it was written by a young person, it might be a fitting conclusion to The Book of Living Verse, which was ready to go to the printer. As indicated, all three of us—Robert, Sara, and I—were embarrassed, but, though the return resulted in strained relations, the poem was (with obviously awkward and evasive excuses) declined.

The last paragraph refers to Vachel Lindsay's tragic death. He had committed suicide on December 5, 1931, a fortnight before the letter was written.]

[Bennington, Vt.
December 19, 1931]

Dear Louis:

I hope you got an uninfluenced judgment from Sara. I shall feel better justified and so will you in delivering the blow it must be to the Mackayes. The poem was fairly good, but was too generous and impulsive a choice for so deliberate a book. I can put myself in the Mackayes' place. Everything down-trodden in their nature will rise to cry robbery at being done out of an honor already within their grasp. Beware their fury. But you have the practiced bravery of a regular and don't even have to summons the heroic to face your duty. (I'm glad it's yours, not mine.) The poem would never have done for your tail-piece anyway. It would have been the only poem a lot of people would have read in the whole book—accustomed as they are from their novel-reading to look first and find out how a book comes out. You can see I must have a bad conscience in the business— I talk so much. I suppose at bottom, away down in my heart, I am incurably sceptical about anything being accepted or rejected on its merits. If anyone doesn't like anything of mine I am sure from of old, it is because he hasn't met me or because I haven't liked something of his, for every reason but a purely critical. Such am I after fifty-six years spent in arbitrariness among the arbitrary. Let him that is without stone among you cast the first thing he can lay his hands on. If I have praise I don't deserve, I say nothing and accept it to compensate for having had blame I don't deserve. I even go further in my optimism: if I have praise I don't deserve I say nothing and

accept it to compensate for someone's else having had blame he
doesn't deserve. Thus injustice cancels injustice and our pleasure is
unalloyed in this easy winter weather while it lasts.

I read what you said about Mrs. Todd's letters of Emily with
admiration for your acuteness. You are at the height of your powers
and ready for the next step beyond the splendid introductions to the
poets of your American Poetry before Whitman. Not for me to say
too definitely what it will be, but surely some sort of original
interpretations of a few of your favorite great ones of any and all
times. How someone is to be understood, and if not so understood
how he will be wholly missed. You have the individuality to consult
for an original impression. You have the language and the strength of
will to have it your own way. You have the scholar in you not to go
off in generalizations at half-cock. You know you are unfolding
into a scholarship you have no right to, not having "been to college."
One thing to say for James Truslow Adams (my mild aversion for
the moment) : he is a better scholar because a livelier, a less
deadened by school, than any of the academics. He has the freedom
of the realm as you never get it in the teacher-taught. He has come to
learning as you come to the table, not the conference round table,
but the dinner table. You could show him the way in the historical
literary. He is better than the hack Freudian explanator.

> Of course we all have a policeman,
> But what we want's a release-man.

That bunk fadeth. But listen to him explaining our lawlessness.
He, no longer trading on Freud, no longer ascribes it to Puritanism
bursting through its age-long repressions. He gives someone credit for
the better idea that it is a lingering frontierism. But he says that is
only partly it. He says we are worse than the other frontiersmen, the
Canadian and the Australian. It must be because, as everyone
knows, we were provoked into lawlessness by British ill-treatment of
colonies before we taught the British good treatment of colonies.
The Canadians and Australians came later and profited by what we
taught the British. Not so original. He trades on the commonplace
assumption of history that the British or anyone else have treated
latter day colonies better for the American revolution. Has Ireland
liked the way she was ruled? Has India? Australia would have gone to

war if strong enough to stop England's using it as a penal colony. Ireland has gone to war. India is going. The dictum is too unoriginal, too unexamined, to base another on. Let's have a try at it ourselves since trials are free and the free mind is known by the way it makes them always fresh. We are lawless because, in theory and largely in practice, we are all of the upper class which has in all times been above the law of marriage, life, and property. Our society is a truncated cone. We cut the point off and little points broke out all over the resultant plateau. We are like a lot of hens that start crowing and treading each other because there are no roosters in the barnyard. Gee I have run on. All of this is just to indicate the realm I think of you as disporting yourself in. Only you'll be better grounded than Adams and I. You have an awful solidity in literature—in all the arts. And you have an American mind, for which reason I am the more yours ever

Robert Frost

Adams has a would-be British mind like a bad Rhodes scholar.

Addendum

Woe is me for Vachel. I feel more as if I had lost a child (with all sorts of foolish little ways) than a brother and fellow-artist. It comes near me. Memento mori, the church says. I do. I will now more and more anyway. To the young death is what it is to Poe, macabre. Someone in a poem he sent to me lately calls it tender. It is subduing.

[Amherst, Mass.
February 23, 1932]

Dear Louis:

Jean writes that where e'er you may roam you worry about me. You should. I'll tell you what we'll do: I'll worry about my family; you worry about me; and let Hoover worry about you. Concerning you are all Hoover's expressions of hope and fear—concerning you and the proletariat you represent or used to when you were an editor of the Masses. Me and mine are below the threshold of legislative cognizance. Beyond participation of politicians and beyond relief of senates lie our sorrows: if any of the farm bloc (heads) chance to heave a sigh, they pity us and not our grief. And the chiefest of our sorrows is that the world should go as it does—that thus all moves and that this is the justice that on earth we find. What justice? Do I have to tell you? Why injustice, which we either have to turn on the other fellow with a laugh when it is called comedy or we have to take like a spear-point in both hands to our breast when it is called tragedy. Laugh no more, gentles, laugh no more. For it is almost too hard for anything to succeed in being divine, though Lionel Johnson sware the opposite. But let what will be be. I am so deeply smitten through my helm that I am almost sad to see infants young any more. I expect to look backward and see the last tail light on the last car. But I shall be going the other way on foot.

Yet I refuse to match sorrows with anyone else, because just the moment I start the comparison I see that I have nothing yet as terrible as it might be. A few of our children are sick or their spouses are and one of them has a spouse still in college. I and my wife are not well, neither are we young: but we mean to be both better and younger for company's sake. That is to say we mean well, though we aren't well.

I thought I'd just lay it on lugubrious this letter. I saw and heard what you said about me in Springfield, but it didn't cure my evil mood because it threw me into a superstitious fear that you would incur for me the jealousy of gods and men. I shall have to tell you some day just how great I can allow you to say I am—that is if Elinor will allow me to set you a limit. (But she says now if you don't go to extremes for me she will.) The gods I am afraid of are your God of Israel, who admits he is a jealous god, and Edna's goddess Venus, who can't deny the love she stands for is a 99 per cent adultery of jealousy. Never mind the names of the men I am afraid of. Now don't for goodness sakes ever take me at my word and incontinently give up praising me altogether.

I admire yours. The book is full of your new-found country answer to the questioning dark—bright answer. What a bright delightful poem that is you fear you stole a shred of from me. You didn't steal anything to mention. Your whole next book is adumbrated in that one poem both its humor and its matter. Or I'm a liar.

I seem slowly to be getting over what I imagined was the matter with me.

Ever yours

Robert

Say, if you're any where in Harriet Moody's neighborhood ask her about her domestic science book will you?

["For it is almost too hard for anything to succeed in being divine, although Lionel Johnson sware the opposite." The reference is to Lionel Johnson's "The Dark Angel," particularly to the stanza:

> *Do what thou wilt, thou shalt not so,*
> *Dark Angel! triumph over me:*
> *Lonely, unto the Lone I go;*
> *Divine, to the Divinity.*

The book to which Robert refers is my Food and Drink, which had just appeared; it contained "Last Words Before Winter," which, in spite of Robert's disclaimer ("You didn't steal anything to mention.") was an Adirondack echo of his New Hampshire "Good-by and Keep Cold."

Harriet Moody, widow of William Vaughn Moody, the Indiana poet and playwright, had become the manager of a large and successful catering establishment in Chicago.

"Edna's goddess Venus" refers to the love poems, lyrics and sonnets, by Edna St. Vincent Millay.]

[Amherst, Mass.
April 8, 1932]

To you, Louis, wherever you are:

Way down in my heart I don't know about your doing that to Robinson.* You and he are old friends. He will suffer if you find it necessary to go back on him too publicly. Your silence about his falling off should be severe enough in the cause of art (which of course must be maintained.) Don't you think so? Jeffers would be my quarry if I were out hunting.

Ever yours

Robert

Amherst still.

*[A projected review of Matthias at the Door, E. A. Robinson's gloomiest and least rewarding study, a book-length narrative poem in which all the characters speak in the same dark, overdeliberate idiom.]

[Although he shuddered whenever some journalist tagged him as "a farmer-poet" and although he never made a profit from any of his farms, Robert never gave up the idea of farming. He hated the "Back-to-the-Soil" cultists who deluded themselves that the country was a guaranteed stimulus for impoverished imaginations, a mental therapy for city-bred sophisticates, and a general panacea for poor health and unhappiness. Yet he quoted Tennyson more or less seriously: "Courage, he said, and pointed toward the land." However, as a shrewd countryman and also as an experienced writer who had to wait a long time to be recognized, he could not help adding this bit of bucolic advice: "Refuse to be rushed to market or forum. Don't come as a product till you have turned yourself under many times."]

[South Shaftsbury, Vt.
May 13, 1932]

Motto:
Courage he said and pointed toward the <u>land.</u> Alfred Lord Tennyson.

Dear Louis:

The land be your strength and refuge. But at the same time I say this so consonant with your own sentiments of the moment, let me utter a word of warning against the land as an affectation. What determines the population of the world is not at all the amount of tillable land it affords: but it is something in the nature of the people themselves that limits the size of the globulate mass they are socially capable of. There is always, there will always be, a lot, many lots of land left out of the system. I dedicate these lots to the stray souls who from incohesiveness feel rarely the need of the forum for their thoughts of the market for their wares and produce. They raise a crop of rye, we'll say. To them it is green manure. They plow it under. They raise a crop of endives in their cellar. They eat it themselves. That is they turn it under. They have an idea. Instead of rushing into print with it, they turn it under to enrich the soil. Out of that idea they have another idea. Still they turn that under. What they finally venture doubtfully to publication with is an idea of an idea of an idea. The land not taken up gives these stay-outers, these loosely connected people, their chance to live to themselves a larger proportion of the time than with the throng. There is no law divine or human against

222

them when you come to think of it. The social tyranny admits of squatters, tramps, gypsies because it can't make itself tight if it wants to. It isn't rebellion I am talking. It isn't even literary and intellectual detachment. It is simply easy ties and slow commerce. Refuse to be rushed to market or forum. Don't come as a product till you have turned yourself under many times. We don't have to be afraid we won't be social enough. Hell, haven't I written all that in my first book? But the point is the unconsidered land makes the life I like possible. Praise be to the unconsidered land. That's all. I haven't got through with the farming yet. When I get these sick children rounded up, we are going to make another big attempt at the almost self-contained farm. Almost. No nonsense. Merely much more self-contained than fools would imagine. I'm in favor of a skin and fences and tariff walls. I'm in favor of reserves and withholdings. I'm in favor of individuals with some age on their time apart. Hams cured in one day. Wine matured a week. The trouble with every-body's purse is everybody is caught out in the big market. The trouble with everybody's mind is everybody is caught out in the big forum. Gee you ought to have seen the document Waldo Frank wanted me to sign. He and Mumford and Wilson got it up. He said follow us and you can be a leader of your generation. They propose to use the class-conscious workers for the time being. I have half a mind to tell the class-conscious workers on them. But always ganging up at Geneva or somewhere else. When all you have to do to be saved is to sneak off to one side and see whether you are any good at anything. Can you cook can you make butter can you write can you think can you shoot can you sleep?

I'll leave the rest of this blank for you to fill out.

Ever yours

Robert

[Bennington, Vt.
May 18, 1932]

Dear Louis:

Internal evidence is that I wrote my last in answer to yours of the 10th enclipping the fence advertisement. Else why so much on the theme of high tariffs and separatism? I was just talking what was on my mind and the aptness was accidental.

I should have said "Sure" to your proposal I have something in the Knopf Leaflets. I should be able to.

What Jean said about Lesley's book was very shrewd considering the distance from which she looks on at a mere detective story. There is writing too good in it for the kind of book. I suppose Lesley knows that but it will do her good to have her own intimations confirmed. You know how Lesley is. I mean you can understand her having to do something reckless and unprecious to take the plunge after all the inhibiting she has undergone from me.

Farm farm for this is also sooth, as Yeats would say. Soothe or soothing.

Ever yours

R.

[The first paragraph of the foregoing letter refers to a clipping I thought would amuse Robert. It was about a prefabricated picket fence, and the advertisement was captioned: "Good fences make good neighbors." Robert had extended the implication in the preceding letter: "I'm in favor of a skin and fences and tariff walls."

In 1929 Robert had contributed a poem ("The Lovely Shall Be Choosers") to a series of de-luxe pamphlets published by Random House. Alfred A. Knopf asked me to organize a similar series of elegantly printed single, hitherto unprinted poems by leading poets. Robert was the first to respond. His "A Lone Striker" was printed in 1933 as one of the Borzoi Chap Books.

Lesley had written a kind of detective story under a pseudonym; Robert regarded it with a mixture of pride and apprehension. His concern about his children was aggravated by his wish to have them educated without subjecting them to formal education. He could never determine how much his strong personality was helping or hindering them. "There is," he said ruefully, "no right way to bring up a child."]

[Boone, Iowa
June 24, 1932]
Aboard the <u>Columbine</u>, Flower of
Travel Comfort

Dear Louis:

Far as I was from you and all your works (farm) when I started last night I am going a mile farther a minute (thirty two telephone

poles by actual count.) I leave home and friends sadly at sixty (or is it
fifty?) and I write letters badly in the lurch of the Columbine.
Anyone sharp enough to discover Archie McLeish's muffled rhymes
in all his archaeology ought to be able to find mine. Columbine
Evaline Clementine! Dandyline! I am bound for where the newspapers grow worse and worse every morning when you wake up and
wonder what is going on over and above the village. But that is no
special privation to me (do you follow my internal rhymes or are they
too occluded now even for you). If I don't like the newspapers I
can spend the day looking out the window at the country I love
wherever samples of it have been taken. You ought to see some time
my latest outbreak into political poetry delivered at Columbia a
month since. I trust you will permit me this new form. You didn't
object to the one I read there some years since, and this is better than
that many many times I'm sure you'll say. I'd quote you some
sentiments from it, only I'd rather you judged it as a whole.

Isn't it too bad we're leaving the pine for the palm. This is my
last summer in absentia. Positively. But consuetude requires that we
should live with the kids where they live. Wherever they ghost I
will ghost, however unreal it makes me feel. Sure; send along the
Elinor Wylie and be thanked, but send it to 261 North Canyon
Boulevard, Monrovia, California (there it is out! I have said it.)
There is no criticism like yours to make me reconciled to my rising
contemptuaries, be they McLeish, Jeffers, Dillon, or Whosis. I hate
not to love a thing like Conquistador, and you make me at least kind
to its imitative (of Anabase) accent. You have to remember the
first poem I ever wrote was a narrative of La Noche Triste at
Tenochtilan. It is hard for me not to be jealous of latecomers in my
field. You poultice the jealousy out of me. I undertake to accept
more or less anything you tell me to with your persuasiveness. I am
going in for the new obscurity by using bad handwriting on a moving
table and asking my printers to use old broken type such as was used
in the edition of Ossian I have had ever since I was fifteen sixteen
seventeen or eighteen. Gee, I feel myself going—to Calif. on the
Chicago and Northwestern. Speak to me.

R. F.

[The summer of 1932 was a difficult one for the Frosts. Robert and
Elinor spent all of it visiting Marjorie, still invalided in Boulder,

Colorado, and in Monrovia, California, where Lillian was now being treated for tuberculosis and Carol, true to the family tradition, was hoping to farm. The new voices and techniques in poetry bothered Robert; he distrusted the departures and dissonances ("muffled rhymes") in Archibald MacLeish's prize-winning Conquistador, which had just been published, and he was reminded that his first poem was on a similar Mexican theme. Alternating with groups of lyrics, he had gone back to the simple but eloquent medium of conversational blank verse in a Socratic dialogue. Voicing his distaste of socialism, "Build Soil," which he called "A Political Pastoral," was delivered at Columbia University on May 31st, shortly before the national party conventions. After the reading he received a Doctorate of Letters degree.

Enclosed in the letter were some gaudy picture postcards advertising the train, the "Columbine" ("Flower of Travel Comfort"), the blossom itself ("Colorado's Beautiful State Flower"), and the Mountain Bluebird, "a favorite among Colorado bird-lovers." There was also a printed poem, part of the railroad's promotional publicity, which ran:

> A dash of the azure of mountain skies;
> The white of eternal snow;
> A tinge of the hidden gold that lies
> Where crystal rivers flow:
>
> The delicate scent of a lovely dream;
> The green of the stately pine;
> A verse in a song of thrilling theme
> Is the mountain Columbine!

To this, R.F. added a comment: "Where have I heard this before? Ans: Last year on the same journey. Allarse!"]

[Monrovia, Cal.
August 20, 1932]

Dear Louis:

This isn't the big dislodger I delivered at Columbia, but a little one back in my old ways to keep you going till I—you—get something else. How—just how great a poem and just how long a poem must you have for the Knopf series? Shall I be allowed to add the greatness to the length, divide by two, and take the quotient for the size?

How will the public take my impudence in charging five dollars for a
book made on that basis? Or aren't we going to charge five dollars?
Is this or is this not a graft? I ask you the foregoing questions.

Yrs.

R.

NOT OF SCHOOL AGE

Around bend after bend,
It was blown woods and no end.
I came to but one house
I made but one friend.

At the one house a child was out
Who drew back at first in doubt,
But spoke to me in a gale
That blew so he had to shout.

His cheek smeared with apple-sand,
A part apple in his hand,
He pointed on up the road
As one having war-command.

A parent, his gentler one,
Looked forth on her small son,
And wondered with me there
What now was being done.

His accent was not good.
But I slowly understood.
Something where I could go—
He couldn't, but I could.

He was too young to go,
Not over four or so.
Well, would I please go to school,
And the big flag they had—you know

The big flag, the red white
And blue flag, the great sight—
He bet it was out today,
And would I see if he was right?

R.F.

Calif.   1932

THE OFFER

I narrow eyes and double night;
But still the flakes in bullet flight
More pointedly than ever smite.
What would they more than have me blink?
What is it? What am I to think—
That hard and dry to hard and dry
They may have said for years?
Am I, are they, or both to melt?
If I supply the sorrow felt,
Will they supply the tears?

R.F.

[Monrovia, Cal.
August 22, 1932]

Dear Louis

I don't want you to think those two poems were an answer to
your letter about being poisoned in the hand. They got away from me
just before your letter came and weren't offered as a charm to cure
you. They'll strike you as untimely I'm afraid, and won't get their
chance.

If you won't think they are for anything but the fun of it I may
send you some more by air mail before we shorten the distance too
much. I have always wanted the chance to fly a few poems. They'll be
little ones, not necessarily ever to be published, especially if they
seem to add nothing to what I have already written. What adds
nothing takes away something, I don't need to be told. You may find
one that will do for the Knopf series. But let's not be thinking too
much about that. The idea is to utilize for poetry the most modern of
modern conveniences the Motor Kite. We can call the set "Air Mail—
flown to L. Untermeyer." We better not name it before it is born
though, lest it fool us by remaining a dream-child.

Take care of your hand. Take care of the children. Take care of
Jean—temper the farming to her urban upbringing. Remember me to
Kelley* if you can, master to hired man.

*[Kelley MacDougall was the man-of-all-work who, under my inexpert guidance,
was trying to make a commercially successful farm of my stone Elizabethtown acres.
My lecture fees barely paid his salary.]

I just heard from Lankes that Wells College has called him to teach art there for a year and three thousand dollars. Much as he is thought of, he has hard times paying bills. That will be the biggest money he ever saw in his life. I hope the text-book he is bringing out on the art of wood-cutting will bring him some more money and get him somewhere. Would Knopf let him illustrate one of the series?

Ever yours,

R.

Monrovia!   California!

1932

P.S.   I sent you One. Here are Two and Three.

R.

THE BIPLANE OF
WILBUR AND ORVILLE WRIGHT*

This figure is the shape of human flight.
Its name to Time shall be First Motor Kite.
Its makers' name, Time cannot get that wrong,
For it is writ in heaven doubly Wright.

LET CONGRESS SEE TO IT

Wainwrights and Wheelwrights from old we've had.
Now comes a Wright to whom we need but add
An honorary Wing to make him Wingwright.
That would not only say right: it would sing right.

R.F.

[Monrovia,   Cal.
September 9,   1932]

Dear Louis:

We're getting out of here for Colorado soon—in a week or so. So if you can afford an air mail stamp back I wish you would use it to tell me where Joe March is. I have let him go till the last minute because I wanted to make sure he would believe me when I said I didn't want to be "shown round." I have no interest in the Hollywood Punch and Judy show either way, for or against it. I don't want to have to see it or to have to refuse to see it. But of course I should feel

*[The first of these quatrains appeared, with an altered first line, in A Further Range. The second remained unpublished.]

229

sorry to miss my chance to talk with Joe again. I am still of the opinion that he is about my only child in poetry. (Not quite my only. There is also Merrill Root.) You asked me a while ago about Hendricks and got no answer. There's a queer case. He's almost somebody. I catch a strange almost baby note in him—or should I say sappy—that is undeniably his own...

You asked about the Wylie, too, but you didn't specially want an answer. She was self-conscious artist enough to see her appointed task. It was to make a false heart ring false. Art forbade that a false heart should ring true. That would have been false art. The rules of the game permitted her, required her, to slip from one pose to its opposite even in the same poem when of moderate length. So long as she kept her high poetic strain, so long as the work was all crystals, sugar, glass, semi-precious and precious, the falser she was the truer she rang. The ultimate test is how a writer takes himself as betrayed in tone, word-font, and collateral advertising. I find the Wylie's way of taking herself, her airs about herself, not very detestable.

As for me I don't care too much whether I am a poet any more. It gives me peace to grant that I may be done with the larger public. I have earned the right to quit and go off trial. Let's play anyway that I am back where I was before I had much of any audience and wrote more for the poem's sake than ambition's. Let me use one or two of you for faithful readers whose praise is of the family familias. I won't send you poems because you are my friend and my severest critic, but because you are my friend and best believer. The fight, what there was of it in me, and there was never much where poetry was concerned, has gone out of me. Or it feels as if it had this summer.

Ever yours,

R.F.

P.S.   Hold your book till we get settled in Amherst. Send it there now so you won't forget it. It will be held for us.

> *[Joseph Moncure March ("about my only child in poetry") had been Robert's most promising pupil at Amherst, although he produced nothing until he was thirty. Then, in 1928, his tough, brusquely rhymed* The Wild Party, *which had been rejected by several firms, was privately published with my foreword and caused a great stir. It was followed by the equally explosive* The Set-Up, *whereupon*

1932

Hollywood dangled its golden lure and March was caught. Except for a few lyrics he wrote no more poetry.

Although "the ultimate test is how a writer takes himself as betrayed in tone" refers specifically to Elinor Wylie, it was also true of Robert—at least of the depressed tone during the time he was unhappy in the West. Deeply troubled about his children, he felt he had "earned the right to quit and go off trial....The fight, what there was of it...has gone out of me." The tone changed as soon as he got back East.]

[Amherst, Mass.
December 13, 1932]

Dear Louis:

All you say is true—too true—except that about the (my) Phi Beta Kappa poem* which I have my doubts about, though it rather stole the occasion for some reason from the great Walter Lippmann. In a way it was a monkey-shine and he needn't have minded poetry's having a little the best of it for once in a political age. But I'm afraid he did mind, whether from wounded vanity or lack of humor; and I'm sorry, for I admire him and should like to count him friend. There is a devil in me that defeats my deliberate intentions. I must show you the poem when and if I get it into closer form. Much of it was almost extemporized.

I larked the same way at a party where I met T.S. Eliot a month ago. He offered to read a poem if I would read one. I made him a counter-offer to <u>write</u> one while he was reading his. Then I fussed around with place-cards and a borrowed pencil, pretending an inspiration. When my time came I said I hadn't finished on paper but would try to fake the tail part in talk when I got to it. I did nine four-line stanzas on the subject "My Olympic Record Stride." (I might write it out and enclose it for you.) Several said "Quite a feat." All were so solemn I hadn't the courage to tell them that I of course was lying! I had composed the piece for my family when torn between Montauk, Long Island, and Long Beach, California, the summer before. So be cautioned. They must never know the truth. I'm much to blame, but I just couldn't be serious when Eliot was taking himself so seriously. There is much to give an old man the fan-tods.

*["Build Soil," the "Political Pastoral" read at Columbia University, May 31, 1932.]

I

231

Won't you be fine and cozy snowed in up there below zero? We haven't had a whole winter like that for a long time, but we mean to have one again soon.

I hope you thought Lankes was making a go of it at Wells.

Ever yours

R.F.

Amherst, December 12, 1932.

MY OLYMPIC RECORD STRIDE*

In a Vermont bedroom closet
With a door of two broad boards
And a back wall of crumbling old chimney
(And that's what their toes are towards),

I have a pair of shoes standing,
Old rivals of sagging leather,
Who once kept surpassing each other,
But now live even together.

They listen for me in the bedroom
To ask me a thing or two
About who is too old to go walking,
With too much stress on the who.

I wet one last year at Montauk
For a hat I had to save;
The other I wet at the Cliff House
In an extra-vagant wave.

Two entirely different grand children
Got me into my double adventure.
But when they grow up and can read this
They're not to take it for censure.

I touch my tongue to the shoes now,
And unless my sense is at fault,
On one I can taste Atlantic
On the other Pacific salt.

One foot in each great ocean
Is a record stride or stretch.
The authentic shoes it was made in,
I ought to see what they would fetch;

*[With a change of two lines, this appeared in *A Further Range* under the title "A Record Stride."]

But instead I proudly devote them
To my museum and muse.
So the thick-skins needn't act thin-skinned
About being past-active shoes.

And I hope they're going to forgive me
For being so over-elated
As if I had measured the country
And got the United States stated.

R.F.

[Amherst, Mass.
May 13, 1933]

Dear Louis:

I assume you are hard at it doing what has to be done.* The
expression of your face in the street lights that night settled it for me
that nobody else's business was mine except very superficially. You
know what you can and can't possibly stand. Having given me notice
of what to expect you have cut me off for the moment to spare me
the harrowing details. There's going to be some one left slain outside
the circle as made up new. But what is the will for if it is not to control
thought and suppress sentimentality. I have caused suffering myself
more or less justifiably in the process of getting anywhere. It's only
by luck, it is not in exactly the same realm. I may get credit for luck,
but I don't take any for it. The saddest thing is for two separately
to live on the same memories. A castoff ring ought not to be buried
where it could be dug up: it ought to be thrown into deep water. If
you have the kind of mind that can't help looking for something or
someone in heaven or on earth to blame, you will write life ugly like
a lot of Americans lately; but if you take it naturally as it comes, you
will write it simply sad some of the time. I should hope one could
be sad when there was anything to be sad about without seeming to
reflect on the state of society or the government of the universe.

I was on your trail in Texas when I heard the best things said of
your lectures. Didn't you like those asTex? And weren't you sorry

*[As stated in a previous footnote, I had remarried Jean. The reunion did not last.
The two adopted boys remained with me; later they were to become friends with
John, my son by Virginia.]

you couldn't be kinder to the poetry of such a lovely person as Karle Wilson Baker of Nacagdoches in the so-called piney woods? Easy on the sentimental, you say. You should have heard the out-and-out sentiment of some of the introductions we got down there. (Elinor was along for a glimpse of the bluebonnets.) Hospitality permitted no bounds. We went it and they went it. We both liked them, Elinor as much as I, I was interested to notice, because I hadn't known what to expect of such an inbred northerner.

I hope this finds you farming as I would like to be right now. A few days more and I'll be let loose in South Shaftsbury to see how my different plants and trees have wintered and how they are going to summer. That's about the extent of my spring efforts lately. I shan't have a garden. I may move a few young trees around by the power of music like Amphion or Orpheus or whoever Amy would have said it was. I heard for a fact this one on Amy, and I can believe it after the way she pronounced Nausicaa in public. Someone was telling her about a vague and remote professor who, by some accident of popular success with scholarly book, got asked into society and made much of by ladies he hardly saw or spoke to. At a crowded week-end party he was overheard saying to himself "Terrible day, terrible day." Wasn't he having a good time? Didn't he like the weather? What was the matter with the day? "Oh everything is perfectly all right. I was just thinking of Marathon." Amy wanted to know what Marathon was. So cheer up.

Ever yours

Robert

South Shaftsbury

June 26, 1933

Dear Louis:

I'm in Middlebury July 3rd. Would you want to meet me part way on July 4th? I could probably get someone to take me across the lake. I want to see you for some talks.

Ever yours

R. F.

234

[Franconia, N.H.
September 7, 1933]

Dear Louis:

I've been sick in bed with a temperature again or you would have heard from me sooner. I rejoice with you in your certainty that you have joined the ranks of the peaceful. As your friend, I have always wished the best possible for you in a rather sad world. You have a lot of life ahead of you, plenty of time to begin all over and, with things near you favorable, make the most of yourself you ever made. So now for it!

I've been inclined to suffer regret for my part in the adoption of your boys. You've as good as told me I needn't by the thoroughness of the adoption. I know you'll be a good father to them. They are such a splendid boyish pair. Don't have them too clever. But I meddle no further in anybody's business.

It becomes a question what the matter's with me that I have to go to bed four times in one year with a temperature. You have to remember I never was any good. My being sick is harder on Elinor than it is on me. I believe I always think of more when I have a little temperature. The Lord knows I don't drink for inspiration and so mercifully sends me fever as a substitute. I shall of course have to pay for the excitement of the last week by dragging around for a few weeks now with no incentive but my conscience.

Ever yours

Robert

Franconia N.H.
September 4, 1933

Franconia Sept. 17, 1933
But write to South Shaftsbury, Vt.

Dear Louis:

Can't you make it a week later and to South Shaftsbury instead of to Franconia? Next week we shall be in transition. By the middle or last of the week we shall have settled back in South Shaftsbury and Elinor will have gone on to New Haven with the children to help them start the new year at college. That at any rate is the plan now.

We are full of problems that shift their aspect while we wait. I'm sure however of the week-end of two weeks from today and tomorrow.

We had a successful expedition yesterday, all of us, into a new north for us, looking for a home, looking for a home. It was beyond the uttermost wild to a township called Columbia the gem of the mountain the home of the free from everything poisonous to mind or body and to a particular hamlet in the township called Cones on the map on Cone's Brook where John's people set out from for Kansas two generations ago. We had quite a mind to it. The mountain we would face is called Lightning because the spark from heaven alights there so often. Our mail would come to us at Stratford. Of course we may never. There is a disease known as Geographic Tongue or maps on the tongue. I certainly have maps on the brain.

Ever yours,
Robert Frost

Amherst,   December 21,   1933

Dear Louis:

This is silence long enough to show the restraint of a humanist which is what I should like to do once in so often but not too often. Our David Morton has been punching a policeman for asking a lady a question nobody but a lawyer has a right to ask. There is something ungenerous about not calling someone a son of a bitch or punching someone or driving a car drunk or trusting others to keep you from falling off a roof or leaving it to your audience to supply a meaning to what you say. Did you happen to notice the terrible kind of death Hemingway wished the humanist in his "Winner Take Nothing" dedicated to your Archie MacLeish? He hoped he would die without dignity or decorum. I suppose he must have been after Irving Babbitt for getting under his skin for a humanitarian sentimentalist. Just about the time he wished it, Babbitt was dying as if with humanitarian pens stuck into his wax figureativeness, which was good as far as it went, but unfortunately for Hemingway I'm afraid he died with Graeco-Roman euthanatos. Hear me use Greek! I feel that it is my peculiar right, nay duty, since my marks in Greek at Harvard were published by Robert Hillyer the other day.

The mercy of my not writing to you lies chiefly in its saving you a lot of rhyme and meter which it would have been if I had written at all. I think it was your spirited poem set me off on my spree: but it's

236

been for the last month or two so that I could think of nothing except in rhyme and that the same rhyme steadily till it was exhausted. For example I wrote a whole lesson in rhetoric in lines ending in words to rhyme with Flaccus (leaning on Austin Dobson for my rhyming dictionary.) The Flaccus* I was talking to (not about) was a protegé of mine just out of Dartmouth, not the Horatius, late of Rome and the Sabine Hills. You ought to have seen it before it was burned. Then again you ought not. You have seen a lot of poetry in your time—a lot of mine. Time you were retired to a pension. I don't mean to imply you act jaded. I heard of you (as well as from you) in Texas. You vivified them down there!

Nobody's with us for Christmas—we're two elders alone with nothing to think about but thoughts and how to keep them out of our poetry so it will be pronounced pure by the authorities on purity self-set up. I am going to give a lecture on What Poetry Thinks presently in prose if I can. I shall begin, Poetry abhors a money-matter. I have carefully phrased it that far so nobody can sing it—can they? I am going to end well, if I knew how I was going to end and get out of the damned thing I shouldn't be as nervous and abstracted in company like a neurasthenic the night before he goes over the top. Why do I get myself in for these things you ask me. So do I ask myself. Principally because you can't be writing poetry all the time or you will produce volumes and volumes till you are self-buried.

Our best to you Toledoans† (I seem to want to rhyme that with Minoans and be off. You hear the Limerick coming. The sub-plot would turn on assart—never mind why. But I spare you.)

Have a merry Christmas with the well contrasted boys. Tease them both very wittily for me.

Ever yours
Robert Frost

[Amherst, Mass.
February 23, 1934]

Dear Louis:

I have been in bed with a bug and a tropical temperature again etiolating and emaciating. Otherwise I should probably have written you sooner about those there two girls' wind-baby that they laid as

*[Kimball Flaccus.]
†[I was, during the winter, living in Toledo, Ohio.]

lightly as a blown bubble on my doorstep so as not to break it with
an odor of pewtativeness I suppose. Probably, but not surely, because
I hardly know what to write either to you or to them. If you could
have got along without two or three of the more physical poems in
the book, you can imagine how much more philosophically I could
with my less cultivated taste. I suspect a hidden joke between you and
them at my expense. There is a fleur-de-mallaisian laughter offstage
at the spectacle of my grey hairs being brought down another peg in
sorrow to the incontestible verities. It is possible to make too much
of the episode—whether joke or clinical experiment. I am well past the
age of shock fixation. But if I promise not to make too much of it,
will you promise too? You won't take it as an infringement of the
liberty of the press if I ask you not to connect me with the book any
more than you have to in your reviewing and lecturing. Don't you find
the contemplation of their kind of collusion emasculating? I'm chilled
to the marrow, as in the actual presence of some foul form of death
where none of me can function, not even my habitual interest in
versification. This to you. But what can I say to them?

Yours ever

R.

[Amherst, Mass.
March 5, 1934]

Dear Louis:

David McCord* was in yesterday talking about what a good
time you all had in Boston. I like the idea of a poet's being in charge
of the Harvard Fund. He runs with all sorts of people, not just the
poetry set. He gets a curious excess pleasure out of the lark of each
particular rhyme in a poem. I like the trait. Its danger is that it might
sound too clever.

You see more of my friends than I do. Did Cowden tell you about
his plans for the big prizes at Ann Arbor? Something ought to come
of them if the Muse can be bought. I'm not trying to put her on her

*[David McCord, poet, essayist, editor of the Harvard Alumni Bulletin, and secretary
of the Harvard Fund Council.]

pride not to be bought. I leave her to her own disposition as our statesmen to their dispositions in the matter of money. I don't see why poetry should abhor a money matter, subject always to the code of nobility.

Those two girls again. They bother me only a little. From a certain way they had in inquiring about E. T.* I am led to wonder if they think all friendships may be like theirs. Maybe I misjudge them. Don't pretend you haven't heard of more such people than I have and even encountered them in polite society. It isn't your fault. You have merely been out around more than I. I am more prepared for them than I was when I went to England in 1911. There I first read of them in The English Review in a series of articles by the heads of the famous public schools—Rugby, Eton, etc. I had just as soon they stayed far from my sphere. It is not my nature to want to slap them in the face. I was tempted to tell them I knew the best poem in the book and would tell them which it was but for the fear of coming between two such with thoughts of rivalry in art.

You are a hero to let anyone down your throat with a knife.† It is thought I must be searched for the source of the rheumatism I have more or less always and inflamatorily when I have influenza. I doubt if I dare to go to the table or whiff the nepenthe. I always notice I am most cowardly when writing or just after writing. I mind the cellar at night worse then.

Ever yours

R.

P.S. I sure did see the letter to Doctor Moore.‡ It was well-nigh deadly. You arrested my development with those figures. 40,000 at a time!

---

*[Edward Thomas.]

†[Scarcely a hero, I insisted on a general anesthetic because I couldn't bear to see (and hear) my tonsils being scraped, sliced, or yanked out.]

‡[Merrill Moore, a dear friend whom I had "discovered" when he was an undergraduate at Vanderbilt University, the youngest of the Fugitives group. Before he died of cancer in 1957, he had written, improvised, or dictated to a soundscriber more than forty thousand sonnets. In 1933, when he was in mid-career and just getting to know Robert, I wrote a semifacetious letter to him calling for a moratorium for poetry. It was published in The Book of Modern Letters.]

[Amherst, Mass.
March 19, 1934]

Dear Louis:

For goodness sake be quick and write me out or print me plainly
the address of that couplet in England. I can't seem to read the
reading of the only letter of theirs I can lay my hand on. And I must
say something polite to them soon or the silence will get too hard to
break. I may judge where I have to, but I wouldn't have them think
I was anybody's executioner. The book has beauties, of course, and
they should be acknowledged.

Ever yours

Robert

Amherst for a while yet.

General Delivery
Rochester, Minnesota
April 29, 1934

Dear Louis:

We are going through the valley of the shadow with Marjorie
we are afraid. She had a baby in Billings, Montana, six weeks ago
and most of the time since has hovered on the verge of death. The
harm must have been done by her first doctor there of course. The
infection was a terrible one. But once it was done her first doctor and
the others we have called in have done everything possible for her.
Three days ago we put her in a small airplane with a doctor and nurse
to fly here. The thousand mile flight seems not to have set her back,
and here we can expect the miracles of modern science. Rosenow, the
great biologist, finds he has a serum for a close cousin of the organism
diffused in her blood-stream. It would be better if it were for the exact
organism. But that and blood-transfusions every other day and
Marjorie's tenacity and Elinor's devotion and the mercy of God are
our hopes. You will probably see us home again alive whatever the
outcome, but it will be months hence and changed for the worse for
the rest of our days.

Always yours
Robert Frost

My favorite poem long before I knew what it was going to mean
to us was Arnold's "Cadmus and Harmonia."

1934

[Marjorie's return to health was the cause of so much joy that the aftermath was all the more terrible. She had recovered from her tubercular condition and had married Willard Fraser, a young archaeologist who went into politics and, later, headed the Bureau of Indian Affairs in Billings, Montana. A child, Elinor Robin, was born a year after the marriage; the girl was as healthy as she was lovely, but Marjorie was struck down with septicemia. She was rushed to the Mayo Clinic in Minnesota, but it was too late to arrest the poison which spread through her system.

Marjorie had written poems in what was recognizably a Frostian key, but she was too reticent to submit any of them for publication. (I printed one of them, a sonnet, "America," in an anthology entitled Doorways to Poetry.) Her parents put together some of her poems in a small, privately printed book entitled Franconia, recalling her childhood home in the White Mountains of New Hampshire; it was designed by Joseph Blumenthal of the Spiral Press and issued in 1936.

The tale of Cadmus and Harmonia ("My favorite poem long before I knew what it was going to mean to us...") is a symbolic legend of a couple who, seemingly blessed, were doomed to misery. A precious jewel had been given to Harmonia, but it proved to be the source of their greatest sorrow. In "Empedocles in Etna," Matthew Arnold describes how

...the billow of calamity
Over their own dear children roll'd,
Curse upon curse, pang upon pang.

Marjorie was the Frosts' dearest jewel.]

[Amherst, Mass.
May 15, 1934]

Dear Louis

I told you by letter or telegram what was hanging over us. So you know what to expect. Well, the blow has fallen. The noblest of us all is dead and has taken our hearts out of the world with her. It was a terrible seven weeks' fight—too indelibly terrible on the imagination. No death in war could more than match it for suffering and heroic endurance. Why all this talk in favor of peace? Peace has her victories over poor mortals no less merciless than war. Marge always said she would rather die in a gutter than in a hospital. But it was in a hospital she was caught to die after more than a hundred serum injections and blood transfusions. We were torn afresh every day between the temptation of letting her go untortured or cruelly trying to save her. The only consolation we have is the memory of her greatness through all. Never out of delirium for the last four weeks her responses were of course incorrect. She got little or nothing of what we said to her. The only way I could reach her was by putting my hand backward and forward between us as in counting out and saying with over-emphasis You—and—Me. The last time I did that, the day before she died, she smiled faintly and answered "All the same," frowned slightly and made it "Always the same." Her temperature was then 110, the highest ever known at the Mayo Clinic where as I told you we took her, but too late. The classical theory was not born out in her case that a fine and innocent nature released by madness from the inhibitions of society will give way to all the indecencies. Everything she said, however quaint and awry, was of an almost straining loftiness. It was as if her ruling passion must have been to be wise and good, or it could not have been so strong in death. But curse all doctors who for a moment let down and neglect in childbirth the scientific precautions they have been taught in school. We thought to move heaven and earth—heaven with prayers and earth with money. We moved nothing. And here we are Cadmus and Harmonia not yet placed safely in changed forms.*

R.

[Franconia, N.H.
September 15, 1934]

Dear Louis:

We have been in our not unusual family confusion, but we see a few days to ourselves ahead, Sunday to Wednesday or Thursday, and wish you could make us your promised visit then. The best day for us to have you come would be the earliest—Sunday—and the best day to have you go the latest. We had thought before this to have found,

---

*[Cadmus and Harmonia were changed into "two bright and aged snakes," trans-ported to the hills,

     ... and there
  Placed safely in chang'd forms, the pair
  Wholly forgot their first sad life ...]

242

bought, and occupied our next farm, our fifth in life. But though we
have sought it with divine unrest we have not attained to its peace
that passeth understanding. There are farms to be had of good
outlook and free from hayfever. I could show you a small one in
Lancaster to be had for eight hundred. I begin to suspect the
difficulty is not with the farms but with me. I may be like an airplane
that has lost its landing gear: I can never alight any more. At any
rate I contemplate with horror the moment when, my gas gone, I
shall <u>have</u> to alight. I dreamed of making a forced descent into a
graveyard and knocking down every gravestone in the place.

It will be part of the fun of your visit for you to see if you can help
us decide on a farm and for us to see if we can keep from deciding on
one. We'll cover Coös County and live off the country. We'll make
the farm problem our entire project. We won't talk too much. We'll
consider politics settled and the question of who went into sheer
landscape first, the writers or the painters. (The writers never went
into it, if you ask me. Nobody reads or writes landscape by the yard
as painters paint it. Not even in the most natural of nature poetry
was nature ever anything but the background to the portrait of a
lunatic, a lover, or a farmer.) Yes, I consider politics settled by the
conclusion I reached last night amid the many movements of my
mind that no change of system could possibly make me a bit better
or abler, the only two things of any importance to me personally.
Now back to my abstraction once more. With Mycerinus I can say:
The rest I give to pleasure.

On the other side of this I give you a diagram not of how to live
but of how to find our cottage at the entrance to the Fobes Farm.

Ever yours

Robert

[The question about "who went into sheer landscape first, the
writers or the painters" emanated from a three-sided discussion in
my Adirondack home. My neighbor, the scene designer Lee Simonson, contended that the writers had never considered the landscape
as anything but a setting, a picturesque but unimportant backdrop,
until the painters gave it character of its own; that until then Nature
was regarded by writers as something composed of fearful heights,
arid wastes, doom-dealing wilds, savage animals, and endless threats.
Robert held that the true poets, as distinguished from the senti-
mentalists, accepted nature from the beginning without making it

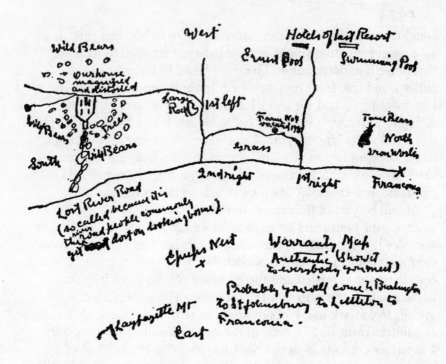

either miraculous or malign. As host, I maintained a neutral position, mumbling Pope's dictum that "all nature is but art."

Robert's slight misquotation from "Mycerinus" shows that he knew Matthew Arnold's early poem in spirit rather than by rote. According to Arnold, who took the legend from Herodotus, Mycerinus, son of Cheops, abjured his tyrannical father's implacable cruelties, was a just ruler, and gave up his throne for "the silence of the groves and woods."

Even in the diagram accompanying the letter Robert could not resist a bit of word play. "Ernest Pool," for example, was not a pond, a mountain spring, or a swimming hole but the residence of Ernest Poole, novelist, whose first book, The Harbor, had gone through many editions and whose His Family had won the Pulitzer prize in 1918.]

["What's this!" in the next letter refers to a clipping of a book review in the Billings Gazette sent by Robert's son-in-law, Willard Fraser. Robert liked to say (with little regard for the facts) that I kept him posted about the new figures and fashions in poetry. His mock outburst was occasioned by the aggressive announcement of Deaf Walls by Edmond Kowalewski. The book, published by the

Symphonist Press of Philadelphia, claimed, among other things, that Philadelphia was destined to be the vortex of an American renaissance. The author maintained that he was the inventor of "the symphonist movement," and he urged "a cataclysmic revolt against the bovine contentment of mediocrity, of that wretched perpetual production by professional writers of verse." His particular discoveries, Kowalewski admitted, were "the imaginative shudder" and the "symphonist penetration of the most secret fibers of man's hidden life."]

[South Shaftsbury, Vt.
September 22, 1934]

Dear Louis:

What's this! Why the Hell don't you keep me informed? I look to you for the wherewithal to do my talking, writing, and thinking. I rely on you to keep me abreast of the times. So does Lee Simonson. So do countless people. I don't like to have to be told things by some reviewer back in the sticks. Did you tell me what to think of Paul Engel? No!

Irascibly

R.

P.S. Expecting you nevertheless here at S. Shaftsbury.

["The Kings" who wanted me (probably prodded by Robert) to come to talk publicly and visit privately were Stanley King, President of Amherst, and his wife. James Agee, whose posthumous A Death in the Family is one of the most moving novels of the period, had just published his first book, a small collection in the Yale Series of Younger Poets, Permit Me Voyage, whose title as well as idiom showed the influence of Hart Crane's "Permit me voyage, love, into your hands." I am afraid my enthusiasm for Agee's delicate perceptions and subtle technique made Robert want to redress the balance and lean somewhat heavily on the other side of the scales.

As to the three poems enclosed in the letter: "The Lone Striker," a reminiscence of Robert's early days as a mill hand in Lawrence, had appeared as one of the Borzoi Chap Books; the indefinite "A" was substituted for the definite article when, two years later,

245

it became the first poem in A Further Range. "A Leaf Treader"
remained unaltered, but "Defense" was renamed, with bow to
Horace, "Triple Bronze," a line was altered, and it was held for
eight years until the publication of A Witness Tree in 1942.]

[Amherst, Mass.
November 2, 1934]

Dear Louis:

Where does one address you at this time of year? Ubiquity,
U.S.A.? Nay but seriously, I've been wishing you were where it would
be convenient for you to visit us before we light out for Salubrity,
Flaw, on November 26th. Maybe I haven't got about this in time to
reach any agreement between you and the office of the President.
Tell me as soon as you can when possibly you could come and what
it would cost the college to hear you on a subject. If I am too late for
now, we shall have to wait for my come-back in April. The Kings
(we never say King and Queen at Amherst) both want you very
much and so do I. Speed is called for.

Ever yours
Robert Frost

Amherst Mass
November 2 1934

And now Agee—Oh gee! Ain't that long one a terrible travesty of
Birches, Home Burial, and The Fear combined! And the psychology
of having a woman so bothered over a still-born child! Take the very
first little lyric in the book. What is such a thing if it isn't pretty
flawless? There are five flaws to eight lines. You can't have anything
between a joy—one joy. "Many could" is painful outside parenthesis.
The euphuism of "everyway" is unpleasant. Why not say every which
way? What does "wind not up" mean? I've heard this being kind
to a boy called winding up a little ball of yarn. Wolfer night doesn't
interrupt love. Night brings lovers together. He means wolfer <u>day</u>. Of
course he means Death, if you'll only help him with a little
understanding. "Climbs!" Why climbs? No luck at all in my first
two dips. What am I going to say to the kid? "Hereafter in a better
book than this I shall desire more love and knowledge of you."

R.

THE LONE STRIKER

The swinging mill bell changed its rate
To tolling like the count of fate,
And though at that the tardy ran,
One failed to make the closing gate.
There was a law of God or man
·That on the one who came too late
The gate for half an hour be locked
His time be lost, his pittance docked.
He stood rebuked and unemployed.
The straining mill began to shake.
The mill though many, many-eyed
Had eyes inscrutably opaque;
So that he couldn't look inside
To see if some forlorn machine
Was standing idle for his sake.
(He couldn't hope its heart would break)

And yet he thought he saw the scene:
The air was full of dust of wool.
A thousand yarns were under pull;
But pull so slow with such a twist
All day from spool to lesser spool,
They safely grew in slender length.
And if one broke by any chance
The spinner saw it at a glance.
The spinner still was there to spin—
That's where the human still came in.
Her deft hand showed with finger rings
Among the harp-like spread of strings.
She caught the pieces end to end
And with a touch that never missed
Not so much tied as made them blend.
Man's ingenuity was good.
He saw it plainly where he stood,
Yet found it easy to resist.

He knew another place, a wood,
And in it, tall as trees, were cliffs;
And if he stood on one of these
'Twould be among the tops of trees,

Their upper branches round him wreathing,
Their breathing mingled with his breathing.
If—if he stood! Enough of ifs!
He knew a path that wanted walking;
He knew a spring that wanted drinking;
A thought that wanted further thinking;
A love that wanted re-renewing.
Nor was this just a way of talking
To save him the expense of doing.
With him it boded action, deed.

The factory was very fine;
He wished it all the modern speed.
Yet after all 'twas not divine,
That is to say, 'twas not a church.
He never would assume that he'd
Be any institution's need.
But he said then and still would say
If there should ever come a day
When industry seemed like to die
Because he left it in the lurch,
Or even merely seemed to pine
For want of his approval, why
Come get him: they knew where to search.

Robert Frost

A LEAF TREADER

I have been treading on leaves all day until I am autumn-tired.
God knows all the color and form of leaves I have trodden on and
    mired.
Perhaps I have put forth too much strength and been too fierce
    from fear.
I have safely trodden underfoot the leaves of another year.

All summer long they were overhead more lifted up than I;
To come to their final place in earth they had to pass me by.
All summer long I thought I heard them threatening under their
    breath;
And when they came it seemed with a will to carry me with them
    to death.

They spoke to the fugitive in my heart as if it were leaves to leaf.
They tapped at my eyelids and touched my lips with an invitation
    to grief.
But it was no reason I had to go because they had to go.
Now up, my knee, to keep on top of another year of snow.

                                      R.F.

DEFENSE

The Infinite's being so wide
Is the reason the Powers provide
For inner defense my hide:
And for next defense outside

I make myself this time
Of wood or granite or lime
A wall too hard for crime
Either to breach or climb.

Then a number of us agree
To set a boundary.
And that defense makes three
Between too much and me.

                                       R.F.

[Robert spent the winter of 1934-1935, one of his many southern
hegiras, in Key West, Florida. He brought his wife, Elinor, and, to
escape the strain of the long winter in Vermont, his still ailing
daughter-in-law, Lillian, his son, Carol, and his grandson, Prescott.
At that time the place was balmy but it was also bankrupt, dismal,
and dirty—scarcely the sort of spot to attract the tourists who, after
the completion of the long causeway, came to crowd it. Elinor felt
sick most of the time. Robert, however, managed to acclimatize
himself and even to write poems as lightly scoffing as "Departmental," a brilliantly rhymed satire on what he considered a semi-
socialistic method of government.

"The Bianchi" (near the end of the second long paragraph) was
Martha Dickinson Bianchi, Emily Dickinson's niece and executrix.

Ezra Pound's "latest" was his third collection of Cantos (A Draft
of Cantos XXI-XLI), which accentuated Pound's magpie erudition
and his ordered (or disorderly) free associations, "a bundle of broken
mirrors." Robert's cinematic pun on Pound's being a "Greater
Garbler" was a critical thrust.]

[Key West, Fla.
January 10, 1935]

Dear Louis:

In this letter I am going to tell you where we got off (the train); in my next I shall tell you where you get off. Is it your idea to have a volume of selections such as the rest of us have had lately? We've just added a dozen to mine—I mean Elinor and I have. Once in so often I get into a creative state where my next composition has to be a new arrangement of my poems. The mood is past in a few hours. I think it comes from utter discouragement. When I get so low I can well agree with Mr. Masters that I have written nothing. Then, slightly recovering my manhood if not my critical sense, I brace myself to a point where I will stand for at least some of what I have written. These anyway! I say the world has got to show cause why they should be dismissed. I set out to have it a very, very small book— just a few almost sure things. But it grows on me from parental fondness. Leaving out one poem in favor of another seems invidious. That's the way The Line Gang, and A Soldier got in, and Waiting (Afield at Dusk) should have got in.

Well, one hundred and fifty miles south of Miami, six hundred south of Los Angeles, three hundred south of Cairo in Egypt, and sixty miles at sea, we reached Key West by train over a string of keys and bridges. It is an island about ten times as big as your farm, and fairly dense with population, equal parts Negro, Cuban, and American, 12,000 now, which is a reduction from 25,000 since the cigar business went to Tampa a few years ago. There is no sanitation. The water is all off the roofs and after it goes through people I don't know where it goes. Everything is shabby and even dilapidated. There are as many stinks as there are nymphs who rule o'er sewers and sinks (Delete sewers). There are mosquitoes. But there is no Yellow Fever any more. There is no malaria. There has never, absolutely never, been a frost. The air is balm. The total winter rainfall is 6 inches. (The climate is separate you see from that of Florida.) The range of temperature is between 70 and 80. There are very few winter visitors— fewer even than the natives would like to claim. The jam on the little main street Saturday evening is entirely native—the opposite to what it is in Miami. You won't see a stranger. You elbow nothing but the Spanish-speaking Cuban and the Boston-accented Negro

and American. (The pirates who founded the city were apparently
from Boston.) Food is cheap, though there is no such variety of it as
in Amherst for instance. The market for everything including note
paper is limited. We are on the point of the island exactly between
the Gulf of Mexico and the Atlantic Ocean. The waves break 20 feet
from our door—Elinor's and mine. Carol, Lillian and Prescott live
down town by the Customs House and Post Office equally distant
from the abandoned Navy Yard and the small Army Post. Havana
is six hours by shallow seas full of coral reefs: Yucatan not twice that.
Airplanes would make Yucatan in two hours. We are almost back in
the flesh where I started to think from. There are said to be traces of
Mayan culture in Key West (Cayo Hueso, which being translated,
should be Bone Key). Hemingway is said to be here much of the
time. But he knows not me and I know not him. He seems to be
less noticeable in town than the Bianchi in Amherst. The only thing
at all socially disturbing is the presence in force of Franklin D.
Roosevelt FERA.* This has been one of the Administration's pet
rehabilitation projects. No taxes had been paid on anything.
Everybody was riding round in cars without silencers and without
licenses. There was talk of transporting seventy five percent of the
crowd. But nobody could think of anybody who would want them. So
the author of a book called Compulsory Spending is here with a
staff to put everybody at work on public improvements, some
building, some tearing down, and some general cleaning up of
filthy vacant lots. We had to get our rent thru them. They are mildly
and beneficently dictatorial. Both the Mayor of the Town and the
Governor of the State have abdicated in their favor. Their great
object they say is to restore the people to their civic virtue. When
in history has any power ever achieved that? You see how much I am
interested.

I did think when I set out I might give you my ideas on Pound in
his latest. But I shouldn't be as interested as I am in the politics and
economies of Key West, and you might not be interested at all. You
have probably already delivered yourself on him professionally. My
opinion would be good in a way, better than of any of the rest of
those annuals. But what a garble of reading and nothing else. The
whole book is made out of newspapers, current non-fiction books,

*[FERA: Federal Emergency Relief Administration.]

and the minor classics you get in advanced college courses in Greek and Latin. Absolutely nothing else—not an idea of his own and not an observation of life, not an experience, outside of print. The best thing in the book is the story of the Afghans who came to Geneva to see if they could buy cheap any guns we might be disarming ourselves of. If only I could be sure Ezra concocted that. He ought to be called Greater Garbler.

Ever yours
Robertus

Key West, Fla. Jan. 10, 1935.

Key West, Florida
January 30 1935.

Dear Louis:

I should like to tell you something that would really help you toward making your book* one projectile. I should like to think of some plan on which all you ever wrote could be rearranged with the sharpest at the point, the broadest at the base, and the explosives in the middle. The sharpest would be made out of your wit, the basic out of your rustic and human sympathies (which is where we come nearest together), and the middle out of the rebel in you. You wouldn't think of a book like that I suppose, and I suppose you are right. My idea would be to have a book like that for now—not unlike my Selected Poems and then later the whole works in the order in which they were written. I know something about it but not everything. I sympathize with others' wish to leave nothing out. That would be one book and ultimately the more important. But right now I could see good war in letting them have the other sort of thing like a bolt from the blues. I should have talked this over with you that day at Broadloaf and found out just how definitely you know your own mind in the matter.

What you asked for, as I remember it, was a list of twenty or so that I should be sorry to see you omit. Suppose I just name you a few that have stayed by me; those that have stuck to me without my trying to stick to them. That can tell a very true story.

*[Selected Poems and Parodies, published in the autumn of 1935.]

After all I decided to play with my plan. Pay no attention to me.
But what an entering book it would be.

Robert

PRELUDE

Jewish Lullaby
Two Jewish Folk Songs
Water, Water, Wine-flower
Stay Here To-night*

(You could well give us a lot more of these adjectiveless folk things.)

THE POINT

Feeble Whistler
Member of the Supreme Court†
Critique of Pure Rhyme
To a Self-confessed Philosopher
Portrait of a Jewelry Drummer
The Flea-bites of Clement Wood‡
Song Tournament
    Etc.

THE LOAD (in three parts)

I. Rebellion

Prayer
On the Birth of a Child
Caliban
Steel Mill
Strikers
To the Child of a Revolutionist
He Goads Himself
    Etc.

II. Race

Lost Jerusalem
Roast Leviathan
    Etc.

*[Actual title: "The Leaf."]
†[Actual title: "Portrait of a Supreme Court Judge."]
‡[Actual title: "Portrait of a Friend."]

III. Istehar

The Eternal Masculine
The Burning Bush

Inhibited   The Woodpecker
Mozart   Feuerzauber
      Etc.

(I find The New Adam least like you in any of your kinds.)

BASIC

Last Words Before Winter
Return to Birds
Scarcely Spring
Dog at Night
Disenchantment
Long Feud
Country Evening
Ten Years Old
Positano—and so on
to the end with,
Rich Return
Transfigured Swan

(Mingling city and country home and foreign parts.)

[Key West,   Fla.
February 17,   1935]

Dear Louis:
    Won't you see Italy as no American has even seen it before? I'm a
haughty devil for a democrat. I hate to be caught touring with the
tourists and seeing only what is advertised to be seen. I refused to
look England in the features the whole three years I was there and
came home safely unable to exchange observations with anybody else
who had ever been there for culture purposes. What I encountered
nobody could have shown me for money; there were no trip tickets
to it. T. E. Hulme for instance. I went as an exporter anyway, not as a
self-accredited importer of European art into our system. You go as
an exporter too. That will give you different eyes and ears.

I only meant to be mildly suggestive about your book. I'd no more think of putting your poems into a plan in a book than I'd think of putting your words together into an idea in a poem. When we go to press, we makers are alone with our Maker. We have the momentary weakness to wish there were human help in deciding what we will keep or reject. But no, we are condemned to loneliness. Nobody can satisfy us but ourselves and we but poorly. (There seems to be exceptions to my rule. Merrill Moore is funny to be able to let you make up his book into six facets of a man not to mention separate his good from his bad. And by the way, what you wrote in the postface was one of the best and most entertaining pieces of your prose.)

And by the way I think you overvalue A. McL's article. It is the prose of a college-educated and practiced publicist trying hard to think. Restated it says publishers ought possibly (he wonders) to play up originality in art more than they do because the originality of today in art is the revolution of tomorrow in politics. He's been reading O'Shaughnessy's poem about us music-makers having built Nineveh and overthrown Babel. Tell me any poetic or belle lettre originality of any day that became the revolution of any day following. Let's talk sense. Wordsworth and Emerson both wrote some politics into their verse. Their poetic originality by which they live was quite another thing. So of Shelley. His originality was sufficient to give him his place. His politics were of the order of Godwins and Orages. If you want to play with the word revolution, every day and every new poem of a poet is a revolution of the spirit: that is to say it is a freshening. But it leads to nothing on the lower plane of politics. On the lower plane of thought and opinion the poet is a follower. Generally he keeps pretty well off that plane for that reason. Who wants forever to be setting to rhyme the greatness of Rousseau? Keats? Browning? Somebody set going the idea that art is an escape. The very word escape can hardly be kept out of the minor poetry since. I heard Thorpe of Ann Arbor make it out that in "Hyperion" Keats anticipated evolution when he had the old gods go down before the new. Hell he did. Keats merely set out to show you the great revolution of form getting the better of power. But why talk about it. A. McL was wrong in thinking the object of the artist is to be untimely—not to be in fashion. The artist's object is to tell people what they haven't as yet realized they were about to say themselves. First they are displeased, then they are pleased at this for psychological reasons we won't go into. The publisher comes in right there to help in the transition between their being displeased and pleased. Don't read all this.

Ever yours,
Robert the Devil

[The Donkey of God, a book of stories written in 1932, had, because of its Italian background and interstitial "travelogue," won an award offered by ENIT, an organization designed to encourage travel in Italy. I was gratified and more than a little amused to learn that the first prize had been split between my book and the work of an author who had written a three-volume glorification of Mussolini, his cultural accomplishments and his august place in history. Instead of accepting the cash, I received a de-luxe passage to and from Italy, including a reception in Rome by Il Duce.

"Merrill Moore is funny to be able to let you make up his book into six facets..." I had been instrumental in placing Merrill's first book, The Noise that Time Makes, with my publishers. Harcourt, Brace also published his second volume which, since the highly talented Merrill had no gift for self-criticism, I had selected from thousands of his sonnets, arranged in six sections, and entitled Six Sides to a Man. "The paradox of creation and conflict," I wrote in an Epilogue by Way of Advertisement, "this order out of chaos is common to every poet. In the case of Dr. Moore the process is more than usually self-revealing. The factor that frequently deranges his aim is that his intuitions and unconscious associations are not in league with and sometimes even opposed to his conscious intentions." The "Six Sides" were an extension of the Five Senses: Hearing, Seeing, Smelling, Tasting, Touching—and Thinking.

Archibald MacLeish had not yet become involved in politics, but he was already busy with polemics and poems with socio-economic objectives utterly unlike his previous subjectivity. He implied and even insisted that the poet should give up his traditional privacy for public affairs and, instead of remaining aloof, become an active force in the community.]

[Key West, Fla.
February 18, 1935]

Dear Louis:

Honest and truly isn't that just a Pound-gang editorial?* The
thesis is our object in life is to be untimely: our publisher's object is
to have us timely. Where then, do we and the publishers meet? Do
they weaken toward us or do we weaken toward them. Or do we
both weaken toward each other? I couldn't be bothered with such
considerations. My object in life is to be first-hand with some things
of the senses and the mind and to strike no false personal note to set
my nerves on edge. Those two matters taken care of, my difference
will follow and take care of itself. With the right nature its
difference will at first brighten it. Imagine seeking, calculating, a
difference; a hitting 'em where they ain't and won't be for a hundred
or two years at least. And imagine Alfred being asked to leave all and
publish such inutility either for glory or profit.

Gee! But of course a man doesn't have to think to be a poet.
A. McL may be as wrong as he pleases if he gives me a quality to savor
in his verse. Do you know the quality may be of wrong-headedness
in his case just as with Joyce it may be cloacality.

I like your sardonix about war. You may think you can stop war
or at least that war ought to stop. That makes you a Quaker. The
position is tenable. It can't be called bad thinking because it isn't
thinking. Pacifism is instructive. It is a dream of wiping out the last
infirmity of noble minds, and so it is the height or last word of
nobility. But don't ask me to listen [to] these technical kids who
believe they can calculate a place to spill where no dog has spilled
before by measuring distances equally from all the posts in town. "No
fair if you don't use a post."

You remember Lawrence Conrad, once of Michigan? He has
worked his way up in the automobile factories and topped off with a
college education, you remember. Henry Ford drove him somewhat
radical. He has been working on a novel about the labor problem
out in Detroit. He calls it "F.O.B. Detroit." What I saw of it I
liked. He wants to know if I have any suggestions about publishers.

*[The article by Archibald MacLeish to which, in the previous letter, Robert
violently objected.]

Do you think you could get Alfred to give him a special chance with his readers? Here is timeliness more or less accidental but quite frank and shameless. Lawrence is a poor devil I wish somebody could use as a novelist.

If I seem irritable it is probably due to the horribleness of having to look on at the redemption of a city that has lost its self respect to the New Deil.*

I brought you into the conversation when I was asked by the Edward Bruce at the head of Art Relief under the FERA. He asked if poetry could be considered an art like painting you could expect to live by. He wanted to be nice to poets if I could assure him there were any. I said ask you. He speaks for the President and the Missus without intervention of Ickes or anyone. So be nice to him if he turns to you for advice. He put the thing on the high plane of encouraging art by pension rather than giving work for relief. He said he was going to reduce the number of painters pensioned from 2600 last year to 1000 next. How many poets did I think there were? I said ask you. I believed you had figured there were 400,000 writing and trying for publication, but I doubted if you would say more than a hundred or two would be worth the pensioning. Elinor said a hundred. I said two hundred. The pensions will run indefinitely and be small—just honorary grubstakes—but honorary, not charitable. He thought a thousand dollars a year would be enough and yet not enough to lie back on. So did I. I couldn't tell what the prospects might be.

Ever yours

R.

[Amherst, Mass.
June 24, 1935]

Dear Louis

Just a min—till I can achieve my independence. Then I will write you adequate. You will never know—no one will ever know because I don't like anyone to know—how busy the afternoon of a quietist can be at times. Reputation is a cumulative congestion. What this child needs is a place to go to. But I was not born an immortal bird

*[Robert's devilish term of derision for Roosevelt and his New Deal.]

to be served up on peacock's tongues among many at a Lucullan banquet. If I am, trust me to be found singing when the pie is opened.

The Adirondack mountains have looked on Mussolini, and Mussolini looks on the Papal See. I shall want to hear all about it. And did he stop (you) and speak to you? What do you say we see each other soon—soon. I can hardly wait to hear my judgment confirmed or reversed on the great Iamb of Italy.

Interesting news about Esther's* being admitted to the bar of New York. I suppose that may mean moving ultimately from Toledo. An office in Albany for the winter would give you week-ends at the farm if you wanted to keep the farm going. But I mustn't make plans for people any more than Franklin D. should be allowed to.

I wish Esther would specialize in cases arising under the New Deal legislation. It was only in a dream, to be sure, but I am still rankling with a new elaborate law I read in very fine print in my sleep last night. It was designed to keep any poet from reading in public for a larger fee than any other poet. It had apparently been drawn up very carefully by the Poetry Society of America to leave no loop-holes. There was a good deal of Latin in it: which comes of my having had insults lately from George Whicher's father, the old man who addressed you so familiarly at the first meeting as Lewis!

I'm in favor of more discrimination and then some more. Here without regret one sees rank considerations and degrees. Go to your more discriminating anthology—so long as in discriminating against others you discriminate in favor of me. It was designed to be a sad world, how sad we won't keep telling each other over and over, as we would have to if our heads were thick. You should have heard me holding forth to the boys at commencement on Our Darkest Concern. I darkened the sunny fine day for them inexorably.

Have any poems you like for the new anthology. Shall we talk about them when we gather?

Remember me to the Duce when you write your guessed letter.

Ever yours

Robertus

Amherst for a few days yet.
June 21, 1935.

*[Esther Antin, a lawyer of Toledo, Ohio, whom I had married.]

[South Shaftsbury, Vt.
July 8, 1935]

Dear Louis:

I wasn't here when your telegram came. No luck. We didn't
subside at Amherst till last Saturday—more than two weeks after
commencement. I had been wondering the last few years what use I
was round the place. Well a use was found for me. I lectured, so to call
it, three times, on How a Poem Picks up Thought, New Ways to
Be New, and Our Darkest Concern. The last proved the best,
though I was scared in it the worst. I burst forth like a Nova in those
last days portending war, pestilence, and the end of the present
Administration at Washington. I rose for the moment from well
below the sixth or visible-to-the naked-eye magnitude to about the
third or second magnitude. Then I sunk back never again to blaze
perhaps. The President thought it best to reward me at once before
my effect was lost. I'll brag a little more when I see you—not much.
I'm a sad old thing now. But tough.

I have several things to talk over with you, your news and mine. I
wonder if there isn't some half way-place where we could meet for a
night's talk. Elinor is not fit for anything. She is trying to save up
energy for a melancholy journey to the terrible scenes in Colorado
and Montana. I am doing my best to dissuade her from such a
pilgrimage. We can't have a soul in the house for a while. And I don't
want to be away from her long at a time.

Ever yours
Robertus Geler*

*["This," in the next letter, was the first draft of Robert's penetrating
foreword to E. A. Robinson's posthumous King Jasper. I had seen
part of it during a recent visit at his farm and Carol's. At that time
Robert had remarked, "I'm not sure how many readers will care,
but at least it should stop some of them from saying that I never
paid heed, let alone a tribute, to Robinson."]

*[Even with Latin Robert could not help playing.]

260

[Franconia,   N.H.
August 21,   1935]

Dear Louis:

I wanted you to see this before I sent it in to Macmillans but they got after me and I had to send it today. They may not like it. If not it will save me the trouble of deciding what I ought to charge for it. I hope you'll like it a little. There is some high, some low, and some Jack (Frost) in it. Game (by which I choose to mean "evaluation") is purposely left out.

Carol and I had a good visit. I came away still feeling full of things I had to say.

Ever yours
Robert Frost

Franconia New Hampshire
August 21, 1935

FOREWORD TO "KING JASPER"

It may come to the notice of posterity (and then again it may not) that this our age ran wild in the quest of new ways to be new. The one old way to be new no longer served. Science put it into our heads that there must be new ways to be new. Those tried were largely by subtraction—elimination. Poetry for example was tried without punctuation. It was tried without capital letters. It was tried without metric frame on which to measure the rhythm. It was tried without any images but those to the eye, and a loud general intoning had to be kept up to cover the total loss of specific images to the ear, those dramatic tones of voice which had hitherto constituted the better half of poetry.* It was tried without content under the trade name of poesie pure. It was tried without phrase, epigram, coherence, logic, and consistency. It was tried without ability. I took the confession of one who had deliberately to unlearn what he knew. He made a back-pedalling movement of his hands to illustrate the process. It was tried premature like the delicacy of unborn calf in Asia. It was tried without feeling or sentiment like murder for small pay in the underworld. These many things was it tried without, and what had we left? Still something. The limits of

*[A sidelong dig at the Imagists.]

poetry had been sorely strained, but the hope was that the idea had been somewhat brought out.

Robinson stayed content with the old-fashioned way to be new. I remember bringing the subject up with him. How does a man come on his difference, and how does he feel about it when he first finds it out? At first it may well frighten him, as his difference with the Church frightened Martin Luther. There is such a thing as being too willing to be different. And what shall we say to people who are not willing but anxious? What assurance have they that their difference is not insane, eccentric, abortive, inadmissable? Two fears should follow us through life. There is the fear that we shan't prove worthy in the eyes of someone who knows us at least as well as we know ourselves. That is the fear of God. And there is the fear of Man: the fear that men won't understand us and we shall be cut off from them.

We began in infancy by establishing correspondence of eyes with eyes. We recognized that they were the same features and we could do the same things with them. We went on to the visible motion of the lips—smile answered smile; then cautiously, by trial and error, to compare the invisible muscles of the mouth and throat. They were the same and could make the same sounds. We were still together. So far, so good. From here on the wonder grows. It has been said that recognition in art is all. Better say correspondence is all. Mind must convince mind that it can uncurl and wave the same filaments of subtlety, soul convince soul that it can give off the same shimmers of eternity. At no point would anyone but a brute fool want to break off this correspondence. It is all there is to satisfaction; and it is salutary to live in the fear of its being broken off.

The latest proposed experiment of the experimentalists is to use poetry as a vehicle of grievances against the un-Utopian state.* As I say, most of their experiments have been by subtraction. This would be by addition of an ingredient that latter day poetry has lacked. A distinction must be made between griefs and grievances. Grievances are probably more useful than griefs. I read in a sort of Sunday School leaflet from Moscow that the grievances of Chekov against the sordidness and dullness of his home-town society have done away with the sordidness and dullness of home-town society all over Russia. They were celebrating the event. The grievances of the great

*[An indirect reference to MacLeish's sociological poems.]

Russians of the last century have given Russia a revolution. The grievances of their great imitators in America may well give us if not a revolution, at least some palliative pensions. We must suffer them to put life at its ugliest and forbid them not, as we value our reputation for liberality.

I had it from one of the youngest lately: "Whereas we once thought literature should be without content, we now know it should be charged as full of propaganda as a child's stocking is with coal when he boasts of having lost faith in Santa Claus." Wrong twice, I told him. Wrong twice and of theory prepense. But he returned to his position after a moment out for reassembly. "Surely art can be considered good only as it prompts to action." How soon, I asked him.

But there is danger of undue levity in teasing the young. The experiment is evidently started. Grievances are certainly a power and are going to be turned on. We must be very tender of our dreamers. They may seem like picketers or members of the committee on rules for the moment. We shan't mind what they seem if only they produce real poems.

But for me, I don't like grievances. I find I gently let them alone wherever published. What I like is griefs, and I like them Robin-sonianly profound. I suppose there is no use in asking, but I should think we might be indulged to the extent of having grievances restricted to prose if prose will accept the imposition, and leaving poetry free to go its way in tears.

Robinson was a prince of heartachers amid countless achers of another part. The sincerity he wrought in was all sad. He asserted the sacred right of poetry to lean its breast to a thorn and sing its dolefullest. Let weasels suck eggs. I know better where to look for melancholy.

A few superficial irritable grievances, perhaps, as was only human, but these are forgotten in the depth of griefs to which he was plunged.

Grievances are a form of impatience. Griefs are a form of patience. We may be required by law to throw away patience as we have been required to surrender gold; since by throwing away patience and joining the impatient in one rush on the citadel of evil, the hope is we may end the need of patience. There will be nothing left to be patient about. The day of perfection waits on unanimous social action. Two or three more good national elections should do

K

the business. It has been similarly urged on us to give up courage, make cowardice a virtue, and see if that won't end war and the need of courage. Desert religion for science, clean out the holes and corners of the residual unknown, and there will be no more need of religion. (Religion is merely consolation for what we don't know.) But suppose there was some mistake; and the evil stood siege, the war didn't end, and something remained unknowable. Our having disarmed would make our case worse than it had ever been before. Nothing in the latest advices from Wall Street, the League of Nations, or the Vatican inclines me to give up my holdings in patient grief.

There were Robinson and I, it was years ago, and the place (near Boston Common) was the place, as we liked afterwards to call it, of Bitters, because it was with bitters, though without bitterness, we could sit there and look out on the welter of dissatisfaction and experiment in the world around us. It was too long ago to remember who said what, but the sense of the meeting was, we didn't care how arrant a reformer or experimentalist a man was if he gave us real poems. For ourselves, we would hate to be read for any theory upon which we might be supposed to write. We doubted any poem could persist for any theory upon which it might have been written. Take the theory that poetry in our language could be treated as quantitative, for example. Poems had been written in spite of it. And poems are all that matter. The utmost of ambition is to lodge a few poems where they will be hard to get rid of, to lodge a few irreducible bits, where Robinson lodged more than his share.

R.F.

[Franconia, N.H.
September 21, 1935]

Dear Louis:

Could you come to see us at South Shaftsbury any time between the twenty-seventh and thirtieth inclusive? We are getting out of here. The frosts come and the Frosts go. I've been bothered a little by the preface to King Jasper. They wanted more and, if I could manage it, a quotation or two from Robinson. They were nice enough about it. I don't feel sure they weren't after an appraisal of King Jasper. I'm no appraiser. But I want to be good when it is easy to be good: so I added an idea more that brought Robinson in a little more. I had said he was content with the old way to be new (1) that his were griefs rather than grievances (2). I went on to say his lesson was that you could go with sorrow with philosophy with confidence in poetry as far as you could go playful—so far and no further. I'll give you the rest of it when I see you.

Of course I am going to your "Adolescence Party."* The equipment spoken of in the invitation I have ordered of Abercrombie and Gibson. I am coming in three changes of raiment, one over the other, which I will start taking off and so continue till you are satisfied. I will stop at nothing anyway.

In haste (never mind about what)

Robertus Geler

[Amherst, Mass.
October 15, 1935]

Dear Louis:

Please make Henry Canby give you back that Lost in Heaven poem. I've got to have all the poems I can muster to meet the editorial demand there has been on me since you published A Leaf Treader. Tell Henry Canby I have promised Lost in Heaven somewhere else. Tell him I say he has already had too much of my next book, and if he hasn't he can say the word and I'll write him some more at once. And another matter: I seem to have lost somewhere one whole note-book with the poem in it about proposing to supply the sorrow felt if the storm will supply the tears: Dammit I wonder in whose house I left that privacy lying round. But never mind that now. Can you let me have a copy of the tears poem? The time draws near for going to press and I must get as many editors as possible implicated in the book beforehand. Ain't I wiley? You remember Amy Lowell the author and poet? Well they's a life of her out and they tell me it's a caution the wileyness she showed with editors and reviewers.

We thought it was a grand party. I got so excited that I came away with the money I cleaned up on my autoholograph lottery and it got mixed up in my pocket with my own: so that I don't know exactly how much it was; but I think it may have been five dollars.

*[A party given to celebrate my fiftieth birthday.]

Now, I am not a habitual gambler and I always like to square myself with God for any ill-gotten gains by giving them to the church or charity. And I was wondering if Mr. Rosenberg would accept the swag in this case and hold it as trustee for a fund to be known as the Louis Untermeyer Fifty-Fifty Birthday Memorial Fund for Indigent Indiginies. Will you tactfully ask him for me? If he refuses the responsibility I shall have no recourse but to administer the fund mysef. I admnistered the interest on it to date to an itinerant bard (Oliver Waye) who blew in on us today from western Kansas. He is the author of The Forgotten Man lately in Moey's New Deal Magazine. Doesn't someone speak of Amaranthine Moley?

(I'm about through with this letter). You tell me if I did right. I stand ready to give an accounting of my trust. The tramp was worthy. I examined him for six hours, or rather he examined me, and I judged him by his judging. He had a very convincing contempt for people who live in houses and know where the next meal is coming from. Anger was his motive—anger at imperfection. You might not suspect it from my impassive exterior, but I have always had the same anger. But I refuse to be driven to suicide or desertion by it. Ridgely Torrence was telling me how he sat with Robinson not so many years ago (thirty), and Robinson was weeping face in both hands for want of being read as a poet. My fury is for more important things and is moreover too tight. All the same no deserter comes near me without my sympathy.

Everurn

R.F.

Amherst
October 1935

[I had been "placing" some of Robert's poems with various editors; "Lost in Heaven" was one of them, "A Leaf Treader" was another. Robert needed them both for the section called "Taken Singly" in A Further Range published in 1936.

S. Foster Damon's Amy Lowell: A Chronicle, a tome of some seven hundred and seventy pages, had just been released.

"Mr. Rosenberg" was my good friend, James N. Rosenberg, lawyer, painter, and writer, who gave the birthday party for me at his country home in Mamaroneck, New York.

266

Professor Raymond Moley, with another professor, Rexford Tugwell, and Judge Samuel Rosenman, formed Roosevelt's private "Brain Trust." The pun on "Amaranthine Moley" ironically suggested that Roosevelt's wizardry—"moly" being a mythical herb with magic powers—claimed to be as time-defying as the amaranth which never fades.]

[Amherst, Mass.
October 30, 1935]

Dear Louis:

Nothing you did in my favor could possibly be presumptuous (I see a pun possible, but I forbear). I merely had a fear Henry Canby might be getting too much of me. If Palmer* was with one, Henry Canby surely should be with half a dozen. He tells me not however. So stet. He and Miss Loveman seem good friends of my arts.

Well, well, now you are probably working too hard. I know I am. With all I stay out of I find I don't stay out of enough. I didn't get as much good out of the summer as I should have if I hadn't got all messed up with Macmillans about the Robinson introduction. I went far far out of my way for worse than nothing. I'm not kicking, but I'm mad at Macmillan—not at you, nor anybody else. I've just come through my four lessons to all concerned at the New School. I like Alvin Johnson.

Ever yours
Robertus Geler

I see another pun possible but I forbear.

[Miami, Fla.
January 22, 1936]

Dear Louis:

I have been sick some more and only communicating by telegraph. But I must write a small letter to put you out of any anxiety you

*[The publisher, at that time, of The American Mercury, of which I was Poetry Editor.]

may have given yourself by finding fault with "frightfully."* To tell
you the truth I thought that word was part of the joke—just like
"mortician" and "out of there"—yet am I mixing up "Janizary"
with "commissary." But get this: Anybody who follows me with the
close attention you displayed in noticing the loss of effect from the
introduction of a good figure in my Wrong Twice story,† can do
anything he pleases with my works up to ten corrections and
suggestions in the rest of my life! This counts one if you stick to it.
I will change it for you without reasons. But remember it counts one.
You have only nine left. Nothing having been said about the size of
the criticisms, you are free to make them as large as you please even
to the suppression of whole poems or even whole books. You would
get the biggest feeling of importance by vetoing my next nine books.
Nothing would be lost. I would only gain in compression. No poem
I give up but appears later as one line or one epithet. It would be
the same with a lost book. It would not be truly lost. It would go to
build soil as in my Phi Beta Kappa poem at Columbia in 1932
before the New Deal had come out for soil-building or much of
anything else.

And speaking of lost books, what a loss you suffered in the one
Whats-his-name had stolen from him.‡ A thing like that would down
me for good. It hurts me somewhere I can't tell you how much. The
only thing worth learning is to be brave, and I suspect the best way to
learn it is not to let our mothers keep us out of danger when we are
young. I was brought up to think self-preservation was not an instinct
but a virtue. That's why I can't get used to the way these fine bold
people run round killing each other in their splendid cars. There
was never such an outburst of individual initiative, responsibility,
and courage since the world began. And we talk about this being an
age of no individual life!

Ever yours

Robert

*[The next letter disproves what some of Robert's critics were saying:
that he never interested himself in the work of younger poets. He*

---

*[In the first draft of "Departmental" the last line was: "But how frightfully depart-
mental." When it appeared in A Further Range, "frightfully" had been changed to
"thoroughly."]
†[Contained in the Introduction to King Jasper.]
‡[A collection of my manuscript poems borrowed by a friend.]

was always ready to respond to anyone who showed an original turn
of mind or phrase. Unfortunately, I did not share all his enthusi-
asms. I liked E. Merrill Root's stubbornly plain manner, but the
downrightness, pleasing enough in single poems, suffered from
awkwardness when stretched through a whole volume. Robert
Francis was Root's opposite. His lyric style, casual yet compact,
reminded me so much of Robert's that, until I learned better, I
thought my leg was being pulled and that Robert Francis was an
alter ego Robert Frost had invented by slightly altering his last
name.]

[Miami, Fla.
February 6, 1936]

Dear Louis:

An unselfish letter. Don't you like the enclosed kind of poetry?
Have you ever considered the enclosed fellow?

And what are we going to do for Merrill Root? His time draws
near for his next book I gather. Are you going to have it at Harcourts
or must I urge him on the Holts. Don't let this drop out of our
minds.

I told you about the Charles Eliot Norton lectures, didn't I?*
Well if I didn't, I can't in this letter because it is by announcement
an unselfish letter. I can't talk about myself in it. I can't talk about
you in it—or I would ask you how you are.

Ever everybody's

R.

BLUE WINTER

Winter uses all the blues there are.
One shade of blue for water, one for ice,
Another blue for shadows over snow.
The clear or cloudy sky uses blue twice,

*[Under the auspices of Harvard University, from which, thirty-seven years earlier,
Robert had declined to graduate, the Charles Eliot Norton Lectures (March 4 to
April 15, 1936) took place. They were given subjects which Robert chose and from
which he departed liberally. The titles were "The Old Way to Be New," "The
Renewal of Words," "Vocal Imagination: a Merger of Form and Content," "Poetry
as Prowess," "Before the Beginning of a Poem," "After the End of a Poem," "Does
Wisdom Signify?".]

Both different blues. And hills row after row
Are colored blue according to how far.
You know the bluejay's double-blue device
Shows best when there are no green leaves to show
And Sirius is a winterbluegreen star.

Robert Francis   December 19,   1935

[Miami,   Fla.
February 13,   1936]

Dear Louis:
    All right Merrill Root is mine. I have had him on my soul for
many years and it is time I put on a front with some publishing house
and got him really published. I don't know what makes me so lame
an advocate unless it is the look in the Court's eye that goes over
the head of my arguments and simply says "Friend of yours?" It is
always more than friendship in me, but it takes the strength and
plausibility all out of me to have it thought merely friendship. I could
tell you a tale of how I fail. Take the present case of Robert Francis
and the majority and minority opinions on it you have handed
down. I feel myself to blame for not having presented it with
assurance enough. I faint at the critical moment as the lawyer for the
AAA* did before the Nine. I should have said his poem had
resemblances to mine, though I don't suppose that appears as
plainly to me as to outsiders. But it has something mine never have.
I'm never concerned with color that much. From childhood I was a
black-and-white boy. Robert Francis was always more the aesthete
than I would have wanted to be. I timidly put him forward for a
rather remarkable person. He went to Harvard, graduated, taught
high school one year, failed (he says) with the children, and went out
to live alone on the little he can earn teaching younger children the
violin. He looks like a puritanical priest. Neither I nor anybody else
own him or very much influences his thinking. His opinions are no
pushovers. He never starts a subject one way and then at the first
sign or look of dissent from you steers it another way. I get a lot of
the pushovers. I just wish he might prevail. His address is Amherst,

*[Agricultural Adjustment Administration.]

Mass. I guess that will reach him all right. I don't know his street and number. I see him perhaps once a year.

I'll write you the name of my next book before tomorrow. Of course I must have a poem for Palmer if he cares enough to ask for it. I thought he was afraid of having too much of me. I'm all in a whirl with thoughts of the book and standing up to them at my old school. But I have poems around I can deliver. Wasn't it rotten I lost that notebook with so many in it. I'm no rewrite man. If any are saved from that loss it will be thanks to the copies you have of them in the Adirondacks. They won't get into the next book.

Ever yours

Robert

3670 Avocado Ave.
Coconut Grove Fla. for about a week longer.

[Miami, Fla.
February 15, 1936]

Dear Louis

David writes he saw a picture of me in the N.Y. Times looking worried beside Hervé Allen and DuBose Heyward at the Pan American Airport Dinner Key Miami Florida. He thinks it was because of all I was in for at Harvard and I let him, as a Harvard man, think so. In reality what was worrying me, if anything, was having to be with too many literary people for too long a time at the risk of losing their respect by being found out; or if it wasn't that it was not yet having hit on a name for my sixth book. The latter defect has been remedied in the last twelve hours and I hasten to share the satisfaction with you. I have it as Archy the Mede is said to have said.

A Further Range

You and Merrill Moore put it into my head and perhaps it may seem immodest of me to say it for myself and let it for the moment it will take the reader to discover by turning a page or two that all I mean by a further range is the Green Mountains after the White. I have a good mind to make you a skeleton plan of the book as I now suddenly see it.

The six Harvard lectures have yet to take shape in my head.

They should make a small book. Shall I write them before or after I deliver them? It's a tight place to be in because too novel. The name of the book and series might well be The Old Way to Be New. Some of the lecture headings may be: The Renewal of Words, Vocal Imagination, Does Wisdom Matter, etc.

Oh dear, I feel a little overburdened I must admit. I have never worked, you know. The Devil is after me. But watch me!

Ever yours
Robert

[The "skeleton plan" of A Further Range came in the shape of a handwritten eight-page booklet. It consisted chiefly of a Table of Contents. It was not dissimiliar to the final table of contents of the volume as published, but Robert's "title page" was a whimsicality.]

A Further Range
Book Six
by
Robert Frost

Henry Holt & Co.
Willing

The dedication page was a direct reply to the suggestion I made in company with Merrill Moore. I suggested that A Further Range might well be taken to mean the further range of Robert's interest in politics and technique. This, instead of pleasing, troubled him. He feared it might seem an unwarrantable immodesty to the readers and a presumption to the critics. Despite this, he dedicated the following to his wife:

To E. F.

for what it may mean to her that
beyond the White Mountains were the Green;
yes, and beyond both these were the Rockies,
the Sierras, and, in thought, the Andes and
the Himalayas; range beyond range even into
the realm of politics and religion.]

[Baltimore, Md.
February 24, 1936]

Dear Louis:

I'm overcome by your editor's request for a poem from my book. I realize this is a great indulgence on the editorial part. You may remember how The Atlantic years ago objected to my having The Ax-helve in a book for six months after it was in The Atlantic. Rules have changed maybe. I prefer to think Palmer is being particularly good to your favorite poet. I wish I had more short ones left. Perhaps his liberality of the moment will stretch to using a rather long piece for once in a way. The Woodward's Gardens one is a good one, don't you think? Probably the Roadside Stand is too long. He might like the political implications. The Woodward's Gardens is a better poem as a performance. And it has philosophical implications and those are better than political. However I leave all to you. Oh, I forgot that Kerker Quinn, Peoria, has a copy of A Roadside Stand which he is holding for his Direction magazine. It was one of two I sent him to select from. I told him to send it back. I don't know why he hangs on to it. I'll wire him if you should choose it.

I am moving northward on Harvard University, Cambridge, Mass., U.S.A. My address there beginning March 1st will be 56 Fayerweather St. Did I or didn't I tell you the titles of any of the lectures: The Old Way to Be New. Does Wisdom Signify. Vocal Imagination. Before the Beginning of a Poem. After the End of a Poem. The third is my never-ending consideration. I'll try to throw more light on it. Should you want to reach me before March 1st write or wire Henry Holt. David has probably told you: he has got me in for more than prose up there. Don't scold me. Scold him. I need kindness at this hour of my fortunes. I go to press with a book in real unhappiness. I wish I could see you for a talk. I try to forget the politics of poetry. But I am no child any more and I can't help a sense of the machinations of the gangs up there in N.Y. You have a book before certain judges at this moment.* You must know that your services to the art as they may be called are not going to help your case. Better that you had never made anthologies.

Ever yours,

Robert

---

*[Selected Poems and Parodies was a candidate for the Pulitzer Prize, which it did not win.]

AT WOODWARD'S GARDENS*

A boy presuming on his intellect
Once showed two little monkeys in a cage
A burning-glass they couldn't understand.
Words are no good: to say it was a lens
For gathering solar rays wouldn't have helped.
But let him show them how the weapon worked
He made the sun a pin-point on the nose
Of first one, then the other, till it brought
A look of puzzled dimness to their eyes
That blinking didn't seem to blink away.
They stood, arms laced together, at the bars
Exchanging troubled glances over life.
One put a thoughtful hand up to his nose
As if reminded–or as if perhaps
Within a million years of an idea.
He got his purple little fingers stung.
The already known had once more been confirmed.
By psychological experiment.
And that were all the finding to announce
Had the boy not presumed too close and long.
There was a flash of arm, a sudden snatch,
And the glass was the monkey's, not the boy's.
Precipitately they retired back cage
And instituted an investigation
On their part, though without the needed insight.
They bit the glass and listened for the flavor.
They broke the handle and the binding off it.
Then, none the wiser, frankly gave it up.
And having hid it in their bedding straw
Against the day of prisoner's ennui,
Came dryly forward to the bars again
To answer for themselves: Who said it mattered
What monkeys did or didn't understand?
They might not understand a burning-glass–
They might not understand the sun itself.
It's knowing what to do with things that counts.
Resourcefulness is more than understanding.

Robert Frost

*[This poem was published in A Further Range with a few minor changes and without the last line, which Robert eliminated as too didactic. However, he used it as a subtitle in the table of contents.]

THE ROADSIDE STAND*

(*Euthanasia*)

The little old house was out with a little new shed
In front at the edge of the road where the traffic sped,
A roadside stand that too pathetically plead,
It would not be fair to say for a dole of bread,
But for some of the money the cash whose flow supports
The flower of cities from sinking and falling faint.
The polished traffic passed with a mind ahead,
Or if ever aside a moment, then out of sorts
At having the landscape marred with the artless paint
Of signs that with N turned wrong and with S turned wrong
Offered for sale wild berries in wooden quarts.
Or a crook-necked golden squash with silver warts,
Or Beauty Rest in a beautiful mountain scene.
You have the money, but if you want to be mean,
Why keep your money (this crossly) and go along.
The hurt to the scenery wouldn't be my complaint
So much as the trusting sorrow of what is unsaid:
Here far from the city we make our roadside stand,
And ask for some city money to feel in hand
To try if it will not make our being expand.
And give us the life of the moving pictures promise
That the party in power is said to be keeping from us.

It is in the news that all these pitiful kin
Are to be bought out and mercifully gathered in
To live in villages next to the theatre and store
Where they won't have to think for themselves any more.
And the greedy-to-do-men-good like beasts of prey
Swarming over their lives enforcing benefits
That are calculated to soothe them out of their wits
Will teach them to sleep the sleep of the safe all day,
Though it spoil their sleep at night the ancient way.

Sometimes I feel myself I can hardly bear
The thought of so much childish longing in vain;
The sadness that lurks near the open window there,

*[When this poem appeared in *A Further Range* several lines were radically altered, the title was changed to "A Roadside Stand," and another subtitle was added in the table of contents. Instead of "Euthanasia" Robert substituted the grimmer "On Being Put Out of Our Misery."]

That waits all day in almost open prayer
For the squeal of breaks, the sound of a stopping car,
Of all the thousand selfish cars that pass
Just one to enquire what a farmer's prices are.
And one did stop, but only to plow up grass
In using the yard to back and turn around,
And another to ask the way to where it was bound,
And another to ask could they sell it a gallon of gas.
They couldn't (this crossly); they had none; didn't it see?

No, in country money, the country scale of gain,
The requisite lift of spirit has never been found,
Or so the voice of the spirit seems to complain.
I can't help owning the great relief it would be
To put these people at one stroke out of their pain.
And then next day as I come back into the sane
I wonder how I should like you to come to me
And offer to put me gently out of my pain.

Robert Frost

W E S T E R N U N I O N

TELEGRAM
1936 FEB 28
NEW YORK NY

LOUIS UNTERMEYER

BIRKHEAD PL   TOLEDO OHIO

WOULD YOU WIRE BACK TONIGHT BY WESTERN UNION CARE WEBSTER
HOTEL NEW YORK WHICH ONE YOU TOOK FOR MERCURY. COULD USE THE
LEAVINGS. CAMBRIDGE AND PROSE TOMORROW. I COULD DO WITH
SOME BEST WISHES.

ROBERT FROST

[Cambridge, Mass.
May 9, 1936]

Dear Louis:

Just a word about the outcome. I know you were prepared not to
mind it. So that if you do mind it you don't mind it so much. I
hate this being automatically entered for prizes by the mere act of
publication. I have suffered nervous collapse in my time from the

strain of conscious competition and learned from it how to pretend
at least that I am below or above it for the rest of my life. And I'm
a good stout pretender when I set out to be. Nobody can catch me
setting my heart on any rewards in this world. I'd as soon be caught
breaking and entering. My days among the dead are passed. The
only comparison I suffer gladly would be with them by them. Con-
flicting claims and the clamor that goes with these among our
contemporaries are next to nothing to me. Next to nothing. I know
too well the personal politics. So do you. We have our farms and
our poems to cultivate.

I don't feel I made too big a hit with the dignitaries and authorities. There was a moment in March when I thought perhaps they
were giving me back my father's Harvard. But probably I was
fooling myself. I'm imperfectly academic and no amount of association with the academic will make me perfect. It's too bad, for I
like the academic in my way, and up to a certain point the academic
likes me. Its patronage proves as much. I may be wrong in my suspicion that I haven't pleased Harvard as much as I have the en-
compassing barbarians. My whole impression may have come from
the Pound-Eliot-Richards gang in Eliot House here. I had a really
dreadful letter of abuse from Pound in which he complains of my
cheap witticisms at his expense. I may have to take him across my page
like this: It is good to be back in communication with you on the
old terms. My contribution was the witticisms: yours the shitti-
cisms. Remember how you always used to carry toilet paper in your
pocket instead of handkerchief or napkin to wipe your mouth with
when you got through? Etcetera.—I suspect the same dirty sycophant
of having reported me to him as reported me to Wallace Stevens.
I think its Mattheson. Never mind. Peace hath her victories no
less renowned than war.

Funny I should have been on the same program (my first here)
with Coffin and Mattheson. Coffin is a peculiar case. He has poetry
in him but too profuse so far. We might take some comfort in
his having got the prize. He gets it I must think for promise, as
Joseph Auslander's wife got it. It is a policy decision. He will go
further than Joseph Auslander's wife.

Which brings me round to your anthology. Do you want to
do something to please me and make me happier on your account?
Good people fail to understand your reason for that sheet of re-

jected poets in the book. Could you leave it out of the next edition or printing or binding? Would you if you could? In my opinion it is bad all round. Honestly. I'm no fool about these things.

You must be back at the farm. Me for Vermont soon.

Ever yours

Robert

56 Fayerweather St
Cambridge   Mass
May 8,   1936

["Just a word about the outcome"—the award of the Pulitzer Prize for Poetry. Encouraged by Robert, I had reason to hope if not to believe that my Selected Poems and Parodies might receive the award. Instead, it was given to Robert P. Tristram Coffin's Strange Holiness; the year before it had been won by Bright Ambush, a pretty, innocuous volume by Audrey Wurdemann ("Joseph Auslander's wife.")

"Mattheson" was Francis Otto Matthiessen, whose declared aim was "to place our masterworks in their cultural setting," and who became chairman of the Board of Tutors in history and literature at Harvard. He was much praised for his scholarly writings, The Achievement of T.S. Eliot, American Renaissance, The James Family, and other books, before he committed suicide at forty-eight in 1950.

In the fifth (1936) edition of Modern American Poetry I had added a Reference List of poets represented in previous editions but who were, in order to make room for additional examples of the more important poets, omitted from this one. As Robert pointed out, it was a mistake; the error was not repeated in subsequent printings.]

[Amherst,   Mass.
June 1,   1936]

Dear Louis

To me that seems the best thing you ever wrote about anybody.*
I had figured that you could go no further in my description. But I was wrong. I must say I indulged myself to the full in your words.

*[A review of A Further Range, which had just been published in The Saturday Review of Literature.]

And it wasn't just the praise I enjoyed: it was even more the re-
velation and the beauty of the prose. I may not deserve it, nevertheless I can take it.

You are back where you longed to be. I have got as far back as
Amherst and my single Amherst acre. It will be about a month before I
get to the freedom of my one hundred and fifty Vermont acres. I am
homesick and sick in bed today. A temperature bug got me in the
nose. I'm not going to write you much.

The anthology books are at South Shaftsbury, thanks. You're to
have one of the Spiral Press specials from me and one of the regular
firsts if it would mean anything to you. My copies have been held up
at Holts till I should settle down at an address.

I choose to be called a Revisionist. Thanks for a new nickname.

I'm a little keyed up with fever and publication. Remember me
rather excitedly to Esther, Larry and Joseph. And have some for
yourself.

R.

Amherst May 31,   1936

*[At one of my lectures in St. Louis I met Cyril Clemens. A distant
relative of the great Samuel, Cyril had capitalized on the family
name. Among other activities, he had "organized" an International
Mark Twain Society and had constituted himself President. The
function of the Society was undetermined, but, because of the il-
lustrious association, Cyril Clemens had managed to persuade various writers to allow their names to be printed on the letterhead.
Its chief function, if it had a function at all, was the "commemor-
ation" of recently deceased celebrities.*

*On June 26th, 1936, he wrote me requesting "some lines either
in prose or verse" to be included in "A Garland of Tributes" to "our
late member, A. E. Housman." He also asked me to get a few
fellow poets to participate—"we shall count on you not to fail us."
I forwarded Cyril Clemens' appeal to Robert with a teasing letter
and, after a week, Robert returned it with this notation scribbled
across the top: "If I didn't return this at once, it was just to tease
you. I see its invaluability."*

*The letter from Robert which accompanied this follows. Inci-
dentally, Robert, in common with many, always added an "e" to
Housman's name.]*

[South Shaftsbury, Vt.
July 3, 1936]

Dear Louis:

I have been getting all sorts of wangle from this source. Clemens
says he heard I was doing Houseman's biography. I'll bet you gave
him a fill! He says one of Houseman's favorite poems was Stephen
Dowling Botts which he knew by heart. He says Houseman doted on
Gentlemen Prefer Blondes. He says Houseman rated my poetry
with these two things. So I am free to bring in a little advertising,
if I am doing the biography!

A funny thing Lesley has just run into. An English portrait
woodcarver named Miller, whom she has been seeing, goes round
spreading the suspicion Houseman never wrote a word of his poetry.
He says he can't see how Lawrence Houseman can keep the secret
much longer. He positively knows Lawrence Houseman knows. I
must say the identicalness of the "Last Poems" and "A Shropshire
Lad" of thirty years before made me suspicious. Nobody can stay in
exactly the same spot even in handwriting for a life-time. All those
poems were out of one young person utterly unlike the Houseman we
knew as scholar and author of the shallow essay on poetry. Probably
you have heard this doubt. Why not rhyme it and offer it to Clemens
as your tribute and mine?

R.

[South Shaftsbury, Vt.
July 6, 1936]

Dear Louis

On that poem it tells you please to return. But if I don't return
it to you, but keep it, as incriminating evidence, you can't return it to
Clemens, and then Coffin will have to write it over for him or write
him another as good, which would be a feat.

I go where the wind blows Chloe and am not sorry at all.

Dowson* is often in my mind these days of Tugwell and the
New Deil. (I told you Tugwell reads him to Mrs. Roosevelt. Elinor
says don't believe a word of scandal I utter.)

*[Ernest Dowson, the "decadent" British poet of the eighteen-nineties.]

Now cooperatives are up for consideration! I have long known them. There was a British one that long since came to grief in Lawrence Mass. There were two orange cooperatives I studied in California. Those were the Irish Cooperátives of my friend A.E. and there was the Coop (Coup) (Coupé) I dealt with in Cambridge. You ask what I think of them. They are one thing. But this is not telling you how to vote in November. I hope we clean up at the Olympics.

Ever yours

R.F.

P.S. Some day I must tell you the story of the taxi-driver who thanked us for cooperation in finding the house we were bound for.

[South Shaftsbury, Vt.
July 25, 1936]

Dear Louis:

Going on from where we left off: the English wood-carver's story wasn't that Lawrence Houseman wrote The Shropshire Lad but that he knew only too well the lad who did write it. He said he was a pupil who entrusted his manuscript to A.E. Houseman before he went away to the East to die young. It seems to me a damned plausible yarn. There are a lot of things about the poems that don't seem to go with what I know about A.E. Houseman. I have always been bothered by the exactness with which the Last Poems coincide in every way with the Shropshire Lad. Thirty years hadn't done a thing to the author apparently. No living person can succeed in not changing so perfectly. However, I merely pass this along for what it is worth as a trouble and fun-maker. I don't necessarily believe a word of it. I want to see someone get all stirred up over <u>something</u> besides national politics.

Don't dare to ask me what luck I am having with the eclogues I am writing to order. My method is this. As I work, mowing and chopping, I entertain myself thinking of good titles such as Where is the Place of the Ideal and Who is its Custodian? When I come in with a load of hay or wood I bring my titles with me and write them down before filling up with water at the kitchen sink. I must have

281

stored more than two hundred already. Put together with just the right flash of inspiration I don't see why they shouldn't make one poem themselves without more than a word of glue added here and there to hold them together. It sounds crazy. Don't pity me, as Wordsworth would say—pity my grief.

We wish you would come over pretty soon. I expect the Thorntons (Henry Holt & Co.) will be going by on Sunday or Monday. How about your coming on Wednesday or Thursday? Have some explanation ready of why Palmer didn't publish your review of my own, my dative book. It's a fairly good book and your review was one of the best I ever had. I hate to be done out of it by a hard-boiled inhumanitarian. What did he think? That the Republican party would repudiate in its toryism everything from old-age pensions and unemployment insurance to rural free delivery, free public school and the graduated income tax! Nock is a wonderful idealist of the old school. No least taint of socialism and paternalism for him. Absolutely all enterprise private. Herbert Spencer I remember was in favor of private armies that should contract with the government to carry on its wars. No such purity of merely presiding government has ever existed.

What do you say to next week, Wednesday or Thursday? I'm not serious about the review. But there are a whole lot of things I can be serious about. I won't submit a list of them.

Ever yours,

R.F.

[The Housman story that Lesley had heard (see the letter of July 3rd and enlarged in the foregoing letter) was a queer confusion of gossip. Housman was, of course, the author of his poems. There was no "pupil" who wrote A Shropshire Lad, entrusted it to Housman, and "went away to the East to die young." There was, however, a young friend, Moses Jackson, to whom Housman was strongly attached and whose rooms in London he shared, and who, greatly to Housman's regret, went away to India. Laurence Housman stated that he had placed in the British Museum his brother's remarkable diary revealing details of the intimacy with Jackson. "A.E.H.," wrote Laurence Housman, "wished it to be known after his death that he was what he was—a man who gave more devoted love than he ever received, and as a result was a lonely man to the end of his days."]

1936

Dear Louis:

We'll expect yous (double plural for emphasis as in Shakespeare)
next Saturday, which according to you is the fifteenth (I have not
this year's calendar to see whether you are right or not—I am dating
my next year's lectures with a last year's calendar—and I have nothing
else to go by but the newspapers which as the Presidential election
draws on I find less and less trustworthy.) Let's see, what was I
saying?

Oh, about lectures. I told you you could get all you wanted
without benefit of bureau.

And going off at another tangent at the point bureau (sp): there's
nothing the matter with the age, if you ask me, but too many officials,
and the fact that everybody who isn't riding round in a car during
what used to be working hours is out spreading fresh dirt like
courtiers spreading cloaks on roses in the road for Roosevelt's royalty
of wealth to ride over.

And another thing to complain of is that ode to oder (sp.) for
Harvard and please don't you add to my misery by asking every once
in so often how about it. Let's not talk about it. Let's not look as if
we were thinking about it. Dave should worry; because he cares for
me and he cares for Harvard. What a position that puts him in if I
should fail, as Macbeth said. To Hell with these baubles gewgaws
kickshaws. I'll write 'em a poem the last night before I face the mike.
I will and be dammed to all the uncontrolled rivers in the country.
(I've got a new slogan for one party or the other. I hadn't broken it
to you, had I? It is the name and theme of an eclogue I have written.
This is it: No Rivers to the Sea! No water shall go back! Meanwhile,
I am mowing some, chopping some, and digging a little. How
could man die better?

But there is nothing in farming either special or general. There
is no class lowly enough in this country to accept the wages of it in
comparison with the wages of industriality in the city. We have gone
so far with industrialism that there is no turning back. Our farming
will have to be done outside of this country by humbler people than
ours will submit to be. You mark my words. And the pity of it!

Signed

R.F.

283

[During late summer in 1936, Robert was in physical agony. He was afflicted with an unusually severe attack of herpes, and the sores of the "shingles" did not heal until the end of September. He and Elinor had planned to spend a week at "Stony Water," which I was foolhardily farming in the Adirondack mountains; but he was too miserable to stay anywhere except at Franconia, where Elinor took care of him and where he dragged himself up to the Fobes' house for one meal each day. He was reluctantly compelled to forego his part in the Harvard Tercentenary exercises. John Masefield, who six years before had been appointed poet laureate, was honored in his place—"I left Harvard to the English," he wrote in the next letter.]

[Amherst, Mass.
November 25, 1936]

Dear Louis

Away back early in September I swore off on letter-writing till I should get well entirely. But I begin to think if I wait till then I shall wait forever. So here I am writing again though from bed.

Don't imagine I haven't been up all this time. I have been up and down. At one stroke I cut out all duties away from Amherst. I left Harvard to the English and I left the American Academy to Billy Phelps. I dropped all the pay engagements. From that moment I was a different man. It dawned on me that all this I had been imperceptibly getting deeper and deeper into wasn't the life of my choice and liking. What a relief to have the spell broken by Herpes Zoster Agonistes! None of my friends would back me to backing down. They probably couldn't bear to see me with my bravery off. It would disillusion them. They left it to God, and God saved me with a charge of bird-shot in my right bump of ideality where all could see my incapacitation. I was in great agony of countenance when I was with you at Bread Loaf, but my stigmata hadn't yet shown on the surface. When it did come out I thought it smallpox and as such something I had better keep still about if I didn't want to start a panic. It was quite a malady. I had hardly noticed it before. That was because it was others misfortune and none of my own, I suppose. I don't mean it is humanity not to feel the suffering of others. The last election would confute me if I did. I judged that half the people that voted for his Rosiness were those glad to be on the receiving

284

end of his benevolence and half were those over glad to be on the giving end. The national mood is humanitarian. Nobly so—I wouldn't take it away from them. I am content to let it go at one philosophical observation: isn't it a poetical strangeness that while the world was going full blast on the Darwinian metaphors of evolution, survival values and the Devil take the hindmost, a polemical Jew in exile was working up the metaphor of the State's being like a family to displace them from mind and give us a new figure to live by? Marx had the strength not to be overawed by the metaphor in vogue. Life is like battle. But so is it also like shelter. Apparently we are now going to die fighting to make it a secure shelter. The model is the family at its best. At the height of the Darwinian metaphor, writers like Shaw and Butler were found to go the length of saying even the family within was strife, and perhaps the worst strife of all. We are all toadies to the fashionable metaphor of the hour. Great is he who imposes the metaphor. From each according to his ability to each according to his need. Except ye become as little children under a good father and mother! I'm not going to let the shift from one metaphor to another worry me. You'll notice the shift has to be made rather abruptly. There are no logical steps from one to the other. There is no logical connection.

Which makes me think of Larry and Joseph. I hope you and Esther and they are all together for Thanksgiving wherever you are, and that you will temper the wind of experience to them for a long time and not let them hear too much, see too much, do too much, or have too much done to them. What we don't know won't hurt us. I know too much for my age, if I may take myself for an example. I can tell you off-hand the difference between a Communist and a Fascist and even between a Nazi and a Fascist. Much discrimination has made me mad at people I don't side with.

There's more to write but it must wait till I am stronger.

Ever yours

Rob't

[San Antonio, Tex.
January 2, 1937]

Dear Mr. Untermeyer:

You may not remember me and my feminine hand may mean nothing to you, though I have met you many times (more often I

confess in books than in person) and I have written to you before
this: but I trust you will pardon the intrusion and bear with me
while I relate how pleasantly I have just come upon you once again.
My little grandson who is twelve years old has become so unwanted
a child in the regular schools on account of the enforced irregularity
of his attendance (not his health nor disposition but the vagrancy
of his family is to blame) that we have had I wont say to send him
to the Calvert School of Baltimore, but to have the Calvert School
come to him by mail. A great merit of that school is the high quality
of the text books it supplies. Among them your "Yesterday and
Today" has come into the house and I have been reading it with as
much interest as my grandson. It is too good to be called a text-book,
but that I hold is what all text-books should be. Your own poems in
it are among the best and among your best. I never wear out your
"Prayer." But in reading it again with my grandson I was prompted
to ask who first justified dissatisfaction. I guess you would now say
dissatisfaction is no more praise-worthy than satisfaction. I think they
are about equal when they stay at the noble height. The dissatisfaction of an ageing Millay however about what dogs are taken out
of appartments on leashes to do at night to posts and curbs in cities
before they go to bed—what brought such unhappiness into her
heart and head? Is she bedevilled by a canine nose for the tracer of
dogs? You have a farm in the Catskills I believe. There at least is
something I can wish you contentment with. Oh sweet oh sweet
content as Dekker says. Some crave the satisfaction of overturning the
state. Give me the satisfaction or dissatisfaction of knowing it wont
be any better when overturned. Overturned is the right word. Only
in interstellar space does top and bottom lose its meaning. No gold
beater can beat sheet so thin that it hasnt top and bottom. But do
you go on to insist on your lofty unrest. I am all for it—whoever I
am—and it need not matter to you. I may say we are of a good family.
Having no ancestors living, I think we can claim to have more dead
than people who have any living. My little grandson can claim rather
near relationship to the Robert Frost represented in your book and
only somewhat distant relationship, I fear, to the Frosts of the Frost
National Bank of this city. (Check enclosed).

Sincerely yours

Read but not signed by Mrs. Frost
113 Norwood Court San Antonio Texas

1937

[The foregoing letter is another of Robert's faintly disguised impractical jokes. Robert and Elinor had gone west again, this time to spend most of the winter with Carol and Lillian who were taking care of Robin, Marjorie's baby. They stayed chiefly in San Antonio, Texas, allaying Robert's sinus condition, and it was from there that he wrote this mingling of amusement and common sense. When I first read the last line I thought that Robert was making another of his offside puns and that the Frost National Bank was a purposeful misprinting of the First National Bank. However, a day later I received a one-sentence note reading:

> *This is the check negligently omitted from*
> *yesterday's letter.   R.*

The enclosure was a blank check from the Frost National Bank of San Antonio, Texas.]

[San Antonio, Tex.
January 5, 1937]

Dear Louis:

If you have anything important or unimportant to say to me will you please say it to me at 947 Agarita St in this town. We are investigating farming in another quarter. It narrows down to this: We will probably end our days growing Tung nuts in northern Florida, Persian limes in southern Florida, Avacadoes (Calavoes) in southern California, prunes in Middle California, garden truck in Texas, or maguy in Soviet Mexico (but only if Trotsky is handsomely received there.) We are in six minds about it by actual count. I have verified this. I say six, but it comes to seven if you include our strongest inclinations of all, which is to stay raising apples (MacIntosh, Golden Delicious, and Northern Spy)* in New England. As a side line we were thinking of Shetland ponies with so many grandchildren to break them in. Gee I'm attached to it up there. I wish I didnt have sinuses. What's the plural of sinus? Sinai? I see where President Hutchins doesn't believe in learning languages ancient or modern. Only grammar (from the Chinese glamour) logic mathematics and rhetoric. Of all the god dam—... Some more of this form-without-content guff. Aint we had almost enough of it pro tem? Kick me under the table if I'm out of order. The best way to learn to swim is out of water, pivoted on a skewer. I was taught all the motions of a screw

*The Northern spy of our Civil War is the only spy I ever heard of being honored like this.

287

driver before I saw my first screw. Very expensive Montessori education at Madam Zitsker's in San Francisco circa 1880—year Garfield was elected. What do you know? Speaking of logic, can you tell me what poet and where rhymes a bare syllogism to be set to music? I think poorly of the merely good at syllogisms. The best minds are those best at premises. The first logical flight from the premise is dangerous, the next from the first conclusion is fatal. Pay no attention to me. I'm feeling very high-strung. Its owing to having the north taken off me too suddenly.

What are you doing? I must know.

R.

947 Agarita St
San Antonio   Texas
January 5   1937

[San Antonio,   Tex.
January 18,   1937]

ANNACHRISTY   PROVINCETOWN*

Dear Mr Untermeyer,

If you will pardon the stationery and not ask where I got it. (Where for that matter did you get your own?) And now to business. I beg of you not to kill the man on my doorstep. Consider my merits and even his enough to let him live till you can catch him somewhere else with his next book.† Perhaps if he is on the downgrade (as we may hope everyone is) he will be worse then and you can have less compunction about slaying him with circumstance. I believe you have some lingering compunction now. You can't help remembering you have encouraged him to think he was a satirist. I have met him but once and then only long enough to learn that you and he have been friends. He spoke of you with admiration. Which averts me with the more dread from the shambles.

Ever yours Louis, with the mask off,

Robert

947 West Agarita Ave.
San Antonio   Texas
January 18   1937

*[An obviously fake letter-head which Robert, in a mock-tribute to Eugene O'Neill, had drawn at the top of the sheet of paper.]
†[The book I was reviewing was Rhyme and Punishment by Leonard Bacon.]

[Robert's preoccupation with education and his worries about teach-
ing—he kept the two sharply separate—came through in countless
talks, trickled into lectures, and leaked through his letters. It was
as a stimulator that he reconciled himself to himself as a teacher.
He decried the kind of education that stressed information without
appreciation. The creative impulse, like ripeness, was all. He never
assigned subjects for any written work. When, as in the incident
related in the next letter, he found that his pupils were not suffi-
ciently interested in what they had written to want their papers
back, he refused to read them, and, without another word, swept
them off his desk. "I wasnt going to be a perfunctory corrector of
perfunctory writing."

This attitude was consistently maintained, whether he taught
elementary English in his mid-thirties at Pinkerton Academy in
the New Hampshire village of Derry or, at sixty-two, simultaneously
provoked and instructed his listeners as Charles Eliot Norton Pro-
fessor of Poetry at Harvard.]

[San Antonio, Tex.
March 11, 1937]

Dear Louis:

How goes the teaching? I never see one of your anthologies but
think you are one of the most natural-born teachers unemployed.
Teaching is a pretty thing if it comes into your life just right. It can
get to be a most innocent and unselfconscious way of holding forth.
I havent even minded the marking in it. It's just another thing to make
play with and show what you mean by education. When I told a class
once I would give A that year only to those buying one hundred and
fifty dollars worth of books, B only to those buying one hundred
dollars worth and so on down to no books and a merely passing mark
everyone was entitled to automatically for having taken my course,
of course I only kept to it long enough for indication. I never taught
long enough to carry anything out. I was a symbolical teacher. After
giving a class a chance to say if there was anything in the bunch of
themes on my desk they wanted to keep and satisfied myself there
wasnt I threw them unread into the waste basket while the class
looked on. If they didnt care enough for the themes to keep them I
didnt care enough for the themes to read them. I wasnt going to be
a perfunctory corrector of perfunctory writing. But I couldnt do that

a second time. I could only tell of it to other classes to shock them into realizations. And I couldnt tell it many times. I have to move on to other acts that would symbolize my pedagogy. Its been fun. There have been more than forty things I have thought of to do in the forty-four years since I had my first small school of twelve barefooted children in a neck of the woods in South Salem New Hampshire in 1893. Thats the year I wrote the first poems I have kept in a book. My weakness has been that I havent carried out my illustrations. I didnt impress them on many. About all that impressed the ordinary run was probably that shameful fact that anybody at all could get a passing mark with me. Let life flunk 'em: I wouldnt.

My connection with Amherst tries in vain to stay somewhat a teaching one. It's partly my fault. I got up a new scheme for this year of four Big Evenings in a Beautiful Room with four sets of forty boys each picked and sent up to me by the departments of philosophy, literature, economics and science respectively. I was half way through it when I came away and I am afraid I am already sick of it. I had one good evening in which I dealt with the anxieties of Conant* and Hutchins† about the unification of knowledge. Now my imitators are having Big Evenings in the Beautiful Room I discovered. One of their Big Evenings was on the subject of Wallis Simpson‡ and the British Throne. I didnt go. I was off somewhere getting farther off the whole idea. I wondered if they discussed what it was the Simpson was able to do for the king that it was said no other lady had been able to do.

In some ways its quite awkward for me at Amherst. I have reason to think they like to have me there. But I am a little too much out in the world by comparison with the others for my comfort and theirs. Both of us try not to mind it. Those least acquainted with me mind it most. It keeps me away from faculty meetings and the faculty club and it keeps me from making practical suggestions. I grow shyer and shyer. You may not realize it but I always was a slinking (slinking I say not shrinking) cuss. I can talk if I have to to almost any rank or condition. But you have no idea what it costs me to brace up, get out of my old clothes and go where people are. I dont know how much longer I am going to be able to stand public or just active life. Harvard

*[James Bryant Conant, educator and President of Harvard.]
†[Robert Maynard Hutchins, educator and Chancellor of the University of Chicago.]
‡[An American socialite divorcée who married King Edward VIII, after his abdication of the throne in 1936.]

wrung Hell out of me. There's something wrong with me in the middle—always was. Maybe that's why I have so much sympathy with the middle classes in their hour of being wiped out by the New Republic—or at least being found out. But I mustnt trifle with the rabidities in their sacredities ever again. All I ask is the bloody showdown soon and warning enough so that I wont be caught among the scattered as in Spain but may have drawn to a hold where friends can take care of my back anyway.

We have liked your Catholic (Roman) friend Mrs Stumpf—what we have seen of her. I hadnt cautioned you that we were in San Antonio as a hide-out. That was what was called for in my case. The nice thing about Mrs Stumpf is that she has understood. So have the two others I was given away to, one by Melcher, one by Amherst. I have had pretty complete rest. All but Payne in the other places have been put off for another year. If we come back, that is. We may and we may not. There are things to say for Texas. It is not a national winter hospital like southern California and Florida. I like ranch hunting. (Im going to do a book on Farm-hunting some day) But there has been little sunlight on our skin and we have kept an undying Vestal fire going for warmth the whole time at an expense of two and one half cords of live oak logs. It could hardly be called salubrious. The nights are often really cold. A few flowers smoulder along, roses particularly. Now and then an Iris opens. But it has been a winter of a kind—sort of English kind—until within the last two weeks. Now the Blue Bonnets are coming out and we hear talk of spring. I believe I hear spring peepers. So the seasons are distinguishable—possibly into our four.

Ever yours

Robert

947 West Agarita Ave
San Antonio   Texas
March 11   1937

[Robert always flattered me by insinuating that I had given him a critical start with my (admittedly partisan) reviews of his early work —"I'm your bonfire that you started without a permit"—yet, although it was an exaggeration, I could not help but be pleased. It was, therefore, easy to share his gratification when, with the publication of A Further Range, the Pulitzer Prize was awarded to him for the third time.

Things were going well for Robert, except for his plaguing sinusitis and a sense of being out of sorts as well as out of place at Amherst. Amherst was the college with which he had become most ambivalently involved. He was soon to leave it and, after another decade, to return to it with more affection and greater honor.]

[Amherst, Mass.
May 6, 1937]

Dear Louis:

I'm your bonfire that you started without a permit from the fire warden and left burning when you turned your back to go in for lunch; and now look at it: it's got away from you, and if it gets into the woods not even the red-shirted fire fighters of the New Republic will be able to put it out. To be sure Im not yet a conflagration. There's a road and a good-sized brook to jump before I'm in the woods. But I'm a menace. At least I seem to myself so, compared with anything I ever expected to be when I was set. Some liberals dont think I am anything to worry about. But you know how liberals are. You know how they were about the Russian Revolution and the German Revolution. You can pack the Supreme Court for all of them. Nothing is crucial. Nothing poetry can do anyway—either in their opinion or as a matter of fact in my own: otherwise I shouldnt be writing so flippantly about my latest little burst into blaze. You don't seriously think it can do any harm for me to have got the Pulitzer a third time? If it does, you can blame yourself more than anybody else. At least twice before this I have caught you pouring kerosene on me to put me out. And I have information that leads me to suspect the genuineness of the extinguisher you used on me this time. All of which is to say you are of my party and I know you will be as glad I got the prize this year as I am sorry that you didnt get it last year. Damn it all what makes me talk so guiltily? I'll tell you what makes me talk so guiltily. I have been made to feel by something in the air here at Amherst today that it had been bad enough lately what with this honor and that. I might have spared them this final high hatting. And I might have if I had known in time and known how. I've grown to be fond of Amherst and I'm going to be sad if she minds my prospering a little in my old age. Let's close the incident before we both weep. I ought to add however I have done my best to maintain some sort of balance between what I do for Amherst and what I do in the world. I've given myself with conscious effort to the college since Stanley King became President. It may come to my having to go farming again. I must be sure first that I am not imagining things.

I'd like fine to see you. I need a talking to and I need it soon. I shall be working hard at home or abroad on the following days in May: 8, 9, 10, 11, 17, 18, 19, 20. I shall be scot free May 13, 14, 15, 16 (four days) and from May 21 on to June 9 (nineteen days). Please make your visit fit in. I should think we'd have more fun—I should be more care free from May 21 on. But you decide. It'll do us both good to talk politics and religion with you.

Yours everly

R.

[South Shaftsbury, Vt.
July 1, 1937]

Dear Louis:

The night of the 5th I shall be at Breadloaf talking, if my purpose holds, on the subject What There Is <u>to</u> You—that's all; so I dont see any reason for your being there till the next day to take me over to Elizabethtown for the night of the sixth (if your purpose holds). It doesnt look at this moment as if I could have Elinor with me. She's too tired from a year of excitements. I finished off at Harvard without her.

The above title should be amended to read The Question of What There Is <u>to</u> You with the accent on the word without a capital. I may not stick to it. I thought of it too long ago. I begin to incline to talk about The Broader the Base the Higher the Apex Ought to be Able to Be—<u>ought</u>. All there is to either talk is in the title. I never recommend anything I do in public. You know how unintentionally I have landed out of a clear sky on the platform. Stay away till the 6th.

What I wanted to be in life besides a poet was a base ball pitcher and a scythe mower. And a philosopher. And a U.S. Senator. I have about realized it as a scythe mower. I have mowed about half an acre since I came home. I have to admit though that Lankes who doesnt like anything says he doesnt like my mowing style. I call for a shorter stiffer blade than formerly. I get into trouble with a long limber blade.

Everly

R.

[*Recognition of Robert Frost mentioned in the next-to-last paragraph in the next letter, edited by Richard Thornton of the Henry Holt staff, was issued in 1937 to celebrate the twenty-fifth anniversary of the publication of Robert's first volume. It was a symposium of critical studies of his philosophy as well as of his poetry; the many contributors included William Dean Howells, Edward Thomas, Ezra Pound, Edward Garnett, Lascelles Abercrombie, Amy Lowell, Elizabeth Shepley Sergeant, Padraic Colum, James Southall Wilson, W.H. Auden, C. Day Lewis, and myself.*]

Concord Corner   Vermont

Aug 23   1937

Dear Louis

Waterboy you are! Where are you hidin? Sometimes I feel as if I deserved a hidin myself for the selfish way I have behaved in life. I heard someone say to an audience in public that he was the opposite from me: Whereas I had never done a thing except for the fun of it, he had never done a thing except from a sense of duty. Its an almost true picture of me. I got into this Concord Corner (so called because there were only four houses left standing in it and my buying two and in fact nearly three of them constituted a corner under the Duffy Sherman act) on an impulse of self-indulgence. I liked the idea of cornering Concord. Heavenly Concord, image of Love, send us thy blessing down from above. Make thy light enter each loving heart. Heavenly Concord, never depart. The reference, I take it, is to the Concord Mass of which the Concord bit I am cornering is but a fragment. Piece piece Orestes-like I breathe this prayer. If Concord is almost synonymous with peace, how much more so is a piece of Concord. You mustnt forget my grandmother was a Colcord which at once connects me with the sea (in poor ablution) through my cousin Lincoln Colcord and again through him with Lincoln Apomattox apotheosis and A PO-Edgar a po of respite-and-Nepenthe fame. But lets see—what was I getting back to?

> What we desperately want
> Of Concord Vermont.

We came into it for peace and it hath given us more publicity than our publishers. The two dirty little houses we bought have got

onto the front page of the St Johnsbury Caledonian, so that now
waitresses ask me to autograph my bill for my meals rather than pay
cash and anybody feels free to stop me on the street and start talking
about the sunset. We may have to scrap these investments and move
on. I am seriously contemplating a number of radical departures, all
based on a profound questioning of the terms on which we have our
lives. I will bear watching in the next twenty-five years, dead or alive.
What I do next wont be so rash that a letter addressed to me at
Concord Corner wont sooner or later find me out. I have spent all
this time and paper complaining of the kind of publicity I hate when
I should have been applying for help in the kind I must have for my
books. What I am to ask of you for my publishers is a contribution
from your already written works to a book to be called The
Recognition of R.F. They need it in our business. We thought it
might be sent to students expecting me to write them my life. There'll
be this that and the other thing all the way down from the beginning.
It should be a story made out of criticisms. I thought of having you
in with a part of your article in the new anthology spliced to what
you had in Mercury about a Further Range. What do you suggest?
You must have been one of the very first to speak out in America.
Where is that speech? How would it come in under some such
heading as A First American Review. Lets have the estimate you like
best. I myself incline to what you have in the Anthology + the review
in Mercury.

If people will let alone of me I shall get to the finishing off of
something for your poetry text book.

Everly

R.

HOTEL STONEHAVEN
SPRINGFIELD, MASSACHUSETTS

[October 4, 1937]

Dear Louis:

I tried two or three times yesterday to tell you that Elinor had
just been operated on for a growth in her breast. I doubt if she fully
realizes her peril. So be careful how you speak in your letters. You can
see what a difference this must make in any future we have. She has

L

been the unspoken half of everything I ever wrote, and both halves of many a thing from My November Guest down to the last stanzas of Two Tramps in Mud Time—as you may have divined. I don't say it is quite up with us. We shall make the most of such hope as there is in such cases. She has come through the operation well, though there was delay over her for a day or so at the Hospital for fear her heart wouldn't stand the ether. Her unrealization is what makes it hard for me to keep from speaking to somebody for sympathy. I have had almost too much of her suffering in this world.

Ever yours

R.

HOTEL STONEHAVEN
SPRINGFIELD, MASSACHUSETTS

[October 5, 1937]

Dear Louis

Say I hate or have come to hate the thought of all the letters I ever wrote. I never intended them to be kept. I cant ask people to destroy them I suppose. But in a particular one like the last about Elinors peril I wish I could make an exception. I cant bear that it should ever become a public matter whether I am dead or alive. Please burn it. Be easy on me for what I did too emotionally and personally. It spoils letters when it gets so they're undeniably collectors items or biographers material. Gee there are some eventualities we didnt bargain for, and I'm going to have them different if I can.

It did me good to hear your voice today and have your assurance of a fifty per cent chance. Thats more than the best batter has when he goes to the bat.

Ever yours

Robert

October 5   1937

[In spite of Robert's request to burn the letter of October 4th, I could not bring myself to destroy it. The threat that the cancerous growth might spread evoked so deep a sentiment that it seemed wanton to expunge both the fact and the force of the emotion. Fortunately, metastasis did not occur.]

[Amherst, Mass.
October 17,   1937]

Dear Louis:

Your triumph was my triumph. It excited you more than me
because you expected it less. Then again you were in the firing line
and I was only at head quarters. I couldnt have had more general
satisfaction if I had been General Foch. You neednt worry about my
conscience: I have no scruples about winning glory at a safe distance
from the danger.—We poets dont even know whether to take each
other seriously. Anyway we hardly hope to be taken seriously by the
bourgeoisie (sp.) (I never wrote the word before and scarcely ever
said it) The enclosed clipping shows we are taken seriously by Stalins
Third International if not by Trotsky's. For Godssake remember me
to Joseph and Lawrence in all this confusion of self consciousness.
We mean to be better and better people, don't we?

Ever yours

Robert

Oct 17   1937

I enclose a fair copy of the poem, Willful Homing.

WILLFUL HOMING*

It is growing late and time he drew to a house,
But the blizzard blinds him to any house ahead.
The snow gets down his neck in a chilly souse
That sucks his breath like a wicked cat in bed.
The snow blows on him and off him, exerting force
Downward to make him sit astride a drift,
Imprint a saddle, and calmly consider his course.
He peers out shrewdly into the thick and swift.
Since he means to come to a door, he will come to a door,
Although so compromised of aim and rate,
He may fumble wide of the latch a yard or more,
And to those concerned he may seem a little late.

Robert Frost

*[This original draft differs considerably from the final version printed four years
later in A Witness Tree.]

[*The "triumph" in the preceding letter refers to four lectures I delivered during October in Johnson Chapel at Amherst College sponsored by the Henry Ward Beecher Foundation. I was somewhat worried that the talks were too informal; but Robert, who had been the prime mover in arranging for them, beamed his satisfaction. He was, nevertheless, a little self-conscious during the last, "The Living Inflection: Humor and Understatement," which was largely devoted to his poetry. The general title of the series was "Play in Poetry."*

The "enclosed clipping" from an unspecified newspaper was headed POETRY PLOT REVEALED *and ran as follows:*

> That poets had their share in the plot to overthrow the rule of Stalin in the Moscow government was the charge made at the meeting of the Writers' Union at Moscow. The controversy centered about the poets Pasternak and Selvinsky, who were backed as the leading poets of present-day Russia by Bukharin and Karl Radek, literary figures of note, condemned as Trotskyites. The poets are supposed to have conveyed treasonable ideas by a "double-meaning" system as "double-dealing in literature."

Twenty-one years later the item took on new significance. The "double-meaning" Pasternak was the same poet who, in 1958, was awarded the Nobel prize and was compelled to refuse it.]

[Gainesville, Fla.
December 24, 1937]

Dear Louis:

I sent you a one-song pamphlet last night, but that cant take the place of all the letters I havent written since I saw you (sober) in Amherst. I dont have any trouble killing time. I find I can sit indefinitely and not do a thing with equanimity. Dont think for a moment that my state of mind is the success psychology of a person whose income from poetry alone etc etc etc etc. I am neither happy nor unhappy (New Year suggests these considerations.) At any rate I can't seem to determine which I am. At any rate I think it none of my business nor anybody else's which I am. What am I talking about it then for? Or for then? I'm not. Im just giving way to my cal cur. Lesley says that last nights paper carried some invective by Edgar Lee Masters against the United States for not buying anybodys poetry but Kiplings and Guests. I blame you largely for

that man's chronic bad temper. I see R-p-t (repetitive) Coffin
is making up to him—snuggling is the current word. I am very
sensitive to political shifts like this. We are choosing up sides,
balancing our powers for the next world war in art. But what I am
getting at is that characteristically of the clouded mind, the
megacephalus Masters is really mad at the critics for not praising him
but makes himself think he is mad at the United States for having
killed Vachel Lindsay. He's like a baby in whom pain isnt localized
or locatable as yet. You pinch its big toe and it thinks it has a
bellyache.

Lets see where did I start off? Oh with my not having written
lately and look where my cal cur has landed me—with both feet on
poor Masters. Neither you nor I wish him harm. Only why doesnt he
write poetry? Or if he cant write poetry why cant he be reasonable?

I read about Heine absorbedly. It is a splendid book and must
solidify your reputation as a critical essayist (not to say biographer).
I don't want to seem to try to steer you, merely to point the way
you should and must go. You can cast them all in the shade, the
Wilsons Eliots and Molly Columists. I summon you to defend your
country from the lot of them and particularly the last named.
She gets credit for being learned. She is not even that. How
does she get credit? By presenting her credentials just like some
one-horse doctor from an unheard of mid western university. She is
eddicated she'll have you understand. By what? Spare us! Your field
is the critical essay (not unmixed with the personal or biographical.)
You can dominate the field both writing and speaking.

The poems are all right—they are a fine job such as only a poet
can do for another poet. They are as near as one poet can come to
another in translation. I have worked too long at translation however
to be perfectly happy about anything that ever comes of it. Your book
is useful. I don't deny its use to those who dont want to miss a great
poet for want of the German to read him with. I like it up to a point
considerably short of your own poetry and essays. Pay no attention to
me. I have congenital limitations.

Lesley is home from Mexico with plenty to tell. The charm of the
situation is that the peons are taking over the land by vote of the locals
so they wont have to work on it any more. That sounds all right for
them. Why work when a living falls out of trees right onto your

head? But how about the government? It simply must have someone to tax for roads armies famine emergency and self perpetuation. It is too easy to think out.

She wants to thank you for your advice about the biographical preface. It will help a lot. She wants me to tell you though that the place where she seems to balk at telling one of my old bed-time stories was not meant to be arch or coy. She didnt have a copy of the story with her and was leaving a place blank for me to fill in. I wrote out a number of stories at the time (circa 1905). The question is whether we can decide on any one of them as good enough to use.

There is talk already of your April visit here. I wish it could be earlier. We must go home April Fools' Day. You can't look in from somewhere in the region earlier I suppose.

Best holy day wishes and then some

Ever yours

Robert

Bay St North
Gainesville   Florida
Day before Christmas   1937

[The Frosts again spent the winter of 1937-1938 in Florida, this time in Gainesville. Robert and Elinor shared a house with Lesley and her two small daughters; Lillian and Carol with Prescott and little Robin settled near them.

"R-p-t (repetitive) Coffin" (first paragraph of the previous letter) was not only a gibe at Coffin's assembled given names, Robert Peter Tristram, but at his repeated and rather blatant campaign for (as Coffin put it) "taking my poems and my ideas about poetry directly to the American people with my own voice ... Poetry is the art of making people feel well about life; poetry is saying the best one can about life; poetry is the art of putting different kinds of good things together: men and plows, boys and whistles, hounds and deer, sorrow and sympathy, life and death," etcetera.

The critics mentioned toward the middle of the letter were Edmund Wilson, T.S. Eliot, and the late Mary M. Colum, all of whom were (contrary to Robert's opinion) far better critics than I.

As to Heine, my two-volume Heinrich Heine—Paradox and Poet had just been published. One volume was a biography; the other was a translation of some five hundred of Heine's poems. The reviews were unusually gratifying, but, knowing how much of the original music had escaped, I appreciated the truth of Robert's epigram (in another connection) that poetry is what is lost in translation.

I was planning (next to last paragraph) a selection of Robert's poems that would appeal especially to young people and act as a general introduction to his work. I had hoped that Lesley, writing from her youthful memories, would furnish a memoir rather than a formal biography, and I expected to confer with her during a southern lecture tour in early spring. When, some years later, the book, appropriately entitled Come In, was published, it was my biographical foreword that prefaced the book because Lesley felt she was too close to the parent, the poet, and the poetry to write with the ease that comes from detachment.]

[Gainesville, Fla.
January 1, 1938]

Dear Louis:

Why dont you manage to see us sometime during the winter? Bring snow on your boots and in your whiskers like the Russians I didnt see myself but some of my friends or friends friends saw coming by train down through western England that terrible first year of the war to save the Western Front.

Our weather has been sunnily lovely except for a rain or two to start spring in the grass.

What I said was the style is the way the man <u>takes</u> himself. It is that shining through that makes you like or dislike both talk or reading. I think it a more damaging test of Masters put that way don't you?—though he comes out plenty bad enough your way. He takes himself for Hell and all. But even if he took thought I doubt if he could manage to take himself any more presentably or engagingly. By his age we are none of us able to revise ourselves very deeply. He went wrong at some point. It would be a good subject of psychological study to determine where. He took the wrong turn in the way he took himself, but why? Maybe because he refused to meet Theodore Roosevelt in the crowd with the rest of us at that party you may remember. He insisted on being invited alone and got invited alone next day. Roosevelt who had condemned his poetry probably because he haughtily stayed away from the party, changed round the next day and decided to like his poetry because he had him at Oyster Bay. Such are the sorrowful chances if you know too much about the politics of art. I mean it isnt innocent of me to be able to tell you the low down on the downfall of a rival. But I'll bet it dates from that display of immodesty.

1938. Now we're getting into years of the century that feel like a repetition of experiences almost personal in the last century. My grandfather spoke naturally of those other thirties. My mother was born in the late forties Ten years more to a rounding out there. Quite a long time to my own birth year again though. Jimminy, do you suppose I can make it. I wish we all could together my relatives friends and I. I'll soon have been married fifty years. Thats half a hundred. Time suggests further considerations, but I won't go into them in prose.

Ever yours
Robert Frost

743 Bay St North
Gainesville   Florida
January 1   1938

[Gainesville,   Fla.
January 18,   1938]

Dear Esther

Don't send a second check. I must have the first round somewhere.* I will destroy it when I find it: and you can make it right with us by sending me a book when you see one you think will do us good by taking us out of politics. I am practically out now with a great sense of relief from trying to think about what was beyond me. Tell Louis from me he lives too near Rockwell Kent for his social conscience. The Kent kind think with the heart and feel with the mind. That is to say they reason about those they should merely love, and love those they should merely reason about. That's why their greatest excitement is always for the dog for the moment undermost in the world's perpetual dog-eat-dog fight. Revolving dogs are intended for a mental exercise and shouldn't enlist sympathy.

We like to hear of your winter weather. Some day we mean to

---

*[At this time Robert needed a little cash and, since he was reluctant to apply to his publisher, I sent him a check from home. He misplaced it. Learning of this while on a lecture trip, I wrote Esther to send another check.]

face it again ourselves. I hope Larry and Joseph know when they are well off. Is there anything better than snow and sunshine when you are young and healthy?

Ever yours
Robert

743 North Bay St
Gainesville   Florida
Jan 18   1938

[Gainesville,   Fla.
February 5,   1938]

Dear Louis:

Thats the first time you ever named a poem of mine I couldnt remember having written.* It gives me the funniest feeling. My "unfoxy vixen"! May be she's a person and you speak figuratively. I should say the only fox I ever spoke of in a poem was the fox in The Quest of the Orchis. Has somebody else been writing my verse better than I can write it or at least well enough to have deceived you? I shan't rest till I hear more. Francis Frost Coffin Lew Sarrett and some of the new proletarians are all suspect. I fear malice somewhere.

Poor Tom Ferrill and poor Ezra—one does for himself and you do for the other—on showings A and B. Such travesties of what we have desired take the spirit out of my old age more than all that can be called defeat. They give me that what's-the-use feeling. I say Let's die pretty soon. I mean a natural death of course if any. I come round all right in an hour or so. This February 5th has lifted its fog on redbud in blossom and mocking bird in song. I read a really noble man-power article on our ideologies and isms last night that encourages me to believe there will be enough of us left for seed whatever happens in New York and Washington. Down with the Stock Exchange! I mean down with the quotations on the Stock Exchange. Money talks and will sooner or later tell us where we get off. The bottom is none too deep. Abase the basement for all of me.

*[An unsigned poem which had been sent to me and which, in turn, I sent to Robert. Later, I learned that, imitating the Frost idiom, it was by another Frost, but no relation: Frances. What with Robert Francis and Frances Frost, the situation was somewhat confusing.]

I wonder if Ezra will appreciate your effort to be temperate with what he has become in memory of what he once promised to be come.

Ever yours

R.

[Gainesville, Fla.
March 10, 1938]

Dear Louis:

Your book is more than a keen interest: it's an out-and-out pleasure.* And how well it shaped up as you cut it for the Saturday Review. As your extra essay rounded off the book I thought Benny DeVoto's editorial capped your article. This accidental team work suggests what you and he and I could do to these times if we wanted to stage a deliberate putch. But we are reserved for better things than steam-rolling over our enemies. Only I confess my imagination is possessed with the magnificence of the forces let loose in action all round us and I am tempted to wish I was one of them instead of what I am. Two years ago I half wanted to be a Senator (none knows how.) Now I'm caught thinking I'd like to gang up with a few friends and run a magazine a few numbers for the rectification of public thought. Luckily this plethoric energy didnt manifest itself when I was younger or you might have seen me a ward politician working for Tammany.

Thanks for the discretion of your Phi Beta Kappa review of my recognition. Gee I have had some queer feelings about that book. We have to remember it is chiefly an advertisement. It can't help making me wonder what I am though. The best of your criticism of me all these years is that you have never treated me as welfare-minded or of social significance. Its an accident that the welfare-minded have made a path to my door. I don't consider myself to blame for their mistake. Ferner Nuhn (Henry Wallace's ghost writer) is still at me for having led him on with North of Boston to expect better of me than A Further Range. Its his damned party politics. I tried to tell him and his like in the Need of Being Versed

---

*[Play in Poetry, the four lectures delivered at Amherst the previous year, with an added chapter (stealing the title from Whitman): "Poets to Come."]

in Country Things that my subject was not the sadness of the poor.
He puts his finger on The Lockless Door with uncanny shrewdness,
but not enough to quite bring him through. He says the rich in their
top hats knocked at my cottage door and though having provided no
way to keep them out I retired through a back window and left
the place to them, it was only to join them mischievously by circling
round behind and taking their view of the house I had built. Funny
but except for one person Robert Von Moschziskes all the rich who
ever came to my door were the condescending welfare minded and
they came under the mistaken impression that what I had built was
a house of the poor. I was flattered by their attention and I decided
to let them have the house any way they would. I wanted to be
honest with them in all gentleness: and I satisfied my conscience
with hints at the truth, as in the last part of the poem New
Hampshire and in The Need of Being Versed in Country Things.
But lately I have been getting cross with their fatuosity. My house
may be only a one-room shack but it is not the Poor House: it is
the Palace of Art. North of Boston is merely a book of people, not
of poor people. They happen to be people of simplicity or simple
truth miscalled simplicity. Before I get through I'm going to drive
these social servitors back to the social settlements or to concentration
camps where I can starve their sympathies to death. For myself I
never sought anyone I wasnt thrown with and I never thought of
anyone I was with as a possible subject for literature or charity or the
literature of charity. I shall be made to realize sooner or later how
clean I am there however dirty I may be in other respects.

We aren't going to be able to wait for you here. Elinor and I
must be in Washington by March 29 for my first platform of the
season.

Tell Esther to make me out a new check. I'll buy candy with it
for myself not for the grandchildren. This not from self pity but from
pitilessness toward all. Ever yours

R.F.

Theres more I want to say but I've used up all my paper—
I should have written smaller.

[On the first of January, 1938, Robert had written: "I'll soon have
been married fifty years." The half-hundred mark was never reached.

Suffering again from respiratory trouble, Robert contracted influenza, but it was Elinor who failed to survive the winter. She died of heart failure on March 20th.

I had visited the Frosts sometime before the catastrophe. The tragic news reached me while I was lecturing in North Carolina. I cancelled those of my southern engagements that I could to be with Robert. From Gainesville we went north to Amherst for the funeral in the college chapel; I was one of the pallbearers.]

WESTERN UNION
TELEGRAM

1938 MARCH 20

GAINESVILLE   FLA
LOUIS UNTERMEYER
LECTURER SPEAKING COLLEGE DAVIDSON NCAR
ELINOR DIED TODAY OF HEART ATTACK

ROBERT

WESTERN UNION
TELEGRAM

1938 APR 4

GAINESVILLE   FLA
LOUIS UNTERMEYER
HOTEL ROOSEVELT NRLNS
UP AND GOING AGAIN, BUT DOUBT IF I CAN STAY HERE TILL YOU
COME. MANY LAST THINGS TO TEND TO AT HOME. WAS HOPING TO SEE
YOU BEFORE THIS. YOU WILL BE BACK NORTH SOON. SEE YOU THERE.
DONT WORRY ABOUT ME

ROBERT

WESTERN UNION
TELEGRAM

1938 APR 7

GAINESVILLE   FLA
LOUIS UNTERMEYER
HOTEL ROOSEVELT NRLNS
YOU WILL BE SURE TO FIND ME HERE

ROBERT

CARPE DIEM*

Age saw two quiet children
Go loving by at twilight.
He knew not whether homeward
Or outward from the village
Or (chimes were ringing) churchward.
He waited (they were strangers)
Till they were out of hearing
To bid them both be happy.
"Be happy, happy, happy,
And seize the day of pleasure!"
The age-long theme is Age's.
'Twas Age imposed on poems
Their gather-roses burden,
To warn against the danger
That overtaken lovers,
From being over-flooded
With happiness, should have it
And yet not know they have it.
But bid life seize the present?
It lives less in the present
Than in the future always,
And less in both together
Than in the past. The present
Is too much on the senses
Too crowding, too confusing,
Too present to imagine.

R.F.

Gainesville, Florida,
April 17, 1938.

[It was hard for Robert to maintain his balance after Elinor's death.
He sold the Amherst house where he and Elinor had lived; he resigned from the college; he talked recklessly, and for the first time
in his life the man whose favorite tipple was ginger ale accepted
any drink that was offered. He committed himself to a long and
wearying lecture trip. He was elected to the Board of Overseers of
Harvard University, but there was a long black period before he
found anything resembling peace.]

*[With slight changes, this appeared four years later in A Witness Tree.]

307

[Amherst, Mass.
May 16, 1938]

Dear Louis:

You have lived a lot of life since I said good bye to you at the door of this hotel and so have I. I went out and did a thousand dollars worth of lecturing last week on purpose to see if it wouldn't improve my symptoms to overwork and to see also how much on a pinch I can hope to earn a year when I am cut off from Amherst College. Fifty two times a thousand is fifty-two thousand. Drop two weeks for vacation in the mountains at Concord Corners and it still comes to fifty thousand, which is in a painfully high bracket for these days or for a poet for any days. But it would be as a moralist rather than as a poet I would be pilloried there.

I don't know myself yet and won't for a long time, if I ever do. I am so quickened by what has happened that I can't touch my mind with a memory of any kind. I cant touch my skin any where with my finger but it hurts like a sad inspiration. In such like condition I spent all of yesterday packing deadly personal things in the desolated house on Sunset Ave. My strength went out of me to the last drop and then Carol carried me back to the house in South Shaftsbury. I feel as a tree that has lost its whole surrounding forest by bad forestry. I've got to have someone to complain to. I promise not to trouble you with the private very much more. Carol stood by me all day like a good boy. He has got himself together. He didn't know what to do those first days.

I read at your new book with admiration for your teaching skill. Your range and exactness of knowledge show that you should have been a teacher. Don't leave farming for any length of time to be either. All the same I wish you could have shared two or three years for an exhibition of your powers at some university.

One more short tour (de force) and I shall be free to 'tend to one or two things in New York and Boston and then free to go home to Vermont. I shall be Freedom itself—

> And Freedom shall awhile repair
> To dwell a weeping hermit there.*

I have much to talk about with you.

Ever yours

R.

*[The couplet quoted is from William Collins' "Ode Written in the Year 1746."]

[North Bennington,   Vt.]
July 4th   1938
S.S.V.

Dear Louis:

Bread Loaf tonight and tomorrow. Then Wednesday I thought if you would have us, Lillian Carol Robin Prescott the dog and I or I and the dog, if I may presume not to yield place to a dog, would arrive with you in the afternoon, all but me for Wednesday night only, I for a couple of nights. I must get over to see John and Irma Friday or Saturday—wherever they are, at Hanover or Concord Corners. We would reach you after lunch Wednesday. You can prevent this landslide by parleys on the telephone and give no offense to

Yours ever
R.

[In 1938, as the next letter indicates, I was treating myself to an indulgence common to many metropolitan refugees: I was in the throes of pleasurable if highly unprofitable farming. Against the advice of the local grangemaster, I was raising Hampshire hogs instead of high-bred horses and hens, which Robert liked and which I not only distrusted but detested. With the help but not the encouragement of a county conservation program I covered a sand hill, where nothing else would grow, with small pine trees which, to everyone's amazement, turned into a forest. I tried to breed Eskimo dogs for work and play—and possible sale—since the winters were appropriately sub-Arctic. I kept faun-colored Jersey cows for their beauty and butterfat cream instead of the far more commercial, milk-bountiful Holsteins. "Stony Water" was the finest place in the Adirondacks for scenery and the worst place for a farm. It took me ten years and the loss of several thousand dollars to find that out.

"The Kents" were Rockwell Kent, the artist, his wife, and, sporadically, his children. "The Smith Senior" was my secretary, Frances Elizabeth Mitchell, who had gone to Smith College and had poetic yearnings.]

South Shaftsbury   [Vt.]
July 14   1938

Dear Louis:

Home is the farmer home from the Untermeyer farm and farming as she is done in the Adirondacks. In spite of certain sins of omission and commission (you omit the domestic hen and you commit the pent-house party, albeit mildly) you're a better farmer than I am or ever thought of being Gunga Din. I gives you your certificate of membership in the Grange or the Farm Bureau and if you want it signed I'll come over and have another game of tennis with you whenever you're inclined. But this time it had better be on the courts of the Kents: unless you think poetic justice hasn't yet been done the Smith Senior for not being a poet. Any self respect I have left proceeds from my having been your advisor in the matter of the damned spot where you planted the pines. You have trees, your own butter, a wealth of cats (untaxable) and a single-barrel smoke house for when your pigs shall litter. I could wish you thought better or rather thought more of horses and liked hens in the least. But if I were Radamanthus or Peter you would get by me for the obviously happy life of the animals that revolve around you—not to mention the children in this letter.

Everly

R.

Concord Corners Labour Day
[September 6]   1938

Dear Louis:

I thought of two things today the first things I have thought of since I was under the influence of your liquor at Stony Water two weeks ago in the company of that first rate fighting intellect Lee Simonson. What a good time I had that day. I had meant to report to you on it, but I had somehow got it into my head that you knew all about it already. However that may be, I am more interested now preparing you for my attempted come-back—to Stony Water. I want to come back next Monday in the car of my daughter Lesley and be left there by her after a day or two pleasantly spent on her part playing tennis with us and then be put on some train by you later in the week after some more tennis on our part exclusively and get about the business of furnishing my tenement in Boston at 88 Mount Vernon Street overlooking Louisburg Square overseeing Harvar(d) College and overlooking any little defects there may be in human nature in the rough. Dont you think so? I mean do you agree? In cutting marble and in drawing with silver point you can't undo what you have done. So may my writing be. Stet is my slogan. And if it can't stand let it set.

But as I set out to say I thought of two things today which shows that I have resumed specious sayments.

The first one was in repartee with a propagandist who came to the door to permote the cause of a thirteen month year. Honestly I said isnt this just the feminist movement in a new manifestation? Who sent you out?

The second was that cooperatives having found that they cant compete with individual private enterprise have hit on the idea of seizing the government and destroying their rivals by force. Then they are communists.

In almost the same breath I thought of you over there not two hundred miles away with your wisdom of this world, a pundit who has punned it without money and without price to all comers. All I have to do if I want advice (and I do) is to come to you in forma pauperis and not pretend it is anything else I am after. I've been crazy for the last six months. I havent known what I was doing. I wonder if you have noticed and could tell me. Thats what I'm coming over to find out. Dont talk too fast. Let it come out as it will by rambling round the subject. Do you think I am still living in this world? Tell me the truth. Dont spare me.

We are about a hundred miles from Bread Loaf which is about fifty from you. We'll have lunch at Middlebury and reach you by five probably or a little earlier. Gee!

Everyours

R.

Monday unless you forbid.

WESTERN UNION

TELEGRAM

1938 SEPT 8

CONCORD CORNERS VT

LOUIS UNTERMEYER

STONY WATER EN

PLEASE WIRE BY WESTERNUNION WILL YOU MEET ME MIDDLEBURY INN MONDAY AFTERNOON THREE OCLOCK IF NOT POSSIBLE NAME OTHER TIME ROBERT FROST

[*The summer of 1938 was a bad one for Robert. He had not yet regained his equilibrium—"I've been crazy for the last six months. I havent known what I was doing," he had written in September. He did not find comfort until Kathleen (usually referred to as Kay) Morrison, wife of the poet and Harvard professor, Theodore Morrison, came to his aid, helped him to move into an apartment on Mt. Vernon Street in Boston, and, as secretary-companion, managed his affairs.*

During this unhappiest time, there was much visiting between our homes on the opposite sides of Lake Champlain. On one of Robert's long weekends, he literally lifted a painting from the wall. Given to me by Alfred Harcourt, it was a "primitive" by a schoolteacher, Hazel Knapp, a winter scene which Robert said belonged with his winter poems. It was so much a part of his mental furniture that I did not let him return it.

Robert was also uncomfortable about his relations with Henry Holt and was again thinking of going to Harcourt, Brace. The Holt firm had undergone various changes in management and personnel; at that time he felt no one there cared much about his poetry. After Alfred Edwards took charge of Robert's affairs in 1946 he was not only reconciled but completely secure.]

Appartment 30

88 Mt Vernon St
Boston   Mass
[October 12,   1938]

Dear Louis:

David brings me the bad news that you wont write anymore letters to me or anyone else if I dont give back the winter picture I sacrificed my virtue to steal. You are mad. Well now let me tell you something. It will be spoiling the picture I have of my self if I give in and give the winter picture to its rightful owner. I am posing as ruthless highhanded and above morals. But of course if you are determined to call my blough, I am like Chamberlain: I wont undertake to face it out. Consider the picture returned and me humiliated and restored to the honor-bright-standard. Anybody could tell I was going to be good in the end. Why hold out in a false position out of resentment against the universe?

Tomorrow I will sing the Take the Road Song from the Beggars Opera and set out for Columbia and Columbus.

Whats eating me at the last moment is how to compose a tactful letter to Edward Bristol to get a friendly release from Henry Holt and Co. I wish I could talk with you about it.

Tell me about the sick and hurt in your family.

Ever yours

R.

88 Mt Vernon
Boston   [Mass.]
[November 28, 1938]

Dear Louis:

The above indicates what it has come to with me.* Be moderately sorry for a poor old man of iron will. Nothing I do or say is as yet due to anything but a strong determination to have my own way. I may show as sick, but it is for practical purposes. I dont know what I deserve for a nature like mine. I was boasting to David this very day that I was clever enough to beat my nature. Did he suppose I wasn't?

Well among the things I don't deserve but hope to get is what I am about to propose from and for you. If you consent to do it you will be doing more than one thing to make my immediate future a joy forever. Not to beat about the bush a page longer it is: Come to Bread Loaf and team up with me in poetry criticism four or five days a week for the two weeks of the Conference. You could go home over the week end and I could go with you. We would make the poetry consultations and clinics a joint stunt to the nation. I got up this idea and Ted Morrison† took to it like live bait. I needn't go into my mixture of motives except to say that they are all honorable by now. I am growing more and more honorable every time the moon comes safely through an eclipse. (Subject for a poem.) I am really a person of good aspirations and you know I am or you wouldn't stay my indulgent friend through all my errancies the way you do. There is nothing to report on my present state of mind but that though it is

*["What it has come to with me." Robert had always lived in a house with acres of fields and trees around him; 88 Mt. Vernon Street was a small apartment.]

†[Theodore Morrison was in charge of the Writers' Conference at Bread Loaf.]

better, it can still be alleviated by any kindness you will do me. I sometimes take it pretty hard to be left in a city apartment alone with the night. Dont think I haven't myself well in hand, though, and beyond the need of psychoanalysis. As I have said, I cut up no ructions but with design to gain my ends even as aforetime when I was a child in San Francisco I played sick to get out of going to school. There's a vigorous devil in me that raises me above or drops me below the level of pity. Nevertheless I sometimes weep internally with sorrow (but not as often as externally at the eyes with cold weather). Grant me my request, oh friend of many many years!

This year I have worked hard in the open, and I think it has done me good. My secretary has soothed my spirit like music in her attendance on me and my affairs. She has written my letters and sent me off on my travels. It is an unusual friendship. I have come to value my poetry almost less than the friendships it has brought me. I say it who wouldnt have believed I would ever live to say it. And I say it with a copy of The Independent containing my first published poem on the desk before me. I was thrust out into the desolateness of wondering about my past whether it had not been too cruel to those I had dragged with me and almost to cry out to heaven for a word of reassurance that was not given me in time. Then came this girl stepping innocently into my days to give me something to think of besides dark regrets. My half humorous noisy contrition of the last few months has begun to die down. You have heard a lot of it and you are hearing it still a little here. I doubt if it has been quite dignified. I am told I am spoken of as her "charge." It is enough to be. Lets have some peace. You can figure it out for yourself how my status with a girl like her might be the perfect thing for me at my age in my position. I wish in some indirect way she could come to know how I feel toward her.

Ever yours

November 28   1938

Robert

[Miami,   Fla.
February 17,   1939]

Dear Louis:

I seem as bad in some ways as when you saw me last. I dragged both Morrisons south with me to Key West and then here to

Hervey's* for a week's stay. After their desertion I was sent to Cuba for five days for obvious reasons and then for the same reasons when I got back was removed from the small house where I had lived with them to another without associations. I am not supposed to be in on the secret of what people think is the matter with me. It's pretty ill we all dissemble. I go north to some more of my fate next Friday morning and should be at my office (88 Mt Vernon St Boston Mass) with my secretary not a minute later than Monday morning February 27th.

I have been talking of you with the Chapins who are living in another of Hervey's little houses. They tell of the good time they and her father, Henry Van Dyke,† had with you in the Bermudas once. I remembered that you had a good time too.

Hervey is the same old historical philosopher as of old only more so. He has many figures, parallels, and ancient and modern instances. To show his sympathy with me he says he hates to see one of the most powerful engines of the country wracking itself to pieces from running wild after the loss of its fly-wheel: also I remind him of a big steam boat with all its lights ablaze and the band on it playing as it passes Goat Island toward the roar of Niagara Falls. I, who never sang played read or wrote a note of music have learned for consolation to play on a "recorder" by ear entirely the whole of The Linden Tree and Wanita. What is to become of me? Will I end up on the concert platform? That is for my friends and well-wishers to puzzle out. I am past feeling that it is any concern of mine.

My secretary has marked down six lectures in March before the sixteenth. Those too are prescribed for my consolation. Money seems to interest me faintly in both the getting and the spending, but only faintly and far away. I got a telegram‡ partly in Latin from the Holts yesterday saying it was their pride to let me know that my latest book

---

*[Hervey Allen who, long before he published his huge best-seller, Anthony Adverse in 1933, had hoped to be recognized as a poet. He founded the Poetry Society of South Carolina and lectured on poetry at Bread Loaf, where he became Robert's close friend and mine. He died of a heart attack at his home in Florida in 1949.]

†[Essayist, short-story writer, poet, pastor of the Brick Presbyterian Church in New York, Professor of English Literature at Princeton, and President of the National Institute of Arts and Letters, Henry Van Dyke deserved his characterization as "an adventurous conservative." Exuberant to the last, he died at eighty-one in 1933.]

‡[The telegram read: "NO SATISFACTION COULD BE KEENER THAN THAT WITH WHICH WE PUBLISH TODAY YOUR COLLECTED POEMS. EXEGISTI MONUMENTUM PERENNIUS AERE (I have reared a monument more lasting than brass)."]

was that day on the market.* The Latin gave me a stir that I never expected to have again in this world from publication. I tell them I am become non-elatable and indisgustable. My chief signs of life are shown in any debate. He [my opponent] interrupted me in company the other night to ask while I was reciting Raleighs The Wood The Weed the Wag what in the world was meant by Wag. I had got to the first time it occurs in the poem: "And they be these, the wood the weed the wag." My answer was the poem itself would have told you if you had had the manners to wait and hear it out. It goes on to say The wag, my pretty knave, betokens thee. I put plenty of accent on where it was needed.

I am still your good friend if only because you still take an interest in such things as the prefaces I write. I call the one in the new book The Figure a Poem Makes; the one in the Bread Loaf Anthology, The Doctrine of Excursions. I haven't read the Anthology. I rather dread it though I am told I have no need to. I remain a sceptic in educational publication.

Have a great success at Michigan and let me hear of it.

Ever yours—

Robert

South Shaftsbury Vermont

June 26 1939

Dear Louis

You are said on good authority to have said of me that I am dangerously apt to get anything I want. Don't worry about me then, but accept the risk that what I want may prove too much for your sense of propriety. There is an old proverb that goes Half a cake, especially if it be the upper half frosted, is better than no bread. But assuming for the sake of argument that for the moment I am at a loss to know what I want, what as a friend do you want for me? What or whom would you prescribe for my unhappiness. For I confess I am not as pleased with myself as I might be. Would you suggest either of the Worlds Fairs or Soviet Russia or farming again with a farmer and his wife to take care of me. This new Harvard entanglement is no help. None at all. I am going to say in my letter of acceptance that I

---

*[Collected Poems.]

wonder at myself for still hanging round education after all these years; but I suppose what keeps me is the reasonable doubt that the college belongs entirely to the scholars. I long for a change of problem. You and I will soon be coadjutors at Bread Loaf. My idea has reached an extremity where I will maintain it against all custom that poets (at least) do not come to Bread Loaf for improvement or correction: they do not come to find a publisher or get help in finding a publisher. Coming to Bread Loaf with manuscript is in itself a form of publication.* To read each other and be read by each other is the object. I have about tapered off to nihilism in school.

I wish I could get over to see you some time soon and hear what you would say to me. Maybe I will manage to. Lets see is there some thing more I was going to say?

Ever yours
Robert

Bread Loaf, Vermont
August 4, 1939

Dear Louis

I should have come out of my dreamy trance before this and at least long enough to tell you some of my dreams for your Freudian delectation and interpretation (with my help) The wonder is I can come out now for a moment for any practical purpose. Look! This is August 3rd isnt it. A week from Saturday will be Saturday the 12th. There will be a lull of three or four days there between the 12th and the 16th when I thought I would visit you to conspire with you against the academic way of teaching poetry. Gee! or should it be Jee! But I say nothing till I satisfy myself that while I was growing less and less (ac)ademic from having lived at the academy, you havent been growing more and more academic from not having lived at the academy. It will make no difference in my regard for you if you have come to think that authors can be corrected into existence. All teaching is below where you and I live. We laugh at it when we don't howl. We believe in it a little. We believe in it a great deal. It is as old and valid as the family. It will be here after Carl Marx has denationalized Russia. It is as sacred as Capitalism. (Capitalism

*[One of Robert's self-contradictions. He used to say that Bread Loaf was a Mecca for the unpublishable in search of a publisher.]

being but another name for the struggle for existence with a little emphasis on the dollar ahead.) But my trouble is that people dont stop getting openly and shamelessly educated early enough. I guess that's my trouble. Never mind what it is. I am good natured and tolerant toward everything even the Writers Project with Alsberg and Gorham B. Munson at the head of it. What the Hell! How does the rather second-rate poem go? "Give a man a horse he can ride." Or is it horse? I quote from memory. How _does_ the poem go?

The Conference begins on the 16th. One or more of the Morrisons might get me as far as Ticonderoga on the 12th or 13th and you might be invited to meet me there to take home.

Ever yours

Robert

Ripton   Vermont

88 Mt Vernon once more. [Boston,   Mass.]
Off for two weeks of Kentuck
and Ioway this 12th Oct.   [1939]

Dear Louis:

I will never be impatient of minor poets again after what one of them did to emancipate me from the insanity of conscience that made me strew the streets of Boston with fifty dollars worth of coppers in three months last year in contempt of property in money land and women and buy two thousand dollars worth of semi-precious stones in contempt of my own character and reputation for the unornate. I begged of you to let nothing I did dismay you, and you listened to my prayer. I shall forever lay up in your favor the evenness with which you took my violence. You will have to concede that I kept my head about everything in the world but myself. I have understood Chamberlain every step of his diplomacy. He was disposed to have England mind her own business. The French with their old vindictive terror are still asking Germany to scotch herself back into a third-rate nation as a guarantee that she wont try to conquer the world. Her best guarantee that she wont try to conquer the world is that she can't conquer the world—not with Russia as powerful as appears and England ruling the waves and the United States always here ready to cast the deciding vote. It is amusing to see Russia yawn and stretch at word that Geneva is delended, and with

one pass exorcise those nonsensical little figments of the French
imagination along the Baltic. I seem never to lack for something to
say to the news of the day. Mind you I may be wrong. But I am able
to give things an intelligibility. Not so my own personal affairs of
late. Part of the time I was acting on the theory that I was plain bad—
yes and <u>talking</u> in public and private on that theory. But for me to
be bad somebody else had to be bad too and that was unhypo-
theticable. Much has followed and will follow on further, give us
time and the patience of the good-natured. I am not usually a
frantic person. I shall be all serene now. Keep this to see if my
prediction doesn't come true. I am more concerned to justify my
prophesies than my moral principles. It is the greatest relief I ever felt
to know that what couldn't be, wasn't. I knew that it wasn't but I
had to be told in form that it wasnt. I had to have it documented.
Blessed be poetry for the clue and more than clue. I owe absolutely
everything I am to poetry—all I know about the pronunciation and
spelling of words, all I know of geography history and philosophy and
all I know of true thought and feeling. I owe my position to poetry;
I owe my income. I owe <u>you</u> to poetry. Actuations must be compre-
hensible. I can see what's eating Gannet easily enough. You got
as good as could be expected from a man so soft on St. Edna.* The
worst fault in his review was his failure to see that you werent writing
about the greatest people in the world but the greatest you knew
personally and could legitimately bring into a book that was after
all your own biography.

R.

[Cambridge, Mass.
December 26, 1939]

You Old Slow Coach
  Is this the upshot of your coaching? Information please.

R.

*[Robert was now suffering physically more than mentally—a serious
operation was impending—but the pain did not stop his raillery. He*

---

*[In his review of my quasi-autobiography *From Another World* Lewis Gannett was
pleasant but not enthusiastic; possibly, as Robert surmised, because I had slighted
Edna St. Vincent Millay.]

had frequently teased me about Nathalia Crane, whom I had discovered years ago in Brooklyn and whom I had hailed as the most remarkable literary prodigy since Marjorie Fleming. Nathalia's first volume, The Janitor's Boy, had been published when she was ten, and the English Society of Authors and Playwrights had invited her to become a member. Opinion about her was divided. Some claimed she was a hoax that would soon be exposed; others prophesied she would surely be destroyed by her genius. Neither prediction was fulfilled. Nathalia Crane continued to write and live normally; she married a gemmologist, moved to California, and taught poetry at the college in San Diego.

Robert's inquiry—"Is this the upshot of your coaching?"—concerns a clipping about Nathalia, then in her twenties, who had presented Mayor Fiorello La Guardia—he was startled to find himself rhymed as "Lord Mayor"—with "A Ballad of New York." It was one of her least happy efforts and, with its "classical" references to Plato, Cervantes, Aesop, and Merlin, proved that she could write as affectedly and ineffectively as any laureate composing to order.]

88 Mount Vernon Street
Boston, Massachusetts
January 15 [1940]

Dear Louis:

Everything goes well if slowly. Robert is still feeling weak enough and in sufficient discomfort to make the hospital discipline bearable. He is putting on what looks like a planned campaign against emotional disturbances and is doing more than his share towards recovery. The doctors apparently did what they consider a record operation and cleaned up what they believe may have been the source of a great deal of infection—probably the cause of both the last outbreaks.

No date for dismissal yet. In all probability another ten days to two weeks.

Best—
Yours—
Kathleen

[Though the preceding letter does not reveal it, Robert was a recalcitrant patient; he refused to go to the hospital until the pains were too much for him. He was finally operated for hemorrhoids on January 10, 1940. When I visited him at the hospital and, later, in his apartment, I learned that he had had the condition for years and that recently an inflammation of the kidneys had set in. Our talk rambled along about other people's illnesses; then, abruptly, we started to discuss T.S. Eliot's lectures published later that year as The Idea of a Christian Society. Robert was serious for a few moments, but I detected a glint that told me something neither cultural nor kindly was coming. "Eliot and I have our similarities and our differences," he said. "We are both poets and we both like to play. That's the similarity. The difference is this: I like to play euchre. He likes to play Eucharist."]

[Boston, Mass.]
March 31   1940
Eve of departure for
Western Pennsylvania, Iowa,
Utah, Indiana, etc.

Dear Louis

In all that concerns me trust your poetic imagination more than anything you hear from my over-anxious friends. I was willing the doctors down in Florida* (Dr Waterman to be precise) and the doctors up here (Dr Moore to be precise) should have me as sick as they pleased if it would get the prescription out of them that I wanted, namely, that I should "go back north where I was born bred look to die." I told Dr Watermans wife in his presence and hearing that he had better look out for me: I wasnt above using him merely to get out of work or get round a woman. She answered I would have to be a pretty smart man to get anything out of her husband that he didnt see me getting and intend me to get. I ventured to say I was a pretty smart man when I had been up awhile and was well awake. Well the result of our fencing was that my aches and pains were authenticated and I got my order to go North for my health instead of further South. Looking each other wickedly in the eyes we both laughed. No money passed between us. In exchange for his treating me I treated him for not knowing infallibly enough how to tell a good quatrain from a bad quatrain; a discrimination I demonstrated

*[He had gone there for his convalescence.]

that lies at the very root of all poetry appreciation. A bad quatrain consists of an epigram of about the extent of two lines which the poet thinks of first but saves for the last and two lines preliminary labored into some semblance of validity or at least plausibility to round out the form. A good quatrain keeps you from knowing which member of the rhyme-twins the poet thought of first. I had the doctor's acknowledgement of value received.

Everly and steadily yours
Robert

[Spring of 1940]

Yes, Louis, this* looks all right as far as my self consciousness lets me look into it. I'm prepared to accept it or anything on your say so. To hell with me anyhow.

R.

[Tragedy overwhelmed Robert again in the fall of 1940. Only two years before, he had lost his wife and, four years before that, his beloved daughter, Marjorie. Now, his only son went out of his mind. Carol, too, had written poetry, but nothing he sent out had been accepted for publication. Like Robert's sister, Jean, he succumbed to a sense of persecution; rejected and despondent, he turned against the world. He had hallucinations; he suspected the men who worked around the place and felt that passing cars were spying on him. Robert tried to restore his balance and talk him out of his conviction of defeat; but, after listening to Robert speaking all night against frustration, Carol said grimly, "You always have the last word." In a fever of total confusion, Carol even threatened his father's life. A few days later, past reason and beyond help, he shot himself.]

[Boston, Mass.
October 26, 1940]

Dear Louis:

I took the wrong way with him. I tried many ways and every single one of them was wrong. Some thing in me is still asking for the

*["This" was a ten-page typescript discussion of "The Homeliness of Robert Frost." It was written by one of my students, Dorothy Tyler Reed, when I was "Poet in Residence" at Kansas City University during the fall of 1939.]

chance to try one more. There's where the greatest pain is located. I am cut off too abruptly in my plans and efforts for his peace of mind. You'll say it ought not to have come about that I should have to think for him. He really did most of his thinking for himself. He thought too much. I doubt if he rested from thinking day or night in the last few years. Mine was just an added touch to his mind to see if I couldn't make him ease up on himself and take life and farming off-hand. I got humbled. Three weeks ago I was down at Merrills telling Lee how to live.* Two weeks ago I was up at South Shaftsbury telling Carol how to live. Yesterday I was telling seven hundred Harvard freshmen how to live with books in college. Apparently nothing can stop us once we get going. I talk less and less however as if I knew what I was talking about. My manner will be intended to indicate henceforth that I acknowledge myself disqualified from giving counsel. Kay says I am not to give myself up. Well then I'll be brave about this failure as I have meant to be about my other failures before. But you'll know and Kay will know in what sense I say things now.

I dont know where you are. I shall be at Cornell College Mt Vernon Iowa Wednesday at Paul Engle's Iowa City Thursday at Ferner Nuhn's 2215 Grand Blvd Cedar Falls Iowa Friday. If you were anywhere near it might help to see you. If youre not all right I'll keep till later.

It was the thought of a real friend to ask Prescott† to Elizabethtown for the winter. That would have been a fine life for him. But his immediate future had already been arranged for with some friends of his and Lillians in the neighborhood. He ought to keep on with his school another year where he is—another year anyway. He had been up all night alone with Carol talking. He heard the rifle go off downstairs. He didn't flee the house. He called the police. He called me. He stood by till the police came. He called his friends the Hollidays and went home with them to wait for me and Lesley. Lillian has lain close to death in the Pittsfield (Mass) hospital for several weeks.‡ She had to be told. She couldnt be persuaded at first that Prescott hadnt been killed too.

I failed to trick Carol or argue him into believing he was the least

*[Our friends, Merrill Moore and Lee Simonson.]
†[Prescott, Carol's son, was sixteen years old.]
‡[Lillian had gone to the hospital for an operation.]

successful. Thats what it came down to. He failed in farming and he failed in poetry (you may not have known). He was splendid with animals and little children. If only the emphasis could have been put on those. He should have lived with horses.

This is a letterful

Yours

Robert

88 Mt Vernon St
October 25   1940

[Boston,   Mass.

January 4,   1941]

Dear Louis

Why don't I take advantage of this season of gladness on earth as it is in heaven to pour out my resentment against you once more for not wearing the same front to your listening audiences as you wear to your reading audience in the article on Yeats Pound Hillyer and Fearing in the current Yale Review? You are the only brains we've got in the criticism of poetry. You are neither a poet spoiled to make a critic nor a poet who had to turn critic in revenge on the Muses for having failed him, nor a professor. You have the poetry in you express and implicit, you have the philosophical and psychological apparatus, and you have the magnanimity. And the rest has been added unto you. I dont want you showing carelessly on the lecture platform as of indifferent and questionable intellectual rank. You read some of the best poems of our time when you were here at Harvard: and they were your own: but you apologized for them and deprecated them. I wasnt the only one who was angry at you for your sin against yourself. And then you joke too much. Im sure. Im sure. Fifty percent too much—seventy five per cent. People who tell you otherwise are deceiving you and possibly themselves also. You have a cause to maintain. You have easily the best critical powers in our day. I am not asking you to carry them any way but easily. But there are times and places where you must take thought not to damage your position of authority by clowning. Clown with your friends clown at home clown at Bread Loaf (on the Tennis court and in

Information Tease.) * But for the confusion and confounding of your enemies and mine I wish I could insult you into an almost punless high literary dignity for the lectures you have it in you to better America with. Sometimes I wonder if you respect your audiences enough considering your political origins. I dont want you to respect the masses too much—just enough. You can lift them to anything you please with your platform skill.

But I linger too long in the negative side of this letter. Go the platform way to perdition if you will. What is one soul lost to me? I write only from a fresh access of pride in you on reading your article in The Yale Review. Let us rest in that and make the most of great things that no little thing can take away from much.

I heard that Prescott had a fine time with the boys. My thanks can be added to his.

Larry† has been here. Kathleen is here daily. She is screwing up my courage for the enterprise I have ahead of me in Florida. I dont see how I am going to develop that estate down there unless she helps me on the spot.

Forever yours

Robert

88 Mt Vernon St
Boston   Mass
January 4   1941
First letter this year!

New Year
and
Christmas Greetings
from
Robert Frost
1940

* [Robert's rebuke was merited, for my lectures had become much too informal; fearing that I might be talking over the heads of the uninformed, I talked down to the ready response. Having been an occasional guest performer on the radio program *Information Please*, I had put on a somewhat more "literary" program at Bread Loaf.]
† [Lawrance Thompson, one of Robert's most devoted biographers; his *Fire and Ice: The Art and Thought of Robert Frost* was published in 1942.]

OUR HOLD ON THE PLANET*

We asked for rain. It didn't flash and roar.
It didn't lose its temper at our demand.
It didn't blow a gale and misunderstand
And give us more than our spokesman bargained for.
It didn't, because we owned to a wish for rain,
Send us a flood and bid us be damned and drown.
It gently threw us a glittering shower down.
And when we had taken that into the roots of grain,
It threw us another and then another still,
Till the spongy soil again was natal wet.
We may doubt the just proportion of good and ill;
There is much in nature against us. But we forget:
The number of people alive has been steadily more.
Take nature altogether since time began,
Including human nature in peace and war,
It must be just a little more in favor of man,
Say a fraction of one percent at the very least,
Or our hold on the planet wouldn't have so increased.

Robert Frost

[Boston, Mass.
March 11, 1941]

Dear Louis:

You know how I am about your Anthology. Being in it I look on [it] as having done more to spread my poetry than any one other thing. I here put it in writing so I can't go back on it however our respective stocks may go on the market of the future. And it feels like aggrandizement (sp) to be given more room with every edition. You say you want Come In and Happiness Makes Up in Height for What It Lacks in Length. And may be a third of my own choice. Anything you single out gains strength in my estimation. I ought not to confess this if I am sure it is a weakness. But after listening to the arguments for and against approbativeness (sp) I am <u>not</u> sure.

I go on being what I am regardless of the commonplaces of cheap psychology.

*[Enclosed in the letter of January 4, 1941, the poem differs considerably from the final version in Complete Poems.]

Mrs. Stumpf wanted particularly not to be forgotten by you if I could keep her from being.

I stayed with intelligent priests in San Antonio and had good talk with them on subjects most Protestants never heard of. Last year I was concerned with the sin accidie. This year it is the idea in the two-word phrase felix culpa.§ It could be turned against me personally and I am willing it should be: I am less and less on the defensive. I am not concerned with my own deserts. But I like the phrase dwelt on largely as with Thomas Aquinas and in a little poem I dont believe you have in your books (I will have it in my Harvard Book of Verse that David still hangs round waiting for).* Oh I should say its about Adam's felix culp in eating the apple—felix because by it Mary became Queen of Heaven. I have to smile at the easy way the church has of saying deeply. I am safe from all its moonshine however significant I can make it seem to myself. I havent a chance of salvation—and as a matter of fact neither have you nor anybody else. Whatever is ahead of us it will undoubtedly be something different with the same name. Felix culpa—that is only the good of evil born in Emerson whose chair I occupy rather reverently (though not so's you'd notice the reverence in the expression of my countenance.) †

To humbler functions, I call you, awful power who as anthologist presidest over the destinies of us poets. Isn't it ironical that —— has got you all attentively fixed up not to leave him out of your great book and indeed even perhaps to increase him into it with some of the wretched little word-plays of his new book: and at the same time such a serious old poet as poor old Percy‡ has to go down on his knees to you in public to beg in if not for his own sake for his dead wife's. God damn much on earth. Kathleen says all you ask of me is lenience to indulge you in being humanly sinful against the light of criticism for Percy. If it were me I should go back and find enough of Percy in his small ones of the past to make a figure of him to represent the first ten years of the century. He hasnt been good for a long time. But how about when he was young along with Will Moody, Robinson and Ridgely Torrence? Pretend not to notice my

§[Happy fault.]
*[David McCord almost talked Robert into making an anthology along the lines of Quiller-Couch's Oxford Book of English Verse.]
†[Robert was the Ralph Waldo Emerson Fellow in Poetry at Harvard from 1939 to 1942.]
‡[Percy MacKaye.]

tears. They are for my own possible fate. Save me from Oblivion
bong Mr bong Mr bong! Say thats a good poem of Kenneth
Fearing's. Save your money and buy a farm in Vermont.

Are you coming down to see my new home at 35 Brewster St
Cambridge and hear my new play on the subject of cider?*

Ever yours helpfully
Robert

[During 1941, Robert and I often shared the so-called poetry "clinics" as well as the tennis courts at Bread Loaf; his tennis partner
was Kathleen Morrison while mine was one of the younger Fellows,
usually Richard Ellmann, who seventeen years later won the esteem
of scholars with his Yeats: The Man and the Masks and again, in
1959, with his comprehensive critical biography of James Joyce.
Robert and I also shared a cottage close to the Inn, where the work-
shops (a fancy name for classrooms) were situated and where the
lectures took place. Robert had acquired the Homer Noble Farm in
nearby Ripton and was putting his house in order—"I wouldn't want
anyone to say I was living in a disorderly house." Once in a while
he would take a midnight stroll and walk to Ripton, where he would
sleep until midmorning. The following note, slipped under my door
on August 22, 1941, was written during one of his restless nights.]

A MANIFESTO
OF MANIFEST DESTINY

Having got up a momentum of expansion into territories occupied
by none but Indians and not knowing how to curb it or where next
to turn it unless into territories occupied by Greasers and Kanucks I
have decided to move my Capital of the World to the Noble Homeric
farm (for the night) at Ripton Vermont (rather than to Berlin
Moscow London or Washington) and clarify the present world
situation by offering to take over everybody's quarrel with Hitler and
to fight the war out with American forces and resources alone. I can
see no other way to establish our national identity and define
Democracy. I would say to all my adherents and coherents, Come ye
out from among the fools who would lose in the confusions of old

*[Besides his masques and a burlesque playlet, Robert wrote a serious full-length
play, which, in spite of his hopes, was never produced. According to a number of
readers it was unplayable.]

328

European casuistry. Give the present war up as a hopeless mess and begin all over with a plain statement of who is opposed to whom and what to what. Then if we win ours will be the loot the glory and the self-realization. If we fail the Indians will have their chance to come back.

The Fearer*

Full of fears but determined to be un<u>afray</u>ed.
Please tell Kathleen at breakfast!

[Cambridge, Mass.
December 15, 1941]

Dear Louis:

Merrill told Kathleen and she wrote to me on my travels that you had had a mishap but her letter did not overtake me till after I got back home where it started from. The first I knew of you was from Lesley when I was in Washington last week. You opened a seam in New Orleans. It wasnt from eloquence but according to one theory from tennis (which I hate to hear blamed for fear you will be expected to stop playing it) and according to another theory from rehandling too many books of poetry and placing it too high (on shelves in your ivory tower).† But here you are back in Elizabethtown all safe and sewed up to go again. I can permit myself some lightness in speaking of what I should have taken seriously if I had been in on it earlier before you knew you were all right. Well we are tied now for hospital honors. Weve both been knifed once. I can tell you this for your encouragement: I am stronger tissued in the cicatrice than anywhere else in my corpus. I seemed to hurt in it severely at intervals for a year nearly but am now painless. Esther's letter of today says you are all right as is also our bargain about Sonny.‡ Good news. You are a main dependence in my life I suppose you wont mind my saying out at a time like this. Tell Esther the name Sonny sticks. Kathleen will write her about it.

At Kathleen's own suggestion I am <u>loaning</u> you the two enclosed

---

*[This pun on Der Führer from the man who reproached me for punning!]
†[I had had a hernia operation, which gave me an excuse to pamper myself for a short time.]
‡[Robert had "bargained" to acquire "Sonny," one of the Morgan colts which were being bred on the Elizabethtown farm.]

photographs to apprize you of what you may have missed in the papers since it got crowded off the front page by world events. Nothing can surprise you—nothing that I do—after your years of experience in business and art. I do not tell you this to surprise you; simply to inform you so you will know what dispositions to make in the premises. It is no secret anywhere as you may gather from the rather sour faces on the right looking in on romance.* Kathleen and I will be at work at 35 Brewster St Cambridge Mass, she says till war permitting me to go south in January. One of the poems in my new book is called On a Serious Step Lightly Taken. (I dont like the way this paper takes ink from a pen.) The book, by the way, is to be called A Witness Tree, a title which if it doesnt explain itself will be ambiguously explained on the next-to-the-title page by the following rhymes:

BEECH

Where my imaginary line
Bends square in woods, an iron spine
And pile of real rocks have been founded.
And off this corner in the wild
Where these are driven in and piled
One tree, by being deeply wounded
Has been impressed as Witness Tree
And made commit to memory
My proof of being not unbounded.
Thus truth's established and borne out
Though circumstanced with dark and doubt
Though by a world of doubt surrounded.

The Moodie Forester†

SYCAMORE

Zaccheus he
Did climb the tree
Our Lord to see.

The New England Primer

A goddess haec otia franget to bring forth a book again.‡

Ever yours bewildered

R.

*[The two photographs showed Robert stiffly posed at a country wedding.]
†[Another of Robert's plays on names. His mother, daughter of a Scottish sea captain of Orkney origin, was born Isabelle Moodie.]
‡[(A goddess) shatters this leisure ...]

[Boston, Mass.
January 15, 1942]

To prayer I think I go,
I go to prayer—
Along a darkened corridor of woe
And down a stair
In every step of which I am abased.
I wear a halter-rope about the waist.
I bear a candle end put out with haste.
For such as I there is reserved a crypt
That from its stony arches having dripped
Has stony pavement in a slime of mould.
There I will throw me down an unconsoled
And utter loss,
And spread out in the figure of a cross.—
Oh, if religion's not to be my fate
I must be spoken to and told
Before too late!

RF.

Dear Louis: You had the first of this from me long ago and I recently had a copy of it back from you. You never saw the end of it. You never saw how it came out. There was no end to it till now that I could write that I <u>had</u> been spoken to and told—you know by whom. This is merely the letter I always owe you and it's all my news for the moment—if it can be called news. It's not such as to get me into the newspapers. I believe I am safely secular till the last go down—that's all. I decided to keep the matter private and out of my new book. It could easily be made too much of. I can't myself say how serious the crisis was and how near I came to giving in.—It would have been good advertising.

R.F.

[Ripton, Vt.
September 21, 1942]

Dear Louis:
I'm alone here all this week. Can't you bring Esther over to cook for us one day or two days. You could bring me a copy of your new

331

book* too which I have just been reviewing sight unseen with David on the telephone. I called him up to say a word for Hyde Cox as a possible assistant to him on The Harvard Bulletin, and did we talk! When he got half way through it was so long that he proposed dividing the toll. You see how that would figure out. After it was all over the operator called me up to make sure of the number of anyone who could afford to talk so long. "Yes 15 MI," says I proudly. David said your book was a great labor and practically flawless. His only doubt was the inclusion of Ogden Nash. He admired your justice to the Millay. This and much more while the toll piled up. I like to hear David talk ordinarily, but when it costs more than the fare to and from where he is I begin to feel bathed in a new experience.

I mean to have a try at a snatch of prose for you in the next few desolate days. Kay is coming back for me next Monday. I shall go back with her to Cambridge the following Friday.

The dog got bitten and the horse I'm afraid got a spavin by getting a hind foot over her hitching rope in the stall for a hard struggle before we found her.

Ever yours

R.

[Cambridge, Mass.
May 6, 1943]

Dear Louis

The prize came as a genuine surprise after what you said about the committee's having decided I couldnt have it though I deserved it. You had prepared me to be satisfied with the golden opinion of the committee. Kay woke me with the news. It struck her breathless and me rather pleasantly thoughtful. Bliss Perry has just been in to explain his vote for Have Come Am Here—his and Cross's. I eased him of his embarrassment. He didn't know how much I knew and I didnt tell him. His conscience wanted him to confess that the authorities at Columbia whoever they are were the ones I had to thank for the award. They had gone over the heads of the committee and it was for the first time. I could see that he had been as surprised

---

*[The sixth revised edition of Modern American Poetry.]

as I was. But really it is you I have to thank for this as for so many
other things. Your accompanying letter to the authorities whoever
they are and your coming out so honestly in The Yale Review no
doubt brought the result. My only objection to it is that my fourth
time estops me from saying much if Roosevelt tries for a fourth term.
What I like best about it is that it defends my old age from the
undertakers. I don't have to tell <u>you</u> who renewed my youth.

Ever yours
Robert

May   1943
Cambridge

*[In 1943 the Advisory Committee on the Pulitzer Prize for Poetry
consisted of two scholars, Bliss Perry, formerly editor of the Atlantic
Monthly, Wilbur L. Cross, Dean of the Yale Graduate School,
founder of The Yale Review, and Governor of Connecticut for eight
years—and myself. It was agreed that A Witness Tree was the out-
standing book of poetry of the year; but both Perry and Cross felt
that Robert had received sufficient recognition and that the award
should be given to the next best, José Garcia Villa's metaphysical
Have Come, Am Here. I made myself somewhat unpleasant by
insisting that though the second-best was good, it was not good
enough to dispute first place, and that, moreover, merit should
not be compromised. Our divided opinion with my minority report
was sent to the judges at Columbia University, whose decision established a precedent when it was announced that A Witness Tree was
the final choice and that Frost was the only author ever to win the
Pulitzer Prize four times.]*

[Cambridge,   Mass.
October 27,   1943]

Dear Louis

Don't I beseech you say a word to anybody about my juvenile
dream of Broadway. And dont let Esther. Be sure. Kay and I may
repent and want it forgotten. Im already scared. There are plenty of
reasons why we shouldnt tempt fate with another ambition. I want to
stay totally uncommitted till I can think what I am doing. Paul
(Osborn) asked if he might drop a hint in the right quarter, but I
positively forbade it. I must at least wait till I am entirely extricated

from the second piece, the Masque of Mercy. It was unlike me to run down there with half a scheme in my pocket. I never seem to complete anything that gets talked about and demanded before it is done. So protect me. It may be we shall decide in the end to content ourselves with the pair of masques as poems and merely publish them as such.

In the Yale Review there is review of a book a Britisher wrote to show how much freer and better England was than the United States of America. How rude of our allies to argue so at such a time. I heard Sir William Beverige say that twenty five years ago. Elsewhere I have just come on another Britisher maintaining we had no apples to compare with the Blenheim Coxes Golden and Ribstone. How rude of them at such a time. At such a time is all I say—when we who at best have but a secondary interest in their goddam war are doing so much to help them through it. Of course for them their freedom and their apples are better than ours. But our freedom and our apples are better for us. No artist is any good who wishes he were some other artist: no nation that wishes it were some other nation. I dont know whats the matter with us but I fear we have too many who wish we were England. Say ten percent (twelve or thirteen million) principally along the eastern seaboard wish we were England and another ten percent (more scattered) wish we were Russia. That may not be enough to worry about since it leaves eighty percent who know that the only way for America to count in art government and social life is by being itself.

I'm happy to know that you are safely out of any office where it might be obligatory for you to say more than you meant in praise of people who may be our allies but are not for that reason necessarily our friends.* What with the air full of falseness, it's a relief to be where you dont have to listen to it or join in it for social reasons.

Ever yours
Robt

[Robert always twitted me with being a "kind of socialist" when I was, at most, a distressed but dogged liberal. Then came the Sec-

---

*[The Office of War Information, which I had joined after Pearl Harbor and which I left to become an editor for the Armed Service Editions, a non-profit organization which supplied the overseas forces with some seventy million selected and specially printed paperback books each year.]

ond World War when, with a horror of dictatorships, I left my Adirondack farm to join the Office of War Information as Senior Editor of Publications. Working with other writers opposing fascism, I tried to get Robert to participate. I was hurt when he stood "above the battle"; the issues involved seemed to me so catastrophic that they would prevent Robert from remaining aloof. This, in spite of the fact that Robert had always prided himself on being a "separatist," a hater of patriotic platitudes and "gang thinking," so that he had made his isolationism mockingly clear in "New Hampshire":

> I may as well confess myself the author
> Of several books against the world in general.

And in "A Considerable Speck" he had emphasized his rejection of anything resembling universal brotherhood:

> I have none of the tenderer-than-thou
> Collectivistic regimenting love
> With which the modern world is being swept.

He had elected to abstain—four years later on a Christmas card he signed himself "a Lucretian abstainer from politics"—and I should have understood the logic of his refusal to write propaganda. He made his position plain in the remarkable, intimate, and hitherto unprinted letter-poem which follows.]

[Ripton, Vt.
August 12, 1944]

Dear Louis:

I'd rather there had been no war at all
Than have you cross with me because of it.
I know whats wrong: the war is more or less
About the Jews and as such you believe
I ought to want to take some part in it.
You ought to know—I shouldn't have to tell you—
The army wouldn't have me at the front.
And hero at the rear I will not be—
I mean by going berserker at home
Like a post warden bashing in a door
To put a light out some fool family
Has treasonably left burning in a blackout
To go off on a round of night-club parties.
I couldn't bring myself Tyrtaeus like
To sing and cheer the young men into dangers

335

I can't get hurt in. I am too untried
A soldier to preach soldiering to others.
And then please recollect I'm not a writer.
I'm good at most things as I ever was
I can't deny (you may deny it for me).
But I was never any good at routine writing.
I always hate in filling out a form
To call myself a writer. It would sound
Pretentious now to call myself a farmer,
But when it was a modest claim to make
I liked to make it. I'm a lecturer
And teacher now on income tax returns,
Though lecturer's another parlous word.
I could no more have taken pen to Hitler
Than taken gun (but for a different reason).
There may have been subconscious guile at work
To save my soul from the embarrassment
Of a position where with praise of us (US)
I had to mingle propaganda praise
Of a grotesque assortment of allies.
False friendships I accept for what they're worth
And what I may get out of them in peace and war,
But always with a minimum of talk
And not for long. I'm bad at politics.
I was born blind to faults in those I love,
But I refuse to blind myself on purpose
To the faults of my mere confederates.
Great are the communistic Soviets!
If nothing more were asked of me to say
I could pass muster with the State Department.
Hull may be right about their being good
As well as great. He may be also right
About their interests lying close enough
To ours for us to help them run the world.
I'm waiting to see where their interests lie.
I hope they will be good to lesser breeds.
I hope John Bull and we two other Bullies
Can get together for the post-war good
Of all the small fry nations, Finland Poland
Roumania Greece Belgium and France,
Yes and our own poor South Americans.*

*I hope we make the little brats be good.

Hull's a nice man, though, and to hear him talk
Diminishes my doubts to unimportance.
You have to recollect as Lesley says
In District of Columbia dialect
Im not a big shot. None of you down there
Would think of me for any liquidation
(Dread word!) or purge the Sandburg-Browder bloc
May have in mind. You told me so yourself.
Nothing I do can matter. I make verse.
In rhyme and meter. You and Kay indulge me
Once in so often I get round to feel
For what support I have in being useless.
Well you know whom I have to count on most.
Guy is a word of slang vicissitudes.
But good guy ought to mean a good guy wire
That stays the smokestack upright in its place.
Four wires it seems are a security.
Well I have had Kay Lesley you and Larry,
Exactly four, the sacred New Deal number—
Four terms four freedoms and four Bully nations.
Thats if you stretch a point and bring in China.
One of _my_ four you'll notice is a Jew—
No credit claimed for either him or me.
The best part of my friendship for your race
Is that I thought of it as lost in ours,
And the long time its taken me to see
It was in part at least a race apart.
And even the part that is a race apart
I sympathize with. Give them back I say
All Palestine. No race without a country
Can be a nation. I take sides with all
Who want a platform they can call their own
To speak their language from—a platform country.
I'll tell Great Britain to be kind to them.
But see Great Britain: plead your cause in London—
If such your cause is. Talk is our ally.
Don't bother me: I have no pull with Arabs.
I am no Lawrence of Arabia.
I am so sick of all the vexing questions
This war has raised about our duty to resist
With force of armament on our allies
Being as just as we expect to be

To small fry nations and minorities,
I wouldnt much care if we never had
Another war. I vow I wouldn't care.
By way of bidding politics farewell,
And speaking of great nations, look at us (US)
The mighty upstart, full of upstart people
Or Shoe-string Starters as I like to call them.
Where have we come from in these hundred years
Up to a place beside the mightiest?
By what traits—virtues and propensities?
All the democracy in me demands
Is that I get surprised at where men come from.
I am not unsusceptible to stories
Of princes of democracy like Lee
And the two Roosevelts who were never forced
To pay their way through school by mowing lawns.
I get as much surprise as I require
In seeing any good come out of Groton.
But as I read the lives I find most pleasure
In those who have come up from being
Clerks, printer's devils, railroad section hands,
Mill hands coal miners elevator boys.
About the extent of my democracy's
A sort of mystical delight
In staying innocent or ignorant
Of the conditions that produce a man.
I like a world where nobody dare say
Or bet his fiat money out of what
Advantages or disadvantages
The hero may not come. A year ago
I thought I had us in the formula
That our democracy was a diffusion
Of quality, such quality for instance
As may sit back with feet crossed on the mantel
Thumbs in the armholes of its vest to doubt
The value of its own prosperity.
Think of how many commoners attain
To the superiority that says
As Solomon the king said Vanity
Of Vanities all all is Vanity;
And in one generation without waiting
The way the Adams family had to wait

For the third to produce a Henry Adams.
You may remember out from my back door
We have a bolt hole the choke cherries choke,
And a path through a patch of bracken snares
To open pasture where the view is free
Across the near horizon of black spruce
To a far off horizon of dim mountains—
Your Adirondacs which to us are you.
They fold you in but we in thought unfold you.
We leave your veil of distance undisturbed
For fear of being charged with lèse-romance,
But fold on fold we lay the ridges back
Till by your house beside the headlong brook
Among the spiring flowers you stand disclosed
In a companionship that loses nothing
By being left in part at least to fancy.
I have an album full of pictures of you
Looking expert as you step up to flowers,
Delphinium, to take their quality.
Or go against a painting on the wall,
Or pick out themes on a piano for us,
Or listen to a poem. Once is all
You have to listen to get every word.
No one can look so aquiline-expert.

Aw come on off your cosmic politics.
Not having heard from you for very long
Sets us to going over what a friend
How many kinds of friend Ive had in you—
She who should be the great authority
Says no one else I know knows who I am
As well as you. That in itself would put
My debt to you so far beyond my power
To pay I can but turn up now and then
And by acknowledging the debt renew it.
I trust the explanations given you here
You only—no one else—will satisfy you
I am entitled to a day of grace.
I'll pay a first instalment pretty soon
I promise you. Hold on! Here's one right now,
An idea for one more anthology.
You say no more anthology, you're wrong.

I know the very name to call your next.
I'll tell you more about it when I see you
I'd take a hand in it if you would let me.

R.

August 12   1944
Ripton   Vermont

[Ripton,   Vt.
July 18,   1945]

Dear Louis:

Before the poet in you amid the many movements of his mind gets to imagining there is anything more to these precautions for peace at Bread Loaf than meets the eye, let me fall all over myself to assure you there is absolutely nothing more. Certain gossip that has seeped into circles here from the direction perhaps of the Rockwell Kents, though not in the least malicious, was mistaken enough to need correction and has left a condition it is just as well to be careful about. Esther's attempt to drag Bread Loaf into the story for the bad publicity may have caused a slight flurry among the Middlebury College trustees. I wouldnt put it past her to be trying to think up right now what next she can legally do to you or anyone connected with you to express her feelings. I dont mean anyone is much afraid of her legalities. Still for the sake of the institution you can see Ted's object in wanting to protect our stained glass windows with a screen of wire netting. Nobody can say a word against Mary's coming as an enrolled member. She has standing as a writer.* The fee wont break you. And once she's here she can be your guest at the table or at Treeman and she and you can pair up for doubles against your old rivals as of old. Oh Gee isn't it fun being discreet at last after all the folly I have escaped the penalty for? It doesnt seem fair or just that an old dissenter like me should live in such an easy going country and so far from discipline that no Stalin will probably be able to lay hands on me to confess me and shoot me in a cellar by a vat of quick lime before I die a natural death. I'd better not brag lest you bring my letter to the attention of Genevieve Taggard, for I have reason to believe that for all my philosophy, I wouldn't prove a very brave man under physical torture. I have heard about things I know I shouldn't be able to stand—such as having my balls crushed. How does the

*[Mary Jane Gaffney, a teacher and writer of short stories, was my pupil.]

340

rhyme go? "One ball for baseball and three balls for tennis." Which puts me in mind to wonder why you have forsaken rhyme in your quandaries. I premeditated laying on weight. I turned to play-writing till you might suspect I had retired of age from little poems. But as I lie awake or walk by myself every week or so a little poem will make in my head as sudden as an exclamation. It beats war and politics by whole laps. So also does play-writing for that matter. After little poems like some of yours and mine come medium sized poems like Lycidas in order of importance, then long poems (but not too long unless by Homer) then short plays like The Importance of Being Ernest or Arms and the Man, then short stories like I am a Fool, The Jumping Frog, Mr. Higginbottom's Catastrophe, Rip Van Winkle or E. V. Laider and then long plays like Mornings at Seven (mentioned here, partly because I admire it so much and partly because its author has just been with us for a visit).* Hattie Flanagan† proposed putting me on somewhere even as she had put on Eliot and Auden but I said Whizz I had rather she thought of me in connection with Wilde than with them two. War and the political future no where.

I failed to see our bite out of the sun. But Ill be seeing you.

July 18   1945   R.F.

The George Ticknor Fellowship in the Humanities

DARTMOUTH COLLEGE ★ HANOVER ★ NEW HAMPSHIRE‡

[Cambridge,   Mass.
January 9,   1947]

—and in opposition to the Sciences by contract. I am not supposed to use electric light to read or write by. I use Roman candles in preference to tallow candles.

Dear Louis Untermeyer:

As I sit here alone watching the old year out with nobody to get ahead of me in exclaiming Happy New Year on the last stroke of

*[Paul Osborn.]
†[Hallie (not Hattie) Flanagan was a director of one of the theater projects supported by the government.]
‡[The letter was sent from Robert's home in Cambridge, Massachusetts, on January 9, 1947, but he happened to have a few sheets of Dartmouth College stationery on hand. The sub-heading seems to have suggested the more or less relevant two sentences about the Sciences as opposed to the Humanities.]

twelve (or should it be on the first? Has any custom been established?), but after all come to consider me by and large, none so
forlorn in my emotional life (there would be no mockery in my being
wished a Happy New Year or at any rate a Happy-go-lucky New Year
—nor in your being, either, I take it)—let's see where was I?—as I
sit here on this anniversary of nothing but one of Time's new begin-
nings it comes over me with a young freshness to write one more
letter to the friend I have written more letters to than to any one
else. (Kay and I promised permission to look those letters over for
anything they ought not to contain. Dull with propriety and
discretion as I am in public on the platform, my breaks in private are
as the waves on the shore. I get going wild, more stimulated than
hindered by any guardian of my accuracy present who tries to laugh
me down. I havent meant much harm in such a character as I may
have given Amy Lowell for instance and if she had been half a man
she would have liked it for its strength of chiaroscuro. This too is
parenthetical.)

The clock on the stroke of midnight was what I was thinking
about. I'll get back to the clock before it strikes one I promise you.
I have a story to tell you about its striking one. I read every story long
and short in your latest.* Atta book, as Hughey Jennings would say.
But between you and me wont you admit that the joke that occurs
twice with you, would be more effective or affecting if the dialogue
went: "And where were you born?" "I was born out of wedlock sir."
"There's some very beautiful scenery in those parts." In those parts
instead of in that country. None of the Little Williest is quite as good
as FPA's cap of the climax. Several times I got what I go mournfully
looking for through the last—I mean on the steep decline of the
West namely the catch of cachinnation. I dont absolutely insist on
that burst of absurdity. I can enjoy laughing inaudibly over what I
have settled down to take calmly. I still am sensible of the greatness
of The Jumping Frog. But long after I had got control of myself in

---

*[A Treasury of Laughter.]

†[Newspaper columnists were still printing ruthless rhymes about a character known
as "Little Willie." They were modeled on a quatrain flippantly written by Harry
Graham, a British soldier in the Coldstream Guards, who signed them "Col. D.
Streamer." This was the original:

> Willie in one of his nice new sashes,
> Fell in the grate and was burnt to ashes.
> Now, although the room grows chilly,
> We haven't the heart to poke up Willie.]

reading that I found the translation of it back from French into English dangerously rupturous. I was hardly intelligible with spluttering when I tried to read Ring Lardners plays to Kay.

But about that clock. Did you see the psychological bull in Latin of the man who startled from sleep or half sleep when the clock struck four cried out, "Nae horologium delirat!* The crazy thing struck one four times!"

Speaking of psychology I heard a man introduce himself on a radio quiz earlier tonight by saying he took a degree in it at NYC University and it had proved a great help in his business of selling furniture. It was what made him think of suggesting the additional purchase of a floor lamp to a customer who had just bought a sofa. Erudita inscitia est which I choose to translate from Scaliger as Erudition is a form of ignorance. The learned Duns Scotus, patron saint of scholars, was so full of things not worth knowing that his name has come down to us spelled Dunce: Sapienteae pars est quaedam aequo animo nescire velle.† Velle is Chinese for very!

You may see what I've been reading lately or you may think you see. You might never guess from any change in my politics that I had been reading a fellow-townsman of yours named Ivins who will have it our vision and art can never be the same again since we have got over our Euclidian geometry. Edna hadn't got over hers the last I heard and you never had any to get over. That leaves me to testify and I am free to depone I never saw arrow or javelin yet fly so fast as to look measurably shorter to my eye or to any instrument in my tool chest. No line can be straight on a curved world moving in circles. Wouldnt it be one on the ribald if bow legs were the only straight legs. Some of the curves we make must offset the curvature of space. It makes you think. But thats all it does. It doesnt alter my vision as a judge of legs at all. Now you take a mermaid, she's out of the running as you might say because she has no legs to run or do anything else with. Kick for instance. To quote Longfellow without starting an anthology:

> "Wouldst thou," so the Hellsman answered
> "Know the secret of the Sea?
> Only those that marry Mermers
> Comprehend its mystery."

*[Verily, the clock is crazy.]
†[There is a kind of wisdom in calmly choosing not to know.]

What is supposed to account for Arnold's melancholy is his having had a friend whose daughter married a mermer and once when she sat with her youngest by him on her knee she heard the sound [of] a bell buoy and mistaking it for church of England got homesick for benefit of clergy and forsaking the whole family rushed right off and by mistake into a seaman chapel, methodist. It made Arnold write oh let us be true to one another for there is no certitude but death and taxes. The kind of children she may have had and had some excuse for deserting may be gathered from Carl's yes-poem:

> "My father was the keeper of the Eddystone Light
> And he slept with a mermaid one fine night.
> And from that union there came three,
> A porpoise and a porgy and the other was me.
>
> One night as I was atrimming the glim
> Asinging a verse of the evening hymn,
> A voice to the starboard shouted "Ahoy"
> And there was my mother sitting on a buoy.
>
> "Oh what has become of my children three?"
> My mother then she asked óf me.
> "One we exhibited as a talking fish
> And one was served in a chafing dish"
>
> Then the phosphorus flashed in her sea-weed hair.
> I looked again and my mother wasnt there.
> But a voice came echoing out of the night
> "To Hell with the keeper of the Eddystone Light."

If you havent that in a single one of your anthologies, the question is Why havent you? Author unknown. Of course not Carl. But it has everything—wildness and everything. And speaking of Arnold, I have decided on his two poems Cadmus and Harmonia and Mycerinus to represent him in my Nil Nisi Book of Verse. Will that seem like straining too hard to avoid your preserves?—Some demon lingers in my viscera that wont be a satisfied till I have written a poem like that Eddystone Light thing.

That was a funny afternoon John* you and I and the Amherst fellow had together. I wish you hadnt had the Amherst
    "   along. He was what was the matter with me. He had a parody

---

*[My son, who was then attending the Massachusetts Institute of Technology.]

344

by Dave Morton of my Stopping by Woods that I had a hard time to keep him from reciting. Where did you get him? The damn fool had heard the need of the times was a Messiah. How can any one fail to see we have one and of the Messianic race, namely Karl Marx. And I'm not joking. F.D.R. came as near being one as I suspect a Democracy can feel the illusion of. Thrice Mayor of London Town. No four times. I've just read that really noble story of two souls with but the single thought of ending poverty. I can lend myself to it for the duration of the piece. It doesnt antagonize me, and their faith never did. But I dont give in to it. We start so far apart that it would be a wonder if we ever got together. Every time, though, I hear of the extinction of another breed of bird fish or animal in our day I get scared about our differences. We'll probably end up all one breed one world and word. The word will be Gee, or is that spelled Jee— Jeez plural. All our declensions and conjugations have practically gone. Who uses the subjunctive anymore? The vocabulary shrinks. They say the universe is a burst to be followed or being followed by a collapse. The bones and struts that hold things apart are softening or rusting away and the muscles and guy wires are pulling us into a small ball. Our last differences are disappearing in saccharine agreement. American political parties are never far apart except for children and childish adults. Only children are deceived into thinking losing an election and being out of office means you must be wicked. It liberalizes the children onlooking to see the parties alternate in office just as if God and the angels didnt know which side to take. Round and round the wheel of Fortune. Theres not much more to it than that. You must tell John (the nice kid) that I wasnt angry at him for despairing of the Republic. I suppose I may have been a little put out at being left no position but of believing in the Republic. Age ought to do the despairing as of right.

My hand deteriorates. I must be getting tired. And I havent said a word about our family troubles. My daughter* has lived in ten houses in the last six months from sheer unhappiness. Kay and I have found most of them for her. We are buying her a small one right now in Acton Mass where her ancestors on the other side landed from the Mayflower. The wear and tear on Kay and me has been considerable. Merrill is for having Irma brought to rest in an institution or at least under a guardian. I find it hard to end anyone's freedom to

*[Irma.]

range to waste and to ruin. Take that away from anyone and what is
there left? Let them run I say till they run afoul. All this represents
some responsibility taken. But for me to be telling you! Merrill has
been telling me about Mary's miraculous survival. You must be
perfection itself to that girl. Let her have absolutely her own way in
everything. I hate so to be crossed I have come to think not being
crossed is the one thing that matters in life. I can think of no bliss-
fuller state than being treated as if I was always right. Gee (or Jee)
I get my share of being indulged. I'm lucky. Lets a few of us make one
another feel lucky. Mary's a gentle soul.

    Signed as probably the first I ever wrote you was signed

Sincerely yours

Robert Frost

[Ripton, Vt.
August 9, 1947]

Dear Louis:

    Merrill tells us there's danger you won't be able to get up to the
Conference to see me. Then we shall have to plan a meeting
somehow somewhere else later at your convenience. I might be
persuaded to come to New York for a glimpse of you. But that
couldn't be very soon. We are distressed by Merrill's news about
Mary. What is it now? Hasn't the poor child had enough?* Merrill
says he will be seeing you next week. He will tell you all about
Irma.† Cast your eye back over my family luck and perhaps you
will wonder if I haven't had pretty near enough. That is for the
angels to say. The valkyries and the eumenides. My only objection
to your communism (socialism for safety) is that realized to
perfection it cant come within three strata of the stratosphere of
touching the reality of our personal life. You know pretty well what
I think and I know pretty well what you think. We dont have
to be embarassed by anything so remote and irrelevant as our
political differences.

---

*[She died of cancer a few weeks after this was written.]
†[Irma had been acting "queer"—there had been a divorce and a long spell of
neurotic invalidism. As friend and doctor, Merrill Moore strongly advised that she
be institutionalized.]

346

I learn with indifference that the New Republic subscription list has increased from thirty thousand to seventy thousand since my former friend Henry Wallace became editor of it. In me your cause could have a more or less detached sympathizer if Moscow would come right out in answer to Balfours crack that you cant make people equally rich; you can only make them equally poor, and say exactly so, we Marxians frankly espouse poverty like the saints. It isnt merely because poverty can make us equal. It can make us better than that. It can make us purer. It can refine us. We Americans suffer from a disgust with our own gross abundance. Witness our writers for the last thirty years. If only we had had Brigham Young for Secretary of State and the Treasury instead of Alexander Hamilton back there in the beginning we might have remained a nation of agrarians as simple as Cincinnatus and the Cincinnati as they called themselves in that old society. We have the Colonial Dames and the Daughters of the Revolution. Where have the Cincinnati (sp.) gone? "Of two such lessons why forget the nobler and the manlier one?" Byronic sounds ironic. The pacifist holds that we neednt hurt each other in war anymore. The Marxian adds, And we neednt hurt each other in peace any more. And we neednt if we all settle back into Franciscan farmers satisfied as in Salimbenes story with a table set forth with no more than a sprig of lettuce and a glass of water.

At every commencement I hear young Americans reproach themselves or their country with the indecency of our success and prosperity. I get sick of it. What are the young (and old) going to do about it? Are the Marxians in earnest in their contempt for American dollars? I wish I didnt suspect them of reasoning from envy. Im afraid they wont despise riches so much if they can achieve it. All that makes them different from us is their belief they can do it better with the enterprise of gain all-centered in one bureau and even one master mind. They may be right and we wrong or vice versa. There is nothing specially noble in the position of either—if nobility is the object in life. I can't be bothered too much to discriminate between them. I was born and brought up to our kind of capitalism and I feel as if I might as well not change it to their form of the same thing. Capitalism is the name for the dollar ahead for security. The only dispute between us is

as to who should be the keeper of it, the state at the capital of the
country or all sorts and kinds of people scattered from boundary
to boundary. I have been taught to think that there is no greater
peril than to cultivate no greatness except in politicians and
statesmen. I should hate it to have all patronage of the arts come
from one source. If I cant get it from the Library of Congress or
the White House or from the Pulitzer Committee I can appeal from
them to publisher after publisher, editor after editor, braving
poverty for myself and children till the society for the prevention
of cruelty to minors catches up with me and I am dragged into
court to justify my sacrifice by a show-down of unpublished
manuscript. In my destitution I should be assigned a lawyer to
defend me and if I lost assigned a professor to cure me of not
knowing how to write. Even that wouldnt exhaust my chances.
I might get to Bread Loaf on a scholarship or fellowship. Hold on!
Where is my logic carrying me off to? Bread Loaf is where I am
now! And happy to be in such a pleasant place* in such blessed
keeping. I wonder why you make me run on to such lengths,
extravagantly and hell-for-spelling. No friend has ever released me
to such letter writing. You must take care of yourself spiritually.

Ever yours

Robert

Ripton   Vermont
August 9   1947

*You come too, if possible.

Ripton,   Vermont.

September 9,   1947

Dear Louis:

Where are you? What now? I thought there was something
said about your coming up to see us. The crowd has been gone for
some time. Perhaps it is a little late for coming here and we had
better wait to see each other when I get back to Cambridge.
I wish life could be always in the country. I go forth to the campaign
of the next season with no great eagerness for the fray. But I
suppose I can be trusted to dodge a lot of it and save myself for
plenty of time in the Book Room at 35 Brewster Street. I would be

1948

writing this by hand but dictating it builds up my self respect
by making me feel like a Dictator.

Ever yours

Robert

The George Ticknor Fellowship

DARTMOUTH COLLEGE ★ HANOVER ★ NEW HAMPSHIRE

35 Brewster Street
Cambridge, Massachusetts
January 12, 1948

Dear Louis:

K. saw the poem written last Fall so I am reciting this letter
about it to her as witness that it wasn't one of the resurrections from
the past that have made you suspicious.* Why don't I tell you
here and now the names of the flagrant cases? "Bond and Free"
was a great deal older than the lustrum of its book. So were "Last
Word of a Bluebird", "Misgiving", "On Going Unnoticed",
"Sand Dunes", "The Flower Boat", "Design", "Not Quite Social",
"One Guess", "The Hardship of Accounting", and "The
Ingenuities of Debt". Some of these turned up after having been
lost awhile. Some, like "The Ingenuities of Debt" lay around
waiting for a last touch. I never thought until last year of the line

"Be sure to sell your horse before he dies"

Perhaps it isn't fair to the critics for me to mingle old and new
this way. I never thought of making mischief. Do you think I ought
to date the intrusions of one stratum into another some time?
But as you must know, I'm pleased you like the brand new of
today as much as you like the brand new of years back.

I am about to telegraph asking if I can have Monday evening
at home with you in Brooklyn.

Ever yours

Rob

*[I had questioned the matter of dating Robert's poems, something that had been
suggested by teachers in so-called creative writing. It was almost impossible to tell
which was a wholly new poem or one which had been waiting to be completed.]

HOMER NOBLE FARM
RIPTON, VERMONT

[July 5, 1949]

Dear Louis:

As my chief upholder in public through two wars and one and one fifth peaces you would have reason to be proud if I ever came to anything. It is a great satisfaction to have lived to hear you say you are proud. Some times I've been afraid the difference between your form of patriotism and mine was bothering you when you had me to defend at some kinds of cocktail parties. But the easy talk we four had together all afternoon there at Lesley's was all the proof needed of how far we hadnt drifted apart. Your touch on my poetry has always been right on the right spot. You "flattered to tears this aged man and poor" by asking (in good faith I took it) if my latest poem, Closed for Good, was not really a product of my earlier lyric years. I've told Time (the personification) not to fail to put that into his list of cates.—Any good news from the courts of law would be gratefully received at this end.*

Ever yours

Robert

July 5 1949

35 Brewster Street
Cambridge, Massachusetts.
October 26, 1949.

Dear Louis:

How about starting a day earlier and dropping in on me for Friday night at Amherst on your way to your Saturday's engagement in Boston? I am stuck fast in Amherst till November eleventh. Some friend and I would meet you at Springfield and set you on the train there again next day. It would be as simple as that. We could have a small dinner party and then an evening to talk together. It would take a whole evening to thank you enough for

*[This concerned litigation regarding my marital status.]

350

getting me out of having to write a Christmas poem for Ed Anthony. How ingenious of you and how generous of him to do what he is doing. These Anthony boys have stayed my faithful friends.*

Come ahead. Let me know about your train at the Lord Jeffery Inn <u>and</u> let K. know here. She'll want to know about our reunion.

Ever yours
Robert

And call us up and have a drink while here!

K.

[December, 1949
On RF's Christmas card-poem,
"On a Tree Fallen Across the Road"]

Most accidents are just to ask us who we think we are. And after all who in Hell are we? Are we mentioned like Bertran de Born in Dante's Inferno? Anyway I am mentioned in the critical writing of Louis Untermeyer, and more than once. So if I put a few airs on my studied humility in spite of myself—

This lecture is running to classroom lengths. I pause for identification.

RF

[In 1950 I put together The Road Not Taken, an enlargement of Come In, which had been published seven years earlier. Like its predecessor, it was, as the subtitle indicated, "An Introduction to Robert Frost," and in addition to the selection of his poetry it contained a biographical preface and a running commentary. It was the commentary that bothered me; the poetry required a minimum of explication, but its background had to be unquestionable. The next two letters, revealing unfamiliar and wholly unknown facts, furnished the precise data I needed.]

*[Both Joseph and Edward Anthony were writers. Edward's career was the more varied and colorful, as detailed in his autobiography, This Is Where I Came In. When this letter was written, Edward was publisher of The Woman's Home Companion and had asked me to try to get a Christmas poem from Robert.]

Box 100–   Route 2
South Miami,   Florida
February 15,   1950

Dear Louis:

I am glad you reminded me of the colleges. We must try to
get a true picture of me with them—of course in your own words—
I'm not trying to write your biographic preface to The Road Not
Taken (as you call it). My special stays have been at Dartmouth,
Amherst, and Michigan, but I have belonged longest, nearly
twenty-five years of the last thirty-five, and belong now to Amherst.
Amherst is the only places where I have had markable classes. I
have made almost a practice of lingering round for several days at
a time to lecture and visit with the faculty and students at many
other colleges. And as you haven't failed to notice I have had
honorary degrees from many.

Perhaps that's enough about me as teacher. Still perhaps you
might find it grist to your mill that I was most really and truly an
all-out teacher back at Salem, New Hampshire, where I presided
over twelve barefoot children under twelve in a district school by
the woods and often sitting on the lid of the woodbox by the stove
wrote poetry (some of it the poetry of A Boy's Will) on the window
sill for my table. I worked the hardest at teaching for my five
years at Pinkerton Academy in Derry, New Hampshire. I got
invited in there on the strength of "A Tuft of Flowers" read aloud
at a village banquet not by me but by someone else with me
sitting by with my head hung down. I liked the job. I never hated
anything new and strange enough to give me ideas.

The way to speak so as to get a true picture of the odd jobs I
took from time to time to help get along with would be to call
them merely makeshift, I suppose. We have to be careful not to
claim for me that I originated as a bobbin boy, cobbler, or like poor
Clare and Bloomfield* as a farm hand. I simply turned my hand
to most and turned it good (or pretty good) in various situations,
as Kipling has it, and never mind what so long as I got by while

---

*[Robert Bloomfield, author of The Farmer's Boy, published in 1800, was often com-
pared to John Clare, a far superior poet.]

furtively fooling with poetry. One year I was up on a ten foot ladder trimming the carbon-pencil lamps over the mule frames in the Arlington Textile Mills. But one year I was editing all by myself the old Lawrence Sentinel newspaper. Another I was writing paragraphs as a sort of columnist on The Lawrence American. But before all that I was getting an audience and hiring a hall in Boston for a Shakespearean reader. I seemed without pride or even without self-respect in those days; I didn't care what I was looked down on for doing. You see the danger of distorting me into too humble a beginning. I always had the keys of the city to play with so as not to take big things too seriously. I walked out of two colleges like nothing at all. I was no rebel. I must have left from failure to see the difference between being intellectual in college and being intellectual outside of college. I got suspicious that it was very much up to me to find out for myself whether I had it in me to write and think. I was shifting my dependence you might say from teachers to writers who had written before me.

You might like to hear a little about the first poem I wrote. I read my first book Scottish Chiefs in my fourteenth year. I wrote my first poem in my fifteenth. It must have sprung full grown, forty four-line stanzas from Prescott's Conquest of Mexico. I gave it to the senior editing our high school Bulletin and saw it in print that month. It exists at the Jones Library in Amherst to this day. The theme was the bad night the Indians gave the Spaniards to my gratification when they drove them temporarily back from Tenochtitlan. There's a lot of history in it and a lot of excitement but not much else. I wrote about ten pieces in rhyme and blank verse in the next two years and then I wrote "My Butterfly", and sent it to The Independent. And in the ten lines there beginning "The grey grass is scarce dappled with the snow" I found myself. Don't you think so?

Expect a second installment of this dictation to K. by the next mail but one (or two). But seriously I mean it. I'll do some more tomorrow. Then we may mention a few poems for you to bring in if you want to indulge us.

Ever yours

Robert

(Written in great haste just before train time)

Box 100– Route 2
South Miami, Florida.
February 21, 1950

Dear Louis:

All right let's have some sort of chronology for your guidance:
I helped elect Grover Cleveland in San Francisco in 1884—
marched in torchlight processions—rode on a fire engine—pulled
by one or two hundred men in one procession. My father was chairman of the democratic city committee. I campaigned through all
the saloons with him—plastered their ceilings with campaign
literature, using a silver dollar to drive in the tack. I didn't go to
school much till I came East in 1885 right after my father's death.

Came to Lawrence in 1885 and started school there in a grade
that would have got me into the Lawrence High School at sixteen
or seventeen. In '86 my mother went to teach district school at
Salem Depot, New Hampshire. After one year and a half of ungraded
school there I went eight miles down to Lawrence and passed by
examination into the Lawrence High School from which I graduated
valedictorian in 1892 about the time I would have entered if my
bad luck had kept me in the city graded schools. My year and a
half of the district school and my four years in the Lawrence High
School were the heart of my education. They suited me perfectly.

I nailed shanks (drove six nails into the hollow of the sole of
the shoes) in a shoe shop and had a mouthful of nails all the
summer of my twelfth year. It was piece work and I earned better
pay than I was to earn for ten years. That was my cobbling.

From then on I spent all my vacations either in a shoe shop or
on a farm as a hired hand till I got through High School. The
summer of 1891 I left a farm for a job pushing a bobbin wagon in
a textile mill in Lawrence—a mistake for my health.

Passed first half of entrance exams for Harvard in 1891 but was
sent in 1892 to Dartmouth by my grandmother whose idea was to
save me from drink. Tended gate at a textile mill summer of '92—
the year Lizzie Borden was being tried. At Christmas or just after
left Dartmouth to come home and take my mother's room in the
grammar school at Methuen, Massachusetts. She had been having a
hard time with some rough boys. I was feeling pretty rough myself

from hazing and all that at college. I asked the school committee to let me see what I could do with the boys. My victory over them though decisive was Pyrrhic and I quit after one term. I spent the summer of '93 farming for myself after a fashion on a rented place near Canobie Lake, New Hampshire. Read advertisements looking for what to do next. Set out to promote a Shakespearean reader but gave him up as not distinguished enough after trying him on a small Boston audience I got together for him—I don't know how. One of the audience was Rolfe the old scholar, another was the dramatic critic of the Transcript.

In '93 began my stretch at trimming lights and tending dynamos in the Arlington Mills in Lawrence, Massachusetts. Must have gone out to teach a spring term of '94 at District School No. 9 (I think) in Salem. See "A Lone Striker."

Spent the summer of '94 alone with a dog in an abandoned farmhouse, the last house away up Ossippee Mountain. Had to get rid of the dog because he was gun shy and jumped on me in bed at the first roll of thunder.

In '94 began as a reporter on the Lawrence American but gravitated to the editorial page where I wrote "paragraphs" some of which though in prose were really eclogues. I remember the subject of two or three. Out of them came "Mending Wall", "The Woodpile", and "Two Look at Two".

Married in 1895 right after Elinor graduated from St. Lawrence University.

For the next five years I took more or less part in my mother's private and tutorial school in Lawrence though I was doing regular work at Harvard for two of the years, '97 and '98. I was of the class of 1901 along with Wallace Stevens but I never heard of him till long afterward. I had a course with Santayana. I ran all to Latin, Greek, and Philosophy till I ran away.

My mother died in 1900 and her school might have fallen to me if I had felt executive enough for the responsibility.

My grandfather had helped me to go to college both times. Elinor now asked him to buy me a farm for my health. I farmed exclusively for five years and then began part-time teaching at Pinkerton Academy to supplement my farming. The extra money enabled us to make our summer trips to Bethlehem New Hampshire to get away from hay fever. I ended up a full time teacher at

Pinkerton and was even urged to be the principal. That scared
me for my freedom and put me to flight. I was only induced to
stay on teaching by the novelty offered of teaching psychology at
The State Normal School at Plymouth. It was agreed that my stay
should be no longer than a year. From Plymouth we sailed for
Glasgow in August of 1912 (might be 1911) in a small boat out of
Boston with a very few passengers on board at that time of year.
Fifty dollars was the fare. There were six of us. The children all
under fare—Lesley, Carol, Irma and Marjorie. The captain hated us
all because he was seasick and believed us all of the servant class
going back to England to find a coat of arms for ourselves. To
show you how little I knew where I was going, I almost got into
a duel with a Scotch schoolmaster on board by miscalling some of
the British navy we saw. I called it the English navy.

I had not a relative or an acquaintance to look up in England.
1912 was right, for it was then soon after we got there that I carried
a sheaf of poems to David Nutt. As you know they appeared and
were rather well received in 1913. I never even knew who read
them for Mrs David Nutt who was the owner of the publishing
house. Almost immediately on top of A Boy's Will I gave her the
manuscript of North of Boston. She liked it better. She didn't
seem very literary herself. I was curious about her advisors. She would
never tell me who they were. A Boy's Will had made me friends
who began to ask "What next?". I let one and another have copies
of "The Death of the Hired Man", "The Code", and "The
Black Cottage". They got into circulation round London and prepared the way for book success. Ezra imposed "The Code" on
Harriet Monroe. He failed to get The Smart Set to take "The
Death of the Hired Man".

As you probably know, everything from then on—that is
May 1914—went rather fine. North of Boston was one of the most
reviewed books of the year. Massingham the editor of The Nation
in summing up the year said so. Edward Thomas was one of
my warmest advocates. We were thrown together very closely for
the rest of our time over there.

Anything further we'll take up in another letter. I may write
it and sent it to K. to send it to you. She's going home to-day.
But I shall be here alone for another week before I set off for four
days at Gainesville, Florida; three at Athens, Georgia, with

Professor Hugh Hodgson; and four days at Wofford College in Spartanburg, South Carolina, in care of Dean Oscar Lever. I am enclosing your questionnaire filled out.

Ever yours

Robert

[Although the preceding two letters supplied invaluable new information, there were still some dates of which I was unsure. Accordingly, I mailed a "questionnaire" to Florida, where Robert was still spending his winters, asking him to fill in the chronological and other references. In the following paragraphs, which were returned with the letter of February 27, 1950, the italicized queries are mine.]

Teacher at Salem, New Hampshire?

I went out there to teach in the spring of 1894 (I think) That was the first time. I took the school in 1895 again (I think) just after getting married. I taught at least twice out there by the woods—maybe three times. It was on impulse to get away.

Period of earning a living as bobbin boy, cobbler, etc.?

I was what you might call a cobbler in my twelfth year, a bobbin boy in the summer of my third year in Lawrence High School.

The year when you edited the old Lawrence Sentinel?

The Sentinel was a dying old weekly we had had sent us from Lawrence when I was a child in San Francisco. I was asked to try putting life back into it when I was teaching private school with my mother. I failed. A young Irishman who succeeded me put so much life in to it that he got put in jail.

The year you were a "sort of columnist" on the Lawrence American?

1894.

The time you trimmed the carbon-pencil lamps in the Arlington Textile Mills?

1893.

What are "mule frames"?

One kind of machine for spinning.

Did you hire a hall in Boston for the Shakespearean reader after or before you supervised dramatics at Pinkerton Academy?

Long long before. It was just before I went into the Arlington Mills. I put on four plays one year at Pinkerton: Dr Faustus,

Comus, The Rivals, and Cathleen Ni Houlihan. I got ready
four more for next year, got out of sorts with another teacher
and called them off.*

*When I speak of your first poem ("La Noche Triste") would you
permit me to quote a little from it—if I can get a photostat from
the Jones Library—or would you prefer I didn't?*

I dont think I should mind if you can find any of it tolerable.
You have to emphasize it that the poem is the first thing
prose or verse in my whole life in or out of school. I was without
benefit of courses in English. The first three poems I wrote
must be in the Jones Library—that ballad about the Spaniards,
some blank verse about Julius Caesar and a lyric in triple rhyme.

*The other teacher thought the plays were over the heads of the
children.

> [Miami, Fla.
> February 27, 1950]

Dear Louis:

A sceptic once taking my hand and turning it inside out to the
light, remarked that it was merely calloused not horny. All right, I
said, if he wasn't satisfied, he could coin a word and call me a farmster.
Anyway, I have hardly been without livestock since I was five, and
practically never without farm property since I was twenty-five. Even
in England we kept hens and tilled a garden. My favorite tools have
been the scythe, the hoe, the ax, the bat—and the pen. (We mustn't
forget the pen.)

Kay isn't here to make me dictatorial, so I'm doing a little by
hand to fall in with your businesslike way of putting things through.
I think I answered all your questions on the questionnaire except the
one possibly about quoting from "La Noche Triste." I can't see
the difference between having intended to do a thing and having
done it when I look back afterwards. You should be the judge of the
poem. Is there a bit of it you could use in contrast with what I was
writing just ten poems later in "My Butterfly." "La Noche Triste"
was absolutely the first thing in prose or verse I ever wrote, in or out
of school. You might be interested, while you are about it, to let
Charles Green of the Jones Library at Amherst show you copies of
the next two poems I wrote, one in blank verse and one in triple

rhyme. I remember distinctly the trance of all those first three and the sudden sense of what it was all about when I fell into the eight lines of the "Butterfly" beginning, "The gray grass is scarce dappled with the snow."—That's where I lost my soul. Those eight lines beside a piece of the earlier stuff might be amusing.

Then some more dates that sometime (not necessarily now) ought to be used to confute those liars, Cowley* here and Shanks† there, who seem to want to take away my credit for being my own man. Maybe I would have been a better poet if I had been more teachable. The dates prove that no one in England at that time did anything to me. Pound told me what I was trying to do was the short story and referred me for models to Les Trois Contes. But several of my eclogues were already in his hands, and all of them were in my publisher's. Edward Thomas never heard of me nor I of him till Ralph Hodgson passed him a typed copy of "The Death of the Hired Man" that had got to going round by the kindness of Gibson, I think, after the mild success of "A Boy's Will." The chronology went like this:

1912	Arrived in England
1912	Gave "A Boy's Will" to David Nutt (his widow)
1913	"A Boy's Will" published
1913	Gave "North of Boston" to David Nutt
1914	"North of Boston" published in May
1915	Left England in February
1915	Arrived in America on George Washington's Birthday exactly thirty-five years ago last week
1914	Late in the year Edward Thomas showed me the first poems he ever wrote. They were not influenced by me but done at my repeated suggestion that his kind of writing would be recognized as poetry if it only declared itself in form. He poured the poetry out as he was drawn on swifter and swifter into the war. He had a fear he had to be disabused of, that I would think he was imitating "North of Boston." He and I were perfect friends (even as you and I) and it's too bad to

---

*[Malcolm Cowley, editor and essayist.]

†[Edward Shanks, an English poet and journalist, asserted that Robert had been influenced by the quiet, colloquial poetry of Edward Thomas, whereas it was Thomas who showed and acknowledged his indebtedness to Robert by dedicating his posthumously published *Poems* to him.]

N

make an issue between us. But fairness to one of us
doesn't mean unfairness to the other. I confess I am
bothered every time Shanks' perversion of the story
turns up.

1893-1912 Poems of "A Boy's Will" written and some besides
1900-1912 Poems of "North of Boston" written. The first of the
eclogues (really too much action in them for true
eclogues) was "The Black Cottage." I had trouble
enough getting it the way I wanted it and no
success in getting it published. In 1913 while
"North of Boston" was getting printed, Ezra hur-
riedly imposed "The Code" on Harriet Monroe
and failed to impose "The Death of the Hired
Man" on Willard Huntington Wright, then editor of The Smart Set. Wright said he had all he
needed of that sort of thing from Harry Kemp!*
Am I repeating? If so, it's because you have got
me busier than I should be by nature.

The theory of my enemies seems to be that I could have trumped
up two books of poetry in a year and a half to meet a new market
demand. As a matter of fact, though treated kindly in general, I was
never really invited into any group over there. I never went to a
meeting of Ezra, the Aldingtons, and Flint. I never saw the Aldingtons
or Amy Lowell. I was no Imagist. I never met Eddie Marsh, who
presided over the Georgians, and never received his Nihil Obstat.
The only fast friend I won was Edward Thomas, and his melancholy
was our cement. Hulme, Hodgson, Davies looked rather quizzically
askance at the stray American intruder, not to say pretender. I
couldn't see that it gave Ralph Hodgson much pleasure to see me
when I called on him with Gordon Chalmers last year at his den in
Ohio.† But I have learned the nice shade of tolerance with which
artists live together. Well well well enough of this. After 1950 and all
its excitements I mean to settle back to my dilatory indulgences again
and so to the end that can't be more than twenty-five years off at
best. I don't feel right that all this shouldn't have gone through Kay's
hands. It would soothe my sentiments if you could have someone

*[Harry Kemp, known as "the tramp poet," was one of the flamboyant figures of the
nineteen-twenties.]
†[Ralph Hodgson, the English poet, had married an American and had retired to the
little town of Minerva, near Canton, Ohio.]

type her a copy of it. Speaking of the excitements of this year you can see by the itinerary we sent you that you and Al Edwards* have got up my expectations perhaps higher than they should be. Disregard them. If nothing comes, why nothing comes. Really now, it's absurd for me to be even interested. I've come a long way on a little, a long way on plenty, and I've had this year of superabundance. If I had foreseen such luck you know what I would have done? I would have treasured my manuscripts and kept some of my early first editions. But all the time I have been scared some lady would jilt me. And Lady Luck, too.

Ever yours, as you can see,

Robert

South Miami   Fla
February 26,   1950

[A copy of the Senate citation, or resolution, was sent to me by Robert with the following scrap of paper.]

[Cambridge,   Mass.
April 14,   1950]

My only comment is the senatorial "no comment."

Senate

Friday, March 24, 1950.

Seventy-Fifth Anniversary of the Birth of Robert Frost

Mr. Taft. Mr. President, I ask unanimous consent that I may present a Senate resolution and have it read, and have immediate consideration of it.

The Vice President. The resolution will be read.

The Chief Clerk read the resolution (S. Res. 244), as follows:

Whereas Robert Frost in his books of poetry has given the American people a long series of stories and lyrics which are enjoyed, repeated, and thought about by people of all ages and callings; and

Whereas these poems have helped to guide American thought with

---

*[In 1946, after William Sloane left Henry Holt and Company, Alfred C. Edwards took over Robert's relationship with the firm. In 1960, Edwards became president of Holt, Rinehart, and Winston, Inc.]

humor and wisdom, setting forth to our minds a reliable representation
of ourselves and of all men; and

Whereas his work throughout the past half century has enhanced
for many their understanding of the United States and their love of
country; and

Whereas Robert Frost has been accorded a secure place in the history of American letters; and

Whereas on March 26 he will celebrate his seventy-fifth birthday:
Therefore be it

Resolved, That the Senate of the United States extend him felicitations of the Nation which he has served so well.

HOMER NOBLE FARM
RIPTON, VERMONT

August [11, 1950]

Dear Louis:

Please plan to come along and bring Bryna.* We are counting on
the visit. Ted was and is still awful sorry you won't speak.†

Robert keeps saying you are one of the few real pleasures still in
his life. He is well and at the moment signing his name fifteen
hundred times for George Macy's courier.‡

Best from all hands

K. (and R.)

HOMER NOBLE FARM
RIPTON, VERMONT

August [12,] 1950

Dear Louis

The papers didn't give us enough to go on.** Neither do you. But
if you say its all right and you won, the details can wait till we see

*[In 1948 I had married Bryna Ivens, a magazine editor.]
†[Theodore Morrison had invited me to address the members of the Bread Loaf
Writers' Conference, but I wanted to visit Robert privately instead of making a public
appearance as lecturer.]
‡[A de luxe two-volume edition of his *Complete Poems* was issued by the Limited Editions Club. It was designed by the famous typographer Bruce Rogers; the decorations
were engraved in wood by Thomas W. Nason; and it carried an introductory essay
which I had written.]
**[The litigation in which I was involved was decided in my favor.]

you. The great thing is to win in war and peace. I have no patience with the casuistry that will persuade undergraduates that neither side wins a war—both sides lose it. Among a lot of liberal Northerners who were talking that way I once asked the only Southerner present who won the Civil War between the States. It was a cruel thing to do—crueler to the liberals than to the unreconstructed Southerner, though it hurt him too. No sir, never from sophistication or anything try to make yourself think meanly of victory. Your antagonist may not yet be convinced you worsted her. You're sure, I take it, that after she has been up through a few more courts she will be. All right then lets go ahead and celebrate in champagne and hexameters.

And speaking of hexameters I never write them. (I wrote one piece in hendecasyllables).* I seem to keep on writing iambics in the teeth of the worlds question why I do. It begins to trickle down to me through her admirers that Willa Cather (my friend you know) in her last testament sort of put away the make-believe of art as a plaything of the young. I put away some games when I got through with them myself; some others I kept on with and only put away when my children got through with them. I can see that decline in my experience. But verse making was never a game in her sense of the word. I feel funny in seeming to go back on one of my oldest notions namely that no matter how terribly serious the theme of a poem the performance was still a play as in the case of Shakespeares Lear. What should you say if instead of going on at this rate I did you out on Kay's typewriter by dictation some recent iambics I have been a prey to. I call one piece Come, Come Ye Disconsolate, or Mist Smoke and Haze. Another will go by the name of Doom to Bloom. Another still A Valentine. It begins to sound like a whole book. I'd better hold on one or two. You want to know what occurs to me? That the best way to stop piping might be to start trumpeting. My nature has shrunk from the idea of taking pen to anything deliberately. Maybe I was being just nice. It might do me good to disestablish a few more rules before the pitcher is broken at the fountain.

How's your farming or dont you do any? Anyway how's your pond. We now have two ponds bulldozed, one to the other in size as Superior to Erier. Why dont we name them that? I see no reason why they should remain nameless. It has been suggested that we call

*[The poem is "For Once, Then, Something." See above p. 90.]

one Loaves because it reflects Bread Loaf and the other Fishes because it has been stocked with minnows and trout though none of them has been heard of since.

Ever yours

Robert

MIST, SMOKE, AND HAZE.*

I don't believe the sleepers in this house
Know where they are.
They've been here long enough
To push the woods back from around the house
And part them in the middle with a path.

And still I doubt if they know where they are.
And I begin to fear they never will.
All they maintain the path for is to seek
Fresh consolation in the evidence
Their neighbors know no better than themselves.
Nearer in plight their neighbors are than distance.

I am the guardian wraith of starlit smoke
That leans out this and that way from their chimney.
I will not have their happiness despaired of.

I am the damper counterpart of smoke
That gives off from a cultivated ground,
But lifts no higher than a garden grows.
I cotton to their landscape. That's who I am.
I lie too low and shapeless to inspire them;
Yet am not so dispiriting a spirit
As to believe a people must be lost
Who don't know where they are. Their ignorance
Is as attractive as an innocence.

Learning has been a part of their religion.
They have long since acquired the native tongue.
They must have asked the Red Man where they were.

They often have and none the wiser for it.
So have they also asked philosophers
Who came a-visiting their universe

---

*[A return to R.F.'s soliloquizing-narrative vein, written a year after the publication of *Complete Poems*. Retitled "A Cabin in the Clearing," and greatly changed, it was included in his last book, *In the Clearing*.]

From Heaven, Paris, London, or Vienna.
One of these had found reason to conclude
The motion of the earth around the sun
Was nothing but the ultimate adjustment
It had to make itself among the adjustments
Everything else in space was making for it
So it could be the one thing standing still;
And men were not mistaken in their sense
Of being stationary and not whirled
And twisted through a dozen curves at once.
But being made the one fixed point there is
Seem more amusing to them than convincing.

I have a way of knowing what they said
The last thing as they came out of the woods
On their way home from church to show their firmness.
The minister had read their title clear
To where they were, whatever place it was,
By taking the three hundred years of Jephthah
(Judges eleven twenty six they said)
As an ennabling text for them to stay there.
And stay they would till they had satisfied
All the conditions to a rounded outcome.
They did not say what the conditions were.

The sleepers in this house are not asleep!
Listen, they murmur thinking with each other
On what must be their day-long theme continued.
The excitement of the day will not die down:

The embers will not die upon their hearth.
Let us eavesdrop as dews drop from the eaves
And try to tell the base from the soprano:

"The reason for our running back to England
Is not too difficult to understand.
We moved in 1607 and 1620
But haven't moved all of our things as yet.
Take Shakespeare's library to Washington,
But still go back to Oxford after Shakespeare."

"It is like gathering wool off into worsted."

"From having thought the land was India
And the inhabitants were Indians,

We've come to wonder if it isn't Europe—
In either case just some more of the same
One old thing or the other over again."

"And I so hoped it would be something new—
Dead reckoning from 1492."

Thus did an outer mist and smoke appraise
The lighter body of an inner haze.

R. F.

AMHERST COLLEGE
AMHERST, MASSACHUSETTS

[October 25, 1951]

Dear Louis—Eighty-Eight Remsen Street Brooklyn New York—all
that to show you I have forgotten neither you nor where you live over
in the town the big city across the bridge jokes about. (And it must
be joking more since the Giants beat the Dodgers) As for you
yourself you're the fellow I used to write more often to than I do
now. I remember you well—and indeed would like to see you for a
long session more than I have ink in my pen to tell you. Kay will be
arranging with you about our getting together next week. I can save
up what I have on my mind if anything till then. You are probably
still joking, if not about Brooklyn, about life in general. I know I am.
When the question comes up or is tactlessly brought up what in the
world are we to do next, the answer is easily either laugh or cry. We
have no other choice. It takes wit to supply the laugh, yes and the
tears too I guess. I remember years ago trying to laugh off the
annoyance college boys gave me in a piece of blank verse I sent you
and you didn't quite like called Young Sure and Twenty. It was in
mockery of conventional young radicals. I never stand young radicals
till I see how long they are going to stay radicals. I hate to see people
get over either their radicalism or their conservatism. You are still
about as radical by the litmus test as you were that Sunday you met
me at the Grand Central and took me down for my first and last visit
with Floyd Dell and Max Eastman at The Masses office. But we
wont go into that any further than we have been accustomed to go.
Rockwell Kent could call you Tom Girdler* when he was mad, as if

*[An industrialist bitterly attacked by the labor unions.]

you had gone to another extreme like Max and I believe Floyd. But you have been pretty steadfast—unless you have weakened lately. So have I been, don't you think? I can change my mind without changing my nature. But where am I getting to? All I set out to say was that I was looking forward to a sight of you and Bryna. Im glad she came through her hand-carving whatever it was. Worse than mine I imagine.* My sculpture was on my face however and had to be joked off by my saying it was what Ridgeway in Asia would call Operation Save Face.

As ever at it

Rbt

for
Bryna and Louis
A new poem by an old pen†
comes to you with Holiday Greetings
and Felicitations (oh for what?)
from Robert Frost an old timer
recently pronounced immortal by
the doctors. He wonders what you
writers and fellow poets will say.

[After Robert reached his mid-seventies there were fewer letters and more talks. I had been editor of Decca Records for some years and had moved to an abandoned farm and a rebuilt Colonial cottage in Connecticut, eighty miles north of New York. Visits from there were easier; either my wife and I drove to Cambridge or met Robert and Kay Morrison at the restored village of Sturbridge, Massachusetts, halfway between our homes.

In March, 1954, after the public celebration of his eightieth birthday given by his publisher at the Waldorf-Astoria Hotel in New York, I accompanied Robert to the more intimate dinner tendered by his fellow poets and professors at Amherst. This is a memorandum I made on that occasion:

*[My wife had undergone a hysterectomy; Robert's operation was for a skin cancer.]
†["A Cabin in the Clearing," R.F.'s Christmas card for 1951.]

It has taken a long time for Robert to show his years, but now he begins to show them. It is not that he looks so old as that he seems weary with age or, perhaps, the age. The scar left by his operation makes his cheek hollow; his walk is slow. But his talk—an occasionally interrupted monologue rather than a conversation—is lively and as peppery as ever. He liked my "remarks" at the dinner, which contrasted with the more formal tributes by Archibald MacLeish, Thornton Wilder, and President Cole of Amherst—George Whicher had died three weeks before the anniversary, and his speech (his last piece of writing) was read by Curtis Canfield. "You know me better than anyone," he said when we were alone. "Al Edwards is still hoping that you'll write my biography, and so do I. Most of the others are writing theirs by wheedling little pieces out of other people."

We talked about how many of our fellow-poets—Robinson, Masters, Lindsay, Fletcher, Amy Lowell, Sara Teasdale, Edna Millay, Elinor Wylie, both Benéts—had failed to survive. "I suppose there's something to the superstition that the good die young—here we still are, me wicked at eighty and you unregenerate at almost seventy. I'm glad it isn't just the good poets who die young! As I said at the dinner, poets die in different ways. Most of them do not die into the grave but into business—which you almost did—or into criticism—as so many of them are doing nowadays—or into philosophy, one of the noblest ways to die. It's the fear of being impractical that turns many people against poetry, and sometimes turns the poet against himself. Often what begins more ethereal than substantial ends by being more substantial than ethereal."

The talk drifted back to the matter of age, and Robert put on the quizzical air with which he delivers mock judgments: "I've said it before and I keep on saying that the danger of old age lies in accumulation—accumulation of other people's ideas and other people's jokes. I know I'm getting older and older when I tell the joke about the old lady again."

"What joke about what old lady?" I asked, dutifully picking up the cue.

"Oh, the one where one of the family says 'Why do you suppose grandma is reading so many books these days?' 'Because,' says another member, 'she's cramming for her finals.' "]

April 16   1957
Cambridge   [Mass.]

Dear Louis

I tried for you at Decca yesterday as one more likely than almost any one for me to share any transports with I might be having. You

may have already heard though it is a solemn secret not to be divulged
till after April 25 that I am to be transported (in a plane) on May 19
to get degrees at Cambridge and Oxford and I have reason to expect,
though it is not yet settled, at Dublin. This is in foreign recognition
of my having become with your help (as you know I know) an
almost national American poet—quite a national American poet we
may as well admit we suspect.

I wanted you in on this. But I also just wanted to see you from
not having seen you for so long.

I'm going out with Merrill for dinner. I havent seen him for long
either. Hear he has a dreadful beard. Something going on there. I
wonder.

This is what I call a scratch sheet. My very first writing of a poem
is in this hand. Sharp pen makes it worse.

My Decca doing all right? People speak of it.

Best to Bryna. Next best to you.

Robt

The State Dept thinks it is sending me to Europe. It doesnt
know how much more I am being sent by Kay. I lift heavily in these
matters.

["My Decca doing all right?" I had been seeing Robert with in-
creasing frequency; during one of his trips to New York I had induced him to come to the Decca studios on West 57th Street,
where I directed a recording of twenty-three of his poems. Entitled Robert Frost Reads the Poems of Robert Frost the album
was successfully launched in late 1956.

The trip to England was a singular honor—Oxford and Cambridge together had not awarded degrees to an American since Longfellow and Lowell. It was an event which Robert regarded with some
trepidation. He had contracted a worrying cough, and he wrote to
Merrill Moore, who had become his reliable friend as well as his
medical consultant.]

The bad cold I hadn't had for a year struck me right in the middle
of everything with a sharp throat that would have stopped me
dead if it hadn't been for the little candies I made you give me to
carry along. I just wanted you to know how much I owed you. I don't
believe in medicine any more than you do, except as a rare exception
to the general rule. I am still coughing hard, but it doesn't matter

too much now that the crusade is over. Now that you've taken care of me, go on from there and take care of yourself and everybody else you find worthy...Good writing. Ever yours,

Robert

[Enclosing Robert's letter, Merrill informed me that "the little candies" were the simple medications that might be needed on the journey, chiefly dramamine, Bufferin, and codeine tablets. The letter was written on June 28, 1957, after Robert's return. Three months later, almost to the day, Merrill, who seemed the most viable and certainly the most vibrant of our friends, succumbed to an intestinal cancer. Robert and I wrote memoirs to his memory; mine appeared as an introduction to Merrill's posthumous Poems of American Life, Robert's was published in the Harvard Medical Alumni Bulletin. Since this rare tribute has never been reprinted and since it presents aspects of a double portrait of both men, I am culling some of Robert's paragraphs.]

"It was a life overflowing with poetic sympathy whether in or out of form. His professional treatments seemed on the principle of poetry toward all. He may have written too many of what it amused him to call sonnets. And then again he may not. Louis Untermeyer was saying the other day he may prevail by sheer force of numbers, and numbers is after all the old-fashioned name for poetry. It can't be expected that the hundred thousand pieces he tossed off and never looked back at will be taken without discrimination. Louis Untermeyer made a beginning on the formidable task. Already he and such admirers as John Crowe Ransom, Dudley Fitts, William Carlos Williams, and Theodore Morrison have penetrated to seeing the trees in the woods.

"Serious physician and serious artist, he had no notion of being taken lightly; still there was something of the rogue there that was a part of his great charm. He seldom more than cracked a smile. The first time he ever called me in on a case, in fact the first time I met him, was thirty years ago after a party at the St. Botolph Club. He had hardly asked if, like a country swain, he might see me home before he asked if he might use me for a visit at that hour of night at the house of a lady patient. It would do her a world of good to talk literary with me, in particular at that hour of night. Anything once, I said. He briefed me: she was a case of wanting to try one more doctor to see if she couldn't be cured of not knowing how to write. It sounded hopeless. Wouldn't he just have to tell that girl to be good? As a last resort he might. I think he would rather tell her to be brave than good. Besides poetry, he dispensed courage...

"No praise would mean anything to him that forgot he was a poet. Poetry was his rapture. He could hardly say it without singing it. I remember an evening out for a ride with him weaving through the traffic when he recited all of 'L'Allegro' and 'Il Penseroso' and, to round them off, with almost the same gentle sweetness and delight, 'The Ballad of the Revenge.'

"I looked for him once at Squantum. He was out swimming in the ocean somewhere between here and Europe. I might have to wait an hour or so; he was a great swimmer. He struck out boldly the same in water as in poetry. As I have said, he dispensed courage as well as poetry. He had courage to spare—enough to go round. He was a soldier poet, a true Tyrtaeus."

[Details of a long visit in October, 1957, remain particularly vivid. My wife and I had driven to Cambridge for an autumn reunion. There were cocktails at the Morrisons, followed by dinner at the Vendôme in Boston, a meal which Robert, in spite of his Puritanical animadversions against culinary refinements, ate with gusto: a fish chowder, sautéed bay scallops washed down with Chablis, and ice cream floating in crème de cacao. Then back to Brewster Street.

Robert never wasted time in a give-and-take dialogue. He did not converse; he spoke. Now, as always, he spoke brilliantly, sometimes bitterly, but never less than provocatively. His thoughts were as logical and precise as though they had been polished and prepared for publication. Like his poetry, his talk, casual and quizzical, formed a language frank and highly flavored, a speech that was not only uttered by the tongue but tasted by the mind. Some of the things he said were startling and, for many of his well-wishers, shocking.

Whenever Robert lectured, he was surrounded by adulators, autograph hunters, neophytes, and even a few discriminating lovers of poetry. They worshiped him not merely as a great poet but a great man. They also regarded him as a benevolent, sweet, serene, and almost saintly person. He was, of course, none of these. He was not a "true believer"; he did not want to "belong"; he liked his differ-

ence; he was proud, troubled, and frankly jealous. Like his Paul in "Paul's Wife" he always was "a terrible possessor." It took years for him to recover from the feeling that every living poet was his potential if not his actual rival—he was put out with me for a while because I had written an article showing W. H. Auden as the most accomplished of the younger poets; the awards of the Nobel Prize in Literature to T. S. Eliot in 1948 and to Albert Camus a few days before our visit seemed not so much neglect as a personal affront.

On this occasion "Togetherness" was the prime object of his scorn. "The best things and the best people rise out of their separateness. 'Togetherness'—that's a word coined to build up circulation for a woman's magazine, isn't it? The word is ugly enough, but the idea behind it is worse. And when it becomes an international slogan it isn't fit to be uttered. The other day a man was here from the United Nations—he was trying to sell me 'Togetherness.' He told me that Sweden had sent over a chunk of iron as a symbol of the strength of unity, and, before it was put in one of the walls, representatives of the U. N. thought it would be a nice idea if I would write them a poem to be engraved on it. I told him that iron was fine for a weapon of war, but it was a pretty curious emblem of peace. Just the same, if they wouldn't mind what I said, maybe I'd write them a poem. So I wrote them a couplet against unity, against 'Togetherness.' I doubt that they'll use it, but this is what I sent them:

> Nature within her inmost self divides
> To trouble men with having to take sides.

"That's what men always have to do—take sides. There's no neutrality—no peace—no let's-get-together-and-protect-each other in nature. A family or a nation that's always crying for protection isn't worth protecting."

This was quite in character. Robert loathed all forms of social service, attempts at interracial understanding, amelioration of national prejudices; he could not pronounce the word "brotherhood" without a sneer. After a remark about "mob feeling" and "mob thinking," he told a story about a young girl who had shown talent as an artist but who had diverted part of her energies into welfare work—later I learned that the girl was his granddaughter, Robin. "'If you want to be a writer or a painter or any other kind of creator, you can't be anything else,' I told her. 'But,' she said, 'don't you believe it's important to do good?' I said it was more important to do well." Robert did not tell me that Robin had had the last word. "All right," she had replied, with a touch of Frostian tartness, "I'll try to do good well."

"Doing well," Robert resumed, "and deciding how to do it is all that matters. Life is a choice of decisions; it is based on challenges and risks—no risk, no life. The dominating nations are those that risked everything to dominate. The rest just survive. We've got to be clear about our choice, about our answerability to ourselves as individuals and nations. Is the United States to be answerable to the United Nations or to itself? That's the question that hangs over us, and you know what I think the answer is. Wilson's League of Nations was a pretty dream, but it was based on an absurdity and it was bound to go to pieces. The United Nations is worse. It was formed out of desperation, and desperation never solved anything— it can't solve a situation or make enemies love each other or stop nations from dominating and making war. War is the natural state of man—remember what Emerson said about Nature being red in tooth and claw—the club, spear, bow and arrow, gunpowder, rocket —anything man can lay his hands on or invent to show he is the better man. The hydrogen bomb is just another weapon, and it doesn't mean total extermination any more than the others. We can't be wiped out. After a lot of the world is swept away, cockroaches and people will come crawling out of the cracks. Then it will start all over again. We just won't die."

Death reminded us of two friends who had died: Merrill Moore and Irwin Edman. I said that, apart from their accomplishments, they were unselfish, outgiving, without a drop of malice in their veins. "Not like me," he said with a wry grimace. "I've got plenty of malice. Haven't you?"

He was, nevertheless, inconsistent in his disdains. He disliked Ezra Pound both as a poet and a person, yet he went to Washington and urged the authorities to let Pound out of the mental hospital to which, awaiting trial for treason, he had been confined. "It wasn't only because I felt I should stand up with Hemingway and Archie MacLeish to save Ezra from the disgrace of coming to his end where he is, and it wasn't from any sentimental sympathy, either. I just couldn't stand the thought of any poet dying among a lot of drooling, obscene idiots. Besides, if he remained there much longer he'd be a martyr for the entire cult."

The word "obscene" reminded Robert that I had recently published a Treasury of Ribaldry and that I had not sent him a copy.

373

"I guess you thought I was too pure to read it," he said. "I could have given you material for it." When I laughed incredulously, he went on, "You don't believe it? All right, do you want to hear a good one—or a bad one?" Then, like a naughty boy, he recited:

> Mary had a little lamb,
> It's name was Jesus Christ.
> God the Father was her ram,
> But Joseph took it nice.

"I like the irregular rhyme, don't you?" he said. "You can pronounce it 'Chrise' to rhyme with 'nice' or say 'nicet' to go with 'Christ.' Do you want to hear another? This one is both better and worse." Whereupon he recited a quatrain which was not only blasphemous and bawdy but unprintable. "That one's for your next edition, if your publishers will permit it. Anyway, don't forget to send me the book so I can see what you consider ribald. One more? Here's a mischievous one for you:

> Consider now the number ten:
> The 0 for women, the 1 for men.
> How often one goes into zero
> Proves man a laggard or a hero.

An hour later I began to droop—it had been a long ride and a long day—but Robert always hit his conversational stride after midnight, and when my wife and I left toward one in the morning he was at his loquacious best.

There was another visit—a most decorous one, for both my wife and Kay Morrison were present—and then in midsummer, 1958, Kay telephoned me that Robert was in distress. He had been deeply hurt at something I had said—or what someone had told him I had been saying. He gathered that I had suddenly gone back on him.

"What can possibly make him think that?" I asked.

"Something you are supposed to have said about the Nobel prize; that you told the committee he didn't deserve it. I'm sure it's not true."

"Of course not. It's a ridiculous distortion," I replied. "I've never had anything to do with the Nobel committee; it's the Pulitzer Prize Committee of which I've been an adviser for years. As to Robert's not deserving the Nobel prize, I said, when interviewed, just the opposite. I added that he didn't need it now, if he ever did."

I immediately wrote Robert something to this effect. The following letter is his reply.]

1958

HOMER NOBLE FARM
RIPTON, VERMONT

August 7, 1958

Dear Louis:

Your masterly letter puts me in my place. You know me and my moods almost better than anyone else. I was once gone back on cruelly although deservedly and ever since I have once in so often had one of these mad paroxysms of unbelief in human faithfulness. I wake up to a feeling that everything had been swept from under me. Thus far I have never shown myself so crazy that I couldn't get back to my senses. K. straightened me out this time by simply talking to you on the telephone. All that about the Nobel prize, too, was just some more of my nonsense. Look at all I've got in friendship and support over and above all I ever dreamed of or thought I had any right to dream of. So let's be easy as becomes us a la Baruch, that build-up of dispassionate dignity. We should see each other once in a while to keep from imagining things. We'll have in mind another meeting in Sturbridge or somewhere this October. Meanwhile write your five books. It's a coincidence that five is exactly the number that Al Edwards is expecting of me, several of them not new except for a preface possibly. I have always wanted to get all my North-of-Boston-like pieces together under one head. Don't you think that would be a good idea?

Ever yours

Rob't

I had this typed to my dictation for the first letter in type you ever had from me.

[In 1958 Robert was appointed Consultant in Poetry at the Library of Congress; he called himself "Poet in Waiting." The following year his official title was Consultant in the Humanities. A few months after the preceding letter I met him in New York, spent a day with him there, and accompanied him to Washington. I went there to speak to Quincy Mumford, Librarian of Congress, about giving my Frost collection of letters, first editions, and various associated items to the Library of Congress, but chiefly to be with Robert for two days.

375

This time his talk concerned politics and poetry only a little; mostly it was about education and religion. Robert's father, a doggedly honest Democrat in a corrupt and hypocritical Republican state, had offended the self-righteous community by rejecting ritual and refusing to go to church. His mother, on the other hand, was a confirmed true believer. Born a Scotch Presbyterian, she became a Unitarian; after studying Henry George, she espoused the Single Tax as well as the Single Standard; after studying Emerson, whom she read to Robert along with Bellamy's Looking Backward, she became a Swedenborgian.

Robert inherited these mixed tendencies. He began as a romantic affirmer (not, he emphasized, a reformer), and became a nonconformist.

"I'll go along with anything that's spoken," he said, "as long as it's outspoken." This led to consideration of an article that made much of Robert's ambiguities and symbolic overtones. "I can't hold with those who think of me as a symbolical poet, especially one who is symbolical prepense. Symbolism is all too likely to clog up and kill a poem—symbolism can be as bad as an embolism. If my poetry has to have a name, I'd prefer to call it Emblemism—it's the visible emblem of things I'm after.

"People who read me seem to be divided into four groups: Twenty-five percent like me for the right reasons; twenty-five percent like me for the wrong reasons; twenty-five percent hate me for the wrong reasons; twenty-five percent hate me for the right reasons. It's that last twenty-five percent that worries me.

"I guess this means I'm not as much of a skeptic as you sometimes make me out to be, especially when it comes to education and people. I still say the only education worth anything is self-education. All the rest consists of schoolwork, textbooks, training, aids to help distinguish one fact from another without helping us to tell true values from false. But that doesn't mean I don't believe in people learning as well as learned people. I'm for educated humanity all the time—except in an undiscriminating way. All men are born free and equal—free at least in their right to be different. Some people want to mix up the weak and strong of mankind; they want to homogenize society everywhere. That's why I'm against the homogenizers in art, in politics, in every walk of life. I want the cream to rise."]

35 Brewster Street   Cambridge, Massachusetts
                                      January 12,   1959.

Dear Louis:

As the last of my fellow jokers about serious things, why haven't
you coming to you now and then some of my nonsense in rhyme and
meters? You will find some enclosed if paper envelope can contain
it. I propose to have a section in my next book called "A Missile
Mix". Forbear to ask me why. No criticism called for. This is just to
make occasion to help you pass the time while we are waiting to
hear from Washington—if we are still waiting. I ought to know what
goes on down there but think it only funny that I don't. We know
where we can turn if our government shows no eagerness to glorify us.
Enough for now. I pause here from self-consciousness from just
having heard myself called "a chain talker". This may look like
writing but it's really talk. If only for the record, I ought to get it in
that this is probably the only letter I ever dictated to you. You can
blame K. for any faults of grammar, punctuation, or spelling in it.
Also for the flippancy.

But if I hadn't been reminded by her, I might have forgotten my
chief purpose in the letter and that was to give you formal permission to make any kind of book you please out of the letters you've
had from me through the great years. You hereby have it. It's K.'s
decision that any share I have in the proceeds should go into my
estate. You know about my will. Remember us to Bryna.

                              Ever yours
                              Robert
                              Frost for legality
                              as always

LINES WRITTEN IN DEJECTION
    ON THE EVE OF SUCCESS*

I once had a cow that jumped over the moon
Not on to the moon but over.
I don't know what made her so lunar a loon;
All she'd been having was clover.

*[With a few alterations, this is included in In the Clearing.]

'Twas back in the days of my Godmother Goose,
But though we are goosier now
And are all tanked up with mineral juice
We haven't caught up with my cow.

But if to the moon I had wanted to go
And had grabbed that cow by the tail,
I'll bet she'd have let out a terrible low
And put her foot in the pail,

Than which there is no indignity worse.
One cow did that to a fellow
Who rose from the milking stool with a curse
And cried "I'll larn ye to bellow."

He couldn't lay hand on a pitch fork to hit her
Or give her a stab of tine,
So he leaped on her bony back and bit her
Clear into the marrow spine.

She probably would have preferred the fork.
She gave him a howl of rage
That was heard as far away as New York
And made the Times' front page.

He answered her, "Damn you! Well, who begun it?"
The question after a war
Has always been that—and not who won it
Or what it was foughten for.

[As I write this, Robert Frost is in his eighty-seventh year. There is
nothing feeble or soft about him, no weakening of posture or power;
he is still wide-shouldered, craggy, tough in texture, solid as New
Hampshire granite. He is still disillusioned about Progress; distrust-
ful of Science, which has taken man deeper and deeper into matter,
further into space, and further away from the spirit. He says he
will call his last book The Great Misgiving.

He continues to think in metaphors, to play with ideas in the old
bantering way; he will take no one, including himself, with complete seriousness. "My ironies don't seem to iron out anything."
He still believes that the only way to be saved is to save yourself;
two of his favorite books are Robinson Crusoe, the self-sustaining
castaway, and Walden, the document of a man who cast himself
away to find himself.

He is still against One World, World Federalism, Universal Brotherhood, unity, conformity, the breaking down of barriers in the interest of Oneness; he is unalterably against One Anything. You may quote him to the effect that "Something there is that doesn't love a wall," but you can be sure that he much prefers the opposed quotation that "Good fences make good neighbors." He insists on Nature's divisions and differences; "in art, as in nature, we want all the differences we can get. In society, too. We want people and nations to maintain their differences—even at the risk of trouble, even at the risk of fighting one another."

He is still the teasing dissident, the stern exemplar of the individualist, unyielding, stubbornly native to the gnarled American grain. As for conclusions, there can be no better finality than the concluding couplet of the very first poem in his first book. Past eighty-six, Robert Frost still makes it clear that:

> They would not find me changed from him they knew—
> Only more sure of all I thought was true.]

[The preceding paragraphs were to be the last in the book which was scheduled for publication in 1961. For some time Robert had been eager to see the letters in print; he had not reread them, but he felt they were a true presentation of what he thought and was, rather than the smoothed-over picture of the poet that a large part of the public wanted to cherish. However, when the manuscript was ready for the printer, he made excuses for delaying its publication. It seemed that he was reluctant to destroy the image his countrymen had formed of him when he read "The Gift Outright" before the leaders of the nation and millions of television-viewers at President Kennedy's inauguration, the first time that any poet in America had been so honored. He was also uneasy about the publication of many critical remarks about his contemporaries as well as other intimate disclosures. The omission of certain letters would have narrowed the full-size portrait to a prettified profile of the man, and this was as unthinkable as it was unwarrantable.

For a while we postponed decision about the letters. During this period, I began to edit a series of books for very young readers, short stories or poems to be composed by eminent authors who did not ordinarily write juveniles. The vocabulary was limited but the range of subjects was not. The series was called Modern Masters Books for Children, and I had already received enthusiastic responses and highly imaginative manuscripts from authors as famous and as unlike as Arthur Miller, Robert Graves, Erskine Caldwell, Pearl Buck, William Saroyan, Shirley Jackson, Victoria Lincoln, and others. When I asked Robert to be one of the contributors to the series I received the following friendly but definite rebuke.

A lover of baseball, Robert's burlesque infield (suggested in his signatures) consisted of himself, Norman Cousins, editor of the Saturday Review, and Edward (Ted) Weeks, editor of the Atlantic Monthly.]

Homer Noble Farm
Ripton, Vermont.
July 11, 1961.

Louis! Louis!

You cruel thing to order of me the kind of book you know I never could write for love or money. You drive me to distraction for a few minutes. You want a whole book by me for children with a vocabulary of twenty five words beginning with the nouns "cat" and "dog" and the verbs "scratch" and "bite" or "meow" or "bow-wow". The form is as strict as a limerick. The sonnet is the strictest form I have behaved in, and that mainly by pretending it wasn't a sonnet. But come up and see us and I will go to work arranging the manuscript for my next book that, until I get it out, stands in the way I feel of your publishing my letters. That ought to be an inducement. You didn't see the picture of me in the hospital, did you? I told the reporters I had my ear operated on to start a new era. For want of me the world's course will not fail. I must try work to see if it does me any good.

To change the subject if any, here's an old one I've just come across that might have gone into my first book to show the mood I was in and gradually escaping from at the time. It's exactly as first written on an old scrap of paper that has come through from the nineties. I must send it to Fleming (Rosenbach's successor) who says I owe him a bit of manuscript on a bet he won about Amy Lowell and her Keats' manuscript. He won and I lost.

> The reason of my perfect ease
> In the society of trees
> Is that their cruel struggles pass
> Too far below my social class
> For me to share them or be made
> For what I am and love afraid.

Yours truly
Robert Lee Frost (at first)
Norman Cousins (at second)
Ted Weeks (at third)

[A little later, when it became apparent that Robert did not want the letters to appear in print during his lifetime, I wrote him that publication would, of course, be deferred. He expressed his pleasure by way of Kay Morrison and his publisher, Alfred Edwards, and followed it up with a letter sent by special delivery, air mail on November 4, 1961.]

35 Brewster Street   Cambridge 38, Massachusetts
                                                  November 4,   1961.

Louis, Louis:

I knew you would have mercy on my irresponsibility. K. and Al and you were the three in the world I counted on most to protect me from myself. You and I have been fond friends. I hated to keep you from publishing my unguarded letters if you thought they would do anything to integrate our lives. But something all the time was telling me there were things in the letters that would expose me to some little and big embarrassments to bother me to the point of wishing I were dead. I lay awake nights over them and had reached a decision that if they came out now, that ended it. I would turn my back on the world and not utter another book. I like to be read as a poet, but I guess I really hate the literary life and hate to be gossiped about for my part in it. I shan't be caring much longer what becomes of my remains. Throw them to the ghouls, who as we know "are neither man nor woman, who are neither beast nor human."

I shrank from looking back at the staleness of my past, and I have only hearsay to go on; but you yourself know the letters are full of indiscretions about people that I may now be better friends with than I may have been at times. I am too apt to amuse myself in private over the foibles and peccadillos of folks I really like. I have just come from visiting with people I wouldn't for anything have meant to hurt by my flippant character sketches. On suspicion and inquiry I learn sure enough the letters have taken them too unseriously. I horrify myself. I simply must try to stop being funny about all this drama and melodrama. Blame me, but forgive me. In a sense I was being personal and confidential in my letters. Publicality was the last thing I was thinking of. Give me time to get good and dead.

                                        Ever yours

                                                  Robert

[The next, and last, letter needs a few asides.

The "long-sustained feud" refers to Long Feud, a selection of what I considered the best of my old poems and a few new ones. We had been over many of the pages together; much of the book had to do with man's combined love and distrust of nature, the "long feud fought silently between man and the growing grass."

Even after all the years Robert couldn't stop twitting me, a puzzled liberal, with being a radical. But, he adds, "The most radical thing you ever did was to stay away from my party." He does not mean a political party, but a semi-official party given in Washington to celebrate his eighty-eighth birthday. Because of a lecture engagement which I could not cancel, I was unhappily unable to attend the festivities.

"I'm glad you found another book in me" refers to something I had written about In the Clearing, which (since it was Robert's reply to certain critics who implied he had written himself out) I wanted him to call, after the title of one of his latest and best poems, "One More Brevity."

The quatrain "by Alphonse somebody" is a slight misquotation from Théophile Gautier's "L'Art," which Austin Dobson paraphrased and entitled "Ars Victrix." The crux of the poem is in these lines:

> All passes. Art alone
>   Enduring stays to us:
> The Bust outlasts the throne,—
>   The Coin, Tiberius;
>
> Even the gods must go;
>   Only the lofty Rhyme
> Not countless years o'erthrow,—
>   Not long array of time.

"Remember me to Bryna and to the Librarians." In 1961 I had been appointed Consultant in Poetry at the Library of Congress and was being reappointed for a second term.]

35 Brewster Street
Cambridge, Massachusetts
April 14, 1962.

Dear Louis:

That's a long-sustained feud but a good natured one all the way.
I followed it pretty closely with admiration for its sureness. You've
never been angry mad and you've never really been at outs with the
whole thing in a lump. You've never been to extremes you had to
repent of. I've often said to 'em that you're about as far left as I
found you. I've enjoyed your evenness. I hope you get the recognition
you haven't been bidding for so much lately. The most radical thing
you ever did was to stay away from my party. But we've been through
a lot together and both know how to make allowances. Business is
business with you in lecture engagements as it is with me in a way.
I think I may say I've never missed a lecture (of my own) or been even
a minute late to one. "All is well and wisely put." If we cannot carry
mountains on our back neither can we crack a nut.

We'll be seeing you and acting like this in a few weeks. I'm glad
you found another book in me. I trust you noticed the one poem in it
not meant to be understood and weren't surprised at my attempt to
keep up with the times.

> Even the gods must go;
> Only the lofty rhyme
> Not countless years o'erthrow
> Or long results of time.

by Alphonse somebody, I think.

Remember me to Byrna and to the Librarians—K. too.

Ever yours

Rob't

POSTSCRIPT

In early December, 1962, Robert entered Peter Bent Brigham hospital in Boston to undergo surgery for an urinary-tract obstruction. The operation was successful but, subsequently, he suffered a heart attack and blood clots settled in the lungs. Thereupon the doctors tied the veins in both legs to ease the clotting.

When he seemed to be recovering, I visited with him on January 22nd at his bedside. Nurses and interns hovered about, but he shooed them from the room and we talked for more than an hour. Robert did most of the talking. Indulging in a reminiscent mood, he spoke lightly of recent honors; of the day at President Kennedy's inauguration when the sun was so strong and the wind so keen that he could not read the lines he had written especially for the occasion and, instead, recited "The Gift Outright"; of the gold medal voted by Congress and presented to him on his eighty-eighth birthday by President Kennedy; of his government-sponsored visit to Russia, accompanied by Stewart Udall, Secretary of the Interior; of his acclaim by the Soviet writers and his interview with Premier Khrushchev.

"He's a big man—he may be our enemy—but he's full of homely proverbs and a great sense of humor. We had quite a give-and-take, through interpreters, of course. He's not afraid of us and we're not afraid of him. When he repeated his idea about 'peaceful coexistence' I countered with a proposal about 'magnanimous rivalry.' He smiled, a broad peasant's smile. A great man, and a great country."

"How about your earlier opinion?" I asked, and quoted a little maliciously:

> I have none of the tenderer-than-thou
> Collectivistic regimenting love
> With which the modern world is being swept.

385

He replied that he still did not believe in crowds or the inevitability of a Brotherhood of Man or the growing Welfare State (a phrase he always uttered with a sneer), but he thought there would have to be a rapprochement between Russia and the United States. "They are beginning to move toward capitalism just as we are accepting certain aspects of socialism—heavier taxation, government control in industry, federal interest in the arts. We are drawing closer whether we like it or not, whether we realize it or not."

I asked him about some of the Russian writers he had met. He particularly liked Yevtushenko, who took him to some of the places where the young poets gathered.

"And there was an even younger poet—not yet thirty—I can't recall his name."

"Was it Voznesensky?"

"I think that's it. Anyway, I was shown some of their work, in translation of course. It looked like a break through the restrictions in Soviet writing. But I couldn't tell anything about it as poetry. I told them, and you've heard me say it—too many times, I expect—that poetry is what is lost in translation."

From Russia he went abruptly to the situation in the Congo and other emerging African nations. "The trouble with undeveloped countries," he said, "is that they are trying to get ahead before they have caught up."

Getting ahead somehow reminded him of the National Poetry Festival held a few months before at the Library of Congress in Washington. The first of its kind ever organized in America, it brought together some eighty poets of all tendencies and temperaments from all over the country. I introduced Robert to a crowded assembly in the Coolidge Auditorium and he made generous acknowledgment to my early championship of his work when it was little known. "Sometimes," he remarked to the audience, "I think I am a figment of Louis' imagination," and then went on to spellbind the listeners with his inimitable "saying" of his poems. We agreed that the national gathering had separated the poetic sheep from the exhibitionistic goats; we took apart one of the participants who was a particularly annoying opportunist. Then Robert seemed to relent.

"We shouldn't be too hard on him," he said.

"Why not?" I inquired.

"Well, we are so near the Day of Doom that anyone—even Gabriel—must blow his own trumpet."

Speaking of poetry made him recall his early days and the time when the Atlantic Monthly returned some of his poems with this comment: "We regret that the Atlantic has no place for your vigorous verse."

"It seemed to characterize the Atlantic more than the poems," he said. "They weren't really so vigorous. Anyway, when I came back from England after North of Boston, the Atlantic asked for something of mine. I sent them the very same poems they had rejected—and they printed them. It makes you wonder about editors, doesn't it?"

I read a note which I had just received from Robert Graves expressing indignation that Robert had not been awarded this year's Nobel prize and adding that he had written a letter to the committee in Sweden proposing America's "unofficial laureate" for next year's award. Robert was both troubled and gratified—he had been led to believe he would be chosen this time—and he managed one of his foxy grimaces.

"Don't tell anyone—it's supposed to be a secret—but I'm getting another prize this spring. It's to be at a reception in England, and you've got to promise to go along. It will be quite a party. Don't forget—this spring."

With that hope I left.

A week later I was waked at three in the morning. David McCord telephoned to tell me that blood clots had formed again and that Robert had died, apparently of a pulmonary embolism. Had he lived another few weeks he would have been eighty-nine.

When the Associated Press asked for an obituary tribute, I thought of what Robert had written for the amended preface to E.A. Robinson's posthumous King Jasper. "Robinson stayed content with the old-fashioned way to be new....His theme was unhappiness itself, but his skill was as happy as it was playful. There is that comforting thought for those who suffered to see him suffer....The style is the man. Rather say the style is the way the man takes himself...If it is with outer seriousness, it must be with inner humor. If it is with outer humor, it must be with inner seriousness."

Robert might have been writing a casual but precise estimate of his own work, and of himself. His was a high stoicism which could mask unhappiness in playfulness, which could even delight in darkness. He could enliven his last book with a couplet as bantering as:

> It takes all sorts of in and outdoor schooling
> To get adapted to my kind of fooling.

The "fooling" was his particular mixture of levity and gravity, of outer humor and inner seriousness.

In "The Lesson for Today" he had written something like his own farewell, a parting apothegm by one who could tease and be tortured, renounce and be reconciled. The poem concludes:

> I hold your doctrine of Memento Mori.
> And were an epitaph to be my story
> I'd have a short one ready for my own.
> I would have written of me on my stone:
> He had a lover's quarrel with the world.